AMERICA'S MARITIME HERITAGE

BY ELOISE ENGLE
AND ARNOLD S. LOTT

NAVAL INSTITUTE PRESS
Annapolis, Maryland

Cover illustration: On 17 July 1812 the U.S. frigate *Constitution* met a
British squadron of five ships off the New Jersey coast. There was no wind,
so her sailors rowed and towed for 36 hours to escape the British guns.
Courtesy: *Harper's Magazine*

Frontispiece photo: J. A. Perrenoud.

Library of Congress Catalogue Card No. 74–31737.
ISBN 0–87021–507–8.

Printed in the United States of America.

FOREWORD

This book has been undertaken to supplement the many high school texts on American history with a concentrated course in maritime history. It includes all the various aspects of America's "maritime heritage"—merchant shipping, the Navy, and other features of salt-water operations which have grown up, especially in recent years. The story has plenty of the "yo-heave-ho" atmosphere of life afloat and "blow-by-blow" accounts of naval actions, but it has even more to say about what brought our ships into being and why they were doing just what they did.

Except for those built as warships or pleasure craft, most vessels were undertaken in the hopeful expectation of paying for themselves and making a profit by carrying cargo or passengers. Although they could sail almost anywhere on the broad oceans, they generally followed well-established "sea lanes" between ports where cargo could be picked up or delivered. By far the most important of those lanes consisted of the 3,000 miles of stormy North Atlantic between the American east coast and the ports of Great Britain and western Europe. The aristocrats of the old merchant marine were the big square-rigged ships; below them, lesser vessels fell off in size through brigs and schooners to sloops and other small craft. About a century ago, steam began to supplant sail, with iron or steel hulls in place of the old "heart of oak."

The Americans had a sizeable merchant marine from early times, but their navy remained relatively small (except during the Civil War) until the end of the last century. Britain, with the world's greatest navy, provided the colonists with defense until they turned against the mother country. The seagoing forces of the United States were badly outnumbered in the American Revolution and in the War of 1812. Then and later the U. S. Navy had very few ships of the line, the ponderous ancestors of the later battleships. Instead, it concentrated on frigates, sloops of war, gun brigs, etc., the cruisers of those times. They were useful for raiding or protecting commerce, carrying dispatches, and showing the flag on distant stations, but they could not challenge the big fleets for command of the seas.

The Civil War came in the midst of rapid naval transition, including steam-powered ironclads and heavy artillery, and there was great naval expansion. Then Americans slipped back to the old ways for twenty-odd years. In 1890 they decided to go in for battleships and before long had built a navy that ranked among the strongest in the world.

The twentieth century has seen many drastic maritime changes. The airplane had a very strong effect on military and commercial operations. Aircraft carriers had supplanted battleships by World War II, and since then jet planes have put the great passenger liners out of service. The submarine began commerce destruction. Tankers, bringing oil from distant areas, have become by far the largest ships afloat. Finally, the rapid increase in recreational boating has put tens of thousands of sailboats and motor boats on inland and coastal waters and given many Americans a better understanding of their maritime heritage.

Robert G. Albion
Harvard University

PREFACE

As the nation prepares to celebrate the bicentennial of American independence, it is appropriate to publish a book that relates how that independence was achieved. Here, then, is an account of how the first American colonists came by sea to establish themselves in a new world, the story of their determined efforts to gain their freedom, and an explanation of how that freedom was won and has been preserved over the centuries, primarily by going to sea and fighting for it.

But while this book takes the reader to sea, it is not solely a naval history. Rather, it is a narration of the exploits of many seagoing Americans—adventurers, explorers, privateers, fishermen, whalers, and sailors of all sorts—in all the seas of the world, and how their accomplishments have affected the lives of all Americans in the United States today.

ACKNOWLEDGMENTS

The primary sources of information used in producing this book were the research and reference facilities of the Nimitz Library at the U.S. Naval Academy, Annapolis, Maryland; the Navy Department Library, Washington, D.C.; the Fairfax County Library, Virginia; and the San Francisco Maritime Museum, San Francisco, California.

Other institutions and agencies which provided assistance in this project were: the U.S. Postal Service, the National Archives of the United States, the Library of Congress, the Office of Naval History, all in Washington, D.C.; the Virginia Independence Bicentennial Commission of Williamsburg, Virginia; the Seamen's Bank for Savings, of New York, New York; the Marine Historical Association of Mystic, Connecticut; the Mariners Museum of Newport News, Virginia; and National Telefilm Associates, Inc., of New York, New York.

Karl Kortum, the Director, and Matilda Dring and David Hull of the San Francisco Maritime Museum were especially helpful in suggesting certain topics to be covered, and in providing the necessary reference material.

For the treatment of the chapter on naval exploration, the recent Naval Institute publication, *Ships, Seas, and Scientists,* by Dr. Vincent Ponko, Jr., Dean of Humanities at California State College, Bakersfield, California, proved invaluable, both as to coverage of the subject and bibliographic assistance.

Information on the modern U.S. merchant marine was provided by Meridith Buell of the American Institute of Merchant Shipping; Albert J. Dennis of the Federal Maritime Commission, Vic Yorsky and Martin P. Skrocky of the Maritime Administration; Homer L. Hendrickson (now deceased) of the American Waterways Operators, Inc.; John Packard of the Lake Carriers Association; and Alfred C. Filiatrault, Jr., of the Propeller Club of the United States.

These shipping lines and shipbuilding companies also provided assistance: American President Lines, Ltd.; Atlantic Richfield Company; Avondale Shipyards, Inc.; Bethlehem Steel Corporation; Calmar Steamship Corporation; Delta Steamship Lines, Inc.;

Farrell Lines Incorporated; Lykes Bros. Steamship Co., Inc.; Matson Navigation Co.; Moore-McCormack Lines, Inc.; National Bulk Carriers, Inc.; Pacific Far East Line, Inc.; Prudential Lines; Sea-Land Service, Inc.; States Steamship Co.; United States Lines; Waterman Steamship Corporation; and American Export Lines, Inc.

In writing this book, we were especially fortunate in having a steering committee of naval officers and educators who reviewed our work; they kept it from deviating onto the rocks and shoals of too much detail on one side and kept it out of the shallow water of too little depth on the other. Our appreciation for this guidance goes to Captain William C. Nicklas, U.S. Navy (Retired) of the First Colonial High School, Virginia Beach, Virginia; Commander Floyd S. Kunkle, U.S. Navy (Retired) of McDowell High School, Marion, North Carolina; and Lieutenant Commander William E. Huddleston, U.S. Navy (Retired) of York High School, Yorktown, Virginia.

The last name to appear here is that of the person who initiated the project. Vice Admiral Malcolm W. Cagle, U.S. Navy (Retired), first saw the need for a book on maritime history, recommended its production, and took the steps that resulted in our having been given a challenging assignment. Our immense satisfaction in its successful completion must be shared with all those, named or not, who made it possible.

CONTENTS

AMERICA'S MARITIME HERITAGE

PART ONE
THE DAYS
OF GROWTH

The earth on which we live is a world of water. Nearly three-fourths of its surface—139,840,000 square miles—are covered with water. Seen from 20,000 miles out in space, it is a misty globe, banded with the white sweep of clouds moving across the vast blue oceans.

Life began in the oceans billions of years ago. Today the earth would be a dead planet if it were not for the oceans. They store the heat of the sun and release it into the atmosphere; without them, part of the earth would be a deepfreeze while the other part would be too blazing hot for any life at all.

Whether you live on an island in the Florida keys, or in mile-high Colorado, you depend on the ocean for far more than you do on the weather. Many of the things you eat, wear, and use every day come from the oceans, or by ship across them, from every part of the world. In years past, even your ancestors came to this country across the oceans.

For thousands of years, the oceans have been the wide highways across which people moved, to spread civilization, trade, exchange ideas, and develop their national cultures. All people in the world share this heritage. And even though you may not be able to look out of a window and see the ocean, you are closely tied to it. This is because your blood has exactly the same density as the salt water in which life first appeared.

The sea was a part of man's existence and growth long before he could read or write—long before he began scratching rude pictures on cave walls. The first primitive men lived near the sea, and some-

On previous pages: During the Revolutionary War, the new Continental Navy won many stirring battles against superior British ships and established proud traditions for the future U.S. Navy. One of the most famous battles, pictured here, took place on 23 September 1779, when John Paul Jones in the *Bonhomme Richard* captured the *Serapis* after uttering his famous battle cry "I have not yet begun to fight!" Courtesy: The U.S. Naval Academy Museum.

times hunted shellfish in the shallow water. Somewhere, perhaps hundreds of thousands of years ago, a daring human ventured onto a floating log. In time, with fire and stone axes, men learned to hollow out a log and point its ends and make it go where they wanted to go. Probably they paddled with their hands before they learned to use poles.

Crude rafts, made of small poles or bundles of reeds tied together, were easier to build than dugouts. The ancient Egyptians and Babylonians used such craft. People still use them today, on the upper Nile River and on Lake Titicaca in the Andes. But no one went very far paddling a raft. Thousands of years ago men learned how to make sails of animal skins or of woven-grass mats. The Egyptians used grass-mat sails on the upper Nile River at least five thousand years ago.

Primitive men also learned that skins could be inflated to make rafts, or stretched over frames to make light boats. About 2,400 years ago, Cyrus the Great, who founded the Persian empire, had his soldiers make boats of skins filled with hay in order to cross the Euphrates River. Julius Caesar wrote of similar boats being used in Britain fifty years before the birth of Christ. Today, in the Arctic regions, Eskimos use kayaks made of sealskin fastened over a framework of bones.

In the Pacific, outrigger canoes carried Polynesian and Melanesian voyagers from island to island centuries before the Portuguese navigator, Ferdinand Magellan, reached that ocean. Using rude charts made of sticks and shells, they navigated by the stars and followed the flights of birds across great distances in double canoes big enough to carry food, seeds, fishing equipment and weapons—everything they needed to make a home in a new land.

In the ancient Mediterranean, the first real ship sailors were people from Crete, called Minoans, who sailed as far west as Sicily. Next came the Phoenicians who roamed everywhere—to Greece, Italy, North Africa, Spain, and Britain. Their slow sailing ships hauled grain from Egypt, wine from Asia Minor, pottery from Greece, and tin from Britain.

The first people to use fleets of ships in naval warfare were the Phoenicians, Carthaginians, Persians, and Greeks. Some of their ships were rowed by as many as 300 men, and helped along with a sail or so.

In northern Europe, the Norsemen, or Vikings, were great navigators and boat builders from about 900 to 1100 A.D. Their "long ships" were built for ocean sailing in stormy seas, and they raided the coastal and river cities of Europe, Russia, the Mediterranean, and England. Then, venturing still farther from home across strange seas, the Vikings sailed west to Newfoundland as early as 1000 A.D., and established settlements in Greenland and Iceland. A descendant of Vikings, William, Duke of Normandy, knew how to use ships; in 1066 he moved an invading army across the English

Channel, won the Battle of Hastings on 14 October, and became known to history as William the Conqueror.

During the Middle Ages, European countries built their own strong navies to protect themselves against the Norsemen. Spain, in the period after the Crusades, developed ships called galleons; they were slow, but bulky, and could carry many heavy guns. The guns were ranged along both sides of the ships, which had to sail very close to one another to do any damage with them.

Medieval Europe was a feudal society, wherein serfs were little more than slaves, and kings and royal families fought for power and kingdoms. Poverty, disease, famine, and ignorance darkened the land until the Crusaders (Christian soldiers) began returning from their long efforts to take the Holy Land from the Moors.

The Crusades lasted for some three hundred years, during which period Europe learned much from the Moslem empire. Crusaders brought back from the Middle East a knowledge of history, mathematics, geography, astronomy, medicine, and tales of great riches in the East. Seaports such as Venice grew to be great commercial cities so that, by the year 1200, about 18,000 Venetian traders were living and doing business in Constantinople (Istanbul) alone.

With expanding commerce, ships putting to sea, and competition between the maritime countries, particularly the Netherlands and Italy, man's thinking began to broaden. In Europe, Thomas Aquinas preached a Christian doctrine. In England, Roger Bacon urged the study of languages and mathematics, and invented an astronomical telescope, a magnetic compass, and an astrolabe. The signing of the Magna Carta in 1215 marked the beginning of a constitutional form of government that other countries would someday follow.

By that time, Europeans had heard there was a great civilization in the Far East, where there was also a wealth of silks, jewels, perfumes, and spices that were unknown in Europe. A young Venetian merchant, Marco Polo, journeyed across Asia and visited the empire of Kublai Khan, the land sometimes called Cathay and now known as China. About 1298 he published an account of his journeys, and it was so filled with tales of vast riches that people began calling him "Marco Millions." People immediately were interested in finding the wealth Marco Polo described. The only known way to reach this land of riches was to sail to the Levant, the eastern end of the Mediterranean, then travel by camel caravan across Syria and Persia to Cathay. But the Ottoman, or Turkish, empire blocked the overland part of the route. The Turks who lived in the interior would not deal with Christians for religious reasons, and those who lived along the coast levied high taxes. For those reasons, European nations bordering on the Atlantic, particularly Portugal, determined to find a sea route to Asia by sailing around Africa.

Prince Henry of Portugal became known as "the discoverer of discoverers," because he encouraged exploration. He promoted advances in ship construction and planned to send out expeditions to explore the western coast of Africa. He also set up a school of navigation, for which he is known as Henry the Navigator. He died in 1460, but his work went on. In 1487, twenty-seven years later, another Portuguese, Bartholomeu Dias, sailed to the southern tip of Africa. Eleven years after that, still another Portuguese, Vasco da Gama, followed the earlier route and went across the Indian Ocean to India, thereby establishing the first all-water route to the riches of the east.

About 1470 a young cloth salesman from Genoa, by the name of Cristoforo Colombo, began hearing stories of the wealth of India. He went to Portugal, and probably to England, and by 1482 had sailed to the coast of Africa. In his travels he heard more about India, and how best to get there. He studied charts, talked with seamen, and when King John II of Portugal refused to finance a voyage to discover a new way to India, he appealed to Queen Isabella and King Ferdinand of Spain.

Finally, in 1492, the Spanish queen decided to provide him with three tiny vessels, a crew of about one hundred men, and an experienced navigator named Martin Pinzon. If successful in reaching India, he was to be promoted to admiral and receive one-tenth of all the pearls, stones, gold, silver, spices, and other treasures he could find. On 3 August, the small ships *Pinta*, *Nina*, and *Santa Maria* sailed from Palos, Spain. The ships were top-heavy, their timbers were rotten, the food and water went bad, and the sailors feared they might sail off the edge of the world. After 69 days, they sighted land—a small island now known as San Salvador, in the Bahamas—on 12 October 1492. Cristoforo Colombo is now known as Christopher Columbus, and because he thought he was in India, all the natives in the New World were called Indians. And for some strange reason, the land he discovered is named *America* after Amerigo Vespucci, a Florentine resident of Seville, who, if he ever did see the New World, saw that part now known as Brazil in 1501–1502.

After exploring Cuba and Haiti, Columbus returned to Spain with a few parrots, slaves, and coconuts, but no treasure. He made four trips to the New World, filling in new lands on the maps and claiming territory for Spain. His trips failed to fatten the royal treasury with the promised riches. He lost favor with Queen Isabella, and died in debtors' prison.

For more than a century after Columbus reached the New World, no one understood the importance of his discovery. It was years before men realized that he had found, not the Indies, but a new land, and even more years before it was determined that beyond the land Columbus had reached, there was a vast continent and another limitless ocean to be crossed before anyone could arrive in India.

But the race to win the riches of the New World, and to find a water route to the Indies, was on. John Cabot (who was actually an Italian named Giovanni Caboto) explored the coast of Canada for England. Next, Jacques Cartier came along to explore the St. Lawrence River for France. The territory was claimed by France and in 1603 Samuel de Champlain set up a trading post at what is now Quebec.

Vasco de Balboa, Hernando Cortez, Francisco Pizarro, and Juan Ponce de León, all in the name of Spain, explored the Americas and in 1513 Balboa crossed Panama and discovered the Pacific Ocean. With Spain now the richest and most powerful country in the world, Hernando de Soto in 1540 landed in Florida and pushed all the way to the Mississippi River. Two years later Francisco Vásquez de Coronado explored the great plains west of the Mississippi, and incidentally gave the American Indians their first horses. And in 1565, the first white settlement in North America was established at St. Augustine, Florida, by Pedro Menéndez de Avilés.

Once men had braved the mystery of the unknown that lay beyond their own small horizons and had proved that they could sail to strange lands and come home again, more and more ships ventured across the wide oceans. Finally, on 20 September 1519, Ferdinand Magellan sailed from Seville, Spain, with 200 men and five ships on a voyage that changed the course of history and science more than anything had in the previous two thousand years. Three years later one ship and eighteen men came back home again. Their safe return meant that no one had to worry about falling off the edge of the world any more—the world was not flat but round, and they had proved it by being the first men to sail around it.

Once the extent and wealth of the new lands were realized, it was only natural for every country to want a share of them. France, England, the Netherlands, Portugal, and Spain all wanted overseas colonies for the raw goods and riches they produced, as well as for national prestige. America, being nearer to Europe than is India, was a logical place to set up colonies; in the century after Columbus, Magellan, and Francis Drake crossed the Atlantic, ships from many lands crossed the ocean. Portugal and Spain planted colonies in South and Central America. France and England and later the Netherlands and Sweden set up colonies in North America. Naturally, the people who constituted the first colonies retained the nationality of their homelands—they were Portuguese, Spanish, French, English, Dutch, and Swedish. For a long time, the only people in America who could be called Americans were the Indians. Everyone else came from somewhere else.

CHAPTER 1
COLONIAL AMERICA

They came by sea, in three small ships—*Susan Constant, Godspeed,* and *Discovery*—sent out from London to start the first permanent English colony in North America. They came on 13 May 1607, to what is now Jamestown, Virginia, but was then a wild and lonely land. Along the shore they could see the spring blossoms of berry and fruit trees; but beyond the shore stood dark primeval forests. What dangers or treasures they might find there, no one knew.

They all knew what they hoped to find—gold. The charter given the Virginia Company of London by King James I called for them to first of all find gold and riches to justify the original investment. Beyond that they were to convert the heathen Indians to Christianity and, if possible, to find a westward passage to the Indies. This bold venture was a direct result of the British defeat of the Spanish Armada in 1588. The British Navy controlled the North Atlantic, and this meant England could establish colonies in America and protect them.

But once the colonists were ashore, England was not much help to them. The settlers at Jamestown consisted of 104 "gentlemen" and boys who had never known hardships or hard work. The long five-month Atlantic crossing, with little food and foul water, killed sixteen of them and during that first summer along the James River, fever and dysentery killed more of the group. Hunger overtook them even as they built their fort, storehouse, church, and log huts. Uninterested and unskilled in farming, they neglected to plant crops and only survived that first terrible winter by trading with the Indians for food.

On previous page: More than 100 passengers sailed for the New World aboard the *Mayflower*. The trip began on 16 September 1620 and lasted two months. Shown here is the *Mayflower II*, a reproduction of the original ship, built in Britain. She sailed across the Atlantic in 1957 to commemorate the voyage of the Pilgrims. Photo: U.S. Coast Guard.

The second season was no better than the first and many more died. And by this time, the Indians had begun attacking them.

Only a strong resourceful leader could save the colony. In 1608, Captain John Smith took over the leadership, put the settlers to work, and bartered with the Indians for corn. His rule, "He who will not work will not eat," meant survival for the group. The Indian maiden Pocahontas who married one of the colonists, John Rolfe, in 1614 helped keep peace between Indians and settlers.

She also introduced the settlers to something that was to become worth more than all the gold they might ever hope to find—tobacco. But tobacco was a mixed blessing—at the same time it

The *Susan Constant, Godspeed,* and *Discovery,* carrying 104 British "gentlemen and boys," landed at what is now Jamestown, Virginia, on 13 May 1607. Replicas of these ships are now on display at Jamestown, near the restored colonial town of Williamsburg. Courtesy: The Jamestown Foundation, Williamsburg, Virginia.

made men rich, it made them poor. Year after year of tobacco crops ruined the land, and plantations big enough to raise tobacco needed many men to work them. In 1619, the tobacco-growers thought they had the answer; a Dutch ship arrived at Jamestown, sold them twenty African slaves, and so changed the entire course of American history.

The "lost colony" at Roanoke
Jamestown was not the first attempt of the English to establish colonies in America but earlier ventures proved that the exploitation of the New World was not to be undertaken lightly. In 1578 Sir Humphrey Gilbert, who believed in the existence of a northwest passage to the Indies, was authorized by Queen Elizabeth to hold and govern such lands in America, not already appropriated, as he might choose to colonize. Loosely translated, this meant, "See what you can do—and good luck!" His first expedition ended in defeat by the Spaniards; his second was wrecked by a storm.

Then, in 1584, Gilbert's half-brother, Sir Walter Raleigh, managed to get a charter to locate another colony which he would diplomatically name Virginia—after the virgin queen Elizabeth. The site for Raleigh's first colony, Roanoke Island in what is now North Carolina, was a poor choice. The Indians were hostile, the climate unhealthy, and the colonists finally fled to the mainland, never to be heard from again. It was presumed that Indians massacred them.

New England
After Jamestown had shown that colonies could indeed survive in the New World, commercial backing was easier to acquire. By 1620 the first permanent settlement in New England had been established on the coast of Massachusetts by the Pilgrims, or Separatists.

The Separatists had broken away from the Church of England which they considered sinful and corrupt and too "popish" for their liking. Persecuted in England, they fled to Holland where after twelve years of hard work and poverty they became increasingly worried about the influence of the Dutch on their children. They wanted a place where they could live and die as Englishmen and worship as they chose. America could be the answer.

With permission from the Virginia Company to start a settlement, the Pilgrims sailed to Plymouth, England, where they were joined by other settlers. In September 1620 the entire band, 103 people, crowded into the *Mayflower* under the leadership of William Brewster and began the long stormy voyage to the New World. Many became ill, one died, a baby was born, but after sixty-five days, the *Mayflower* reached what is now Plymouth, Massachusetts.

The winter of 1620–21 was miserable and cold; only 44 out of the 103 survived and at one time only seven were well enough to bury the dead. Yet, when the *Mayflower* returned to England, not one of the band left with her. "It is not with us as with other men, whom small things can discourage," one of them wrote.

The Pilgrims stayed on, and survived. Friendly Indians taught them to plant corn and catch fish and finally to trade in furs. The autumn of 1621 brought a bountiful harvest and the first Thanksgiving celebration in New England.

Soon there were bustling fishing villages, trading posts, and other settlements on the storm-lashed shores of Massachusetts Bay. The most important and populous of these was the Massachusetts Bay Colony, settled ten years after the arrival of the Pilgrims. During 1630, seventeen vessels brought 2,000 persons to what is now Boston. Ten years later, that number had increased to 16,000. As usual there was immense suffering from hunger and cold. That first winter, a fifth of the settlers died. The others survived by eating clams and mussels, nuts and acorns. They soon realized that their lifeline would be the sea; fishing, shipbuilding, and trading.

Why they came

Why did people risk the hazards of the sea, the greed of sea captains, the uncertainties of life in an unexplored and wild land? Some of them, at first, sought gold and quick wealth. Others came for religious reasons. Protestant England thought of the New World as a legitimate field for missionary work, particularly since Catholic Spain had already won so many converts to Catholicism. English leaders felt that annoying dissenters from the established church would be less troublesome carrying Protestantism and the British flag on American shores than they would be at home. For the people themselves, it meant a chance to have at least a limited amount of religious freedom.

Another motivation was the chance to escape poverty. Only a very few people in England—the titled landowners, and some merchants—were wealthy. Following her wars with Spain, England had many discharged soldiers and sailors. There was no one to care for the paupers any more because Henry VIII had closed the monasteries; monks and nuns were themselves paupers. It was reasoned that if the excess population of England could be drawn off to other lands, those who remained behind would have jobs and money.

Among those sailing to the new land were of course criminals, adventurers, and those wanting to escape a tyrannical father or a nagging wife. But the greatest appeal was the chance to own land which in Europe was a symbol of status; estates and land went to the oldest son in a family. Younger sons with no chance of inheritance came to America in the hope that they would eventually own land. The very poor came as indentured servants which meant they agreed to work for four to seven years for the person who paid their passage.

For the poor, life in the new colonies of America offered the greatest opportunity in history for a person to benefit from his own labor or skill. With determination, anyone could raise himself through the dignity of his work and diligence. The Puritans held that "piety bred industry, and refusal to work was a sin against God."

But all these individual reasons were secondary to the desires of European merchants and governments alike to promote trade. Gold and silver from the New World had stimulated all commerce. Wealthy people demanded luxuries such as spices, sugar, and tea. They wanted rich furnishings for their mansions and were willing to pay high prices for them.

Dozens of trading companies were chartered by the English government during the colonial period. The most successful, the British East India Company, was formed in 1600 to exploit trade with India. The Levant Company built up a prosperous trade with the eastern Mediterranean, as did the Muscovy Company with Russia. America could furnish another such business opportunity. If English manufactured goods could be sold high, in return for cheap raw materials from the colonies, that would mean a favorable balance of trade.

Then too, sailors still hoped to find a "northwest passage" to the Orient. If it existed, America could be a halfway station to the Indies—an all-English route.

Even if there was no "northwest passage," America still offered something no country in Europe could match—land. For nearly two centuries after the first colonists arrived, no one really knew how big America was, but everyone knew there was plenty of land. Cheap land, which turned out to be more valuable than all the gold of the Indies, was the biggest attraction to draw thousands of people to America.

Life in the colonies   In the 1600s and early 1700s, the colonists struggled to maintain their precarious hold on the narrow coastal plains. The sparse settlements were scattered over vast distances and cut off from each other by unexplored wilderness. No one had any idea of what lay beyond the inland mountain ranges.

Travel between most places was by water and even when a land route from New York to Philadelphia was established, travelers had to cross the Hudson and Delaware rivers by ferry. It was, in fact, easier to cross the Atlantic from Virginia to London than to journey along the coast from Virginia to New York or Boston. Even after land travel improved, Alexander Hamilton spent three days going from New York to Philadelphia by horse.

Because of travel conditions and the necessity for trade with Europe, which was all dependent on water transportation, few colonists even in the late 1600s lived more than ten or twelve miles from salt water.

Colonists not only faced disease, fever, starvation and bitter cold in New England and suffocating heat in the south; they soon met another mortal enemy—Indians. Once civilization was established along the Atlantic shores and the organized colonies began to grow, the "Indian problem" arose.

The "Indian problem"

In the beginning, the population balance was on the side of the Indians. The colonies were poorly defended and open to stealthy attacks. Open battles were usually avoided. But as the settlers took over vast tracts of land which the Indians considered theirs by right of ancestry, there were disputes which invariably led to the war path and bloody slaughters.

Even today, there is an "Indian problem." Many modern misunderstandings between the government and American Indians are rooted in colonial times. Undoubtedly some early settlers could not have survived without the help of friendly Indians. Indians taught the newcomers how to plant corn, fertilize the New England soil with fish, hunt game, and use boats on the rushing rivers. Undoubtedly too, if the settlers had not introduced guns, rum, and disease to the Indians, unnumbered lives would have been spared.

Settlement of the thirteen colonies began in 1607. By 1760 the white population along the Atlantic seaboard numbered about 1,600,000. Fifteen years later the population had increased to about 2,500,000, which meant it was doubling about every twenty-three years. In colonial times, people expected to have large families since children meant more hands to plow, weave, or chop trees. Early marriage was encouraged and an unwed maiden of twenty-one was considered "an antique virgin." Benjamin Franklin was one of fifteen children born of two mothers, and William Phips, the Massachusetts governor, was one of twenty-seven—all by the same mother.

The multiplying colonials

Immigration from Europe also swelled the population. The Dutch settled in New Amsterdam (now Manhattan Island) and the Swedes in Delaware. Both colonies were later taken over by the English, who settled the middle colonies of New York, New Jersey, Delaware, and Pennsylvania. Georgia, founded as a buffer between Spanish Florida and the Carolinas, was settled in 1733, under the leadership of James Oglethorpe, and became a haven for English debtors.

**British control
of colonial trade**

During the early years the English kings paid little attention to the American colonies which were allowed, in effect, to become semi-independent republics. There was little worry in England about enforcing British trade regulations in America.

The colonies were operating under what was called the *mercantile system*, common during the seventeenth and eighteenth centuries. Briefly, that meant that they existed solely for the benefit of the mother country. Wealth was created in the mother country by selling the colonies manufactured goods at a high price and buying their raw materials cheaply. The American colonies insured Britain's naval supremacy by building ships, providing ships' stores, seamen, trade, and products such as sugar that would otherwise have to be bought from foreign countries.

Eventually, to control the system to British satisfaction, a number of measures were passed by Parliament. The most famous of these were the Navigation Laws which restricted commerce to and from the colonies to English vessels. In 1651, further restrictions required that European goods bound for America had to be landed first in England where customs duties were collected and British middlemen took a cut of the profit. Other curbs required certain "enumerated" products such as tobacco to be sent to England only, even though a foreign market would pay higher prices.

The colonists were annoyed even more by restrictions on what they could produce at home for export. Woolen cloth and beaver hats, for instance, could not be sold outside the colonies.

Although aggravating, the Navigation Laws were not much of a burden to people who had become experts in smuggling. The laws were not very well enforced and bribery of customs officials was considered a routine business transaction. Many fortunes were made in this way. John Hancock of Massachusetts came to be known (perhaps unfairly) as "King of the Smugglers."

The British mercantile system was not all bad for the colonists. The British government paid handsome bounties to colonials who produced ships and ships' stores, even in competition with envious English builders and merchants. Virginia tobacco-planters enjoyed a complete monopoly of the British market, even though they were forbidden to ship to other countries.

All in all, the average colonist was better off financially than the average Englishman. It was not until the colonies were ripe for revolution that the British authorities made their biggest mistakes. Probably the worst effect of the mercantile system was that Americans were not allowed to buy, sell, ship, or manufacture under conditions they felt were most profitable. To the freedom-loving colonists, it was debasing. Benjamin Franklin wrote in 1775:

We have an old mother that peevish is grown
She snubs us like children that scarce walk alone:
She forgets we're grown up and have sense of our own.

The colonists endured the Navigation Laws until the 1764 Sugar Act demanded the seizure of vessels caught at smuggling. Prime Minister George Grenville then proposed to raise the revenue required for enforcing the Sugar Act by imposing a stamp tax on about fifty items. This alarmed the colonists who were already paying heavy local taxes. The prospect of paying double taxes did not sit well at all.

"Taxation without representation is tyranny," became the protest of thousands. Actually they did not want direct representation in the British Parliament; in the colonies, many small farmers, religious dissenters, and back-country pioneers had no vote even in local elections. What they really wanted was a return to the old days before the French and Indian War, when the Navigation Laws were loosely enforced.

Although the Stamp Act was repealed in 1766, the seeds of American independence had been sown. Colonial protests, with the Sons of Liberty crying, "Liberty, Property and No Stamps," whetted the freedom zeal. Unpopular stamp agents were hung in effigy and their houses wrecked. Trouble raged in Britain as Englishmen protested paying taxes to protect nearly two million colonials who refused to pay even one-third of the cost of their own defense.

Americans were happy with the repeal and New Yorkers erected a statue of King George III which was made of lead. A few years later, it was melted down into thousands of bullets to be used against King George's British troops.

The growing colonial resentment

CHAPTER 2
EARLY MARITIME DEVELOPMENT

Most of the early arrivals in the colonies were laborers, craftsmen, and farmers. There were a few seamen, but after the six-to-eight-week Atlantic crossing, most of them swore never again to set foot aboard ship. As America's maritime history shows, they soon did however, not only for survival but for adventure, wealth, fame, and eventual independence.

As they worked to make a home in a strange, crude, and different world, thousands of miles from their ancestral dwellings and family graveyards, the settlers saw the small ships in the harbor as their only link to the mother country. Ships brought mail, livestock, clothing, clocks, furniture, trinkets for trade with the Indians, guns, and ammunition. As early as 1716, a little lighthouse was built at the entrance to Boston Harbor to guide ships past the treacherous shoals there.

The thirteen colonies along the Atlantic coast had little communication with one another except by sea and by navigable rivers emptying into the Atlantic. Water travel was the strongest tie binding the colonies together, and even that was slow and often dangerous. Eventually, rough trails grew into roads between the principal cities. Land travel was through clouds of dust or seas of mud in summer, and more mud or snow in winter. There was not a single hard-surfaced turnpike anywhere in the colonies until about the middle of the eighteenth century when horse-drawn carriages and stage coaches could finally be used. Riders on horseback, following crude wilderness trails, took twenty-nine days to carry the news of the Declaration of Independence from Philadelphia to Charleston.

Scattered along the dusty roadways and main streets of coastal

On previous page: New Englanders turned to the sea for their livelihood. Many of the sailors were teenagers and their skippers were not much older, but they were known and respected all over the world. The merchant ship *Hercules* of Salem is shown here coming to anchor in Naples, Italy, in 1809.

towns, taverns and inns provided rest for hungry, weary travelers —and a stable and hay out back for the horses. These were often informal social clubs of sorts, offering strong liquor and gambling. Newspapers were scarce, so the inns were also clearinghouses for news, gossip, rumor, information, and misinformation about what was going on elsewhere. Much of the '76 Independence fever grew in these inns.

Workaday America

The hard-working, adaptable colonists were soon at home on both land and sea. They hacked at the forests to build log cabins and fishing vessels. They cleared land for crops and gardens, hunted game, and fished the rivers and coastal waters. The whole family worked together and gradually the one-room shelters progressed to roomy dwellings; oiled paper was replaced by glass for their windows.

The colonies of Maryland and Virginia began shipping tobacco across the Atlantic, while the middle "bread" colonies exported grain. By 1759, New York alone was sending 80,000 barrels of flour a year to England.

Fishing and whaling were profitable in all the colonies, but they were major industries in New England whence great shiploads of salted cod were sent off to the Catholic countries of Europe.

This bustling commerce, both coastwise and overseas, enriched all the colonies, especially New England, New York, and Pennsylvania.

Homemade and homespun

Life in the colonies was slow and humdrum by today's standards, particularly for those who did not go to sea or strike out for the frontier. Everyone worked. There were no welfare programs. People made most of their own furniture; even their cedar shakes and timbers were hand hewn.

About the only manufactured items used in an average home were glass for the windows and a limited number of nails; the family produced everything else it needed. The women hooked rugs, sewed quilts, and knitted garments. They made their own bread, cheese, and cider, butchered and smoked or salted their own meat, and preserved or dried their own fruit. Spinning wheels produced the material for homespun clothing, and home-tanned cowhides were turned into homemade boots and shoes.

Although cash was scarce, there was plenty of cheap, though monotonous, food. The poor ate corn bread, hominy, salt pork, and wild game, and drank beer, hard cider, or rum or whiskey manufactured locally. Brandy and fine wines from Europe were only for the rich. People rarely drank water, which usually made them sick. No one yet knew about contamination.

Prosperous colonists began building two-storied houses of stone and brick in the Georgian style, with many chimneys and fire-places. Later there were tall-columned porticoes such as George Washington had on his home at Mount Vernon. Wealthy men wore silk stockings, breeches made of silk or velvet, and expensively trimmed frock coats of broadcloth. And, in the high fashion of the day, wigs. Colonial dames danced the minuet in silk, hoop-skirted gowns.

Although society was not democratic in the strictest sense, rich and poor alike all shared the common discomforts of the day. No one had central heating, running water, indoor plumbing, or window screens. Ashes and garbage were dumped into the streets where hogs ran loose to root among the debris. Everyone had rats, flies, and mosquitoes. Disease killed more people than did the Indians.

Amusements of the day depended on where one lived and how much money was available. Most people lived in villages or on farms, and ready cash was scarce. New Englanders attended church, public meetings, and lectures—mostly on religious topics. They frowned on celebrating Christmas because it was too "Catholic." "Yuletide is fooltide," they pointed out. Dances, theater, gambling, horse-racing, and fox-hunting were strictly for the southern colonies where living was more pleasant.

For the hard-working pioneers along the seaboard there was little time or energy for socializing, so amusements usually combined work and play. People got together for log-rollings, husking bees, quilting bees, house-raisings, weddings, and funerals.

A fairly adequate school system was set up early in New England; preparing young people for leadership as good Christians was the prime goal. Schools in the middle colonies and in the south came along later—with the emphasis on religion, Greek, and Latin. Private and public schooling was a grim and gloomy business, yet nine colleges were established during the colonial period.

New England seafarers

New Englanders soon realized that their short growing season for food, their fine harbors, and their endless supply of tall timber meant that they would have to turn their efforts towards ships for fishing and trade.

Turning to the sea was the logical thing for them to do. By character, New Englanders were descendants of Vikings from the Scandinavian countries of Denmark, Norway, and Sweden who had settled in England. They had plain ways and plain speech and they prided themselves on their self-sufficiency. They were island people to whom the sea was no stranger. The storm-lashed coast of New England was the ideal home for them.

Josiah Quincy described the whole spirit of early New England when he said: "New Englanders would rather see a boathook than all the sheep crooks in the world. . . . Concerning the land, of which the gentleman from Virginia and the one from North Carolina think so much, they think very little. It is, in fact, to them only a shelter from the storm, a perch on which they build their eyrie and hide their young, while they skim the surface and hunt in the deep. . . ."

It was this spirit that sent seafarers from Boston, New London, New Bedford, and Nantucket on long dangerous voyages around Cape Horn to the Indies and China. The usual route east and around the Cape of Good Hope was a familiar one to the less adventuresome New Yorkers and Philadelphians, who thought only of the end justifying the means. For the New Englanders the voyage itself was what mattered.

The hardy Yankees considered life at sea a challenge, a contest, and an escape from the bleak, gloomy Puritan life on land. Sailing to the frozen Arctic, the mysterious Orient, the balmy South Seas, collecting their riches, spices, tea, and tales of the other side of the world were the great rewards. These sailors changed the peoples' taste in dress and home furnishings, they tantalized their appetites at the table. Ebony and carved ornaments, rich cloth, and even patterned Chinese wallpaper began to brighten the austere New England household. Even today, oriental treasures brighten the old mansions of sea captains who first sailed to China from New England's rocky shores.

Yankees were superior seamen

Yankee ships and seamen became known and respected in ports all over the world. These sailors were generally young, rugged, tough, individualists. Although life at sea was harsh, brutal, and hazardous, it was the great opportunity for youths who had no interest in dull clerking jobs or life in a wilderness corn patch. For example, John Boit, Jr., when he was only 19, took the 84-ton sloop *Union* around the world to Canton, China, and home again. John Suter also took a ship to China when he was 19. John Perkins Cushing, at 16, took charge of his uncle's firm in Canton. William Sturgis was 16 when he first sailed to China; at 19 he took command of a vessel. These voyages and responsibilities required quick wit, endurance, and great skill in dealing with strange peoples. Many of the young sailors worked on a farm or in a store when they were not at sea, and skills were passed down from father to son, as New England's maritime history progressed.

Southern shipping

Great plantations grew along the navigable rivers in the middle and southern colonies. "Tidewater" country, the area was called. Swift American-built schooners with tall masts and wide sails ran a lively trade between Charleston and the British West Indies. They carried indigo and cotton to the islands and brought European luxuries back to the colonies. These small, fast ships, could outsail the British, who chased them to collect revenue, and escape through narrow channels barred to larger ships.

In Virginia, plantations with private wharves on the James, York, Rappahannock, and Potomac rivers were self-contained shipping centers. Tobacco by the hogshead went from private wharf to England, and back came Chippendale furniture, gowns, books, and mail for householders of the great Georgian mansions. Virginia's country gentlemen were, in fact, transplanting London culture to the riverbanks of the New World.

For the planters, the rivers were their highways. Shallops and canoes took them on Sunday visits; scows and sloops carried their produce to market. Ketches and barks from New England sailed from wharf to wharf peddling wines, sugar, salt, tin, and candlesticks.

The first fisheries   Fishermen and fur-traders had been active on the coast of Maine and New Hampshire for several years before the founding of Plymouth. The first settlers were saved from starvation by living on herring caught during the spring spawning runs. They soon realized, however, that the big meaty codfish running along the shore by the millions in spring and fall were better than herring and worth more than gold. The "sacred cod" replica on display at the Massachusetts State House in Boston testifies to the importance this big fish had for the early colonists.

Yankee fishermen soon thinned out the grounds near shore and began venturing farther out to sea, to the Acadian Coast, and finally to the "green fishery"—the Grand Banks, off the coast of Newfoundland.

Different kinds of ships were required, once fishing became a commercial contest rather than a mere matter of eating. Fishing fleets became the training centers for young sailors and ship-designers. Local shipyards grew as cod fisheries stimulated the export trade and more ships were needed, mainly to haul fish to the Catholic countries of Spain and Portugal and to the British West Indies.

At first the Yankee fishermen dried their catches on racks near the shore. They cut down trees to make camps for salting and dressing the fish. The "dry fisheries" became more elaborate and numerous as the profits from shipping dried cod abroad increased. The Indians did not like the deforestation, and the French did not like the Yankee invasion of their fishing grounds. These dislikes became the causes of the French and Indian War or, as the Europeans called it, the Seven Years' War.

Before the colonists came, American Indians not only killed and ate whales that became stranded on shore, but hunted them from canoes as they fed close inshore. They used stone and wooden harpoons attached to floats to slow the whales down. Eventually they speared the huge beasts with lances which let them bleed to death.

Around 1650, Long Islanders began hiring Indians to help in their whaleboats. The Yankees had better boats than the Indians and better ideas; they tied the line to the boat instead of to the floats, and stayed with the whale.

Whaling communities sprang up at Southampton, Martha's Vineyard, and Nantucket. A century later, Dartmouth (New Bedford) had the largest whaling fleet in the world.

In its early days whaling was a simple business. When lookouts in watchtowers on shore spotted the great gray hulk and the white jet of vapor shooting skyward, they called out "Whale off." Then everybody ran to the shore, jumped into whaleboats, and gave chase.

If they were able to catch the whale, they dragged it ashore, stripped the blubber with cutting spades and boiled out, or "tried," the oil in huge pots. The smell was hideous and some towns passed laws forbidding the trying of oil near where people lived. Bad as the smell was, it had to be endured. Whale oil was valuable. Cities were growing; their streets and buildings needed light, and machines needed lubricants. Gaslight was not used until well into the nineteenth century and electricity much later. Petroleum "rock oil" had not yet been discovered, so everything depended on whale oil.

It was an uncertain system of whaling but it was a livelihood for many communities. Once when a whale came into Nantucket, no one in town had a harpoon. The whale stayed three days—long enough for the Nantucketers to make a harpoon and catch him. By 1700 Nantucketers were whaling offshore. In 1726 they pulled in 86 "right" whales that came in close to shore to feed.

The whole whaling industry changed one day in 1700 when a sperm whale was washed up on the Nantucket shore. A sperm whale is larger than a right whale, and its oil is purer. Furthermore, the waxy substance, spermaceti, that filled its head made fine candles.

Sailors soon learned that there were plenty of sperm whales to be had, but they were far out to sea, away from the relative safety of coastal waters. Three years after that first sperm whale was caught, six Nantucket sloops were chasing whales as far away as Newfoundland. Fifty years later, all whaling was a deep-sea operation.

Then, instead of being boiled on shore, the blubber was "tried out" aboard ship, and the resultant oil was stored in barrels. Voyages were limited only by the provisions that could be carried aboard ship. Ships usually stayed at sea until their barrels of oil filled the hold—even if it took three years.

Whaling

Whalers sailed first to the South Atlantic, then to the Brazil banks, then to Madagascar in the Indian Ocean; finally they sailed to the Pacific, to the coast of Japan and the "grounds" off Kodiak and Kamchatka. By 1775, Nantucket had 150 whalers at sea. They were joined by others from Provincetown, Eastham, Chatham, and Yarmouth on Cape Cod, Edgartown on Martha's Vineyard, Sag Harbor on Long Island, and from the villages of Rhode Island and Connecticut.

Whaling ports were busy with shipping coming and going. Vessels at the docks made a forest of masts. The wharves were stacked with oil casks and "naval stores," rope, masts, and spars. The air was filled with the smells of cordage and tar, the cries of seagulls, and the rattle and clatter of cargo-handling. In all, the colonies were operating about 360 whalers, manned by about 5,000 men and boys, many of whom were between ten and fourteen years old.

Whaling was a wretched kind of life for the ordinary seaman, yet the lure of the sea was irresistible. The ships were crowded, damp, and smelly; the food was terrible and the drinking water was bad. Discipline was severe and there were long days and months of boredom, punctuated by the terrifying dangers of the sea and the battles with the mammoth prey. Pay was low. A boat-steerer could sign on for the 75th lay, which meant his share would be one barrel of oil out of every 75 taken. The Captain might get one out of seven; a boy's share might be only one barrel out of the 125 taken. Their meager supplies were charged against the money due them after three or four years at sea. It was possible for a man to come home from a long, unsuccessful cruise and be in debt.

Outfitting a seaman

Seamen were outfitted by the ship's owner but their supplies, which were to last three or four years, were charged against their eventual earnings. The pine chests issued to them contained the following:

Straw mattress filled with hay	Two pairs of overalls
Quilt	Two jumpers
Blanket	Two white caps
One quart pot and pan	Two chip hats
Spoon	Three bars of soap
Two pairs of shoes	Razor
Two pairs of thick pants	Pipe and 10 lbs tobacco
One reefer or jacket	Pair of drawers
An oil coat and hat	Pair of mittens
Two woolen overshirts	Lamp and wick
Two hickory shirts	Needles
Two undershirts	Two jackknives

Whales were not the only sea creatures hunted by the seafaring Yankees. Sea-otter pelts were usually collected by trading with the Indians, particularly along the Northwest Pacific coast. The sealers were something different. They cornered the seals on a rocky beach, cut off their water retreat, and clubbed them to death. Pelts were removed, stretched, and pegged on the ground to dry, like salt codfish. Shore gangs "worked" the beaches while the ship was handled by a skeleton crew. Sea elephants' body fat was stripped, cut into "horse pieces" a foot wide, like that of a whale, and carried to where trypots were set up.

Seals, sea otters, and sea elephants

It was rough work and a cruel business, one which in later years kept the Coast Guard busy enforcing laws that were passed to protect seals and other sea life.

Whaling, fishing, and sea-hunting called for more, stouter, and faster ships. Colonial shipbuilders designed the kinds of ships that would best suit their needs. They were skilled craftsmen; their ships were sturdy, fast, and capable of outrunning the British revenue vessels. The craftsmen commanded great respect; often they had their meals with the families of their employers—a custom not practiced in the Old World.

Colonial shipbuilding

The magnificent forests also furnished the beginnings of naval stores. Tar, pitch, rosin, and turpentine—highly prized in England—brought generous bounties. Shipbuilders moved into New England forests and set up sawmills to take power from the swift rivers. Tall trees suitable for masts were reserved for the British Navy and anyone cutting down "reserved" timber was subject to a fine. There was one exception—if the trees were blown down by a windstorm, then they could be taken and sold. This meant unexpected income for the lucky finder; from that came the modern term for a bit of good luck—windfall.

CHAPTER 3
COLONIAL SEAPORTS

Early towns in America sprang up on the seacoast or along rivers, where boats could load and unload their cargoes. These towns became cosmopolitan centers of culture where water traffic brought the people news and goods from other colonies and, later, from the West Indies, Europe, and China.

The most precious cargo aboard the early ships was people—people to till the soil, build sail ships, manufacture things, and start shops or businesses. More people meant new families and children, churches, and schools—all of which led to culture and stability in the New World. Almost all the first English settlers were men but in 1619, ninety young women were sent to Virginia to become wives of the settlers. A man had to pay his bride's "fare," 120 pounds of tobacco.

As more immigrants crossed the ocean to America, the look of "colonials" changed. For the first 100 years almost all the people were English. By 1763 about half of the colonials were German, Dutch, Irish, Scotch, Scotch-Irish, French Huguenot, and Jewish. And by that time, the colonies had a half-million Negroes, brought from Africa as slaves.

America was already a "melting pot" of nearly four million people: slaves, indentured servants, criminals, tailors, traders, weavers, religious zealots, idealists, scholars, "gentleman" farmers, pirates, adventurers, and wanderers who came to the New World to see what was there.

Colonial towns were not especially convenient or healthy places to live. Streets, muddy trails at best, were rutted, sometimes cluttered with cattle, pigs, or sheep, and filthy with garbage. Disease

On previous page: Early colonial towns were situated on rivers or bays where ships could handle cargo. From such towns, seafarers sailed on long voyages to the Indies and China. Mystic Seaport, Connecticut, shown here, is a reconstruction of a nineteenth-century seaport, complete from cobblestone streets to square-riggers. Photo: Louis S. Martel, Marine Historical Association, Inc.

was common, and infants and young children were frequent victims. Superstition and strange home remedies were poor substitutes for proper medical treatment. Only the very hardy or lucky people reached old age.

Since houses were of wood, heating and cooking was by open fire, and light was furnished by candles, fire was a constant hazard. There were no fire mains—every household had a fire bucket and ladder for use in fire fighting.

In New England, public punishments were as unreasonable and severe as they were in Europe. Many offenses were punishable by death. Even idleness (drinking beer for more than an hour during working hours) could bring a public whipping. A scolding wife could be ducked in water at the end of a pole or have a wooden clamp placed on her tongue for part of the day. Gossips could expect the same punishment. Public whipping and use of the pillory were common. Counterfeiters, runaway slaves and servants could be branded with a hot iron or have their ears cut off. The hanging gallows was a prominent feature of the public square.

Prosperous New England merchants and rich southern planters lived in grand style. For common people, life was simple and food was cheap. There were fish, oysters, and clams in rivers and bays. Deer, waterfowl, and other birds came almost to the doorsteps in villages and towns. Every home had a kitchen garden, and apples, cherries, pears, and berries were grown. Beer and cider were plentiful—a New England family would put up as much as ten to twenty barrels of cider for the season.

Homespun and homemade clothing lasted for years. Only rich people wore clothing imported from Europe. Furniture was also homemade. Later, this became a profitable business for the skilled cabinetmaker. Plates and kitchen utensils were of wood, and forks were a rarity before 1700. Table napkins from England were a status symbol and used only for impressing guests.

The first settlers brought their manners and ways of life with them from Europe. But once on American soil they began to change. The way of life in the new land was different; America was growing, and communities developed their own individuality. Seaport towns became cities that were so different from each other they might as well have been little republics.

Portsmouth

The people who settled along the south bank of the Piscataqua River in New Hampshire were a rugged lot. Many came from England as indentured slaves; they worked for their masters until they could buy their freedom. Others came as squatters from Plymouth to escape the religious persecution and restrictions of the Puritans. There were also desperate criminals from London jails and poor people from the slums. The settlement, located as it was between Boston and settlements on the Gulf of Maine, soon became known as Portsmouth. It also became a rough and brawling port and an important colonial shipbuilding center. By 1760, only Massachusetts produced more ships than New Hampshire.

The Piscataqua shipyards and ports flourished from the earliest days. Ships sailed from Portsmouth with huge white pine timbers which became masts for ships of the Royal Navy. The government paid a bounty of one pound a ton for the "King's masts," which weighed about 20 to 40 tons each. Between 1694 and 1775, some 4,500 of them were sent from New England forests to British shipyards. It took as many as 40 oxen to haul each mast through the woods to a waterway where it could be sent downriver to a special mast port. The masts for Admiral Lord Nelson's famous flagship, HMS *Victory*, came from forests above the Piscataqua. The ships *America* and *Ranger* of the Continental Navy were built on the shores of the Piscataqua. The Royal Navy suffered through the Revolutionary War with decaying masts that could not be replaced because Americans cut off their supply.

Portsmouth also sold products sent downriver by farmers in the interior. In 1671 Piscataqua ports exported 500 tons of fish and thousands of furs; imports that same year included 2,000 tons of salt and 300 casks of wine and brandy.

Along the coast, New Hampshire crews of eight to ten men in their marvelously seaworthy whaleboats, delivered the mail, carried tools, pots and pans, a little tea, Bibles, eyeglasses from Boston, perhaps an ear trumpet or two, and the usual rum. They were Indian-fighters and sailors; they took turns at the oars, used jib sails when the wind was good, and camped on shore when darkness came.

By 1760, Portsmouth had 4,500 people and fortunes were being made in shipbuilding, fishing, and trading. Vessels built there were in such great demand that a Portsmouth shipmaster could sail a ship and her cargo to England, sell it all, return home on a passenger ship, and still make a profit. William Pepperell began as a fisherman, but finally had 100 vessels on the banks of Nova Scotia, and sent others to the West Indies, Spain, and Portugal with dried cod to trade for salt, iron, cordage, wines, and fruits. Prosperous Portsmouth soon began trading fish and furs for London fashions, combs, lace, shawls, spices, and wines.

Boston   That first winter, 1630, showed the Puritans that their survival, livelihood, and eventual prosperity in their new land would depend on the sea. Of the 800 settlers, 200 died of sickness and starvation; those who survived ate fish.

Within four years, the original settlers were joined by 4,000 more. By then, shipbuilding was already underway. Shipyards sprang up all over Boston Bay—at Newbury, Ipswich, Salem, Gloucester, and along the Mystic River—and built small, single-decked smacks, shallops, pinnaces, and ketches in the early years.

The Puritans put up one-and-a-half-story houses of crudely hewn beams, and planted flowers in small fenced dooryards. They laid out streets and a common grazing ground for cattle. They lived on salted cod, venison, clams, mussels, and Indian corn. Their manners were stiff and their clothes plain. Bostonians became famous for their unyielding laws and severe punishments. In 1660 Mary Dyer was hanged on Boston Common for being a Quaker. Three others, Mary Jones, Mary Parsons, and Ann Hibbins were hanged as witches.

Bostonians accepted smugglers, but would not allow husbands and wives to kiss in public. Sea captains returning from long voyages were severely punished for this kind of outward demonstration of affection. Hospitality to travelers was carefully watched. It was prohibited to entertain strangers without giving the town authorities a description of them and a statement of their reasons for being in Boston.

Yet, in spite of its cruelties and absurdities, Boston in 1690, with its 7,000 people, was the largest town in the North American colonies.

Boston's Fishing and Commerce   Fishing first kept the people from starving, then created trade, and later built great fortunes. Within a generation, sometimes in only a few years, a poor man could become wealthy. Shipowners, shipmasters, shopkeepers, farmers, sailors, artisans, and fishermen were all involved one way or another with sea enterprises. Before long, Boston dominated all the commerce along the Atlantic coast from Maine to New Amsterdam. When Virginian plantations began using African slaves, Bostonians were only too happy to supply them with poorer grades of cod for feeding the slaves.

Before 1700, Boston ships were sailing overseas—to the eastern Mediterranean, to the coast of New Guinea, to Madagascar and other parts of the Indian Ocean. Boston merchants were both importers and exporters. Ships sailed for England and Holland with wheat, rye, and furs, and returned with linens, woolens, shoes, stockings, and dry goods. Barter was the common form of exchange until 1652, when the Bay colony began minting the first coins in America.

London versus Boston Merchants   Boston merchants actively competed with London merchants, who wanted to divide New England into provinces with a governor-general over the whole. But the Puritans resisted and won. Their faster sailing ships could carry better merchandise at lower prices and they hung onto their Atlantic trade.

Nearly all the Boston merchants were part owners of shipyards, warehouses, and wharves. They also owned the ships that carried the goods. They invested in ironworks, sawmills, breweries, and distilleries. Their business network soon reached all over the world —to Russia, to England, and even to China.

The Boston waterfront was busy all year round. Sleek ships and rough schooners filled it. Long Wharf, built in 1710, was more than 2,000 feet long and was crowded with warehouses, wagons, carts, cranes, and sail lofts. The whole area was a colorful, pungent patchwork of crafts and goods of all kinds; sailing coasters from Virginia unloading tobacco, cotton, and turpentine, or Cape Cod shallops stacking their barrels of whale oil, casks of rum, or West Indian sugar.

Boston had neither good weather nor a good harbor; it was Bostonians themselves who made the city great. They mixed greed, religion, and daring for a philosophy that said, "profit is to be considered above everything else." Boston shipmasters were known all over the world for their ruthlessness in doing business. Money and profit meant everything. At home, they were very important people in the community, ranking just below ministers and judges.

Salem   Salem was second only to Boston as a great and busy seaport. Its Puritans lived by and off the sea; giant forests and fur-bearing animals made shipbuilding and trading profitable businesses.

The people of Salem built their big, dark houses right beside the water, facing the wharves and countinghouses. Ten-year-old boys went to work as countinghouse clerks until they had learned enough to go to sea. They usually worked about twelve hours a day, six days a week, and were paid five or six shillings—a couple of dollars. Clerks shared rooms in attics; had their breakfasts of tea and johnnycake, and suppers of codfish stew. It was a dull life but there was a promise of better things. With skill and hard work, a countinghouse lad could go to sea in a couple of years and become master of a ship by the time he was eighteen years old. By the time he was thirty, a master could retire as a rich "old" man.

As with all Bay colony ports, the people in Salem believed in training their boys young. Youngsters were taught to fish, row, sail, and navigate almost from the time they could walk. Boys were taught to hunt, too, but they did not much care for it. Most of them preferred going to sea.

Probably much of the lure of faraway places had to do with the Puritans' gloomy home life. Not that there was no excitement. People were always being punished, or standing up in church to confess their sins, or being whipped and run out of town. And then there was the witchcraft trial in 1692 where nineteen people were convicted of casting evil spells, and hung.

Salem's shipyard was begun almost as soon as the town was

settled, and Salem became a convenient harbor for unloading the Marblehead and Gloucester fishing boats and sending their cargoes on to Boston.

The town was a very close community. The people looked after their own—and those who believed as they did. Richard Derby, for example, would accept only Salem boys for training in his countinghouse. His son, Elias Hasket Derby, took over the business and set up a seamanship class for boys in the countinghouse. Using the brig *Rose* as a training ship he taught them navigation on trips to the West Indies. Such seamanship training brought great wealth to Salem, particularly in trading with China. Salem youths were not only fine sailors, they became shrewd bargainers and diplomats in their Canton offices.

Bristol and Newport

Bristol and neighboring Newport were founded between 1636 and 1643 by people from Massachusetts who were seeking religious and political freedom. The founders included Quakers and other religious dissenters. Both ports flourished, trading along the coast in rum, timber, and furs. Their ships sailed to the West Indies with red onions and the small, chunky horses known as Narragansett pacers.

Newport's population increased to 7,000. Religious freedom continued. The Quaker meetinghouse, the oldest in America, was built in 1699. Newport also had the first public library in America, donated by merchants who had made great profits from the sea. Beautiful mansions were built as the town continued to compete successfully with Boston as a New England port.

Bristol, with a population of about 1,000, tried to keep up with Newport but the shipowners and the people became cynical after a while. They did not keep their liberal attitudes towards religion or people's rights. Their attitudes came to light right after what was known as King Philip's War. Philip was the son of the friendly Indian chief, Massasoit, who had asked the General Court in Plymouth to give English names to his two oldest sons. Philip went on the warpath, uniting Indians against the white settlers.

This war had cost the Plymouth colony and the Massachusetts Bay colony £100,000, and 600 men—one-tenth of their fighting force. As punishment, the General Court decided to sell 500 Indians to the West Indies as slaves.

The average selling price for an Indian slave was 32 silver shillings or 12 bushels of corn—or 100 pounds of wool. But the plantation owners in the West Indies soon found that the Indians were not a good bargain; they were proud and stubborn and they did not want to have children born into slavery. The Bristol traders disliked the idea, too, because they were a little afraid of the Indians.

But it became known that there were plenty of slaves to be purchased in Africa. Soon, Bristol ships loaded with leg irons, rum, and cheap trade goods were headed for the Slave Coast. The ships sailed with crews of about twelve men, whose wages ranged from $8 a month for a cabin boy to $30 for a master. The profits for delivering slaves to Cuba or South Carolina were nearly 100 percent.

New York   The Dutch settlement of New Amsterdam was at the lower end of what is now Manhattan. It contained Fort William, several churches, and some windmills. Its houses were yellow brick or were white-washed, with high-peaked roofs and gable ends. Trees grew in tidy rows along Wall Street and many of the houses had little flower beds in their front yards. Housewives swept their paved walks every morning. Some of the houses had furniture from Holland and colored tiles framing the fireplaces.

The people dressed plainly and lived quiet, serious lives. The town covered only about one square mile until some time after the Revolution.

In the summer of 1664, five British frigates entered the harbor. The British took the town over without a fight and renamed it New York.

New York prospered, trading in furs—mostly beaver—and products sent downriver from the Hudson valley where thousands of English and German farmers produced great quantities of wheat, corn, and flax. Fleets of sloops sailed the Hudson River, along with small fast boats and timber rafts which were sometimes occupied by whole families.

The character of New York began to change when France and England went to war in 1689. The English issued *letters of marque* which gave ship captains a kind of patriotic license to steal from French shipping. By 1700 privateering had become outright piracy. New York became the most popular pirate rendezvous on the Atlantic coast.

Pirates wearing rough-cut, shoulder-length hair and a single gold earring were seen all along the waterfront. Their "uniform" consisted of short loose smocks, wide-bottomed pants, and wide leather belts with murderous cutlasses hanging on the left side. Most of them went barefoot except in winter, even though many carried fortunes in stolen loot. These men were openly recruited by merchants and government officials to sail in pirate ships.

With only a couple of dozen men in the City Watch, there was not much law enforcement. Watchmen carried clubs and lanterns and used wooden rattles to warn of their presence so that criminals could get out of the way.

The poorly lit waterfront was actually a deadly maze of alleys and canals. Streets were "lighted" by means of a lantern placed in the window of every seventh house. Pirate gangs roamed the coves and wharves on foot or in canoes and skiffs, stealing anything of value. They stripped vessels of equipment and cargo and no one dared stop them. Sailors hanging out in waterfront taverns were a rough bunch who did not expect to live past forty. If the fever, smallpox, or storms at sea didn't get them, French privateers or buccaneers would.

Not all pirates were riffraff. Many leading citizens were openly friendly with them. The Royal Governor, Benjamin Fletcher, entertained in his home such seagoing rovers as Moston, Coates, Tew, and Glover. Wealthy merchants had parties for them when they returned with their valuable cargoes. One of these pirates, William Kidd, was a well-established citizen who married a wealthy New York widow, and lived in a fine house at Hanover and Pearl Streets. However, Kidd was eventually caught by the British and hanged in London. After his death, piracy faded away. Men who remained pirates were mostly stupid, lazy, or weak, and the navies patrolling the seas gradually got rid of them.

Philadelphia

The Dutch and Swedes came first, in the 1620s and 1630s, and settled along the Delaware and Schuylkill rivers. Then, in 1682 William Penn, under a land grant from Charles II of England, founded a town which he called Philadelphia (from the Greek word for "brotherly love") and the province of Pennsylvania.

The "City of Brotherly Love," as it was known, lies 30 miles upriver from Delaware Bay in the center of what was then a rich agricultural country. Penn intended the city to "afford asylum to the good and oppressed of every nation." There was to be religious freedom, free speech, petition and trial by jury, no capital punishment, and no fighting, swearing, or lying. Pistols, daggers, or other unusual weapons could be carried only by military officers and strangers traveling on lawful errands.

Penn's appeal for settlers spread over western Europe and, within a year, 23 ships had arrived carrying German, Welsh, and English Quakers. Some of the immigrants were tradesmen and laborers; many were the sorry illiterates so typical of the seventeenth century. There were long-bearded Dunkers, Moravians, Schwenkfelders, and Mennonites. Many of them landed sick or dying of ship's fever and dysentery. Food was always scarce; in one ship, people lived on rats for a week.

All sects, however, shared the Quakers' beliefs in non-violence. Life would be quiet, sedate, with no bearing-of-arms. As the colony expanded, Welsh Baptists arrived, along with Scottish Presbyterians from North Ireland. The big fiery-tempered Scots, with their bagpipes, Highland flings, and brawls at the local taverns, found frontier life away from town more to their liking.

After 50 years, the colony had become a weird mix of nationalities, religions, and languages. Dutch, Germans, Swedish, and Welsh all clung to their native tongues. Dunkers shouted at the yelling Welsh, while the Quakers spoke soft "thees" and "thous."

By 1730, Philadelphia held 50,000 people and, by 1763, 200,000 people. It become the second largest city in the British empire.

Ships sailed from the port of Philadelphia to the West Indies, to western European ports, and to England. They carried wheat, flour, corn, flaxseed, barrels, casks, skins, furs, and ginseng, and brought back manufactured goods from England. Young men like Robert Morris made fortunes in shipping. Morris joined the powerful mercantile house owned by Charles Willing and became a full partner at the age of 20. A few years later he owned more ships than any other man in America.

As river traffic expanded, the need for ship and boat construction required shipyards. Vessels were needed to haul flour, rye, and wheat to the city and to the mills at Schuylkill. Rivermen in buckskin, handling their huge rafts, brought white pine, spruce, cedar, oak, and fir to the shipyards and to shops for making furniture. Almost every religious creed or ethnic group had a boatyard. There were orders for brigs, brigantines, schooners, and shallops, as Philadelphia merchants began bartering in the West Indies for rum, molasses, and indigo. Dressed leather for shoes, saddles, harnesses, and furniture were demanded in England and western Europe.

Blacksmiths' shops turned out nails, spikes, chain plates, block sheaves, and rudder irons, while anchors were made at special forges. Other shops produced tinplate, kettles, coffee pots, saucepans, and fine glass and pottery. Bookbinding, begun as a shop industry, produced reading materials, and books went along with the early newspapers—the *Pennsylvania Packet* and Benjamin Franklin's *Pennsylvania Gazette*—in coastwise ships.

The effects of piracy were felt in Philadelphia during the 1680s and 1690s. Loot from the Red Sea found its way to the city merchants, many of whom approached the pirates directly for oriental silks, pearls, gems, bars of silver and gold, "pieces of eight," and even pistols. The pirates were a bad lot—they engaged in carousing, looting homes for pewter and silver, gambling, and harassing offshore fishermen.

For a while they were socially acceptable; one handsome pirate became engaged to the daughter of Edwin Markham, the governor of the province. Then, William Penn returned from England with the news of pirate trials and hangings. The colonies would no longer have to transport pirates to England for trial. Special courts with full hanging powers were set up in the colonies and, after 1700, piracy was no longer a serious public problem.

Baltimore   Established in 1729, Baltimore was a small town of back-country German and Scotch-Irish farmers. It served as a port of entry where seagoing vessels could safely anchor. Not far away was the Great Eastern Road which ran from Philadelphia to Georgetown (now a part of Washington, D.C.) on the Potomac River. Other towns had grown nearby. Joppa developed around a courthouse built in 1709 on the Gunpowder River. But Baltimore with its better harbors soon outdistanced Joppa in business and citizens.

The port was a trade center where ships loaded cargoes of corn and tobacco for England, and unloaded manufactured items when they returned. By 1756, a Baltimore ship had sailed to the West Indies with tobacco and corn and returned loaded with sugar, rum, and slaves.

Shipyards sprang up all along Chesapeake Bay. Every sort of locally built craft could be seen: gundalows, sloops, ketches, brigs, schooners heaped with oysters, and log canoes loaded with vegetables. Eventually, Baltimore's skillful ship-designers gave up the old-fashioned ideas that called for a ship's beam to be one-third of her length. Instead, the Baltimore clipper schooners were long and lean with flared bows and raked masts. American boys dreamed of those ships, ". . . long black Baltimore schooners under a cloud of snowy-white canvas, reaching across the wind. . . ."

Baltimore's schooner-rigged privateers and slavers were the fastest craft on the oceans. They were forerunners of the tall-masted, square-rigged clippers, the most beautiful ships in the world, which were queens of the sea from about 1830 to 1855.

Annapolis

In 1648 a group of Puritans in Virginia, looking for a place to practice religion as they chose, were allowed by Lord Baltimore to move to Maryland. They built the little town of Providence (now Annapolis). The sheltered waters of the Severn River offered them transportation and a means of trading and shipping tobacco abroad.

For the first 90 years after it was settled, Maryland had only two towns: St. Mary's and Annapolis. Because of its location halfway up Chesapeake Bay, Annapolis—named for Princess, later Queen, Anne of Great Britain—became Maryland's capital. For a short while, from November 1783 to August 1784, it was the capital of the United States. It later became famous as the home of the U.S. Naval Academy.

The English Royal Governor, Sir Francis Nicholson, planned the city around Church Circle and State Circle, the two being connected by School Street. The city was planned so that wealthy people could live quietly, away from the noise and hubbub. The town allowed modest lots for workmen's homes, space for pungent work such as that done in blacksmiths' shops and tanneries, and docks for ships and fishing.

Rivers and the Bay were the highways of those days. People used to visit back and forth from one plantation to another, to the Eastern Shore, and to other cities and towns. The *Maryland Gazette*, begun in 1727 (and still being published) was for a long time the only newspaper in the colonies. The people of "Water town" ordered their goods and sent their letters by sea; they had a theater and there were balls, racing events, musical gatherings, and parties. Their ferry service on the Severn River operated until 1887 when it was replaced by a bridge.

Annapolis still has the look of colonial times. Some of its old homes were built before the Revolutionary War. They face on walks and streets paved with brick, and their stately parlors open onto gardens filled with ancient flowering trees.

During the month of December 1774, 20 ships arrived in the port of Annapolis from overseas, and 22 ships departed for destinations overseas. A partial listing of these movements (quoted from *Naval Documents of the American Revolution*) reveals the variety of imports and exports and the wide range of the ships' operations:

Arrived

2 December — Brig *Peggy*, Abraham Walton, Master, 50 tons, 9 men, from Tortola with 15 hogsheads muscavado* sugar, 12800 pounds brown sugar.

3 December — Ship *William*, Jas. Thomas, Master, 200 tons, 15 men, from Bristol with European goods, 105 convicts and 4 servants.

14 December — Ship *John*, Chas. Poaug, Master, 140 tons, 10 men, from Cork with 350 yards Irish linen, 10 servants.

17 December — Sloop *Betsey*, Jas. Avery, Master, 35 tons, 6 men, from Hispaniola with 60 tierces† and 19 hogsheads molasses.

19 December — Ship *Dick*, Thos. Pearce, Master, 200 tons, 17 men, from Liverpool with 9,680 bushels of salt, 5000 bricks, $14\frac{7}{12}$ chaldrons‡ of coal.

Departed

1 December — Brig *Geddis*, John Harrison, Master, 50 tons, 7 men, for Liverpool with 3500 bushels of wheat, 1400 staves and heading.§

24 December — Ship *Richard Penn*, Isaac All, Master, 200 tons, 10 men, for Leghorn with 12700 bushels of wheat, 20 barrels of flour.

24 December — Snow *Potowwmack*, Archibald Graham, Master, 140 tons, 12 men, for Cork with 200 hogsheads of flaxseed, 200 barrels of flour, 10000 staves and headings.

---

* Raw sugar.
† A tierce is 42 gallons.
‡ A chaldron was a unit of measure that varied between 32 and 72 imperial bushels.
§ Sides and ends of barrels.

By 1680 a number of places in Virginia had been selected as likely sites for towns. Each had deep water and was accessible to ships. Among the early towns that became official ports were Hampton, Norfolk, Nansemond, James City, Powhatan, Yorktown, Queensborough, and Alexandria. They soon grew and had churches, court houses, prisons, private dwellings, and warehouses along their wharves. Everyone lived on or near water.

Alexandria

Indian dugout canoes were the first ferries used in Virginia. Sometimes two canoes were lashed together. Thomas Chalkley, a Quaker minister and merchant mariner, observed at Yorktown in 1703: "We put our horses into two canoes tied together, and our horses stood with their forefeet in one and their hind feet in the other. . . ." Later, settlers in Virginia used anything that floated to cross streams and rivers: canoes, flatboats, scows, even sailing boats. Finally, with the steady increase in population, there was a demand for public transportation across creeks and rivers. In 1636 the first public ferry began carrying passengers between Norfolk and Portsmouth. It was a skiff rowed by slaves. A second ferry went into service in 1640 at Hampton.

Of all Virginia's ports, Port Hampton handled the largest amount of shipping. An early observer wrote: "Norfolk hath a depth of water for a 40-gun ship or more and conveniences of every kind for heaving down and fitting out large vessels; also a very fine ropewalk. There is a passage boat from Hampton to Norfolk and from York to Gloucester. . . ." In the third quarter of the eighteenth century, Norfolk replaced Alexandria as Virginia's principal seaport. Norfolk got the commerce, but Alexandria kept its colonial charm.

Alexandria, a long way inland from the mouth of the Chesapeake Bay, on the lower Potomac River, began as a colonial seaport and shipyard. Tobacco and grain were shipped from there, and by 1776 caravans of "flour waggons" were coming from as far west as Winchester to load ships for England.

Colonial Alexandria had fine taverns for accommodating travelers and entertaining "gentry"—the Washingtons, Fairfaxes, Masons, and other plantation owners who maintained mansions in or near town. Scottish merchant-shippers, such as the partners Carlyle and Dalton, built handsome town houses, as did George Washington. There were lavish parties and balls; and in the market square fairs, political rallies, and other gatherings.

Washington raced his own horses and was a steward of the Alexandria Jockey Club. He recruited troops in Alexandria and drilled them in the market square before marching against the French in 1754. The town was incorporated in 1779; its seal shows "a ship in full sail with a balance equally poised above the ship." A few of Alexandria's streets are still paved with cobblestones that were put down by Hessian prisoners of war during the Revolutionary War.

Charleston   Charleston was founded in 1670 by an English expedition from Barbados. King Charles II wanted a trading post on the mainland to supply the West Indies with food and timber. He also saw that Barbados had become overpopulated because so many slaves had been brought there. Charleston soon became the center for an immense trade area that stretched north to Virginia and south as far as Spanish Florida.

The people of Charleston had bitter memories of the British, and later fought fiercely against them during the Revolution. Many of them were of Irish or Scots descent and, whether their ancestors came to this country because they had been caught up in the Irish rebellion of 1649 or whether they had been sent overseas for some small crime, they were proud and desperate people.

They were self-made men, the planters, merchants, and craftsmen, who turned Charleston into perhaps the most urbane of American cities. There was a semi-public library, and there were bookstores, newspapers, milliners who were in touch with Paris fashions; horse racing, dance assemblies, and easy-mannered men's clubs. Charleston had America's first orchestra with paid musicians. Young men were sent to Europe to be educated at Oxford, Cambridge, London, Edinburgh, Leyden, and Geneva. Young ladies went to "dame" schools where they learned French, drawing, and needlework.

Charleston, with its heavy roof tiles, wide piazzas, jalousied doors, and ironwork fences, resembled a West Indian port town. Its wealth came from indigo, a dye extracted from the West Indian indigo plant, developed by Eliza Lucas between 1741 and 1743. The other crop, rice, was always in demand in England.

The city is on a peninsula where the estuaries of the Ashley and Cooper rivers meet. As with the other colonists along the seaboard, Charleston planters took their families on boats up and down the rivers and tributaries. Some of their boats, built of cypress, were 50 feet long and had collapsible or movable cabins. Their six-to-twelve-man crews were smartly uniformed in white straw hats, red flannel jackets, and wide-bottomed white trousers.

The colony was given a charter in 1729 and divided into North Carolina and South Carolina, and although it remained small for a number of years, the population gradually swelled. A large number of French Huguenots came in the 1690s and later many planters came from Haiti when the slaves there revolted against the French in 1794.

Charleston also became a haven for pirates. One of the more famous was Edward Teach, a flamboyant, rum-drinking killer who was usually called Blackbeard, and who was said to have a dozen wives in West Indies ports.

When the Royal Navy began harassing him in his favorite haunts he sailed for Charleston. Eventually most of his men were killed in fights or captured. On 12 November 1718, 24 of them were hung, but Blackbeard escaped, only to be killed later that same month at Ocracoke Inlet, North Carolina, when some naval ships sent out by the governor of Virginia caught up with him.

The first ships anchoring at Savannah shared the river with alligators. The port was 18 miles inland from the sea, but the tide let deep-water ships tie up at wharves built there. Flatboats brought deerskins down the Savannah River from what is now Augusta—a four-to-five-day trip to the coast. Then they sailed along the inland channel, across Port Royal Sound, and among the islands to Charlestown. The return trip against the current could take as long as a month. **Savannah**

Georgia, the last of the 13 colonies to be settled, was called "The Great Experiment." General James Oglethorpe, whose friend Robert Castell had died in a debtors' prison in England, set out to establish a haven for debtors and people from the London slums. There was much public sympathy in Europe for his cause, and cash donations to help free debtors rolled in.

The 35 families who sailed with him in the *Ann* landed at Charleston on 12 February 1733. The group moved to Savannah, where each family was given a building lot in town and outside the town a garden plot for a total of five acres. Georgia became a mixture of debtors and various religious refugees.

During the 1760s the colony exported silk, leather, lumber, staves, hoops, indigo, rice, peas, corn, and livestock to the West Indies. At first nearly all the crews of vessels sailing the coastal channels, bays, creeks, and sounds were indentured white men, Indians, and Negroes who had bought their freedom. They used poles and sweeps and sometimes, with a good wind, could erect a crude sail on a mast. Navigating the treacherous waterways required great skill and could only be done during daylight.

But the colonists didn't like working the fields—they preferred letting slaves do the job. Some deserted to Carolina or Virginia. The agricultural programs, such as cultivating exotic plants and vineyards, were abandoned as unprofitable. The colony, which had 5,000 people six years after its founding, dwindled to 500.

Although Oglethorpe disapproved of slavery and rum but allowed beer and wine, rum was smuggled in quite openly. It was only when the British allowed slavery and rum that Savannah began to prosper again.

As merchants and sea captains grew rich from trading in the Western Hemisphere, adventuresome Yankees began loading their ships with trinkets and trade goods and sailing for the Far East. The **Trade with China**

Portuguese had led the way in 1516 when they bartered with the Chinese for silks and camphor. The Dutch arrived in 1634, followed by the English "red-haired devils." Finally the Americans, the "flowery-flag devils" entered the race for Oriental treasures.

Elias Hasket Derby, of Salem, sent the *Grand Turk* to Canton in 1787. At that point, Salem had 182 vessels sailing the world's oceans.

In 1790, the *Columbia* of Boston, captained by Robert Gray, returned after a three-year voyage that carried the U.S. flag around the world. Soon, other Yankee captains followed the *Columbia*'s course around Cape Horn, hoping to do business with the Chinese.

But that was not always easy. For one thing, Chinese culture was ancient and well developed—the Chinese had everything they needed and were not interested in trinkets. If foreigners wanted their teas, silks, spices, camphor, ivory, and porcelain, they could pay for them in gold and silver. If Americans did not have money, gold, or silver, they would have to bring something else just as good.

Fortunately, America produced things the Chinese liked as much as gold and silver. One was ginseng root; it grew wild in the forests of North America. The Chinese believed it was a potent aphrodisiac, and bought it eagerly. Another thing they liked was fur—particularly the luxurious pelts of the Pacific sea otters with which the wealthy Mandarins could trim and line their robes.

Ships began sailing around Cape Horn loaded with trinkets, guns, and tools which they traded to the Northwest Indians for pelts. Hardy adventurers soon found their way to the Antarctic and South Seas in search of sealskins. Others sailed to the South Pacific to load fragrant sandalwood. They tempted the Chinese appetites with their favorite treasures from the sea: sea cucumbers, sharks' fins, and edible birds' nests. Eventually the Yankee traders coaxed the Chinese—who had long worn fine silk—to buy American manufactured cotton.

By 1776, Americans had sailed their ships across the seven seas in search of trade and adventure. But soon, they went to sea in a better cause—freedom.

CHAPTER 4
THE REVOLUTIONARY WAR

The American Revolution and the war for independence were not the same thing. The spirit of revolution had existed for a century and a half before the actual revolution began. The first permanent settlers carried with them an "insurrection of thought," against the ways of the Old World. John Adams wrote, in 1818, "The Revolution was effected before the war commenced. The Revolution was in the minds and hearts of the people. . . ."

The road to rebellion

Serious trouble with the colonies began in 1760 when George III became King of England. His German-born predecessors, George I and George II, had been content to let Parliament rule England and her colonies. Not so British-born George III. Working hard to restore power to the throne, he surrounded himself with yes-men. He was a good enough man but proved to be a bad ruler. Many of his problems could be traced to his periodic fits of insanity. He was soon in great difficulty with the American colonies over taxes.

Britain had defeated France in the Seven Years' War which ended in 1763. She had one of the biggest empires in the world but, less happily, the biggest debt. The colonials were not asked to help with this burden, but they were expected to pay one-third of the cost of keeping 10,000 Redcoats on American soil. To accomplish this, in 1765 a Stamp Tax was levied on about fifty items, including newspapers, almanacs, playing cards, and legal documents.

The colonists were furious. They were working hard to wrest a living from the wilderness. They reasoned that if they were forced

On previous page: Prints of naval actions were popular during the early history of the country. This lithograph, printed in Paris, depicts a battle between two English and two American vessels, none of them named. Although Congress ruled in 1777 that the flag would show thirteen stripes and thirteen stars, there was great confusion on the subject. Flags were depicted with from eleven to thirty-six stripes.
Courtesy: The Franklin D. Roosevelt Collection.

to pay a penny now, someday they might have to pay their last penny. In Boston, Samuel Adams told shipowners and merchants that they did not have to pay the taxes: "No Englishman could be made to pay any tax to which he had not given his consent."

Patrick Henry, of Virginia, said the same thing at a meeting of planters in Williamsburg. Groups of men calling themselves the "Sons of Liberty" began destroying the stamps and insulting the King's officers. The colonies got together for the first time when leaders from different parts of the country met in the Stamp Act Congress, which convened in New York in October 1765. Opposition was so heated that England repealed the act. But it was followed by a new tax law. Colonists would now have to pay taxes on things they bought from England: china, paints, glass, paper, and tea. When the colonists refused to buy the merchandise under such conditions, two British regiments were sent to Boston to quiet disturbances. On 5 March 1770, after a snowball attack on some troops, they fired on a group of agitators, killing eleven of them in what came to be known as the "Boston Massacre."

The colonists were also greatly distressed by redoubled British efforts to enforce the existing Navigation Laws. With widespread unemployment in England and complaints to Parliament by English merchants, the law was again repealed, but not completely.

Stubborn George III, just to prove his point, left the tax on tea. In December of 1773, three English ships loaded with tea sailed into Boston Harbor. The harbor master refused to accept the cargo and the British captains refused to sail away until he did.

Samuel Adams cooked up a plan to get rid of the tea. On the night of 16 December 1773, a band of men dressed as Indians boarded the ships, shouting war whoops, smashed open the chests, and dumped the tea—worth about £18,000—into the harbor. That was a sizable fortune which the East India Company could not afford to lose. And, as the "Boston Tea Party," the affair has become a part of American history.

The Intolerable Acts

Britain decided the colonies should be punished for their brazen act of defiance. More Redcoats or "Lobsterbacks," as British soldiers were derisively called, were sent over to the colonies.

Parliament passed a number of acts known as the "Intolerable Acts," which stripped Massachusetts of many of its chartered rights. Among other things, the acts called for offending British officials to be sent to England for trial instead of facing colonists for their crimes. The Quebec Act, providing for the administering of the 60,000 conquered French subjects in Canada, extended the boundaries of Quebec all the way south to the Ohio River. It also guaranteed their Catholic religion and customs. Anti-Catholic, Protestant colonists were not happy at giving up all that land.

"There ought to be a jubilee in hell over this gain for 'popery'," they said.

The worst of the Intolerable Acts was the Boston Port Act which closed that port until the East India Company had been paid for the dumped tea. This amounted to a siege, and many of Boston's 16,000 people would have starved had it not been for the help of the other colonies.

Colonies unite   Flags flew at half-mast in America on the day the Boston Port Act took effect. The other colonies supported Boston; even faraway Charleston sent rice. John Adams, in Boston, and John Dickinson and Benjamin Franklin, in Philadelphia, joined the chorus of protest. In Maryland, Charles Carroll voiced his sympathy. The House of Burgesses in Virginia passed a resolution declaring that "an attack made on one of our sister colonies to compel submission to arbitrary taxes is an attack made on all British America." Patrick Henry said, "I am not a Virginian, I am an American!"

On 5 September 1774, representatives from all the colonies met at the Continental Congress in Philadelphia. Bostonians wanted freedom from England, but others were still loyal. It was decided to ask King George III to restore the colonists' rights as Englishmen. The representatives would meet again in May 1775 to study the King's reply.

When no reply came, Patrick Henry said, in a speech at St. John's Church in Richmond, "I know not what course others may take but as for me, give me liberty or give me death!"

Meanwhile, Virginia planters began training companies of soldiers, with George Washington in command. Massachusetts farmers, calling themselves Minutemen, because they said they could fight at a minute's notice, met on village greens four times a year. They had no uniforms or insignia of rank and they carried their own muskets of every size, weight, and caliber—the same guns they used for hunting rabbits and squirrels. They went through loading and unloading drill, marched, and probably held target practice. The day's "training" ended with a sermon and a cider-drinking bout at a local tavern.

On the night of 18 April 1775, Bostonians learned that 700 British soldiers were on their way to seize gunpowder and arms stored at Concord and, perhaps, to bag the leaders, Samuel Adams and John Hancock, at their Lexington refuge. A lookout was stationed in the steeple of Old North Church to signal with his lantern when he saw the soldiers.

The Boston patriots despatched Paul Revere to spread the alarm. At Lexington he was joined by William Dawes and Dr. Samuel Prescott. Near Concord, a patrol captured Revere. Dawes managed to escape, but Prescott galloped on with his cry, "To arms. To arms. The British are coming!"

The next morning about 70 Minutemen gathered on the village green at Lexington, facing a company of British soldiers. No one knows who fired the first shot, but eight Minutemen were killed and ten were injured before the Redcoats marched off for Concord. As battles go, it would not make headlines now, but as the Battle of Lexington in 1775, it showed that the homespun Americans were ready to fight and die in the war for independence.

**Lexington
and Concord**

The British marched to Concord while, from behind trees and stone walls, American snipers picked them off like squirrels. They headed back to Boston. By the time they got there, they had lost 247 men, and England had a war on her hands.

It looked like a one-sided fight. The Americans had rebelled against the mightiest empire in the world. Britain had more money, more people (7½ million to 2½ million for America), and a navy spread around the world. The Americans had a few merchant ships and some guns. The British had a professional army of about 50,000 men. American money and supplies were scanty; firearms and powder were in such low supply that Benjamin Franklin seriously proposed going back to using bows and arrows.

A British comment that "The American war would offer no problem that could not be solved by an experienced sheep herder" was not so funny then as it sounds now. The fact was, Americans were *not* soldiers. They were not exactly sheep, either, ready to follow the leader; the fact that one man in a company was appointed captain did not always convince the others that he knew any more about fighting a war than they did. One Rhode Island detachment was known as the "Ragged, Lousy, Naked Regiment."

Although militiamen were numerous, they were unreliable. Finally about 8,000 regulars were whipped into shape by the non-English-speaking German "Baron" Friedrich von Steuben. Even so, there were demoralizing problems in the American society, as profiteers—the get-rich-quick crowd—capitalized on the patriots' problems. The sad truth was that only a select minority of American colonials were selflessly devoted to the cause of independence.

Yet, America was blessed with outstanding leadership at a critical time in history. A remarkable band of statesmen and patriots were ready—John and Samuel Adams; Christopher Gadsden; the master diplomat, Benjamin Franklin; James Otis; Patrick Henry; Robert Livingstone; and John Hancock. And, in the quiet splendor of Mount Vernon, high above the Potomac, George Washington. Never has a company of better men been active at one time in any country. This group was joined by a few European noblemen-idealists: Thaddeus Kosciusko, the Polish statesman and general who served in the American army and designed the fortifications of West Point; the wealthy young French nobleman, Marquis de Lafayette, who became a major general in the colonial army at the age of 19; and the Polish count, Casimir Pulaski, who was killed at the siege of Fort Monmouth.

The Americans had one important advantage—they were the "home team." Fighting a defensive war on their own territory gave them a certain moral advantage at home and in the eyes of people abroad. Sometimes it even helped make up for the jealousies and the disunity of the states. Because of their inability to "get organized," the colonials fought almost the entire war before they produced a written constitution—the Articles of Confederation—in November of 1777.

George Washington

As a result of the bloodshed at Lexington and Concord in April 1775, some 20,000 Minutemen moved in to Boston to fight the British. The following month on 10 May, the Second Continental Congress met in Philadelphia to draft new appeals to the British people and the King. Anticipating a rejection of their appeals, the delegates also adopted measures to provide themselves with an army and navy. Their most important single action was the appointment, on 23 June 1775, of George Washington to lead the colonial troops.

Washington was then 43 years old, a tall, dignified Virginian gentleman planter. He was not a career military man—his only command had been a 1,200-man militia during the French and Indian War, 20 years earlier. But by inheritance and marriage, he was a man of wealth; he served without pay but kept a careful expense account.

For a while, a war of curious inconsistency was fought. Loyalists to the King were trying to patch things up while at the same time shooting down His Majesty's soldiers. Then, in May 1775, a small American force captured the British garrisons at Ticonderoga and Crown Point in upper New York, and obtained powder and artillery for the siege of Boston. The next month it seized nearby Bunker Hill, from which an attack could be launched.

British General William Howe ordered his 2,400 troops into a frontal attack against the 1,500 defending Americans. There were later claims that the ensuing slaughter was a display of American sharpshooting. But in truth, even the most near-sighted Yankee could hardly have missed the packed scarlet ranks of British soldiers at a distance of fifty feet. Almost half of the latter were wounded and 226 were killed. British regulars had been defeated by the American rabble in arms. American casualties were 450 (140 killed) and most of these occurred when they had to give up the hill after their ammunition ran out.

After Bunker Hill, there was no hope of reconciliation with the King. In August 1775 Britian formally proclaimed the colonies in rebellion. The next month 30,000 Hessian mercenaries were hired to help crush the Americans, who were shocked that outsiders should be brought into a "family" quarrel. There was nothing left to do but fight.

In October 1775, just as winter was coming on, the British burned Falmouth (Portland), Maine. Two thousand Americans daringly invaded Canada, hoping to add another colony to their cause and to cut off that base from British use. They were almost successful but were finally beaten back.

A real war

There was bitter fighting elsewhere in the colonies. In January 1776 the British set fire to Norfolk, Virginia. In March, they were forced out of Boston. (Bostonians still celebrate March 14 as Evacuation Day.)

The Americans won two victories in the south in 1776, one at Moore's Creek Bridge in North Carolina and the other against an invading British fleet in Charleston Harbor.

Despite the war, many Americans still did not want independence. As late as January 1776, officers of General Washington's mess near Boston continued to toast the King's health. But gradually Americans were realizing that such acts as the hiring of Hessians and the burning of Falmouth and Norfolk made unity with the mother country impossible.

In January 1776, the most potent pamphlet ever written in America was published. Thomas Paine, a flaming liberal who had been a poor corset-maker's apprentice in England a year before, wrote *Common Sense*, and within a few months it had sold 150,000 copies.

Common sense

A few words of that pamphlet are still well worth reading:

"These are the times that try men's souls. The summer soldier and the sunshine patriot will, in this crisis, shrink from the service of their country; but he that stands it now, deserves the love and thanks of man and woman...."

Paine called the colonials' namby-pamby inconsistencies contrary to common sense. He asked: why should the tiny island of England rule the vast continent of America? He called the King, "the Royal Brute of Great Britain." America had a moral obligation to the world to set herself up as an independent, democratic republic.

Americans who had been on the fence made up their minds. They realized how foolish their position had been. They also saw that, unless they openly broke with Britain, they could not hope for help from France.

On 7 June 1776, Richard Henry Lee, of Virginia, at the Philadelphia Congress, moved that "These United Colonies are and of right ought to be, free and independent states...." There was great de-

The final break

bate, but the motion was adopted nearly a month later on 2 July 1776.

This was the original "declaration" of independence. In fact, John Adams wrote that thereafter, 2 July would be celebrated annually with fireworks. But it was decided that a more formal declaration ought to be made, particularly for the benefit of foreign nations who might give the Americans aid. The Declaration of Independence, in its final form, was approved on 4 July 1776. That declaration was formulated two hundred years ago, but it still makes good sense:

> "We hold these truths to be self-evident, that all men are created equal, that they are endowed by their Creator with certain inalienable Rights, that among these are Life, Liberty and the pursuit of Happiness. . . ."

The deed is done   Now the air was cleared. Benjamin Franklin said that the Patriots must all hang together, or they would all hang separately. Or, as the Declaration stated: "We mutually pledge to each other our lives, our fortunes and our sacred honor." It became the inspiration for other revolutions around the world.

The British used New York as a base of operations. There were many Loyalists there, and the harbor offered good shelter for ships. At that time the Royal Navy's North American Squadron had, on the Atlantic coast, twenty ships armed with 450 guns; about half of them were in New York and the others were scattered from Maine to Carolina. But elsewhere the British had many more ships; the Royal Navy was the biggest in the world. The Americans had no navy at all; if they were going to fight, they would have to use fishing schooners and squirrel guns.

Washington had command of about 18,000 poorly trained and badly equipped troops. They panicked that fall in the Battle of Long Island. Washington managed to withdraw them to Manhattan Island, then retreated southward, crossed the Hudson River to New Jersey, and finally got across the Delaware River, with the British in hot pursuit.

General William Howe, who had led the British troops at Bunker Hill, did not stop the ragged patriots as they fled pell-mell. He estimated that General Washington could just about be counted out of the war. It was the wrong estimate.

At Trenton, on 26 December 1776, after having sneaked across the icy Delaware River, Washington's forces surprised and captured a thousand sleeping Hessians. A week later, leaving his campfires burning to deceive the British into thinking he had not moved, he surprised and defeated a smaller British detachment at Princeton.

The British wanted to capture the Hudson River valley in order to cut off New England from the rest of the colonies. General John Burgoyne was to lead his troops down the Lake Champlain route from Canada and meet General Howe's troops near Albany. A third force, commanded by Colonel Barry St. Leger was to come from the west.

Hudson River valley

However, there was the American general, Benedict Arnold, to contend with. He was still holding his battered army in the Lake Champlain area. The British were stuck until they could gain control of the lake. To do this, they would have to construct a fleet—a larger one than Arnold had. This gave the Americans a strategic victory, in that while the British were building a fleet, they could have whipped the army.

There were furious battles on the lake and the tiny American flotilla was finally destroyed. But with winter coming on, the British were forced to move north to Canada. Had it not been for Arnold's skill, the British surely would have invaded as far south as Ticonderoga.

General Burgoyne began his invasion from Canada in 1777, with 7,000 troops, many of whom had their wives along. As they hacked their way through the forests, American sharpshooters lay in wait. General Howe, instead of pushing north to join Burgoyne's forces, attacked Philadelphia. He thought he had enough time to finish off Washington's forces and still help Burgoyne.

Washington's troops were defeated in battles at Brandywine Creek and Germantown. Howe then settled down to a happy, gay life in Philadelphia, leaving Burgoyne to flounder in the wilderness of New York state. Benjamin Franklin, who had been sent as envoy to France, told his friends that Howe had not captured Philadelphia —Philadelphia had captured Howe.

Washington moved his troops to winter quarters at Valley Forge, northwest of Philadelphia. They were ragged, cold, and hungry; their suffering during that long winter was terrible.

Meanwhile, Burgoyne's troops were constantly attacked by the Americans. Finally the British Army was trapped. The Americans drove back St. Leger's forces coming from the west. Burgoyne could neither advance nor retreat. On 17 October 1777 he surrendered his entire command at Saratoga.

Saratoga ranks with the decisive battles of American and world history. It gave hope and courage to the weakened, demoralized Americans—and, more important, it brought foreign aid.

The French wanted revenge for their defeat by the British in the Seven Years' War. Sentiment for the Americans' cause became the fashionable thing in Paris. Few people knew, however, that French sympathy included supplying Americans with powder and ammu-

The French come in

nition. In fact, through a dummy corporation, the French provided 90 percent of the gunpowder used during the first two and a half years of the war.

All negotiations were in secret because France did not want to provoke open warfare with the British. Besides, she could not be sure which way the colonies would go. After the Declaration of Independence and the smashing victory at Saratoga, those doubts were swept away.

In 1778, France offered the Americans a treaty of alliance. The allies bound themselves to wage war until the United States had won its freedom and until both had agreed on terms with the foe.

France had powerful fleets operating in American waters, mostly to protect her own valuable West Indies holdings. This threatened Britain's blockade of America's supply lines. The British decided to leave Philadelphia and concentrate their forces in New York. Washington attacked them at Monmouth, New Jersey, where many men died during an indecisive battle. The British finally made good their escape to New York. After that, except for his brief time in Yorktown, Washington spent 1781 in the New York area, moving in on the British.

In the summer of 1780, the French landed 6,000 regular troops, commanded by Comte Jean-Baptiste de Rochambeau, at Newport, Rhode Island. Preparations were soon under way for a joint Franco-American attack on New York.

Just when things were going so well, the Americans were shocked to learn that General Benedict Arnold had turned traitor. He had plotted with the British to sell out the stronghold of West Point for £6,300 and a commission. The plot was discovered, Arnold fled to the British, and Washington asked sadly, "Whom can we trust now?"

Meanwhile the British went after the southern colonies, where many of the people were still loyal. In 1778 and 1779 Georgia was overrun and in 1780 Charleston fell. It meant the loss of 5,000 men and 400 cannon—a devastating blow to the Americans. Fighting in the Carolinas was bitter and bloody, with loyalists fighting their patriot neighbors. By 1781, General Nathan Greene, the "Fighting Quaker," had exhausted his foe, General Charles Cornwallis. Georgia and South Carolina were finally cleared of the enemy.

Inland, the frontier was often ablaze. The Indians who were allies of George III fought with torch and tomahawk. The year 1777 was called "the bloody year," as the British reputedly paid bounties to the Indians for American scalps.

The fighting at sea   Britain thought her North American colonies could be beaten by sea power alone. There was even talk of withdrawing the entire army and leaving matters to the Royal Navy. And it was true that neither side could win without control of the sea. Washington knew that sea power was "the pivot upon which everything turned."

The British were convinced that the powerful Royal Navy, so recently victorious over the French, could blockade American seaports, seize waterways, and control all trade and transport. There were no fortifications along the hundreds and hundreds of miles of coastline. The Americans had no navy and no protection against the squadrons based at Halifax in Canada and Jamaica in the West Indies.

But although the Americans had no navy as such, they did have a lot of sailors—fishermen and traders who knew how to handle small, fast ships. They also had another big advantage—they were familiar with much of the coastline. They knew where the safe channels were, where reefs and bars were, and they could sneak a small, fast schooner past a big deep-draft ship of the line at night and get into shallow water where they could not be reached.

What the Americans did not have, and needed badly, were guns and ammunition. George Washington was deeply concerned about the situation. Even though he was a gentleman farmer, soldier, and aristocrat with no experience at sea, he knew he would have to have a navy of some kind—and soon.

One of his first moves on taking command of the Continental Army in July 1775 was to request the Governor of Rhode Island to send an armed vessel to Bermuda to raid the British stores of gunpowder there. With these supplies, he would be able to break the blockade of Boston. But there were no warships to do the job. Washington appealed to the Congress in Philadelphia to create a colonial fleet.

At that time, Congress was unsure of itself. Many members still thought the rebellion was a temporary thing. A navy, they said, would aggravate George III and make the break a final one. But by the time John Adams asked "What think you of an American fleet?" the British had brought in hired mercenaries and burned American villages. Congress was ready to act.

On the 13th of October 1775, Adams was able to persuade the Continental Congress to authorize the fitting-out "with all possible despatch" of two vessels to be used for capturing British shipping. Two more were approved by the end of the month. An official naval committee was set up: John Adams, Silas Deane, John Langdon, Christopher Gadsden, Stephen Hopkins, Joseph Hewes, and R. H. Lee. It was the beginning of the U. S. Navy. Esek Hopkins, of Rhode Island, became the first commander in chief of the Continental Navy.

The merchantmen that were converted into warships by having a few cannons quickly loaded aboard, were the *Alfred, Columbus, Andrew Doria,* and *Cabot*. Later, two schooners, the *Wasp* and the *Fly,* and the sloops *Providence* and *Hornet* were added.

America's first sea battle

Patriots had been troublesome to British shipping for some years before the Navy was officially born; Newporters had boarded and burned the British customs ship *Liberty*, and men from Providence had destroyed the British customs ship *Gaspee* at Narragansett Bay.

On 12 June 1775 trouble broke out in the little seaport town of Machias, Maine. There had been a crop failure, and two British sloops, covered by the armed cutter *Margaretta*, had brought food to be exchanged for lumber for the British troops in Boston. The people knew about the battles of Lexington and Concord, and did not want to help the British by supplying them lumber. At a town meeting they voted to exchange only for enough to eat. But the British captain, Ichabod Jones, said he would give them food only if they voted his way.

At an indignation meeting, they decided to try to catch the British sailors in church. When that was unsuccessful, they marched to the wharf to strip the British merchant sloop *Unity* of her cargo. Midshipman Moore, commanding the *Margaretta*, got wind of the plot, raided a local sloop of her captain, and forced him to pilot his ship out of the harbor the following morning.

Meanwhile the locals gathered around the *Unity*. Jeremiah O'Brien and 35 other lumbermen, armed with guns, swords, and pitchforks, scrambled aboard to pursue the *Margaretta*. The *Margaretta* was a slow sailer, but she was armed with four 3-pounder guns. Luckily for the patriots, she was never able to use them. A shot cut her sails and another killed her helmsman. Finally the two vessels locked together and the colonials clubbed their way aboard; British resistance collapsed.

The Massachusetts General Court directed that the *Unity* should be fitted out with the *Margaretta*'s guns and sail under the name *Machias Liberty*.

Washington's little fleet

By the fall of 1775, Boston was in the hands of the British, and Washington's troops at nearby Cambridge had been without powder and military stores for six months. The promised ships were slow in coming from Philadelphia—so slow that Washington told his military secretary, Joseph Reed, in exasperation: "I fear your fleet has been so long in fitting, and the destination of it so well known that in the end it will be defeated."

Desperate to get going, Washington rounded up some fishing vessels to raid enemy shipping in Massachusetts Bay. The first was the schooner *Hannah*, which he commissioned on 2 September. She sailed out and returned two days later with her first prize, a British sloop loaded with naval stores. Finally there were six little schooners, fitted out with officers and soldiers. Each carried from four to six guns and flew the Pine Tree flag.

"Washington's Navy" was commanded by John Manley, a Marblehead fisherman who had been a boatswain's mate in the Royal Navy. He sailed his fleet down the wintry New England coast and captured the British supply ship *Nancy* with her cargo of 2,000 muskets, ammunition, and a 13-inch mortar, which Washington later used to drive the British out of Boston.

While the British were in Boston, the little fleet captured 35 British vessels carrying military cargo worth $600,000—enough to make it possible for Washington's army to last the winter. In the spring they would take Boston. Equally important was the demonstration to Congress that even a little sea power could make an enormous difference.

Now came the rush of sailors, skippers, and fishermen to enter the service as privateers. Congress specifically authorized them to prey on enemy shipping. Carrying small arms and *letters of marque*, these privately owned vessels hounded the British up and down the Atlantic. Altogether, over 1,000 American privateers responded to the call of patriotism and profit and put to sea with about 70,000 men. They captured some 600 British prizes. The British captured about as many American merchantmen and privateers. In 1777 Franklin declared that American shipping had grown richer by privateering than it had by commerce.

Although there were frequent squabbles over "prizes" and the government had little or no control over the free-lance captains, their dashing victories provided a badly needed morale booster.

So many British ships were captured by privateers and the Continental Navy that British insurance rates went sky high. Merchantmen were forced to sail in convoy, and British shippers brought increasing pressure on Parliament to end the war on honorable terms.

The infant American Navy was only a handful of nondescript ships but it soon established a brilliant tradition. At its peak strength in 1777, it had only 34 ships and 5,000 men, commanded by daring officers. The most famous was the hard-fighting Scotsman, John Paul Jones. It was he who carried the fight to British shores and destroyed shipping close to home. A song critical of the Royal Navy began:

John Paul Jones

"The tradesmen stand still, and the merchant bemoans
The losses he meets from such as Paul Jones."

Born as plain John Paul in 1747, Jones went to sea when he was 12 years old. He began as a cabin boy, became an apprentice, and then a mate. After receiving his master's license at the age of 20, he commanded the Scottish merchantman *John* for two years.

Charged with murder in the West Indies, he proved his innocence, but then faced a second charge of cruelty to his crew. Friends advised him to go to America to wait until a fair court-martial could be assembled.

In the colonies, unknown and unemployed, Jones went to Philadelphia where he hoped to make himself useful in the new American Navy. He decided not to return to Tobago, where he was to face charges, and at that time changed his surname to "Jones." Because of his friendship with John Hewes of North Carolina and Robert Morris of Pennsylvania, both influential members of the Continental Congress, he was commissioned a first lieutenant on 7 December 1775.

Aboard the *Alfred* he participated in several successful battles off the New England coast. In 1776 he received command of the *Providence*, with which he captured 16 ships.

Promoted to captain, he assumed command of a small fleet and continued his raids on British merchantmen for ammunition and supplies. In a single cruise, his American fleet captured the transport *Mellish* with its cargo, a privateer, and several smaller vessels.

In 1778 Congress gave him command of the sloop *Ranger*, the best American ship afloat, and ordered him to France to report to the American commissioners there. He had been promised command of the frigate *Indien*, but when he got to France he learned that she had been given to the King of France to increase his interest in helping America.

Jones reported to the commissioners, then sailed the *Ranger* to the Irish Sea, where he attacked the English town of Whitehaven and burned English ships in port. He invaded Scottish soil and terrified the British coastal villages. These attacks were urged by Benjamin Franklin who wanted retaliation for British atrocities in America.

Next, Jones took command of the *Bonhomme Richard*, which was originally the French *Duras*, renamed in honor of Benjamin Franklin and the practical advice he gave to readers of *Poor Richard's Almanack*. She was small but fast, and carried 40 guns. In September 1779 he put out from France, accompanied by the frigates *Alliance* and *Pallas*, each carrying 32 guns, and the brigantine *Vengeance*, carrying 12 guns.

At dusk on 23 September, off the coast of northeast England, they sighted a British convoy escorted by the *Serapis* and the *Countess of Scarborough*.

Jones signaled his ships to stand by while he made for *Serapis* in *Bonhomme Richard*. The *Alliance* stood off at safe distance while the *Pallas* went after *Countess of Scarborough* and eventually captured her.

The first broadside fired by the *Bonhomme Richard* ended in disaster; two of her three heavy guns on one side burst, killing the gun crews and blowing up the deck above them. Her third gun was abandoned. The only chance was to fight the British hand-to-hand. Jones sailed his ship alongside the *Serapis* and his men lashed them both together. Then, for three hours the ships pounded each other at point-blank range.

The *Bonhomme Richard* was so badly damaged by shells that only the steady use of pumps kept her afloat. Water seeping into her magazines ruined most of the gunpowder. Both ships were afire.

At first it seemed that the *Serapis* would win the battle. Her guns splintered the *Bonhomme Richard*'s rotten timbers and sent them flying, knocking out one gun after another. Finally Jones had only three guns left. Fires were breaking out all over the ship and the water was gaining on the pumps. Still he fought on.

When the captain of the *Serapis* shouted out "Do you surrender?" Jones replied "I have not yet begun to fight." The British attempted to board the sinking ship and Jones led the fight that repulsed them. By that time his ship was a near-wreck but, under the direction of American officers, French marines in the masts had cleared the enemy rigging of British seamen and were pouring heavy fire into the *Serapis*. Sniping, hurling grenades, belaying pins, and cutlasses, they cleared the enemy decks. Then a chain of explosions rocked the *Serapis* from bow to stern. Jones later wrote "The scene was dreadful, beyond the reach of language."

A half-hour later the *Alliance* took up a raking position off the Britisher's bow. Some of her shots struck the *Bonhomme Richard* by mistake, but enough of them hit the *Serapis* to force her to surrender.

Jones put his wounded men aboard the *Serapis* and the next day, when his own ship sank, he took command of the British ship and sailed her to Holland with his flotilla and the captured ships. Jones had lost his ship but he won a tremendous battle. By his refusal to surrender in the face of a superior force, he had humbled the British naval pride and given the Continental Navy one of its greatest victories and a lasting tradition.

Yorktown

The decisive battle of the Revolutionary War was fought at Yorktown, Virginia. It ended on a note of triumph, in large part, because of the aid given the Continental Army by Lafayette's fellow Frenchmen, Admiral François de Grasse and General Rochambeau.

The Yorktown campaign began on 30 August 1781 when a French fleet of thirty-six ships under de Grasse converged on Yorktown, where Cornwallis and 8,000 British troops were encamped. De Grasse successfully blockaded the Chesapeake Bay and cut off British supplies, reinforcements, communications, and escape. On land, Washington and Rochambeau encircled Yorktown with a combined force of 16,000 men. By September Cornwallis was surrounded by the Allies. The siege itself began on 28 September and continued until 17 October when Cornwallis sent out a white flag of truce.

The surrender came on 19 October 1781. The French played military music as the soldiers went into line. Opposite them, moving proudly to the lilt of Celtic fifes and drums came the tall Americans, some in brown hunting shirts and some in blue and buff.

George Washington, Rochambeau, and de Grasse stood their horses until the gates of the fort were swung open and, to the slow beat of drums, British Brigadier General Charles O'Hara rode out to meet them. Cornwallis pleaded illness and sent his deputy to surrender for him. O'Hara handed Cornwallis's sword to General Benjamin Lincoln, because a deputy must surrender to a deputy.

The scarlet-coated British and the Hessians in their brilliant blue and green uniforms, stacked their arms, as a military band played, "The World Turned Upside Down." Lafayette solemnly remarked, "The play is over; the fifth act has come to an end."

When the news of the surrender at Yorktown reached Lord North in London he cried:

"O God, it is all over!"

And it was, although fighting sputtered on for another year, chiefly on the western frontier.

On 3 September 1783, the Treaty of Paris formally brought the War of the Revolution to an end. On 23 November, the British army sailed home from New York.

In the wave of economy that followed the Revolution, the Continental Navy was disbanded. By 1784 the last remaining ships had been sold. Most of the captains went to sea in merchant ships. Jones left the United States to serve in the Russian Navy. With the nation at peace, there seemed to be no need for a navy. For the next 10 years, the new nation which had whipped the British Navy at sea had no navy at all.

CHAPTER 5
SHIPS OVERSEAS

When the Revolutionary War finally ended, the United States settled down to become a nation. Americans, who had been in prison for many years after their capture by the British, returned home. The last two vessels of the Continental Navy, the frigates *Alliance* and *Hague*, were sold for badly needed cash. The 300 privateers still afloat were put to peaceful use. The names of these small fighting ships reflected the spirit of the men who sailed them and they became a proud part of America's maritime heritage: *Bloodhound, Black Snake, Disdain, Panther, Revenge, Retaliation, Viper, Wild Cat,* and *Liberty,* to name a few. Their masters who had captured wartime prizes with skill and daring would now have to go to sea on peaceful enterprises if the infant nation were to survive.

The new country   The United States of America finally had a firm foothold on the Atlantic coast. Inland, settlements were scattered south from the Great Lakes to Florida and west to the Mississippi, but that was about all. Most of the 3½ million people lived in seaports or a few miles inland. They had won the war but had ruined their trade and industry. The people were poor, prices were inflated, and agriculture was inadequate. There was virtually no knowledge of the rich land beyond the coastal ranges. It would be up to Boston, Salem, Nantucket, New Bedford, New York, and Philadelphia to send ships out again to find profitable world trade. But that was easier said than done.

On previous page: "Oh, the times wuz hard, an' the wages low, *leave* her Johnny, leave her! But now once more a-shore we'll go, oh, it's *time* for us to leave her!" This capstan chantey was sung only on the last day a crew served aboard ship. The whaler *Stafford*, shown overleaf, was built in Kingston, Massachusetts, in 1848. Well into the next century, came the time to leave her, empty and alone, in New Bedford.
Courtesy: The Office of Naval Records.

Competition for trade and territory everywhere, both far and near, was fierce. The British, Dutch, and French had monopolies on distant markets, while nearer home, Spain dominated trade in the Gulf of Mexico.

As soon as peace came, the sailors of Nantucket set out to reestablish their sole industry—whaling. Their fleet of 32 whaleships was bringing in oil by 1781. One of them, the *Bedford*, made history.

Carrying the new flag

After a trip to "the Brazils" late in 1782, she loaded 487 butts of oil and sailed to London. She arrived off the coast of England on 3 February 1783, moved up the Thames, and dropped anchor near the Tower of London. Sensation! From her masthead fluttered the bright new flag of the young United States—the first Stars and Stripes ever seen in any British port.

Right behind the *Bedford*, the brig *Industry*, loaded with whale oil, cleared for Europe. Two more craft sailed from Nantucket in January of 1783, but one, the *Speedwell*, was captured and sent to Jamaica. When news of the provisional treaty of peace arrived, Captain Whippy, her skipper, immediately displayed the Stars and Stripes. On return home, he took the *Speedwell* to Quebec and displayed the flag for the first time in Canada. Two years later the frigate *United States* (one of many ships to carry that name) was the first to display the new flag in India.

The success of these ventures soon encouraged others. In 1783 and 1784, Nantucket had 60 vessels of various kinds at sea. Other New England ports reentered the whaling industry: Bedford village; Falmouth on the Cape; Boston; Plymouth; Wellfleet; Newport and Bristol, Rhode Island; Sag Harbor on Long Island; and New London, Connecticut. The whalers found that whales had increased their numbers during the war years, and most ships returned with full cargoes.

But this kind of good fortune did not last. Soon the market became flooded with whale oil. Prices fell rapidly and the whole industry went into a depression. People who had used the less expensive tallow candles during the war were reluctant to pay high prices for whale oil which gave a brighter light. Some shipowners decided there was no future in whaling so they began fitting their ships for different trades.

Nantucket, specializing in sperm oil, was not hit at first because most of her oil went to Britain. But the British, trying to build up their own whaling industry, set a duty of £18 per ton (about $100) on American whale oil. In trying to secure a commercial treaty in 1783, John Adams argued with William Pitt: "We are all surprised that you prefer darkness and consequent robberies, burglaries, and murders in your streets to the receiving, as a remittance (for colonial trade) our spermaceti oil. The lamps around Grosvenor

Square, I know and in Downing Street, too, I suppose, are dim by midnight, and extinguished by two o'clock in the morning and chase away, before the watchmen, all the villains, and save you the trouble and danger of introducing a new police into the city. . . ."

Many Nantucketers grudgingly admitted defeat and moved away to found other whaling colonies; some even joined British and French whaling enterprises. The British actively chased down American whaling crews, impressing them into their own under-manned fleets—an activity that would involve Britain and the United States in another war. Nantucketers who managed to hold out during the doldrums of 1783 through 1786 made a quick recovery during the succeeding six years. They discovered new markets; whale oil which was first sold in French- and Dutch-owned West Indies, could also be sold in France, Holland, Germany, Sweden, and Russia. Americans, led by Nantucketers, were able to compete successfully with Europeans and carry on the industry.

Perils of independence

Whalers were not the only seafarers with problems. All Americans had trouble as they tried to make it on their own. The Founding Fathers, wise in so many respects, somehow did not foresee what would happen to the country, once she became England's rival in trade, rather than her protected dependency. Following the peace of 1783, British policy was that of a haughty parent with a wayward child. Britain closed her ports to trade with Americans, as well as with all foreign nations, unless a duty was paid. Navigation laws cut off the lucrative West Indies trade which had long been a rich market for colonial fish, corn, lumber, cattle, and horses.

Formerly, American shipyards had built hundreds of ships for the British at half the price it cost them to build their own. Furthermore, American ships had been allowed to carry only products of the states from which they sailed. After the war, Parliament ruled that no more American ships could be bought, and the only American products that could be brought to England in American ships were naval stores the British lacked; masts, spars, pitch, tar, turpentine, and indigo.

Because their government lacked sufficient power to promote a policy on which all states would agree, the Americans were unable to pass an effective navigation law of their own. States began competing with one another, levying port dues and taxes on their rivals. Coastal trade suffered badly and many merchants and traders looked beyond their homeland for solutions, but there were problems overseas too.

Before 1775, American shipping had been protected by the Royal Navy. Now, that luxury had gone, along with the skimpy Continental Navy. American privateers could no longer afford to carry heavy armaments and large fighting crews for protection against pirates and privateers on the high seas. In the rich trade areas of the Mediterranean, the Royal Navy had no intention of rescuing the recently traitorous Americans; it concentrated solely on enforcing Britain's treaties with the pirate regencies of the Barbary States. The Americans had to fend for themselves.

They managed this on the sly in the West Indies. Americans put to sea, ostensibly to trade at the French islands, then sailed into British ports "in distress." They were permitted to sell their cargoes to make way for repairs. They then carried away the "overstocks" of local merchants.

It was obvious that Americans would have to do more than seek trade in ports that were not barred by the Royal Navy. It seemed equally obvious that they had been eased out of the big markets. Older nations had established monopolies either by warfare or international agreements. Chartered organizations such as the East India Company were like nations unto themselves, complete with armed forces and diplomats. There was just no way of competing. When actual occupation of a territory was not worth the expense, monopolists bribed various princes and set up protectorates.

There were only two lucrative trade routes open to the merchants and shipowners of the United States; the Far East, and the northwest coast of America.

China

Seafarers had long been trading with China. The Portuguese came in 1516 and established their colony at Macao in 1557. Next came the Dutch in 1634, the British in 1635, the French in 1698, the Danes in 1731, the Swedes in 1732, and the Russians in 1753. In China, it was every man for himself—a rare opportunity for anyone willing to play the game according to the rules set down by the Emperor of China. All *fanquei*, or "foreign devils," were under his strict control.

The emperor allowed trade only at the port of Canton, far up the Pearl River; no one was allowed to do business at Peking or Shanghai. Westerners were confined to about 500 yards of fenced-in waterfront and the nationals of each country stayed within their own high-walled factory.

Foreigners did their business with the "co-hong" of 10 to 12 Chinese merchants. The "hoppo," chief of customs, was usually pleasant and worldly and could often be bribed with gifts of musical snuffboxes or "sing songs," and cuckoo clocks.

The game consisted of "hong" merchants accommodating visitors, "depraved by the education and customs beyond the bounds of civilization," who brought "gifts" or "tribute." In exchange they were allowed to load their ships with tea, porcelain, and delicate fabrics. After the War for Independence, it was America's turn to join the "game."

A dangerous journey

Americans contemplating a voyage to China faced many dangers and uncertainties. Lacking proper navigational instruments and accurate charts, and carrying only light armament, they risked running aground on treacherous shoals and reefs, or attack by pirates. The accepted route would take them eastward toward the Canary Islands. From there they sailed south to Capetown, Africa, then across the Indian Ocean, and through the Sunda Strait (between Sumatra and Java) to Canton. Pirates from the Barbary States prowled in the Atlantic. In the Java Sea, native islanders were just as dangerous. China also had her fair share of pirates.

The journey was so treacherous that there was a strong temptation to trade in Capetown for less profit rather than risk losing all in a dash for the Orient. Such trade was possible because East Indiamen, returning from China with their tea, silks, and spices, were allowed by the company to barter 56½ tons of the ship's cargo space for the master's personal trade venture. An example of this was the 40-ton *Harriet* of Hingham, Massachusetts, which sailed from Boston in December 1783, loaded with ginseng. At Capetown, an English captain offered the *Harriet*'s skipper two pounds of fine tea for one of ginseng. He was only too happy to agree to the bargain.

The *Empress of China*

Any number of former American privateers were just waiting to be purchased, refitted, and sent to sea on trading expeditions. One of these was the 360-ton *Empress of China*. Financed mainly by New York merchants at a cost of $120,000, she set out on 22 February 1784, bound for China. Major Samuel Shaw, former aide-de-camp to General Henry Knox, who sailed as supercargo, provided a written account of the historic voyage. The unfortunate choice of skipper was John Green, a veteran of the Revolution.

The ship's bill of lading listed 242 casks of ginseng, about 30 tons. This root, regarded by the Chinese as a splendid aphrodisiac, would hopefully yield a fine profit.

The *Empress* rounded the Cape of Good Hope uneventfully but Captain Green missed Sunda Strait by many miles. He poked around for days until he found his landmark, Java Head. Eventually he had the good luck to fall in with the French *Triton*. The *Triton* had been convoying merchantmen to and from Macao and was only too happy to accompany her recent wartime ally through the reef-studded South China Sea.

The *Empress of China* anchored at Whampoa, 14 miles below Canton, on 28 August 1784. Samuel Shaw wrote: "We saluted . . . with 13 guns, which were returned by the vessels of each nation." This one-for-one saluting suggests that the American ship would not have been entirely helpless had she been attacked by pirates. The Yankees found themselves being welcomed to the family of nations as brave and resourceful equals rather than as ragged provincials and privateers of the recent independence war. It was a turning point in the politics of American seafaring as well as in the sailor's view of himself. The French helped the *Empress of China* to a good berth, with anchors and cables; the Dutch sent a boat to help, and both the British and Danes sent officers "to welcome your flag to this part of the world."

Trade commenced in short order and it was fortunate that the *Empress of China* carried a mixed cargo. John Swift, her purser, wrote to his father: "We brought too much ginseng. A little of the best kind will yield an immense profit . . . unfortunately this year ten times as much arrived as ever did before." This problem of overloading the market sometimes did happen in a time of slow communication. Men who often bragged about the enormously profitable voyages they made sometimes said little about the times they lost money. Ginseng probably never was as highly valued as some people claimed; it was even less profitable when the market became glutted. A dollar a pound for the superior quality was the usual, but that depended on the amount available.

The *Empress of China* reached New York on 11 May 1785, after a voyage of 13,700 miles. She had a full cargo; 3,000 piculs of tea (a Malayan unit of measure meaning a manload—about 130 pounds), spices, silks, and chinaware. The ship's despatch said, "it presages a future happy period for our being able to despense with that burdensome and unnecessary traffick . . . with Europe . . . to the future happy prospects of solid greatness."

Unhappily, the profit of $30,000, or 25 percent of invested capital was not enough to satisfy the investors. But it did set off a wave of interest and hope. That first China trip affected young America like his first dollar does a boy—if one felt good, more would feel even better.

New Englanders on the high seas

New Englanders were annoyed that they had not reached China first, but otherwise they had the situation well in hand. They would reach China in good time, and numerous other ports as well, enriching everyone from shipowner and captain on down to apprentices and seamen. They carried on their business in a peculiarly personal way, and for them it worked. Shipowners gave their captains almost unlimited freedom to swap for profit and take advantage of every opportunity they found at distant ports.

Young sea captains, carrying the awesome responsibilities for the safety of their crews, their ships, and the investments of their ships' owners and merchants, surely led foreigners to suspect that America must indeed be a nation of youngsters. In Salem, from the very beginning, sons followed their fathers to sea. Boys began their countinghouse experience and training at an early age and by the time their fathers "retired" to their farms in their early 30s, their 12-to-14-year-old sons could put to sea.

The system led to a remarkable burst of prosperity and world fame for Salem. The town had only 8,000 people when the war ended. It was the only seaport whose maritime commerce had increased during the Revolution. Trade to the West Indies had sustained the city nicely, though the people were poor, mostly illiterate, and lived in simple wooden houses. Within 20 years, Salem became the richest and most distinguished city on the American continent. Some years later, an admiring lady, Harriet Martineau, declared it to be the richest city of its size in the whole world. When the War of 1812 began, Salem was ranked with Genoa and Venice as a trading port.

Salem's riches were made possible, in large part, by Elias Hasket Derby. In making Salem rich, he also became America's first millionaire shipowner. Most shipping enterprises were owned by many partners, but Derby owned all of his ships outright and was the sole investor. In fact, he owned a tenth of all American ships from all ports touching the remote Mascarene Islands between 1786 and 1800; a total of 578 ships. His word was law—a law which allowed his countinghouse apprentices to put their savings into small "adventures" in foreign trade for which he gave them space in his vessels. Even seamen were allowed 800 pounds of freight apiece to exchange for foreign products. Although boys and young men grumbled about Derby's harsh work rules and strict conduct requirements, they were a bit cocky about being "Derby's boys."

His training and trust were well placed because time after time, when crises occurred or important decisions had to be made thousands of miles from home, Derby boys proved worthy. In 1793, the 161-ton *Benjamin* of Salem anchored at the Indian Ocean island of Mauritius. None of her officers were more than 24 years old. One of them, 19-year-old Richard Cleveland, had been in Derby's countinghouse from the time he was 14 because his father wanted him "to acquire a love of naval affairs, and a taste for commercial adventure."

Nathaniel Silsbee, master of a ship at 20 years of age and wealthy at 28, "went ashore." Before then his two brothers, William and Zacariah, were in the business; both were shipmasters by the time they were 19.

The six sons of George and Mary Crowningshield all worked in the countinghouses as boys, and five of them had command of ships before they reached the age of 20. The sixth died of fever at Guadeloupe.

The *Grand Turk* Derby was anxious to open up trade wherever it could be found. He realized that American sugar could replace Europe's traditional sweetener, honey. Sugar from America was plentiful and popular, especially when it was discovered that fruit could be preserved in it and jam could be made with it. Consequently, on 15 June 1784, he sent the bark *Light Horse*, under Nehemiah Buffington, with a cargo of sugar to St. Petersburg in Russia to open up the Baltic trade. The ship brought back canvas and hemp—both of which were scarce items in America.

But Derby really had his sights on China and had been cautiously exploring such possibilities for some time. In November of 1784 he sent the 300-ton converted privateer *Grand Turk* under Captain Ingersoll to Capetown, Africa, to gain more information about the China trade. The *Grand Turk* carried 22 guns and a mixed cargo worth $27,000, which Captain Ingersoll could exchange for anything of profit except slaves.

At Capetown, Ingersoll made friends with several English captains and gathered bits of news and gossip. When he was offered a big price for the rum on board the *Grand Turk*, he became suspicious. He finally learned that the island of St. Helena had run out of liquor and was completely dry. He immediately sailed there, sold the rum for a fine profit, and then headed for the West Indies to sell the rest of his cargo. He returned to Salem in the fall of 1785 with a profit of 100 percent.

Derby sent the *Grand Turk* out again, this time under Captain Ebenezer West, an ex-privateersman who had spent four years in a British prison. In the Mascarene island of Ile de France (now called Mauritius), West sold miscellaneous items such as candles and prunes, then headed for Canton where he found the *Empress of China* on her second trip. He sold his cargo, which included musical snuff boxes and cuckoo clocks, loaded up with tea, silks, and chinaware and returned to Salem after a voyage of 17 months which again produced a profit of 100 percent.

Derby sent the *Grand Turk* out that same year, bound for Mauritius and possibly Canton. His 22-year-old son Elias Hasket Derby, Jr., a Harvard graduate of the previous year, was in command. The *Grand Turk* carried 17,000 pounds of tobacco, 2,482 gallons of rum, 610 firkins of butter, 300 barrels of fish, and other items. But because of the decreased demand—only two casks of ginseng.

Mauritius needed almost everything he carried, so Derby sold his cargo quickly. Then he learned the island was short of ships, so he sold the *Grand Turk*, worth $6,500, for $13,000.

Trade with the Far East

American ports hummed with activity as ships, large and small, set out for the far corners of the earth. Even groups that had no capital or knowledge were determined to try for the profitable trade in the East. As one southern gentleman sarcastically remarked, "Every little village on every little creek with a sloop that can hold five Yankees was now planning to embark on the far eastern trade."

The *United States* left Philadelphia in March 1784 to trade in French India, while the *Recovery* sought out possibilities at Ile de France for the coffee trade. The *Chesapeake* and *Betsy* traded in Calcutta and the *Hope* did business in Canton. The smallest vessel to reach China from New York was the 80-ton Hudson River sloop *Experiment*. She was commanded by Captain Steward Deane, an ex-privateersman who sailed with a crew of 11 men, one officer, and two boys. They carried two guns, two swivels, pikes, muskets, pistols, and cutlasses for self-protection.

The China trade became so profitable that in 1789 there were 15 American ships in Canton at the same time.

The Northwest fur trade

When the ginseng trade with China fell off, it was plain that an appealing substitute would have to be found if the riches of the East were to continue to pour into America's markets. What seemed to be a logical and very appealing solution was offered by John Ledyard, who based his suggestions on good logic and solid experience, including extensive travel in the Orient.

Around 1773 Ledyard dropped out of Dartmouth College and signed on board a ship bound for England. There he joined the third exploring voyage of Captain James Cook to the Pacific. After Cook's death in Hawaii, Ledyard and Lieutenant Gore brought the expedition's vessels back to England. There Ledyard learned that his native country had declared her independence. He promptly transferred to a British blockader headed for Long Island Sound, jumped ship there, and made his way to Hartford, where he wrote the first American book which told of Cook's world-ranging journey.

But long before any account of the Cook expedition was printed, Ledyard went to Philadelphia to tell Robert Morris, a financial wizard, an amazing story about the Chinese. He told his story from memory.

When the expedition reached China, the Chinese were so eager to get worn-out furs lying on the sailors' bunks that they paid $100 apiece for them. These were sea-otter furs obtained from American Indians on the Northwest coast, for perhaps six pence each.

Ledyard proposed that a vessel be sent to the Northwest by way of Cape Horn, to trade a few trifles to the Indians for furs. She would sell the furs in Canton, reload with tea, silks, and spices and return by way of the Cape of Good Hope to New York. The problem was, no American vessel had ever bucked her way westward around Cape Horn. The accepted route to China was east around the Cape of Good Hope.

Morris liked the idea but the plan was finally dropped. He

could not raise expenses, and there were doubts about the untried route around Cape Horn. Finally, as has been earlier stated, the *Empress of China* went around the Cape of Good Hope.

Two years after the *Empress of China* returned to New York in 1785 from her first voyage to Canton, Bostonians prepared to send their own expedition on the route proposed by Ledyard. Six investors bought the 212-ton three-masted *Columbia* for $50,000. Built in 1773, and armed with ten guns, she was considered old by standards for wooden sailing ships, so it was decided to send a tender along with her, the 90-ton sloop *Lady Washington*.

The *Columbia*

John Kendrick, of Wareham, Massachusetts, was given command of the *Columbia*. Robert Gray, of Boston, had command of the *Lady Washington*. Both had been privateersmen.

The vessels sailed on 30 September 1787, carrying a cargo of knives, iron, tools, toys, and beads. Their orders were to sail via Cape Horn, then up the coast of South America without touching any Spanish ports. They were to deal fairly with the Northwest Indians for furs, then proceed to Canton to trade for tea and other items. They were to return to Boston via the Cape of Good Hope.

The voyage commenced uneventfully. But when they reached the Cape Verde Islands, off the coast of Africa, signs of disagreement between the two captains appeared. Gray wrote to Joseph Barrell, the expedition's organizer, "We spent 40 days there, 36 more than I thought necessary." Their guide, who had been with Captain Cook, and the surgeon, both jumped ship.

They reached Cape Horn in April, a stormy season. The *Columbia* nearly capsized in a fierce storm and the ships lost sight of each other. As Gray later reported, "I had the good luck to part company . . . and I made the Coast six weeks sooner by being alone. . . ."

Gray took the *Lady Washington* north, exploring the coast from Oregon to Vancouver Island. He anchored often to trade with Indians, who were sometimes fierce, refusing to put aside their weapons. On one occasion, on 16 August 1788, they attacked a shore party gathering fruits and vegetables, and Captain Gray's black servant boy from the Cape Verde Islands was killed.

The *Columbia* finally limped in to the rendezvous point, Nootka Sound, at Vancouver Island. Her crew was weak with scurvy and there had been two deaths en route. This is hard to explain because Captain Cook had shown ten years before that scurvy could be prevented by eating fresh fruits and vegetables or drinking lemon or lime juice.* Two English ships were anchored there, and their

---

* Many years later, scientists discovered that fruits and vegetables contained vitamin C.

officers regaled the Americans with horror stories of the bitter winters and fierce natives in China, then sailed off to Canton with their loads of furs.

The Americans soon learned that the British took with them all the ready supply of furs and the Indians were not much interested in trinkets any more. They wanted iron or copper tools and weapons. The Americans settled down for the winter, living aboard ship and fashioning tools, particularly chisels. (In the spring of 1789, one chisel was worth one otter skin. Later, "inflation" raised the price to eight chisels for one skin.)

In the spring, Gray took the *Lady Washington* to Alaska, exploring islands and inlets and looking for Indians still willing to trade furs for chisels. Returning in June, he found two Spanish ships in Nootka Sound. They had been sent by the viceroy of Mexico to check up on the Russians, who might be headed for California. Finding no Russians, the Spanish commander busied himself with searching British ships in the area and from time to time claiming the land for Spain.

At this time Captain Kendrick did a very strange thing; he turned the *Columbia* over to Robert Gray and on 31 July 1789 sent him to Canton to sell the furs. Kendrick took command of the *Lady Washington*, traded a few months longer, then sailed for China. He did poorly in his transactions, and finally sold the *Lady Washington* to himself for tax purposes. He never returned to Boston and the investors never received any return for their money.

Robert Gray took the *Columbia* into Honolulu. She was the first American ship to visit the Sandwich Islands, as the Hawaiian Islands were then called. After provisioning with fresh fruits, hogs, and water, and taking aboard two natives, he sailed to Canton, arriving there in November.

His troubles were far from being over. Either he simply was not a shrewd bargainer or the Chinese merchants took unfair advantage. The furs brought only $21,400, of which half went in import duties and other payments to the wily merchants. Gray only had $11,241.51 with which to buy tea. The *Columbia* sailed for Boston in February 1790, where she arrived six months later.

Ships and shore guns exchanged a salute of 13 guns, as crowds rushed to the wharves to welcome her. The *Columbia*, home after nearly three years, had circumnavigated the globe—the first American vessel to do so. She had made Ledyard's dream come true.

More salutes and cheers followed Robert Gray and his officers and men, as they marched up State Street. With them was Gray's Hawaiian cabin boy, Atoo, wearing a helmet and exquisite cloak of yellow and scarlet feathers. He was the first Hawaiian that Bostonians had ever seen, and was accorded the dignity of "crown prince of the islands."

The owners of the *Columbia* took another look at the venture, decided it was a failure, and two of them pulled out. Along with the other disappointments more than half of the tea was water-logged.

First martime legislation

While the *Columbia* sailed around the world, the federal Constitution had gone into effect in March 1789 and George Washington had been inaugurated as the first president of the United States on 30 April 1789. Congress began passing "privileged discrimination" acts to protect America's merchant marine from European competition. One of these was the Customs Act which gave American vessels a 10 percent discount on tariff rates on imports and doubled the rate on tea brought to the States in foreign ships.

Next, Congress passed an act which permitted American-owned and -built ships to enter home ports with only 6 cents a ton duty, while foreigners paid 50 cents a ton.

Also, foreign ships engaged in coastal trade were required to pay duty at each port of entry, while American vessels paid only once a year. With this kind of encouragement, merchants and ship-owners began building and fitting out more and more ships. In December of 1789 there were only 123,893 tons of American shipping registered for foreign commerce; a year later that figure had jumped to 346,254 tons.

The new government improved working conditions for seamen. In 1790 Congress passed an act requiring that seamen have a written contract stating the pay rate and duration of voyages they signed on for. Shipmasters' responsibilities were defined, and captains were forced to consider the welfare of their crews as well as the profits of the ships' owners.

The *Columbia*'s second voyage

The *Columbia*'s first voyage had been a financial loss but Joseph Barrell, with faith unshaken, immediately made plans for a second expedition. He refitted the *Columbia* with new masts and spars and persuaded John Hoskins to go along as supercargo. It was hoped that Hoskins, a shrewd merchant, would make up for Gray's weak business sense. A young fifth mate, John Boit, Jr., went along to keep careful records of the trip.

The ship sailed from Boston in late September 1790, and reached Nootka Sound in June 1791. By that time Gray and Hoskins were getting on each other's nerves. Hoskins complained in a letter to Barrell that Gray was calling him a "damn clerk," and telling the crew that he was a company spy.

Meanwhile, young John Boit recorded his personal observations. On 23 April 1791 he paid tribute to the ship's goat: "Departed this life our dear friend Nancy the Goat having been the Captain's companion on a former voyage. . . . At 5 PM Committed her body to the deep She was lamented by those who got a share of her Milk!" Nancy, who had been taken on board at the Cape Verde Islands in 1787, might possibly be the first goat to sail around the world.

The *Columbia* was supplied with better trading goods than before; woolen cloth, muskets, sheets of copper, and plenty of iron chisels which hopefully would coax sea-otter skins from the Indians. Generally the Indians were not unfriendly although there were several clashes. John Boit described them: "The Men go quite naked, except a skin over the shoulder. The Women are entirely cover'd with Garments of their own manufactory, from the bark of the Tree. . . . (they) have an incision cut through the under lip, which they spread out with a piece of wood about the size and shape of a Goose egg. . . . their lip pieces was enough to disgust any Civilized being, however some of the Crew was quite partial."

During the summer the *Columbia* roamed the bays and inlets of the northwest coast. When winter came the crew built a log cabin and moved ashore. They used their time to assemble a 44-ton schooner on a frame brought from Boston. The *Adventure*, as the schooner was called, would be the *Columbia*'s tender.

In the spring, Gray was eager to sail again, this time to the south. He had heard reports of a Spaniard, Bruno Hecate, who had sighted the mouth of a great river in that vicinity. On the morning of 12 May 1792 he took the *Columbia* across the sand bars and through the breakers to enter the "Great River of the West." He named it Columbia's River and, according to the custom of the day, claimed the territory for the United States of America.

The rest of the summer was spent trading along the coast. There were several unpleasant brushes with the Indians. Once the ship went aground. On their return to Nootka Sound, they were entertained by a courtly Spaniard, Don Juan Francisco de Bodega y Cuadra. John Boit wrote: "Fifty four persons sat down to Dinner, and the plates, which were *solid silver*, was shifted five times, which made 270 plates. . . ." Boit was certain of this because he noted that "they never carried the dirty plates or Dishes from the Hall where we dined."

By October, the *Columbia* was ready to sail. She had a full cargo, helped by selling the *Adventure* to the Spaniards for 75 otter skins. After a stop in the Sandwich Islands for fresh provisions, they reached Canton in December. The Chinese merchants were as tricky as ever, but Gray and the "damn clerk" Hoskins were wise to their game this time. Even though pelts were selling at the low price of $30 apiece, the Americans made a good bargain for tea, cottons, and other goods.

The *Columbia* sailed for home in February, by way of Sumatra and the Cape of Good Hope, and reached Boston on 29 June 1793.

Her crew did not get a hero's welcome but it got a warm one. Joseph Barrell was pleased with his profits and Gray had the personal satisfaction of having discovered the great river and establishing the furs-to-China trade that would last for the next 50 years.

Of the men aboard the *Columbia*, Gray went on to command other merchant ships; John Kendrick died a year later in Honolulu when a ship accidentally fired a round of grapeshot for a salute, killing him on the quarterdeck; John Boit had command of his own sloop in the China Seas by the time he was 19. He later had his own countinghouse, married a Newport girl, and raised seven children in his big home on Beacon Street.

Although Philadelphia, New York, Providence, and Bristol all sent ships on the sea route established by Gray and the *Columbia*, Boston continued to dominate the Northwest "triangle" trade—so much so that Northwest Indians thought Boston was the whole country. **Profits from furs**

Profits from that trade were enormous. During the first 30 years, Americans took to Canton 1,800,000 sealskins which netted them $3.5 million. Some 160,000 sea-otter skins brought $4 million. In all, for about $4.5 million in trade with the Indians, they gained furs which they sold for $20 million. With that sum, they brought back from China products that were sold in America and Europe for still larger profits.

The Dutch had dominated the pepper trade ever since they took over the East Indies. They deliberately bought less than was offered by eastern princes in order to keep the price high. Then, in 1798, Captain Jonathan Carnes, of Salem, sailed the brig *Cadet* to Madeira, India, and China, for miscellaneous peddling. In the port of Mencoolen, he heard that pepper grew wild on the northwest shore of Sumatra. When he returned to Salem, he whispered the news to Jonathan Peele who promptly fitted out the schooner *Rajah* and sent Carnes out to the Far East with her. **Riches in pepper**

Eighteen months later, Carnes returned with a cargo as precious as gold. Soon the rare spice had all Salem sneezing from end to end of Derby Street; everyone was frantic to learn where the spice came from. It yielded a 700 percent profit, and Jonathan Carnes was not about to tell.

Despite the close watch rival merchants kept on him, one moonless night he slipped out of the harbor for another trip to the spice islands. But he was followed by another vessel that tracked him half around the world to Mencoolen. The two ships dropped anchor, but the next morning, the skipper of the rival ship awoke to find the *Rajah* had gone. There was nothing for him to do then but go on to Canton, load up with tea, and head back to Salem. When he got home, there was the *Rajah* unloading another cargo of pepper.

Pepper made Jonathan Peele a rich man, but the secret could not last long. Others discovered that his source was Sumatra, and for a decade following October 1799 pepper re-exported from Salem supplied most of the world.

The pepper trade proved to be the most dangerous of all East Indian ventures. The natives of Sumatra had a habit of cutting off the heads of foreigners. Entire crews of Salem ships were massacred by Malays. But because the trade was so lucrative, Yankees continued to risk their lives for pepper.

Sealing in the Falkland Islands

Trading with the Northwest Indians for sea-otter skins proved to be an expensive and troublesome business after awhile. Besides, the supply began to drop off. Another source would have to be found if the fur trade with China were to continue. The familiar Newfoundland seals would not do for the luxury trade. Their fur made good clothing but lacked what the Chinese Mandarins thought of as beauty.

The answer was found in the Falkland Islands, 7,000 miles from Boston, at the southern tip of South America. Seals swarmed at the rookeries there; all one had to do was club them to death and skin them.

The first American ship to reach the Falklands was the *United States*. She was owned by an Englishwoman, Mary Haley, then living in Boston, who bought the 563-ton former frigate from the Royal Navy. Ebenezer Townsend, aboard the New Haven sealer *Neptune* at the Falklands, wrote on 20 November 1796: "States Harbor derives its name from a ship of that name which lay here two years to obtain sea-elephant oil and hair seal skins. She was a very large ship, toward 1,000 tons, from Boston, fitted from there soon after the Revolutionary War, and the first ship that we know of that took any fur seals. She was owned by Lady Haley, living in Boston."

When the *United States* reached New York, she landed sea-elephant oil and 13,000 fur sealskins which brought a low price of 50 cents apiece. No one seemed to know quite how to dispose of them at a profit so they were loaded aboard the ship *Eleanora* bound for Calcutta, that postwar trading center for all the Eastern markets, and a merchant there paid two dollars each for the skins. He sold them in Canton for five dollars apiece.

Sealing in the South Pacific and Atlantic reached its peak in the last decade of the eighteenth century on the island of Mas Afuera —off the coast of Chile. More than three million skins were taken

from this island in only seven years. They first sold in Canton for
three dollars or four dollars a skin, but prices soon dropped as low
as 35 cents. The wholesale slaughter of seals, along with ignorance
of their breeding habits, almost killed them all off.

The morality of keeping slaves was first questioned by the Quakers **Postwar slave trade**
in Pennsylvania. In 1700, New England's Samuel Sewell wrote that
it bothered his conscience to see Indians and Negroes being rated as
taxable assets with horses and hogs. Yet, by 1775, there were
450,000 slaves below the Mason Dixon Line and 60,000 above it.

In all, vessels owned by white men transported from 15 million
to 20 million black African slaves to the Americas. Probably twice
that many were killed when native villages raided one another for
slaves, or died of disease in tightly packed slave ships.

There were a number of anti-slavery societies in the mid-1700s,
some of which were started by shipmasters who were sickened by
the practice. Both John Paul Jones and Esek Hopkins, first commander in chief of the Continental Navy, had firsthand experience
in the slave trade. Jones, at the end of his second voyage from
Africa, asked to be let go because of the "abominable" nature of
the trade.

After the Revolutionary War, state and federal laws were enacted to stop the inhuman traffic. None did any real good. And
even as New Englanders voiced their disapproval, they built adaptable vessels and supplied versatile men to carry on the trade. Few
shipowners were against the practice, so long as it made a profit.

In 1819, the United States authorized slave patrols at African
trading ports and along the U.S. coast and, the next year, slave-
trading was made a crime, the same as piracy—punishable by
death. But there were not enough patrols to enforce the laws;
slavers were too clever and fast to be caught very often. Not until
1862, after the Civil War had begun, was an American captain,
Nathaniel Gordon, caught and hung.

British anti-slavery efforts were far more effective than the
American. They had more patrols and faster vessels. But they were
not allowed to stop and search ships flying the Stars and Stripes
until 1862 when they were given permission under certain conditions. Offenders were tried before international courts.

Seafarers of those early years sailed to the far corners of the world **Nathaniel Bowditch**
with only the most primitive and inaccurate methods of navigation.
They depended largely on the "seaman's eye," or "seaman's feel,"
and often just plain luck to reach their destinations. But all of this
was changed by a young Salem scholar, Nathaniel Bowditch.

Bowditch was not a sailor or a writer. Instead, he was a self-taught mathematician and master of the Latin, French, and Spanish languages. He approached the subject of navigation in a scholarly, scientific way, rather than the accepted guesswork of his day. He actually went to sea only five times between the years 1795, when he was 22, and 1803.

From the standpoint of future seamen, the most important voyage was a trip to Manila in 1796 by the *Astrea*, a ship owned by Elias Derby. Bowditch was aboard the ship as supercargo; he spent most of his spare time recomputing the mathematics of John Hamilton Moore's inaccurate work on navigation, and preparing a new book on the subject. *The American Practical Navigator*, first published in 1802, became the most valuable single work for seafarers that was ever published. It has since been through 80 revisions and is internationally accepted as the basic text on celestial navigation. Young Bowditch's work was the most trustworthy method for determining longitude when out of sight of land.

At the time of his death in 1838, the East India Marine Society adopted a resolution: ". . . as long as ships shall sail, the needle point to the north, and the stars go through their appointed course in the Heavens, the name of Dr. Bowditch will be revered."

(More about Dr. Bowditch can be found in Chapter 8.)

East India Marine Society

Yankees sailing the seven seas, particularly to China and India (generally called "The Indies"), developed a close comradeship with others from home. They had a special sense of history as they brought back exotic treasures to display in their homes. East India captains brought back all sorts of specimens, artwork, birds, animals—even people they had come across in their journeys. The first elephant ever seen in the United States was brought from Bengal by Jacob Crowningshield in 1796.

Not surprisingly, these voyagers joined together to form the East India Marine Society (now the Peabody Museum in Salem), with membership open only to shipmasters and supercargoes who "shall have actually navigated the Seas near or beyond the Cape of Good Hope or round Cape Horne." Each member was given a certificate and a blank journal in which he would log his voyage, make sketches, and give descriptions of distant coasts and waters. He was also asked to bring back trophies for the collection.

Captain Jonathan Carnes, returning from his second pepper voyage to Sumatra in 1799, contributed an elephant's tooth, a Battak pipe, and a rhinoceros-horn goblet.

The smell of pepper has gone from Salem's streets, and the old square-riggers no longer come in from the seven seas, but thanks to East India captains, what is now Salem's Peabody Museum is filled with priceless treasures unmatched anywhere in the world.

CHAPTER 6
PERILS OF INDEPENDENCE

After the Revolution, American merchantmen trading in distant ports returned the country to its prewar prosperity—but not without severe penalty. With no Navy to protect them, they were always in danger of being raided by pirates. In the Mediterranean, Barbary pirates held captured men for ransom, or sold them into slavery.

Tribute for the Barbary states

Algiers, Tunis, and Tripoli, three small countries on the north coast of Africa, had lived for 200 years by piracy. Each was ruled by a Dey, or Bey, or Pasha, who kept a small garrison of harsh, cruel, professional soldiers. Most of the inhabitants were Moslem Arabs and Berber tribesmen. Small nations paid tribute to the Barbary powers as a bribe to leave their shipping alone; Britain, France, and Holland paid subsidies to keep the pirates active against commerce of neutral nations.

A Dey or Bey or Pasha might well declare war on a small nation by simply cutting down the consul's flagpole. Then he would send raiding vessels out to capture its ships, whose crews would be put into slavery or forced to man oars in a war galley. Prisoners, with iron rings around their ankles and a diet of only black bread and vinegar, could rot in jail for years before they were finally ransomed, or died. Captured ships were sold at a fine profit and when

On previous page: In a fierce fifteen-minute battle off Boston on 1 June 1813, HMS *Shannon* defeated the USS *Chesapeake*, whose captain, James Lawrence, fatally wounded, shouted "Don't give up the ship!" It was a war of slogans—the seagoing ancestors of bumper stickers. Here, the *Chesapeake* flies a flag bearing "Free Trade and Sailors Rights." Three months later, in the Battle of Lake Erie, Oliver Hazard Perry's flagship carried a flag reading "Don't Give Up The Ship." That flag is now at the U.S. Naval Academy. Courtesy: The Office of Naval History.

a new peace treaty was signed it was usually accompanied by a handsome "honorarium."

The first such insult to Americans came when the schooner *Maria* of Boston was stopped off the coast of Portugal on 25 July 1785. A nondescript vessel fired a round shot across the *Maria's* bow and suddenly 21 Turks and Moors, brandishing weapons, swarmed aboard her. Their leader demanded to see the schooner's flag, and when Captain Isaac Stevens showed them the Stars and Stripes they were mystified. They had never seen a flag like that before. They hustled the crew off to see an old Moor who gave them bread, honey, and coffee and advised them to make friends with their father, the King of England. He did not believe the Revolution was over. He did not turn them loose, either.

Five days later the Philadelphia ship *Dauphin* was captured 150 miles west of Lisbon. The number of Americans in Algerian captivity was then 21. Later the total reached 110.

By 1792, public anger forced the American Congress to choose between war or tribute. For some time there had been talk about reviving the Navy but nothing was actually done about it. Instead, Congress chose to pay tribute and approved payment of $100,000 annually to Algiers, Tunis, and Tripoli; a $40,000 ransom would be paid for the Americans already held in slavery. John Paul Jones, at that time living in France, was appointed to negotiate a treaty of tribute with the Dey of Algiers, but died before he could accomplish the shameful task.

Meanwhile, events in France began having a profound effect on America. The French people, encouraged by the American Revolution, stormed the Bastille (a prison in Paris) in 1789, dragged Louis XVI back to Paris from his palace at Versailles and beheaded him on 21 January 1793. France became a republic, ruled by a National Convention. During the succeeding reign of terror, led by Maximilien Robespierre, thousands of French aristocrats and sympathizers were guillotined. Sickened and alarmed by these excesses, the Convention acted, and Robespierre was executed in July 1794. By that time France and England were engaged in a series of wars that would last 20 years. All Europe became involved, with France and England blockading ports and capturing ships as lawful prizes. At first, the United States was not directly involved. The country was neutral, and had ships, and food and supplies that were badly needed by the warring nations.

Yankee merchantmen began sailing the Mediterranean in larger numbers. Even though tribute had been paid, the Algerians continued their old tricks. Soon they had captured eleven ships and imprisoned their crews. President Washington proposed to Congress that a naval force was the only way of dealing with the

Revolution in France

bandits. But many members of Congress did not want to spend the money. Besides, they said, a Navy might aggravate Britain . . . provoke something unpleasant. Finally, a bill was passed in 1794, authorizing the building of six frigates, but it contained the proviso that construction would have to stop if a peace treaty with the Algerians was signed. The shipbuilding proceeded at a sporadic rate, depending on how many American ships were molested; it finally stopped when Congress accepted a treaty that cost over $1 million—one-sixth of the annual budget—and agreed to give Algeria a 36-gun ship. That, of course, would only be used to capture more Christian slaves. Washington finally persuaded Congress to go ahead with the building of three of the frigates.*

Quasi-war with France

By 1797, French privateers (150 of them in the West Indies alone) were running out of business. British merchantmen were no longer an easy capture—most of them were heavily escorted by the Royal Navy. The French government then decreed that any ship, neutral or otherwise, which might be carrying goods to an enemy country was subject to confiscation. This included Americans; before long at least 27 American ships had been taken in this manner and Yankee skippers were protesting to the Secretary of State.

President John Adams sent three commissioners to negotiate with the French, but they received only insults. France, in fact, demanded 32 million Dutch florins as a loan and a gift of 1,200,000 gold *livres*. Americans realized that their old ally had become even stronger in her demands than the Barbary pirates. To add insult to injury, French privateersmen began entering American ports to spend the money they had stolen from American ships.

In discussing the payment of tribute, Charles C. Pinckney, the American minister to France, was said to have banged a table with his fist and shouted: "Millions for defense, but not one cent for tribute!" Americans cheered, even though what he really said was ". . . but not a damned penny for tribute." Yet while all this talk was going on, 26 barrels of blackmail dollars were being shipped to the pirates.

The following year Congress finally moved to finish construction of the new Navy ships, and authorized the purchase or hire of 12 more vessels, to be armed in the same manner as the Revolutionary War privateers. Sympathetic shipping men of Philadelphia, New York, Salem, and Boston, gave money to build ships as gifts from their cities. On 30 April 1798 Congress passed an act establishing a Navy Department. Benjamin Stoddert, of Maryland, was named first Secretary of the Navy. Assisted by six clerks and a

---

* Two of them still float; the *Constitution* ("Old Ironsides") in Boston, and the *Constellation* (the "Yankee Racehorse") in Baltimore.

messenger, he added 49 ships to the Navy in his first year of office.

Many senior officers of the old Continental Navy were given commands again; Captain Richard Dale, the *Ganges*; Thomas Truxtun, the *Constellation*; Stephen Decatur, Sr., the *Delaware*; Commodore John Barry, the *United States*; and Captain Samuel Nicholson, the *Constitution*.

The new Navy

When President Washington received authorization to build the Navy's six frigates, he turned to Joshua Humphreys of Philadelphia. Humphreys had been a junior partner in the firm of Wharton & Humphreys who had laid down the plans for the Continental ships. Now, it was determined that American naval construction should be on a standard better than anything abroad. Humphreys reported to Washington: "We are to consider what size ships will be more formidable and be an overmatch for those of the enemy: such frigates as in blowing weather would be an overmatch for double-deck ships and in light winds to evade coming to action. Frigates will be the first object, and none ought to be built less than 150-foot keel, to carry 30 24-pounders on the gundeck. Ships of this construction have everything in their favor, their great length gives them an advantage of sailing, which is an object of the first magnitude. . . ."

Humphreys was actually recommending that American frigates should be, in size and strength, midway between the British double-deckers carrying about 50 guns, and single-deckers carrying about 30 guns.

British two-deckers carried their 24-pounders on the lower deck where the gunports could not be safely opened in high seas. Humphreys reasoned that those ships lost half their effectiveness because the guns on the upper deck were 18-pounders.

The first three frigates built for the new Navy were the *Constellation*, 38 guns, *United States*, 44 guns, and *Constitution*, 44 guns. They were fast, maneuverable vessels of medium tonnage with three masts and square sails. They had only one gun deck: a few guns were mounted on an upper deck known as the spar deck. In good weather, they could use all their guns. Their low wind resistance would allow them to escape upwind from a stronger double-decker. Each vessel carried a crew of several hundred men.

Wages and rations

Along with Humphreys' ingenious new ship designs, John Adams had his own ideas on recruiting crews. Americans would not impress sailors from the merchant marine as did the British; instead they would make naval duty attractive enough to get highly motivated volunteers. Wages were set at $15 to $17 per month—$7 more than merchantmen were paid. Captains were instructed to take in as many boys as possible because Adams wanted Navy men to grow up in the service. There would be prize money for all at a fixed rate, and it would be doubled if the enemy were of superior force.

Sailors were invited to visit the new frigates. They could even sample a meal, and learn that their rations for two days were the equivalent of a British ration for a week.

Considering that the only way of preserving meat then was to salt it, and hardtack bread was so tough it could be whittled like wood, the diet was not bad at all. Rations for one man for a week were:

Sunday—1½ pounds of beef and ½ pound of rice
Monday—1 pound of pork, ½ pint of peas, and 4 ounces of cheese
Tuesday—1½ pounds of beef and 1 pound of potatoes
Wednesday—½ pint of rice, 2 ounces butter, and 6 ounces molasses
Thursday—1 pound of pork, ½ pint of peas
Friday—1 pound of salt fish, 1 pound of potatoes, and 2 ounces of butter
Saturday—1 pound of pork, ½ pint of peas, and 4 ounces of cheese

Every man got a pound of bread and either a half-pint of rum, or a quart of beer each day.

The officers fared better than did their Continental Navy predecessors. A captain drew $75 a month plus six rations a day figured at 28 cents each. Lieutenants made $50 and three rations, surgeons an equal amount; warrants $20 plus two rations. The officers' blue uniforms had epaulets on one shoulder denoting rank. The buttons were brass and the breeches and facings were buff-colored.

War again   When the shaky peace between Britain and France collapsed and they went to war again, the United States was caught in the crossfire. And it was soon learned that the Barbary pirates were not the only enemies of Yankee merchantmen on the high seas.

Neither France nor England cared about the rights of neutrals. Each declared the other's ports to be blockaded. Any vessel caught trading with the enemy, even outside the blockaded waters, was subject to search and seizure.

The British, having exhausted the supply of jailed criminals and felons, and unable to take men from their own merchant ships, began grabbing American seamen on the pretext that they were really Englishmen carrying false papers.

The French closed U.S. ports to belligerents, ignoring the President's proclamation of neutrality. They brazenly refitted in U.S. waters, recruited men ashore, then waited offshore for ships loaded with cargo bound for England or the British West Indies.

The new Navy was given orders to drive French privateers from American waters. The orders to the two squadrons set up by Adams and Stoddert were later expanded to include French men-of-war. This resulted in the most famous battle of the undeclared war, that between the *Constellation* and the French *Insurgente*, reputed to be the fastest frigate in the world.

The *Constellation* and the *Insurgente*

The *Constellation* was commanded by Thomas Truxtun, veteran of successful privateering during the Revolution. An intellectual, tough taskmaster and disciplinarian, he drew up a long series of letters and instructions to his officers and petty officers which carefully spelled out duties and responsibilities. These, with other regulations laid down by John Adams, became the basis for the first Navy regulations. Truxtun's first lieutenant was John Rodgers, and his midshipman was 19-year-old David Porter. Some crew members soon decided Navy life was not for them—it was just too tough if Truxtun's ship was any example. Those who stayed on, however, showed what a spirited, well-disciplined crew could do. A lieutenant wrote home: "With these officers and men, I should feel happy to go alongside the best 50-gun ship of the conquering French."

Truxtun did just that on 9 February 1799, off the Caribbean island of Nevis, when the *Insurgente* hove into sight. Though the two ships were almost the same size, the American frigate could fire a total broadside weight of 432 pounds against 282 for the enemy. In less than an hour, the *Insurgente* hauled down her colors and surrendered. She had seventy casualties against three in the *Constellation*.

Captain Truxtun ordered John Rodgers and David Porter to take a 12-man detail aboard the *Insurgente* to claim her as a war prize and supervise the transfer of her battered crew. The Americans found themselves in a precarious position, with 173 Frenchmen aboard the half-wrecked, blood-spattered *Insurgente*. A sudden gale drove the two frigates out of sight of each other, but they managed to sail their prize into the harbor of St. Kitts in the Caribbean.

A few months after this victory, Commodore Barry's squadron, with the *United States* and *Constitution* in the eastern Caribbean, captured twelve French privateers. By the end of 1799, twenty-five French ships had been taken. In 1800, the frigate *Essex* sailed around the Horn and swept through the Pacific where she recaptured several American ships and drove off the French who, until then, had ranged that ocean unopposed.

The sea fights with the French gave the new Navy valuable experience which could be used in the wars with the Barbary States that followed. John Adams later wrote, "The new Navy had effectively protected American commerce and successfully discharged its first mission. . . ."

A better cause   Thomas Jefferson, a passionate champion of individual freedom, distrusted large standing armies for fear they would invite dictatorships. A Navy, he eventually conceded, was not as much of a threat because it could not sail inland and endanger people's rights.

When he took office as president in 1801, he cut the military establishment to 2,500 officers and men. The Navy was reduced to a peacetime skeleton force; all ships were sold except for five light frigates and eight heavy ones, plus the little schooner *Enterprize.* Only nine of the 28 captains remained on the active duty list.

But thrifty Jefferson shortly changed his views on navies and war. Less than three months after he became president, the Pasha of Tripoli, dissatisfied with his share of "protection" money, virtually declared war on the United States by cutting down the flagstaff of the American consulate. At the same time, he demanded $250,000 to set it up again.

The challenge was thrown squarely in the face of Jefferson, who now realized that no compromise with the Barbary States was possible. The words he had uttered during Washington's administration came back to haunt him: "Tribute or war is the usual alternative of these Barbary States. Why not build a Navy and decide on war? We cannot begin in a better cause or against a better foe."

With war declared, Jefferson sent a squadron to the Mediterranean to blockade the entrance to the harbor of Tripoli. The ships, commanded by Richard Dale, were the heavy frigates *President* and *Philadelphia*, the light frigate *Essex*, and the schooner *Enterprize.* It was an uneventful period except when the *Enterprize* fell in with a 14-gun corsair, shot her up, killed 20 men and wounded 30; she finally sailed home empty-handed since the squadron had no authority to take prizes.

Dale soon had to lift the embargo because his men, who had signed on for a one-year enlistment, were anxious to get home. They were to be replaced by another crew with two-year enlistments, to be commanded by Truxtun. But when Truxtun learned that he would have to command his own flagship as well as direct the entire squadron, he resigned. Captain Richard V. Morris was appointed in his stead. For a number of reasons Morris was a dismal failure. In two years he was recalled for court-martial and was dismissed from the service.

Meanwhile, the Tripolitans were becoming more aggressive so Jefferson sent yet another squadron to protect American interests.

This time the commander was Edward Preble, a stiff disciplinarian and frosty-faced veteran of both the Revolution and the French War.

Preble complained that he had been sent to war with "a bunch of school boys," because all his captains were less than 30 years old—and some were in their early 20s. But after a few months of campaigning, "Preble's boys" proved themselves, and the "old man" was the first to give them praise.

William Bainbridge, in the new frigate *Philadelphia*, in October 1803, had the only U.S. ship off the harbor of Tripoli. Preble was in Tangier with the remainder of the squadron, negotiating a peace with the Sultan of Morocco. On 31 October, Bainbridge chased a corsair too close to shore and the *Philadelphia* hit an uncharted reef. She was heeled over by the outgoing tide and unable to use her guns. Bainbridge bored holes in the *Philadelphia*'s hull, hoping to sink her, and surrendered.

"The most bold and daring act of the age"

The Tripolitans quickly plugged up the holes, raised the frigate, and floated her into the harbor. The Pasha was ecstatic over this fine prize, bigger and better than anything in his navy. She was soon flying the Pasha's flag, ready for action against the Americans.

Commander Preble planned a scheme to retake the *Philadelphia*. It began with the capture of a ketch which the Americans renamed *Intrepid*. Lieutenant Stephen Decatur, Jr., then commanding the USS *Enterprize*, volunteered to handle the ketch. He picked 84 volunteers from the *Enterprize* and the *Constitution*. They would disguise themselves as Mediterranean seamen and destroy the *Philadelphia*, even though she lay at anchor under the guns that defended the fort.

At night, with superb seamanship and luck, they sailed to within 100 yards of the *Philadelphia*. With them was a Sicilian pilot who talked to the pirates in their own tongue, and got permission to moor alongside for the night.

As the Tripolitans hauled away on the *Intrepid*'s mooring lines, they suddenly noticed the hidden American sailors and sent up the cry of alarm. But it was too late. Decatur led his men in a fierce fight, swarming over the bulwarks and through the gunports. Some Tripolitans were killed, others were forced overboard; some managed to swim to shore while the Americans went after the ship, and set her afire.

The *Philadelphia* was soon a blazing inferno as Decatur and his men returned to their vessel. Even then they had to work down the harbor in the brilliant light of the fire with the fort guns blazing away. The bombardment was tremendous, but oddly ineffective. Not a single American was wounded. When the little ketch reached Syracuse, in Sicily, the crew was greeted by cheers from the crowds. The Sicilian pilot was granted American citizenship. Decatur was later awarded a captain's commission and a gold sword. Admiral Lord Nelson called Decatur's feat "The most bold, and daring act of the age."

For the next two years, the Americans kept a tight blockade on the harbor of Tripoli. In August 1804, Preble launched a series of five attacks against land and sea defenses of the harbor—with heavy damage to the city. Preble's men also sank three enemy gunboats and captured four. Many engagements involved hand-to-hand combat. The sole object was to teach respect for the Stars and Stripes. Tripolitans learned that the new republic across the Atlantic refused any longer to bear insults or pay blackmail for her right to sail the high seas.

Preble's successor in the Mediterranean, Samuel Barron, with the support of a famous land operation, finally brought the war to an end. The American Consul at Tunis, William Eaton, and Lieutenant Presley O'Bannon, of the U.S. Marine Corps, led a motley assortment of Marines, soldiers, sailors, and tribesmen on camels across the sands from Alexandria.* Their aim was to restore the deposed ruler of Tripoli, Hamet Caramanli, to the throne. Faced with a double threat, the Pasha of Tripoli was only too happy to make peace. A treaty was signed in May 1805, providing for a man-for-man exchange of prisoners and a ransom of $60,000 for 200 seamen of the *Philadelphia* who were in excess of the number of Tripolitans held by the Americans. The Mediterranean Squadron sailed home in triumph.

The Pasha was not the only observer to be impressed by the performance of America's new Navy. Admiral Lord Nelson said at Gibraltar, as he watched the *Constitution* from the quarterdeck of his flagship, *Victory:* "In the handling of those trans-Atlantic ships there is a nucleus of trouble for the Navy of Great Britain."

The Barbary campaigns marked the beginnings of career naval service. There was no longer any prize money involved. Thereafter, officers and seamen fought on land and sea for glory and honor. Formerly, when a war ended, officers had resigned their commissions in large numbers, but when the Barbary campaigns ended, very few left the service.

It has been said that while Truxtun supplied much of the background for the new Navy—regulations, for example—it was Preble, working in close harmony with his officers and men, who gave the Navy its fighting spirit.

The pattern was set; the punishment of the other North African corsairs continued until after the War of 1812. The Navy gained valuable experience while strengthening its blossoming traditions. Foreign nations developed respect for the young country willing to defend herself with blazing guns and deeds of gallantry.

* The phrase "to the shores of Tripoli," in the Marines' Hymn refers to this operation.

In the United States at that time, the penny-pinching administration of Jefferson unfortunately decided that naval defense meant only coastal defense. The home front would be protected, but Federalist New England merchantmen on the high seas could look out for themselves. Consequently construction on all new frigates was stopped, and instead, Congress authorized the building of 278 small gunboats for coastal service. While only 178 of them were built, all the timber that Stoddert had saved for the construction of heavy ships was used up.

Soon dubbed "Jeffs" or "the mosquito fleet," the gunboats were armed with only one gun. Loading and firing took half an hour. Even then they could not fire unless they were at anchor or the boat would capsize. The gunboats were more hazardous to their crews than to any enemy they might encounter. During a hurricane in Georgia, one of them washed eight miles inland into a cornfield, much to the glee of the New England Federalists.

Jefferson's cheeseparing economy backfired in the War of 1812 when, except at the Battle of New Orleans, the whole fleet of gunboats was virtually useless. British frigates and sloops were able to go in and land troops at will. The money for the Mosquito Fleet could have been used more wisely in building eight or more frigates of the *Constitution* class.

Jefferson's "mosquito fleet"

There was no way for America to stay out of European squabbles, no matter how wishful the thinking. Decisions made across the Atlantic directly affected the survival of Americans—even those living in the wild frontier. In 1800, in a secret pact, the King of Spain ceded to Napoleon Bonaparte the immense Mississippi valley region of Louisiana, which included New Orleans. The fact became known to Americans only when the Spanish authorities withdrew the right of deposit, guaranteed by the treaty of 1795. This meant that frontier farmers no longer had the privilege of floating their produce down the Mississippi to New Orleans for export. The pioneers were furious, and threatened to attack New Orleans.

It was a terrible problem for peace-loving Jefferson. New Orleans in Spanish hands had been no threat to America, but its control by Napoleon posed a new and fearful danger. So, in 1803 in order to quiet things down, Jefferson sent James Monroe to Paris to join the U.S. minister, Robert R. Livingston, in trying to buy New Orleans and as much territory to the east as they could. They were authorized to offer $10 million.

Jefferson was prepared, if that mission should fail, to think in terms of an alliance with England against France. It was a strange dilemma for the President to be in. He hated war, he opposed entangling alliances; England was the traditional foe, and he had loved France since his days as minister there. Now he was contemplating joining with England in a defensive war against France!

The Louisiana Purchase

Napoleon suddenly decided to sell all of Louisiana and give up his dream of a New World empire. He had been unable to conquer sugar-rich Santo Domingo, for which Louisiana was to serve as granary. In 1791 the angry ex-slaves, led by the Negro, Toussaint L'Ouverture, had led a bloody resistance against the French, and yellow fever finished the job by killing thousands of French soldiers. Napoleon also saw that with Britain ruling the seas, he would probably lose Louisiana to his old enemy anyway. Perhaps a strong America would put a crimp in the British style.

The haggling between the French Foreign Minister and the Americans lasted a week. Livingston could hardly believe his ears (he was deaf) when the French set the price of $15 million for the entire package. Treaties were signed on 30 April 1803. With one bloodless stroke, America bought at 3 cents an acre the western half of the richest river valley in the world, whose area is 828,000 square miles.

Even though it was Jefferson's most glorious achievement as President, he was at first appalled. His two envoys were supposed to buy territory *east* of New Orleans for $10 million. Now the government was pledged to pay $15 million for an area that included an enormous territory to the *west* which no one knew anything about. It was estimated that about 50,000 red, white, and black people lived there.

Lewis and Clark

Jefferson was triumphantly re-elected in 1804, even though many Federalists said his Louisiana deal was political suicide. Now he determined to consolidate his territorial gains by finding out just what he had bought. Perhaps exploration would reveal that the headwaters of the east-flowing Missouri River and the west-flowing Columbia River, both originating in the Rocky Mountains, were so close together that a water route from the Mississippi to the Pacific might be established. This would open up the new land to fur-trapping and encourage settlers to move west and establish farms.

Jefferson chose two young army officers, Meriwether Lewis and William Clark, to lead the expedition. They were to map the new territory, observe animals, plants, geology, geography, and the people.

When Lewis and Clark reached St. Louis in December 1803 they ran into trouble. Not then knowing of the transfer of Louisiana from Spain to France and subsequently to the United States, the Spanish commander refused to let the two explorers pass. They had to wait through the winter.

In March 1804, the Spaniard finally got orders to turn Louisiana over to France. He hauled down the Spanish flag which was replaced by the French tricolor. But the French knew of the sale to the United States, so on the same day they lowered their flag and the Stars and Stripes were raised. St. Louis had flown three flags in one day.

Lewis and Clark and their party were the first white men to cross the continent and their reports were of tremendous importance. Their explorations were the first steps in the westward tide of emigration which was already beginning, while east of the Mississippi, the nation was challenging the might of the British Navy, and parrying military thrusts by British regulars from Canada.

After giving up his plans for Louisiana, Napoleon unleashed a new storm in Europe by renewing his war with Britain.

The United States as a neutral

The United States, whose ships had been the world's leading neutral carriers since 1793, enjoyed great profits for about two years, but in 1805, all that changed. At the Battle of Trafalgar, the British fleet under Lord Nelson smashed the combined French and Spanish fleets, thus making Britain supreme controller of the seas. At the Battle of Austerlitz in Austria—the Battle of the Three Emperors—Napoleon crushed the combined Austrian and Russian armies and made France master of the land. England and France then were forced to use indirect blows at each other's lifelines, and this involved America.

Britain began the struggle in 1806 with a series of Orders in Council which closed to foreign shipping the ports under French continental control. France struck back by ordering the seizure of all merchantmen, including those flying the American flag, that tried to enter British ports.

American merchantmen considered the risks and sailed anyway. They reasoned that the greater the risk the greater the profit, and they steadfastly claimed their right to carry neutral goods in their vessels.

"Impressment," the forcible enlistment of able-bodied subjects, had been used as a form of conscription by the British and other navies for four centuries. The standard equipment for the "press gang" was club and stretcher. In this way, waterfront inns and bars were cleaned out, and men were forced into naval service, whether they liked it or not.

British impressment

According to British naval custom, each ship captain was responsible for keeping his ship fully manned; failure to do this meant loss of command. If he was unable to find enough men ashore, he could stop any British merchantman and take the men he required to fill his crew.

Problems arose when the British began seizing seamen who were American citizens, claiming they were deserters from the Royal Navy. This was done particularly when the experienced seamen the British desperately needed after years of war were involved. Records show that between the years 1808 and 1811, 6,000 bona fide U.S. citizens were impressed. Many were killed in service or died of disease, leaving embittered families back home.

The British had complaints of their own. They claimed that American warships and merchantmen lured British seamen away from their "floating hells," from cat-o'-nine-tail floggings, and from meager rations. Americans, they said, paid higher wages and offered better shipboard life. Furthermore, the Yankees even passed out fraudulent naturalization papers for one dollar apiece. His Majesty's press gangs laughed at such papers. "Once an Englishman, always an Englishman," they said.

It was especially common for a Royal Navy man to desert in an American port. An American prisoner in Dartmouth, England, wrote in his journal: "An American in England pines to get home while an Englishman or Irishman longs to become an American citizen."

The British insisted they could not give up impressment as a means of filling their ships. America was making money, they said; England was making war. And without her Navy, England would lose the war against Napoleon.

It was galling enough to Americans to have civilians snatched from merchantmen, but unbearable when a U.S. man-of-war was boarded, as happened in 1807, when HMS *Leopard* overhauled the USS *Chesapeake* about 10 miles off Norfolk, Virginia. The British boarding party bluntly demanded the surrender of four alleged deserters—Americans who had been pressed into the British Navy but had escaped to serve in the U.S. Navy. Captain James Barron, skipper of the *Chesapeake,* though unprepared for a battle, refused to give up the men. The British then fired three devastating broadsides at close range, killing three Americans and wounding eighteen. Barron hauled down his flag and gave up the four seamen.

The country was outraged. There had been nothing like that since the French insults of 1797. Britain admitted to being in the wrong, which aroused Americans even more. But peace-loving Jefferson delayed action in the hopes of forcing the British to renounce impressment altogether. And this the British refused to do.

Jefferson's costly embargo

Jefferson was opposed to a large-scale foreign war. The Navy was weak and the Army even weaker. A humiliating defeat would be disastrous. Yet, national honor could not tolerate mistreatment by the British and French.

At this point, all the warring nations of Europe were dependent upon America's raw materials and food. Jefferson decided that if America were to cut off all exports to the offending powers, they would be forced to respect American rights. Consequently, the Embargo Act was passed by Congress late in 1807. The result was disaster for New England shipowners and sailors. Shipping ceased, and empty ships turned the waterfront into forests of bare masts. Unemployed seamen lined up at soup kitchens, as their ships rotted at their moorings.

Farmers in the south and west fared no better as harvests of cotton, grain, and tobacco accumulated. It was soon realized that the embargo was actually doing more harm to Americans than it was to the European belligerents.

Some Americans got around the embargo by building up an enormously profitable illicit trade along the Canadian border. Armed Americans on loaded rafts overpowered federal agents, loudly cursing the "Dambargo." As New Englanders seethed with secession talk, Congress, on 1 March 1809, repealed the embargo. A new measure banned trade only with France and England.

The embargo was actually three times more costly to the country than armed hostilities would have been. With only a fraction of the money lost, a strong Navy could have been built—a force strong enough to have commanded respect for American rights on the high seas and, possibly, to have prevented the War of 1812.

On 4 March 1809, James Madison took office as President. The following year Congress took desperate steps to uphold American rights without resorting to war by enacting a bill which was, in fact, a bribe to the belligerents. It stated that the United States would restore non-importation against any nation that did not repeal restrictions on U.S. trade.

James Madison takes office

Napoleon loved the idea. A non-importation boycott clamped on Britain would not only serve as a partial boycott but would lure America into a war with Britain. On 10 August 1810 he announced that his objectionable decrees had been repealed, while at the same time he secretly ordered the sale of confiscated American ships.

Madison, mistakenly believing Napoleon, reestablished non-importation against England. The infuriated British saw that America was teaming up with France against them. Britain and the United States were moving hopelessly into war.

Logically, the United States should have fought both countries to establish her right to freedom of the seas. France had, since 1803, seized 558 American ships, while England had taken 917.

The War of 1812

Part of the reason why this was not done was that England was the hereditary enemy; the Jeffersonian Republican party was traditionally anti-British and pro-French. Also, Napoleon's misdeeds were carried on far from home, while British impressments and seizures often took place within sight of American shores.

From a profit viewpoint, a victorious war with England would mean that American privateers could go after the richest merchant marine in the world. But most significant of all was the illusion that taking Canada from the British would be absurdly simple, "a frontiersman's frolic." Not only would this punish the British for supplying Indians with the guns and firewater that enabled them to raid frontier settlements, but it would also settle the fur-trading rivalries.

Except for individual action by American frigates on ocean and lake, the War of 1812 was on the whole very poorly fought. There simply was no great collective anger, as there had been in 1807 after the *Chesapeake* outrage. The people were not united behind the war effort and, despite warnings since 1793 when Britain and France went to war, U.S. military and naval forces were woefully unprepared.

Many Federalists, particularly, did not want war at all and talked of New England withdrawing from the Union. The men in Congress who influenced President Madison were actually a minority.

The American military   Although there were some six million whites in America in 1812, one million of whom were males of arms-bearing age, no more than seven thousand were ever mustered for any one battle. Army troops were widely scattered and ill-trained; the militia was even less well trained.

At sea, the U.S. Navy had 14 ships to pit against the Royal Navy, which had over 1,000. Fortunately, in the beginning the majority of the British ships were occupied elsewhere in operations against France.

North to Canada   In Washington, it was decided the best way to hurt Britain was to go after Canada with land forces. Since roads were few and poor, the population had settled along the St. Lawrence River and its tributaries and the Great Lakes. All supplies, both military and civilian, had to be transported over these waterways. If Montreal could be captured, all the supply routes could be cut off.

Unhappily, America's war planners did not push through in one big thrust. Instead, they wasted precious time and energy on a three-pronged invasion. One force, under General William Hull, started in Detroit. He soon retreated to his base and surrendered his army to inferior forces without firing a shot. The second American force wound up with the New York militia refusing to cross the Canadian line because their countrymen on the other side were being killed or surrendering. The third force marched for Montreal along Lake Champlain, but turned back when the troops refused to cross the New York border into Canada.

Conversely, the British and Canadians showed great enthusiasm and energy. First, they captured an American fort at Mackinac Island, in Lake Huron, off the coast of northern Michigan. From there they commanded the upper Great Lakes and a large Indian-controlled territory to the south. The Canadians were ably led by the British General Isaac Brock.

With American land forces taking a drubbing and morale plunging ever lower, Captain Isaac Hull in the *Constitution* won the first victory of several that followed in short order, by defeating HMS *Guerrière*, in a deadly, hard-fought duel. Hull had sailed the *Constitution* alone, and without orders, out of Boston. Off Newfoundland the ship took several minor prizes. Then, on 19 August, 800 miles off Cape Cod, Hull sighted the British frigate *Guerrière*, commanded by the able and experienced Captain James A. Dacres.

Hull hoisted the Stars and Stripes. Then, clearing for action, the *Constitution* moved in on the enemy frigate for close action. The *Guerrière* replied with a broadside, and then another. The British shells bounced off the *Constitution*'s thick oak hull, earning for her the lasting title "Old Ironsides."

For forty-five minutes the ships skillfully maneuvered for advantage. Hull seized an opportunity, closed to "within half pistol shot" and opened a heavy fire. The *Guerrière* soon had all her masts shot away and a third of her crew wounded or killed. Captain Dacres was hit in the back by a musket ball.

The *Guerrière* finally struck her colors. On surrender, Hull met the British captain saying, "Dacres, give me your hand. I know you are hurt." Hull tried to tow the *Guerrière* back to port but she was so badly damaged that she sank. Ten days later the victorious *Constitution* returned to Boston.

Perry at Lake Erie   Again, in 1813, the United States was forced to retreat. The Canadians, many of whom were Loyalists from the Revolutionary War days, were powerfully motivated to defend their new homes. They were fighting mad and justly so. After all, they had been rejected by the United States, and they had not been guilty of impressing American seamen or supplying Indians with weapons. Why should they be attacked in the first place?

If the Americans were going to get any place at all they would have to gain control of the Great Lakes. On 27 March 1813 Oliver Hazard Perry, then only 27 years old, assumed command of U.S. naval forces on Lake Erie. Arriving at Presque Isle (now Erie, Pennsylvania) with 150 seamen and Kentucky riflemen, his mission was to assemble and man a fleet to take Lake Erie from the British.

The men worked in freezing weather, transporting timbers, pitch, pine tar—everything—through blinding blizzards.

On 10 September 1813 British and American forces met in a desperate battle. There were terrible losses on both sides. Perry's flagship *Lawrence* became a shambles; her decks ran with blood and 80 percent of her crew were casualties.

Taking his battle flag bearing the legend "Don't Give up the Ship," Perry transferred to the uninjured *Niagara*. From there he led the U.S. forces to a complete victory. His report on the battle was short and to the point: "We have met the enemy and they are ours. Two ships, two brigs, one schooner and one sloop."

With Lake Erie in American hands, the British soon lost Detroit. To finish the job on the retreating British, Perry donned boots and spurs, and rode in a cavalry charge at the Battle of the Thames. It was at this battle that the Indian leader Tecumseh, whom the British had commissioned a brigadier general, was killed.

The Battle of Lake Erie, 10 September 1813. Ships of the British squadron had more guns, but the American guns fired heavier shot, and Perry's Kentucky riflemen in the rigging picked off British gunners. With his flagship *Lawrence* a wreck, Perry transferred to the *Niagara* (at right) and won the battle. The *Niagara*, once sunk, and then restored, is now displayed at Erie, Pennsylvania. Painting on display in the Capitol, Washington, D.C.

The Battle of Lake Champlain   In 1814, after Napoleon had been defeated, the British could send 15,000 British troops to Montreal to fight the war the Americans had declared. This mammoth force assembled and prepared to strike New York along the lake-river route. The Americans had to stop the advance.

On 11 September 1814 an inferior American fleet under Thomas Macdonough challenged the forces on Lake Champlain in a battle near Plattsburg. It appeared the Americans would be defeated but Macdonough, using stream anchors and hawsers to swing his crippled vessel, gave the enemy a powerful broadside that led to the defeat of the British ships.

Had the British been victorious, America would certainly have been forced to cede some of its northern territory in the peace settlement. Their defeat was momentous. The British army retreated; New York was saved from conquest, the Great Lakes and the old Northwest were spared British domination, and New England decided not to separate from the Union after all.

The victories of Perry and Macdonough on Lake Erie and Lake Champlain involved only 23 ships and a flotilla of gunboats. They caused fewer than 300 deaths on land and sea and they required less than six hours to decide, yet they were by far the most important events of the war. Macdonough, like Perry, is a bona fide American naval hero, but he is often overlooked in popular accounts because he did not compose any blood-tingling slogan.

Invasion of Washington   In August 1814, British warships landed a force of about 4,000 troops in Chesapeake Bay. As they marched towards Washington, the 6,000 American militiamen at Bladensburg, in nearby Maryland, panicked. The British invaded the nation's capital on 24 August. Dolly Madison barely had time to cut a portrait of General Washington out of its frame, roll it up with the original draft of the Constitution, and escape in a coach. Some officers entered the White House and ate a meal that had just been prepared for President and Mrs. Madison.

The British set fire to most of the public buildings, including the Capitol and the White House (the "Yankee Palace"), while President Madison and his aides watched the blaze and smoke from the nearby hills. The troops then busied themselves, looting private homes.

When the British fleet appeared at Baltimore, the tough defenders of Fort McHenry fought it off, despite "bombs bursting in air." Francis Scott Key watched the bombardment and wrote the words of "The Star Spangled Banner." It was soon set to the tune of an old English tavern refrain. American land forces, originally in disarray, pulled themselves together and forced the British to withdraw.

The attack on Washington was no credit to the British. At the time, they claimed they were retaliating for an American raid on some public buildings in Toronto in 1813. The British public thought the attack would be a serious blow to the Americans and compared it to an attack on London but, compared to the big city seaports of Philadelphia, Baltimore, Boston, and New York, Washington was not very important. Only 12 years old, it was still a raw, struggling marshland village of 8,000 inhabitants. Nevertheless, the burning of public buildings in Washington enraged and united the Americans as nothing had in the past.

The Battle of New Orleans   In 1814, the British sent 8,000 battle-seasoned veterans to strike at New Orleans in a move which, if successful, would menace the entire Mississippi valley.

On the American side was Andrew Jackson, the hawk-faced Indian fighter who had just returned a hero from the Battle of Horseshoe Bend in Alabama. He had command of the defense forces of 7,000 sailors, regulars, pirates (including the glamorous Jean Lafitte), Negroes, Frenchmen, and militiamen from Louisiana, Kentucky, and Tennessee—a wild assortment of individualists fighting in what were probably the worst of disease conditions. But morale was high as they sang lines from "The Hunters of Kentucky":

> Behind it stood our little force
> None wished it to be greater
> For ev'ry man was half a horse
> And half an alligator.

The British launched a formal frontal assault against the entrenched Americans, and met the most devastating defeat of the entire war. It was, in fact, the only decisive land victory for the Americans. More than 2,000 British were killed and wounded in half an hour, as compared to 70 Americans. The slaughter was as stupid as it was useless because the peace treaty had been signed just two weeks before. Word simply had not gotten through in time.*

The news from New Orleans reached Washington early in February 1815; two weeks later came the news of the peace. Americans, however, believed that the Battle of New Orleans had beaten the British to their knees "for the second time."

The war at sea   Man for man, and ship for ship, the Navy gave a better performance than the Army did in the War of 1812. In spectacular ship-to-ship battles with British men-of-war, American frigates and

---

* In those days, it took five or six weeks for news from Europe to reach America.

sloops won twelve out of thirteen actions. Americans were better shiphandlers than were the British. They had better gunnery, and their volunteer crews were anxious to avenge the dishonor of the *Chesapeake*.

The British were humiliated by their defeats. They had laughed at America's few "fir-built frigates, manned by a handful of bastards and outlaws," but in only a few months they had lost more ships to the Americans than they had to the French and Spanish in years of fighting. The "invincible" Royal Navy was badly criticized at home, particularly after the U.S. frigate *Constitution* defeated HMS *Java* on 29 December 1812 off Bahia, Brazil. The British publication *Pilot* said: "This is an occurrence which calls for serious reflection. . . . upwards of five hundred British vessels captured in seven months by the Americans. Yet down to the moment not a single American frigate has struck her flag. They insult and laugh at our want of enterprise and vigor. They leave their ports when they please and return to them when it suits

Left: Joshua Barney entered the Navy when he was 16 years old, and became a privateer captain. In the Continental Navy he won the last notable battle of the Revolutionary War when, in command of the *Hyder-Ally* on 8 April 1782, he outmaneuvered four British ships and captured one, the *General Monk*. Barney commanded a gunboat squadron on the Patuxent River during the War of 1812, and led soldiers and sailors against the British in the Battle of Bladensburg. Barney Circle, in Washington, D.C., is named for him. Courtesy: National Archives. *Right:* James Lawrence entered the Navy as a midshipman at the age of 17. He took part in the war with Tripoli, and was second in command when Stephen Decatur destroyed the *Philadelphia*. He commanded the *Hornet* in the War of 1812, and later the *Chesapeake*, where he was killed in the battle with HMS *Shannon*. He gave the Navy its famous battle cry, "Don't give up the ship." Courtesy: The U.S. Naval Academy Museum. Painting by Gilbert Stuart.

their convenience. . . . nothing chases, nothing intercepts, nothing engages them but to yield them triumph."

The English finally had reason to celebrate a victory. The bad-luck *Chesapeake*, going into battle with an inexperienced crew, had been captured off Boston by the British frigate *Shannon* on 1 June 1813. From the dying lips of Captain James Lawrence came the words: "Don't give up the ship. Blow her up." This action clearly pointed out the need for better training in the U.S. Navy.

The privateers' war The 500 American privateers did great damage to the British and they had a great effect on the outcome of the war. Built to escape warships rather than fight them, they could skillfully dart in and out of familiar coves along the block-aded coastline. In all, they captured or destroyed about 1,350 British merchantmen, taking home prizes worth $39 million. Yankee privateers chased British merchantmen all the way into the English Channel and the Irish Sea. Finally Lloyds of London refused to in-sure unconvoyed merchantmen.

Privateering had its drawbacks. Being so much more profitable than military service, it diverted valuable manpower from the Army and Navy. A number of privateering vessels were lost. Still, they brought badly needed money into the country and prevented arms, munitions, and other supplies from reaching Canada. They also attacked the purse strings of British manufacturers and ship-pers who, in turn, pressured Parliament to end this costly and foolish war. At one point, the prices of sugar and coffee rose 100 percent in London, which infuriated the average Britisher.

The Royal Navy finally established a blockade all along the Atlantic coast, choking off America's entire economic life, including fishing. Without customs revenues, the U.S. Treasury could not pay its outstanding bills.

The Treaty of Ghent, signed in Belgium the day before Christ-mas of 1814, called for the British and Americans to stop fighting and restore conquered territory. It was not a victor's peace so there was no territorial booty to be won back. There were wounds, but time would heal them. The treaty was immensely welcome in both countries.

The new nation gains respect Although America did not gain formal recognition of her rights on the high seas, the British no longer sneered over "striped bunting" and "American cockboats." Britain and other nations developed a new respect for American sailors' rights to sail and trade wherever they pleased.

Naval officers like Perry and Macdonough proved that well-directed broadsides could be effective diplomacy. American diplo-mats abroad were again treated with respect.

The brilliant exploits of the young U.S. Navy in operations against the mighty Royal Navy of Great Britain united the nation and established a high standard of naval tradition. At long last, America had been emancipated from Europe.

PART TWO
THE YEARS
OF ACHIEVEMENT

For long years after they first came to America, the colonists clung to the Atlantic seaboard. It was almost as if people were reluctant to leave the sea that had brought them to the new land, and that offered escape if the sometimes-hostile environment should turn completely against them. But despite all odds, the struggling colonies reached out to one another across the wilderness, united with one another, turned against the richest and most powerful nation in the world, and became a nation in their own right.

It was a small, weak, and undeveloped nation, but it had people with imagination and a yearning for adventure. Beyond the coastal hills, a vast continent offered room for unlimited expansion. Slowly, as one generation followed another, settlements spread from Maine to Florida and into the inland valleys. Two hundred years after the establishment of the first settlements, venturesome settlers began moving westward across the Appalachian Mountains, some going as far as the Mississippi River. Their wagon trains started the trails that ended only when their descendants reached the Pacific Ocean.

The country was so big that, after two hundred years, the settlers had made little impression on it. As late as 1790, the census showed only five towns with more than 8,000 people in them. They were Boston (18,000), New York (33,000), Philadelphia (42,000), Baltimore (13,000), and Charleston (16,000). All of them were seaports.

In 1800 the population of the United States reached 5,300,000, and that year the country built 995 ships. There were far more men in the country who had crossed the oceans to China or Africa

On previous pages: The nineteenth century saw American shipping progress from sail to steam, from side-wheelers to turbine-driven, twin-screw ships, and from rackety packet boats to trim liners such as the Inman Line's *City of New York*, built in 1888, shown here. She could make 20 knots, but never did so with sails spread, as pictured; such paintings are essentially architectural renderings, prepared in great detail, to hang in the office of the owner. Courtesy: Mariners Museum, Newport News, Virginia.

than had made the long journey across the mountains and valleys to the Mississippi River.

There is no magic in the mention of the year 1800, except that it marked the opening of the nineteenth century. No one who knew its history could have foreseen that in the coming century America would become a great and wealthy empire. But just as some Americans had explored the oceans of the world, so would others explore the continent. As the nation began to grow, men for whom the mysteries of distant seas or limitless plains held no appeal entered into explorations of yet a different kind—they began searching out the secrets of unknown worlds in science, engineering, and physics. Their inventions were an essential element in making America an industrial and commercial giant. Those first machines

A forest of masts lined New York's South Street in square-rigger days, nearly hiding the three steamships and one ferry boat caught by the camera. All dockside freight was moved by horse-drawn vehicles. Photo: Black Star.

were primitive, but they worked. Men immediately set about making them work better, and the world still uses them—type-setting machines, reaping machines, plows, sewing machines, typewriters, rotary printing presses, phonographs, telegraphs, electric lights, and motion pictures.

As technical developments opened up new horizons for business and industry, the country opened its geographical horizons during an era of great territorial expansion. By purchase, conquest, or annexation, the United States acquired Louisiana (1803), Florida (1819), Texas (1845), Oregon (1846), Alaska (1867), Hawaii (1897), Puerto Rico and Guam (1898), and the Philippine Islands (1899), for a total of more than 2,950,000 square miles.

As the nineteenth century ended, the population had increased to approximately 76,000,000. The value of exports and imports had increased from $70 million in 1800 to $1.5 billion in 1900. This vast commerce, which did not include that carried on within the continental limits of the country, moved on and across the seas—to Europe, Africa, Asia, South America, and Oceania—by ships. In 1900 slightly more than 28,000 ships entered American ports to load and unload the millions of tons of international cargo which added to the nation's wealth. Ports on the Atlantic, Pacific, and Gulf coasts were thronged with the maritime commerce without which the country could not survive any more than the colonies, two centuries earlier, could have done. By that time, more Americans lived inland than along the sea coasts, yet they were all, to some degree, dependent on the oceans they might never see.

CHAPTER 7
ALL SHIPS—
ALL SEAS

After the peace of 1815, Americans entered a period of great nationalism and pride, sometimes called the "era of good feeling." They even got along with each other. People called themselves "Americans" first, and citizens of their respective states second. A national literature was born, with Washington Irving and James Fenimore Cooper in the 1820s becoming the first writers of importance to use American scenes and themes. British school texts were replaced by American ones, and the intellectual magazine *North American Review* began publication in 1815. American painters depicted the American landscape rather than that of the Old World.

In Washington, D.C., a handsome new capitol was built to replace that burned by the British. Congress authorized a standing army of 10,000 men. The Navy, with its record of heroism, began receiving satisfactory support. A new Bank of the United States was established, with $35 million in assets—3½ times that of the original bank.

It was a time, too, for westward expansion to populate the nine frontier states that had entered the Union by 1819. Eastern tobacco-farmers abandoned their worn-out land and headed west. The westward trek was joined by many of the thousands of immigrants from Europe who moved out of the cities to follow their dreams toward the setting sun. Many traveled along the Cumberland Road, which was built in 1811 and ran from western Maryland to Illinois. That same year, the first steamboat on western waters, the *New Orleans*, began operation. Even the Indians were quiet after the crushing blows dealt them by Generals William H. Harrison and Andrew Jackson in the northwest and south.

On previous page: Eight of the biggest and most luxurious liners in the world berthed in New York in July of 1964. From front to rear, they are the *Sylvania, Queen Mary, Leonardo da Vinci, France, Bremen, United States, Hanseatic,* and *Constitution.* High-speed jet aircraft have put these giants out of business. Photo: Flying Camera, Inc.

In an effort to bolster America's merchant marine, Congress on 3 March 1815 offered to drop all discriminating duties on the goods of nations who would do the same for U.S. exports to them. Sweden and Algiers accepted the proposal: Britain went along with it on the condition that she retain for herself the trade between North America and the British West Indies; lumber, salt fish, flour, and livestock would have to be carried from the United States to the West Indies in British ships. In this way, Britain built up a comfortable triangular trade—bringing goods from England to America, reloading with American products for the Islands, then carrying raw materials back across the Atlantic. This practice caused American shippers and manufacturers to suffer badly, and in March 1817 Congress passed the American Navigation Act which forbade foreign vessels from engaging in coastal trade.

Britain was not moved by the Act, and stubbornly held onto her British West Indies policy until 1849. In the meantime, American traders went back to the old game of smuggling and bribery.

With the war over, Americans could put to sea without fear of being captured by privateers. Yankee ships began carrying the flag to ports all over the world, and roaming the seas for new fishing grounds. Ships were needed, and the shipyards began turning them out—more than 100,000 tons of shipping (ships weighing more than five tons each) just after the war; over 130,000 tons in 1826 and more than 250,000 tons in 1833. Small schooners sailed from port to port along the coasts, hauling anything and everything. Whalers set out for the ends of the earth on three-year voyages.

Along the eastern seaboard, the smallest villages developed a worldly-wise attitude. The people of Edgartown, Barnstable, Nantucket, Salem, Sag Harbor, and New Bedford learned from their sailing folk about exotic places in the far corners of the world. The sea affected their schooling, their gossip, their newspapers, and the style of things in their homes.

Until this period, most merchant ships sailed the North Atlantic between America and Europe or England in the spring or fall and tried to avoid the storms of winter. There was no set sailing time. Ships sailed only when their holds were full and the weather was fair. Passengers often had to wait days for ships to sail. The system was costly to merchants because a delay in shipping meant a delay in payment.

There was a clear need for the movement of freight and passengers to be regularized. In 1816, a group of merchants formed a company to provide a scheduled service for passengers, mail, and freight between New York and Liverpool. They called it the Black Ball Line* (each ship had a big black ball painted on her foresail, and the "house flag" was a red square with a black disc on it), and

The merchant marine

---

* This Line is referred to in the old sea chantey that commences: " 'Twas on a Black Baller I first served my time. . . ."

announced that ships would sail on the 1st of every month, full or empty, fair weather or foul.

The first "Black Ballers" were the *Amity, Courier, Pacific,* and *James Monroe,* rugged ships of about 400 tons each. The service opened on 5 January 1818, when the *James Monroe* sailed as scheduled—in a blizzard.

Sailing east to Europe was said to be "downhill" because the prevailing winds blew west to east and the eastward-flowing Gulf Stream helped ships to make good time. The return trip to America was "uphill" because ships had to buck both the wind and the Gulf Stream current. Before the Black Ball Line packets put to sea, the downhill trip to Europe took a month; the uphill trip to America took three months. The Black Ball ships went to Europe in 25 days, and returned in 43 days.

The Black Ball Line enjoyed a comfortable monopoly until 1821, when the Red Star Line began dispatching ships on the 24th of every month. The Black Ball Line countered by adding a second sailing on the 16th of every month. Then the Swallow Tail Line filled the gap in service that occurred at the beginning of every month. Next, Philadelphia investors started a coastwise service between New York, Charleston, New Orleans, and Vera Cruz, Mexico. These ships fed the transatlantic service out of New York—thus making that city a great trade center. By 1838 the Dramatic Line was operating huge 1,100-ton ships whose main decks were 170 feet long. Each was named for a theatrical celebrity: *Shakespeare, Garrick, Sheridan, Siddons,* and *Roscius.*

Most of the freight carried to Europe by the packets consisted of raw materials—especially cotton from the South. The ships brought back English cutlery, hardware, fine cottons, woolens, seeds, books, chronometers, spices, twine, and other manufactured goods. They also carried French wines, silks, ribbons, and laces.

Captains of ocean packets   The packets offered speed and safety. Their object was to cross the Atlantic as quickly as possible. To do this, packet captains, most of whom were ex-privateersmen, drove themselves, their ships, and their crews unmercifully. They were a blend of ruffian and gentleman. Courteous and suave, their dinner guests often included royalty, diplomats, and such international celebrities as Charles Dickens and Nathaniel Hawthorne. Italian opera stars and famous ladies of the London music halls were ceremoniously pampered by the smooth-talking, handsomely uniformed skippers.

On deck, the captains were something else. Masters of seamanship and navigation, it was up to them to decide how much punishment their ships could take from icy winter gales and huge Atlantic waves. Writing of the packets, Historian Carl Cutler said: "They were driven to the extreme edge of safety at all times. They carried sail until it was worth a man's life to go aloft . . . speed meant not only more money for the owners and fame and future patronage for the ship, but it was the all-important factor in keeping out foreign competition. . . ."

Captains had to be physically strong because they would sometimes be on deck for days, driving themselves and their crews. A British lady passenger in an American ship noted with satisfaction that the captain "constantly looked after us and our safety . . . not even bothering to change clothes during the whole voyage." Sailors went aloft to trim the sails in freezing weather and high winds, climbing as high as 100 feet in ice-coated rigging. They were some of the roughest, toughest men who ever to put to sea but, even so, many were killed. When a man slipped and went overboard in a storm, there was no hope of stopping and going back for him.

Captains were paid about $30 a month, plus 5 percent of the freight charges, 25 percent of the cabin passengers' fares ($100 to $140 per head), and the money paid for the mail (2 cents for each American letter and 2 pence for each British letter). A captain could take his wife and family along, free of charge, if he chose. In all, he could make about $20,000 a year, and he was worth every penny of it.

Crews of ocean packets   Most of the men in the crews of the first packet ships were Americans in their teens who were paid about $15 a month. There were said to be two kinds of seamen in the packets, "them as likes it and them as don't." Those who did not like it soon left to sail in ships where working conditions were not so hard.

Their places were taken by "packet rats," or "Liverpool Irish," from Liverpool or New York—ruffians who lived on the waterfront. They were usually brought aboard ship drunk or drugged by crimps who got up to $80 for each man. Sometimes dead men were passed off as drunks, which meant the regular crew at sea would have to double up on the already heavy duties. Although the seamen normally did not steal from one another, they did rob the passengers (even taking shoes as the passengers slept) and they knifed officers they disliked.

After a while, American seamen refused to sail with the Liverpool Irish, and the Atlantic packets came to be manned almost exclusively with Irishmen.

Passengers on ocean packets   Gone were the days of the "floating dungeons"—the notorious "coffin brigs." With the packets came the luxury of a floating hostelry, offering "extensive and commodious" accommodations. On the *James Monroe,* sparkling marble slabs supported a decorative arch in the saloon. Chairs had seats of black haircloth and the tables were of gleaming mahogany. "Sleeping closets," or staterooms as they were beginning to be called, were about seven feet square, paneled in satinwood. Over the entrance to each was an arch held up by pillars of white marble. Lighting was by candle, extinguished by the steward whenever the captain so ordered. Water for washing was doled out in little basins.

Passengers enjoyed themselves with gossip and playing dominoes, whist, and other parlor games. Sometimes when the ship was becalmed they could swim or fish or have target practice from the decks. Much of their time was spent in eating, which they did four times a day; there was even fresh bread and meat. Ships carried pigs, sheep, egg-laying hens, and sometimes a couple of cows.

Immigrants on ocean packets   At first the packets catered to the aristocratic and well-to-do but, when economics showed that the elite were limited in number, shipowners began finding large spaces in steerage for "live" cargo. By stuffing in immigrants, each paying £5 passage money, a profit of 100 percent could be made.

For his money, the immigrant got transportation, "firing" (a place to cook), drinking water (often tasting of indigo or tobacco because the casks had been used before), and a place to sleep. Each person provided his own food and bedding. Alleyways close to the Liverpool landings soon became a vast bazaar selling bread, potatoes, and cheap cooking gear.

Packed in like cattle, the immigrants fared little better than did the slaves from Africa. The filth was beyond description. Marine historian W. S. Lindsay wrote: "It was scarcely possible to induce the passengers to sweep the decks after their meals or to be decent with respect to the common wants of nature; in many cases in bad weather, when they could not go out on deck, their health suffered so much that their strength was gone, and they had not the power to help themselves. Hence, 'between decks' was like a loathsome dungeon." On some voyages, up to 10 percent of the immigrants died.

In 1819, Congress passed a measure which would reduce overcrowding and curb disease. A second statute, passed 18 years later, guaranteed each passenger 14 feet of clear deck space. The British government also clamped down with regulations to prevent the poorly provisioned passengers from begging. The weekly ration per passenger was set at 21 quarts of water, 2½ pounds of biscuits, 1 pound of wheat flour, 5 pounds of oatmeal, 2 pounds of rice, and 2 pounds of molasses.

At one point, some shipping lines boasted in their advertisements that they had more births than deaths aboard their ships. Americans began fining captains $10 for every person who died aboard their ships.

Packets and their mixed blessings   Although there were never more than 50 of them in service at one time, the packets were the best ships of their day. American leadership in the building and operation of sailing ships was not contested, even by the British. The British scientist Augustin Creuze wrote: "The mercantile navy of England is the least speedy and most unsafe that belongs to a civilized nation. America is not only in possession of a better mercantile navy, with which to compete with us, but she has also the vantage-ground of superior knowledge and a far more extended experience from which to start for future competition."

By 1824, the packets were carrying most of the passengers and freight that crossed the North Atlantic. But the ships were roughly used and wore out at an early age. Many were sold and refitted as whalers.

While they sailed, however, the packets brought a flood of comments about shipboard experiences. Ralph Waldo Emerson sailed for England in October of 1847 aboard the *Washington Irving*. In three days she made only 134 miles. "A nimble Indian would have swum as far," he observed. The dour New Englander wrote: "I find sea life an acquired taste, like that of tomatoes and olives. The confinement, cold, motion, noise and odor are not to be dispensed with. The floor of your room is sloped at an angle of 20–30 degrees, and I waked up every morning with the belief that someone was ripping up my berth. Nobody likes to be treated ignominiously, upset, shoved against the side of the house, rolled over, suffocated with bilge, mephitis and stewing oil. We get used to these annoyances at last, but the dread of the sea remains longer. Is this sad-colored circle an eternal cemetery?"

But for all the complaints of seasick, frightened passengers, there were those who had great praise for their thrilling seagoing adventure, "riding the high billows in a brisk breeze. . . ." For some, the packets were a symbol of national pride. Marine historian John Malcolm Brinnin wrote: ". . . a ship with her sails loosened and her ensign abroad was already an American image of romance as potent as an Indian on horseback acceding to the sunset." Coming alongside another American packet, a traveler wrote: "It was a glorious sight when we were abreast of her and saw her swelling canvas—royals, studding sails, and all—and her bright high sides, rising from the waves like a walled city, and plunging again into the glittering abyss of waters. . . ."

Probably the most lasting effect of the packets was the transport of hardy peasant immigrants to the United States at a time when they were badly needed for the country's development. Americans producing large families, along with new people from Europe, had swelled the population to 13 million by 1830—three times that of 1790. Between 1830 and 1840, 50,000 immigrants came by packet each year. In the ten years after 1840, that figure rose to 150,000 per year. The Catholic Irish settled mainly in the cities; many furnished cheap labor to build railroads and canals. The majority of the English stayed around seaports, while the German immigrants moved west to the rich farmlands of Wisconsin and Missouri.

America held onto her transatlantic supremacy until the middle of the nineteenth century when the splashing paddlewheels and smoking funnels of steamships began replacing sails. The British Cunard Line, whose steamships were sturdy, reliable, and safe, was subsidized by the British Post Office to carry mail from Liverpool to Halifax. This meant it could afford to service Boston also, and it was soon taking passenger business away from the American packets.

But running a steamship line was costly, and anyone competing with the British would need government help. Edward Collins finally got a subsidy from the U.S. government and entered the race with four new steamers: the *Atlantic*, the *Arctic*, the *Pacific* and the *Baltic*. He offered large staterooms, luxurious dining saloons with fancy French cooking, and elegant barber shops. To compete with Cunard, he also promised more speed.

At first he was successful. The *Atlantic* on her second round trip broke the speed record in both directions. But speed was costly, and before long Collins was back in Congress asking for more money. He got it, and the *Baltic* set a new record—nine days and thirteen hours from Boston to Liverpool.

Then, in 1854, the speed craze caught up with the Collins Line.

The side-wheel steamer *Baltic*, of the Collins Line, was built by Wm. H. Brown, in New York, in 1850. She carried masts and spars so as to spread sails in case her engine failed. The *Baltic* had no bridge or pilothouse; her course was directed by a man standing atop the wheel box. Courtesy: Mariners Museum, Newport News, Virginia.

The *Arctic*, racing along the Grand Banks in a winter fog, was rammed by a small French steamer, which punched a hole below the *Arctic*'s waterline and, as the captain of the latter headed for Newfoundland, the water rose over her engines. The *Arctic* began to sink and some of her crew made off with all the lifeboats except one, leaving the passengers to go down with the ship. Among the casualties were Collins' wife and two of their four children.

Eighteen months later, the *Pacific* left Liverpool in midwinter and was never seen again. Collins then launched the *Adriatic*, the largest and grandest of all his ships. But by then, Congress had lost interest in subsidizing an American merchant marine and Collins went bankrupt. The safe and sturdy British Cunard Line ships gradually evolved into the great floating palaces of the *Queen Mary* class.

Other countries joined in taking over the Atlantic trade; France, Germany, Italy, and The Netherlands. Eventually, traveling by transatlantic steamer became *the* thing to do. People whose names appeared frequently in newspaper headlines crossed the Atlantic regularly. Sailing day for a big ship was a social event.

After World War II, Atlantic travel began to diminish, as air travel became common. In 1952 the United States made a bid to regain it with the SS *United States*, a 990-foot liner built for speed with the idea that the Navy would use her as an auxiliary in wartime. The *United States* set an all-time speed record for crossing the Atlantic—82 hours and 40 minutes. But jet air travel soon put the transatlantic liners out of business—no one wanted to spend four days getting to London or Paris by sea when they could make it by air in six hours. Liners became white elephants; no one could afford to run them. Two of the last big ones may still be seen; the *United States* is tied up in Newport News, Virginia, and the British *Queen Mary* is in Long Beach, California.

Trade with the Spanish   Trading with the Spanish-held islands of the Caribbean was a precarious business at best. There were hurricanes, smugglers, and pirates to contend with, and it was impossible to know what kind of duties had to be paid from island to island. They varied, according to the bribes and greed of local officials. After the U.S. take-over of Florida in 1819, anti-American sentiments ran high; the duty on ships entering Cuba went as high as $2.50 a ton and in Puerto Rico it was $1 a ton. Spain saw the error of her ways when Congress put similar high duties on Spanish ships entering American ports, and lowered the duties she imposed.

American merchantmen sometimes endured great hardships on what should have been short voyages. When the 130-ton brig *Polly* sailed from Boston for St. Croix, a trip that should have taken only a few days, she ran into a tropical gale. Only her load of lumber kept her from sinking. The crew cut away her masts and righted her, but they could not sail her, and drifted helplessly in the blazing sun. When, after 18 days, their fresh water had gone they managed to catch rainwater in some sails. Some of the men died; the survivors ate shark meat, small fish, and barnacles scraped off the hull. When they were finally rescued by an English merchantman, they had been shipwrecked for 187 days and had drifted 2,000 miles.

Trade with China   By 1815, the China trade had become enormously important. In that year, American vessels carried to the United States 14½ million pounds of tea which, alone, was valued at more than $4½ million. They also brought back silks, sateens, porcelains, chinaware, and sandalwood. In all, the value of American imports from China in 1815 was nearly $6 million. To protect American merchantmen and their cargoes in the area, the U.S. Navy established the East India Squadron in 1835. This action was in line with the Board of Naval Commissioners' policy whereby warships were sent to stations in various distant parts of the world. By 1843, seven such stations had been established: the Mediterranean (1815), the West India (1821), the Pacific (1821), the Brazil (1826), the East India (1835), the Home (1841), and the African (1843).

Americans carefully observed the trade regulations laid down by the Chinese emperor. At Canton, there were commission houses where agents bought Chinese products for shipment home, and arranged to sell cargo shipped out from the States. Americans working in Canton had a good life there: they had servants and enjoyed many comforts they could not have afforded at home.

Trade between the East Indies and China   An important sideline to the direct U.S. trade with China was the business carried on between the Dutch East Indies and China. A steady stream of American ships engaged in this dangerous but profitable trade. Cargoes were mainly pepper, sandalwood, tortoiseshell, and bêches-de-mer, or sea cucumbers. Collected from the reefs by natives, the sea cucumbers were boiled, dried, and sold in China for making soup.

One of the Sumatran ports most frequented was Quallah Battoo, in a part of the island that was not under Dutch control. The natives were described as "a treacherous and warlike people, much given to piracy." It was here that America's postwar policy of enforced respect for the Stars and Stripes was clearly demonstrated.

In February 1831, the Salem vessel *Friendship*, peacefully trading at Quallah Battoo, was treacherously attacked by Malays. Since she was practically without defense, most of her crew were murdered and she and her stores plundered. When news of the outrage reached the United States, several merchant captains appealed to President Jackson for protection. He sent the frigate *Potomac*, under Captain John Downes, "to obtain redress for the wrongs."

The *Potomac*, disguised as a Danish merchantman, landed a force of 282 seamen and Marines at Quallah Battoo. The Sultan who was responsible for the attack on the *Friendship* was killed, along with 150 other offenders; the town was burned to the ground and the forts were stormed. Emissaries from Quallah Battoo begged for peace, which was accepted on the condition that future security for American ships be assured.

Opium and the opening of China   In 1833, the British schooner *Jamesina* sailed from India to China with a cargo of opium worth £330,000. With swift little vessels such as the 100-ton *Ariel*, the 150-ton *Zephyr*, and the brig *Antelope*, Americans then began competing for the rich opium trade. For the "opium clippers," speed was all-important in escaping pirates and getting to China with the first opium crop of the year.

The Chinese government tried to stop the traffic in this evil drug, and in 1839 destroyed the foreign-owned opium at Canton. The British considered this action a just cause for war and, in early 1840, sent a squadron to China to redress the wrongs. They blockaded Canton and attacked a northern port. Since these acts threatened American commercial interests, the government in Washington decided to send a squadron to China to protect them. The ships, *Constitution* and *Boston*, were commanded by Commodore Lawrence Kearny, a veteran of the War of 1812 who had later conducted operations against pirates and slavers in the Mediterranean and the West Indies.

Kearny arrived in Macao on 22 March 1842, two years after the beginning of the Opium War. His orders directed him to protect American interests and citizens on the coast of China. He was to observe the laws of neutrality and to respect Chinese customs. Above all, he was to emphasize to the Chinese that his mission was "to prevent and punish the smuggling of opium into China either by Americans or by other nations under cover of the American flag."

Commodore Kearny maintained excellent diplomatic relations with both the Chinese and the British. While at Hong Kong in September 1842 he learned of the signing of the Treaty of Nanking, by which peace was restored. The treaty ceded Hong Kong to the British and opened to their trade the ports of Shanghai, Ningpo, Fuchau, Amoy, and Canton. In an effort to get the same commercial rights for America, Kearny dispatched copies of the treaty to the United States. The following August, 1843, these efforts were successful.

The Catholic Church had been active in China for centuries. Protestant Americans wanted to set up missions to save Chinese souls, too, but their austere approach to religion had nowhere near the appeal of the Catholic pageantry. Nevertheless, Daniel Webster, President Tyler's Secretary of State, sent Caleb Cushing to China as the American Commissioner. Cushing negotiated a treaty, signed on 3 July 1844, which regularized American trade at the treaty ports. At the same time extraterritorial privileges were extended for American citizens in China, most of whom were missionaries. The U.S. Navy was freed from its responsibility to enforce China's anti-opium regulations.

Whaling   After the peace of 1815, whaling sailed into a wonderful era of prosperity. It became one of the most important of all the country's far-flung enterprises. Ships were large and costly; voyages might last years, as whalers roamed distant seas. America was in the industrial age and new machines needed whale oil as lubricants. Prosperous Americans wanted and could afford the high-priced spermaceti candles that burned so brightly. High fashion called for whalebone in corsets and hoop skirts, in buggy whips and umbrellas.

All whaling ports were busy during the golden age of whaling, from about 1830 through 1860. In 1833, there were 392 ships and 10,000 seamen in the American whale fleet. Ten years later, that number had doubled. New England whale fisheries grew at an astonishing rate. Not even England could compete with the New Bedford Quakers. Before the Civil War, half of all American whale ships dropped anchor at New Bedford. Profits were enormous. In New London, a banker named Sebastian made more than $10 million and all he did was handle the whalers' cash.

It was a profit-sharing business in which the captain received perhaps $1/8$ of the take, and seamen $1/250$, but there was always the chance of a dry voyage with no one getting any profits at all. This would leave a captain and his crew wide open to tavern ridicule, gossip, and scorn—a fate no man could abide. For this reason, almost as much as for money, whalers often took desperate risks at sea.

Whalers were probably the ugliest vessels ever to slide into the water from American shipyards. Merchant and naval seamen in their sleek craft poked fun at them: "Whale-ships are built by the mile and cut off in lengths as you want 'em." Nevertheless whalers did the job for which they were built. They were square-rigged, about 400 tons, with heavy bluff bows, stout masts, tough rigging, and copper bottoms. They carried four or five whaleboats —28 feet long, with a 6-foot beam—lightly built, round-bottomed, but extremely strong. They had no use for speed, but were strictly functional, durable, and built to last for years of brutal punishment wherever they sailed. Some stayed in service for 50 years. Every inch of space was filled with gear of one sort or another and the holds were designed to carry vast cargoes of whale oil.

A whaler's life at sea   The captain of a whaler was an absolute ruler aboard ship; he was all things to all men. He was minister to those in need of guidance, legal advisor, agent for his owners in port, and doctor when medical treatment was needed. Injuries and illness were common, and no matter what ailed a man, the captain acted as surgeon—a job for which he had no training whatsoever. If a hand or foot had to be amputated, he used the only tools available; a carving knife and carpenter's saw. The patient would be loaded with rum and held down by a few crew members who did not mind noise and blood. Whalers experienced a dreary procession of ailments: pneumonia, venereal disease, typhus, dysentery, and scurvy—the last being a disease caused by lack of the vitamin C found in fresh fruits and vegetables. The captain treated them all with a dose of salts, calomel, or castor oil.

Life aboard a whaler was rugged beyond belief. A crew of 30 or more men lived for years at a time in the filth and squalor of a crowded forecastle. The only ventilation came from a small hatch that was dogged shut in bad weather. The only light came from candles or oil lamps. Bunks were not much more than wooden shelves built in tiers of three. If there were no rats or mice present, there were always plenty of smaller types of life. Each man had a small "ditty box" for his personal possessions; slop buckets lined the floor and often overturned in bad weather, fouling the air in the crowded forecastle.

A political reporter from Washington, D.C., J. Ross Brown, decided life aboard a whaler would be an interesting experience. He published his memoirs in 1846: "It would be difficult to give any idea of our forecastle. In wet weather, when most of the hands were below, cursing, smoking, singing, and spinning yarns, it was a perfect bedlam. Think of three or four Portuguese, a couple of Irishmen, five or six rough Americans, in a hole about sixteen feet wide . . . so low that a full-grown person could not stand upright in it, and so wedged with rubbish as to leave scarcely room for a foothold. It contained twelve small berths, and with fourteen chests in the little area around the ladder, seldom admitted of being clean. In warm weather it was insufferably close. It would seem like exaggeration to say, that I have seen in Kentucky pig-sties not half so filthy, and in every respect preferable to this miserable hole; such however is the fact." At first, whaling crews were Yankees, often neighbors from the same village, but in the mid-1800s a few old-timers might have to put up with a bunch of "greenhorns" from several counties.

The quarters of the "specialists," boatsteerers, coopers, and stewards, were in steerage, aft of the mainmast, but were better than those of the seamen. Officers had cabins in the stern. The captain lived in the splendid privacy of his cabin on the starboard side. He often brought his wife who busied herself sewing, keeping a diary, and entertaining her husband. Whale crews had mixed feelings about having a woman aboard ship: some considered it bad luck and refused to sign aboard any "hen frigate."

Everybody ate about the same food, which was generally awful.

Three times a day they ate salt pork or beef; the officers got soft bread while the crew had hardtack—a granite-hard concoction of flour, lard, and yeast. The crew's food budget was 30 cents a day per man. One whaleman described mealtime as "dropping bread into hot coffee to soak out the worms . . . then skimming the worms off the coffee before drinking it."

On shore, a whaling man was often a nuisance in taverns and bordellos. After a long voyage his pockets were full of cash and he wanted liquor, women, and a fight. His escapades often cost him a nose or an ear.

In spite of the discomforts, being a whaleman was something to be proud of. Unlike other seagoing men, whalemen were helpful to one another. They shared their knowledge of new grounds, points of danger along certain routes, and other matters of mutual concern. In addition to the profits to be made, crews had a good time—particularly when they reached the sunny islands of the Pacific. Seeing native girls swimming out to meet their ships and enjoying the "frolic" that followed had far more appeal than shivering through a New England winter.

A career for the young   Whalemen generally started out young. Captain Nathaniel Cary of Nantucket went to sea in 1815 when he was 14 years old and remained a whaleman for 62 years. He made 14 voyages as master, four as sailor, boatsteerer, and first officer. He lost two "gallant ships" on the coral reefs in the Indian Ocean and Pacific. Records show that he brought back 40,000 barrels of whale and sperm oil.

Captain Charles Rawsom put to sea at the age of 15. Once when he was in his whaleboat, a great sperm whale attacked and smashed the boat's bow. The boat capsized, and Rawsom held on to the bottom by putting his finger into the plug hole. One by one his companions lost their hold and drowned, but Rawsom clung on until a boat from the ship reached him. He had to tear his finger out of the hole, stripping off the skin and flesh as he did so. He retired in good health at 45 years of age.

Captain William Swain, Jr., died in March 1870 at the age of 93, after completing a career begun aboard his father's whaleship when he was 15 years old.

Captain Benjamin Worth, of Nantucket, began his seafaring life in 1783 at the age of 15 and retired 41 years later after being a whaling master for 29 years. In all that time, he was home only seven years. He had sailed 879,960 miles, circumnavigated the globe twice, rounded Cape Horn sixteen times, the Cape of Good Hope twice, and visited more than forty island groups in the Atlantic and Pacific oceans. He had traveled the entire coast of South America, sailing as far north as the Columbia River. He brought in 20,000 barrels of whale oil, and never lost a ship or a man, except when he was captured during the War of 1812.

Offshore and other grounds   After the peace with Britain, whalers first set sail for the familiar grounds off the Peruvian coast but three years later the whales had been so thinned out it was hardly worth the effort to go after them. In that year, Captain George W. Gardener decided it was time to look elsewhere. He headed west, and 1,500 miles out found a huge school of whales. When he returned to port with his haul, he passed the word to his friends, touching off a scramble for the famed "offshore grounds." Two years later, 50 vessels were there, hauling in whales.

In 1819, Captain Winship, sailing home to Massachusetts from Canton, stopped in Hawaii for water and provisions. Hawaii was the main whaling port in the Pacific then, and Winship had news of great interest to whalers; there were sperm whales off the islands of Japan. The *Syren* and *Maro* set out immediately and, within three months, both were full to the hatches and on their way back to Nantucket. Shortly after, the Japanese whaling grounds were lively with activity, and by 1823, with more and more whalers from Hawaii cruising offshore, the Japanese emperor forbade outsiders to enter his country. Unlucky whalemen whose ships were wrecked along the dangerous uncharted coasts were promptly imprisoned.

In 1835, Captain Barzilai T. Folger in the *Ganges* of Nantucket took a right whale off Kodiak Island, thereby opening up the northwest whale fishery whose main port became San Francisco. Bowhead whales were found off Kamchatka eight years later, and in 1848, Captain Royce in the bark *Superior* of Sag Harbor found them in the Arctic Ocean.

Despite warnings of smothering fog, mysterious currents, crushing ice, and erroneous charts with no piloting data, whole fleets sailed for the Arctic Ocean. In 1849, 154 ships took 206,850 barrels of whale oil and 2,481,600 pounds of whalebone. The following year, 145 ships returned with 243,680 barrels of oil and 3,654,000 pounds of bone. By 1859, whalers were bringing in a quarter of a million barrels of oil per year.

Whalemen as explorers   American whalemen were not just blubber-hunters. They were also explorers, filling in the fine points of the voyages of their great predecessors; James Cook, Ferdinand Magellan, Francis Drake, William Dampier, Louis Bougainville, Jean La Pérouse, and Abel Tasman. Steering into uncharted regions, locating islands that had never appeared on charts, whalemen recorded their impressions, observations, and their often-harrowing experiences. They discovered 400 Pacific islands and gave them Yankee names.

Richard Macy, captain of the *Maro* out of Nantucket, wrote to a friend in 1824: "Impressed with a strong belief that great numbers of sperm whales existed among the numerous islands in the Pacific, generally known as the Society, Friendly, Feejee and

Caroline Islands, I resolved to spend three months among those islands. I steered first for the Society Islands . . . to procure wood and water. The island I selected for that purpose is called Eimeo, and lies 20 miles west of Otaheiti. I entered the harbor on the north side . . . which is not to be surpassed for access and safety by any harbor in this ocean. I took my ship two miles up the beautiful harbor (entirely land-locked) and tied her to an old tree. The scene that surrounded me was truly romantic. The shores were covered with all kinds of tropical fruit, such as oranges, lemons, limes, coconuts, pineapples, bananas and plantains. The beautiful mountains which encompass the harbor and exhibit a lofty and majestic appearance, commence within a quarter of a mile from the shore and gradually ascend to the height of 2,500 feet, covered with trees from the bottom to the top. I found the natives much more civilized than I had expected."

A few exploring whalemen whose ships were wrecked in the South Seas wound up in cannibal stewpots. Sailors attacked by fierce tribesmen defended themselves as best they could with double-edged blubber knives, spades, lances, and even harpoons. One log recorded that the "cook defended his castle alone, driving off every attack with boiling water."

The decline of whaling   The peak of American whaling came in 1846 when 678 ships and barks, 35 brigs, and 22 schooners made up the fleet. This represented a capacity of 233,189 tons and a value of $21,075,000. Foreign whaling fleets numbered 230 ships; all told, the world's combined whaling fleet consisted of more than 900 vessels.

Although 1859 saw whalers bringing in a quarter of a million barrels of oil, it also saw the beginnings of the petroleum industry in Pennsylvania. Petroleum could be converted into kerosene and used for lighting; later on, gaslight dealt the final blow to the hunters of whale oil. Meanwhile, other damaging forces were at work as tempers flared on the eve of the Civil War. There were riots at a number of ports and many West Coast ports had to be closed.

In 1861, the government bought 25 whalers, filled them with rocks, and sent them to Charleston harbor where they were sunk. The object was to block that Confederate harbor—but the whole maneuver was useless. The following year the Union forces sank 14 more of the "stone fleet" in another unproductive attempt.

The Confederates went on the offensive and the raider *Alabama* sank 14 whaleships before she herself was sunk off the coast of France. In 1865, the gunboat *Shenandoah* went after the Arctic whaling fleet in the Bering Strait. She captured and destroyed 29 vessels in just four days.

There were still whalers and plenty of optimism, however, and the fleets struck out again, sailing farther and farther into the

Arctic. There, in 1871, the greatest whaling-ship disaster of all time occurred. That year the Eskimos told the whalemen they would be jammed in the ice if they hugged the American shore too closely. But that was where the whales were. Seven of the forty captains headed south; the others pushed on.

The first disaster came on 14 June when the barkentine *Oreole* was stove in by the ice. The others kept on and by June all of them had passed the Bering Strait and sailed into the Arctic Ocean. They were given another warning at East Cape when the survivors of the American whaler *Japan* came aboard, after their long winter's stay ashore among the natives. Their ship had been caught and crushed in the ice the previous October, and they had begun the long trek to the Siberian shore; eight of their number had perished.

A few months later, disaster struck again. On 29 August the wind hauled to the southwest, driving the ice back toward the American shore and pinning the whaleships between shore and ice. Some of the ships anchored on the shoals in four or five fathoms of water. Snow and squalls swept down.

The brigantine *Comet* was crushed on 2 September. Five days later while the crew of the barkentine *Ramon* was cutting up a whale, the ice closed in on the ship and crushed her like an eggshell. Forty-five minutes later there was not a trace of her.

The barkentine *Awashonka* was crushed next day. By then the captains of the various vessels were seriously concerned. They decided to abandon their stricken vessels and head south where the seven whalers that had separated from them earlier were standing by. It was a heartbreaking decision but it was the only solution. On 14 September the crews of 29 whalers abandoned their ships as they lay fast in the ice. Boats were lowered, provisioned, and loaded with wives, families, masters, and rugged whale-hunters. The women prayed and the men cursed or sang as they rowed through the churning sea. But there was no hysteria and there were no tears, for whalers lived by an unwritten code that demanded courage in the face of danger. Their wives and children were equally courageous.

At last, the refugees reached Icy Cape and boarded the rescue vessels which took them to Plover Bay. From there, they sailed for Honolulu. In all the annals of ship disasters, this story is the most remarkable. For, in spite of the fact that an entire whaling fleet was crushed by ice, not a single life was lost.

Five years later the Arctic claimed 12 whalers and in 1888, five more went down in a gale.

During this period, the whalers had shifted their operations from New England to San Francisco because it was only in the Pacific regions that whales were still being caught in large numbers. Even so, the herds had been badly thinned by over-fishing. Finally, even San Francisco became a shadow of its past as a whaling port. By the 1890s whale oil was worth only 30 cents per gallon and in

1897 whalebone was down to $4.00 a pound. Women's fashions changed; the large hoop skirts went out of style, ending the need for flexible whalebone. Kerosene, and then gaslight, ended the demand for whale oil for lighting.

The western whaling fleet was reduced to 51 vessels in 1905. Steam whalers appeared and the old ships with their billowing sails became museum pieces or ended up as scrap.

The *Charles Morgan*   One of the more famous of the old whalers was the *Charles Morgan*. She sailed out of New Bedford on her maiden voyage on 4 September 1841. She returned three years and four months later after having twice rounded the Horn and cruised the little-known waters of the Pacific. She brought back a catch of sperm oil, whale oil, and whalebone worth $56,970.

During her 80 years of whaling she made 37 voyages. Taken together, her catches probably amounted to more than $2 million. She made more money than any other all-sail whaling ship, but finally gave up whaling in 1921. Still in good condition and the last one of her kind in the world, she is preserved at Mystic, Connecticut, as a fine example of American shipbuilding skill.

New England fisheries   Fishing was often a family business. Entire crews of eight to ten men and boys might consist of uncles, cousins, sons, and in-laws. Ten-year-old boys could make the three-to-five-month trip to the rich but perilous fishing grounds at George's Bank and the Grand Bank, off Newfoundland. The boys were paid according to the number of fish they caught. They were called "cut-tails" because they cut pieces of the fishes' tails as proof of the number they had caught.

When "cut-tails" grew to manhood they became an important part of the intensely personal community in which they lived. These fisherfolk had no interest in the opening of the West to new settlers. For them it was the challenge of a life at sea, the gamble, the constant change that made the struggle for survival worthwhile. Fishermen lived in the villages and ports of Gloucester, Marblehead, and Newburyport. Others went out from Provincetown, Portsmouth, and Boston, in brigs, schooners, and sloops, to haul in cod and halibut on the Grand Bank.

Congress subsidized the fisheries with bounties and, in 1813, enacted a bounty law which provided $2.40 a ton for vessels between 20 and 30 tons, and $4 a ton for vessels over 30 tons. This was raised in 1819 to $3.50 a ton for vessels of between 5 and 30 tons, if they stayed at sea for four months; and $3.50 a ton for vessels over 30 tons, if they stayed at sea 3½ months and the crews had 10 or more men and boys. The bounty helped, but it was still a hard life for fishermen. Few made more than $18 a month, even as they risked their lives in gales and fog. They could afford only the barest essentials for their large families. Much of the New Englander's habit of thrift or "tight-fistedness" can be traced to these lean times. Wealthy Boston bankers of later generations still practiced thrift—long after their need for it had passed.

By 1820, 530 vessels, nearly all schooners, and carrying 6,000 seamen, could be seen fishing off the coast of Labrador. Thousands more worked off the coast of Newfoundland. Sometimes a fisherman gained sole ownership of a vessel or of a fleet of four or five vessels. But most of the fishing boats were community properties, entire villages owning shares in them and their enterprises.

In 1846, the United States went to war with Mexico, an action brought on by friction between American settlers in Texas, or "gringos," and the inhabitants of Spanish Mexico, or "greasers."

War with Mexico

Americans began moving into Texas as early as 1823, and by 1835 had increased their number to about 30,000. In 1836 Texans declared their independence and flew the "Lone Star" flag. That same year, Mexican forces under Santa Anna wiped out an American garrison in the Alamo, a fort in San Antonio; then Sam Houston captured Santa Anna. Texas remained an international hot spot for years, with both sides spoiling for a fight. All that was needed was an incident, and one was provided on 25 April 1846 when Mexican troops crossed the Rio Grande and attacked General Zachary Taylor's command. Sixteen Americans were killed or wounded. American troops then crossed the Rio Grande, captured the Gulf coast town of Matamoros, and proceeded to invade Mexico.

Meanwhile the Navy's Home Squadron, under Commodore David Conner, maintained a close blockade of Mexico's east coast. The army under General Taylor marched into northeastern Mexico but, in order to defeat Mexico, it was necessary to take the capital, Mexico City. For this, an army of 14,000 troops under Lieutenant General Winfield Scott was moved into the Gulf in Army transports, early in 1847.

The army force and the Home Squadron met at Antón Lizardo, the anchorage for Vera Cruz. The actual landing, on 9 March 1847, was the largest amphibious operation in U.S. naval history until World War II. Over a hundred ships were involved. Gunboats lay offshore, ready to bombard if there should be enemy resistance. Sailors rowed the surf boats ashore in waves. The attack force, which landed without losing a man, included some 1,200 sailors and Marines. It joined up with the army and took Vera Cruz on 29 March. Marines fought with the army until Mexico City was taken on 14 September. This is the basis for the phrase in the Marine Hymn "From the Halls of Montezuma."

American successes   Land operations in the Southwest and California were completely successful. When war broke out, the dashing explorer, Captain John C. Frémont, "just happened" to be in California, where he led a small "army" of some 150 civilians— early settlers, scouts, and others—that operated with 100 regular army troops under Brigadier General Stephen W. Kearny. Mexican troops in California were few in number and not well organized; opposing sides met in a few skirmishes and battles, after which the Americans proclaimed the short-lived California Bear Flag Republic at the settlement of Sonoma and raised a banner featuring a golden bear, which is still on the state flag of California.

The only naval force in the Pacific was a four-ship Pacific Squadron under Commodore John Drake Sloat. There was no Mexican naval opposition. Naval forces cooperated with the army in a few actions against the Mexicans in southern California. On 7 July a party from the USS *Savannah* went ashore at Monterey, raised the U.S. flag, and claimed California for the United States. Two days later a similar ceremony took place in Yerba Buena, when a party from the USS *Portsmouth*, under Commander John B. Montgomery, went ashore and raised the flag over what is now San Francisco. Montgomery's next move was to send a man to Sonoma with a new U.S. flag to replace the "bear flag." Thus ended the Bear Flag Republic.

The war with Mexico was a small war, as wars go. It cost 13,000 American lives, most of them taken by disease. But the territorial gains were enormous. Counting Texas, the total expanse of the United States was increased by about one-third—an addition greater than that of the Louisiana Purchase.

Years later, Americans realized that the Mexican War was a blood-splattered testing ground for the Civil War. The campaigns brought invaluable experience to officers destined to become leading generals in the forthcoming conflict: for example, Captain Robert E. Lee and Lieutenant U. S. Grant. The Military Academy at West Point, founded in 1802, fully justified its existence through its well-trained officers. The Navy's crippling blockade around Mexican ports rendered invaluable service. The Marine Corps, which had been in existence since 1798, won new laurels.

But the most important result of the Mexican War was that the United States acquired a second seacoast, on the Pacific. The nation had spread across the continent. In order eventually to defend itself in the Pacific, it would have to maintain a navy in the Pacific.

CHAPTER 8
THE PATHS
OF THE SEA

Colonial Americans were good sailors; they would take a ship anywhere they could expect to make a profit. Sometimes, however, they did not know where they were headed until they got there. This was not the fault of the men. They did the best they could with the equipment they had, but navigation was pretty much a hit-or-miss proposition until nearly the end of the eighteenth century.

All navigation depends on exact measurements of time, distance, speed, and direction. In colonial times, sand-filled hour glasses, which were turned over every 30 minutes, marked the time; even now, aboard ship, the number of bells struck is a count of the half-hours. A ship's speed was measured by estimating how fast a line with a piece of wood on the end of it—a chip log—would run out. Direction was estimated by a primitive compass marked off into 32 points; a helmsman had all he could do to keep a ship within a couple of points—22 degrees or more—of her course. Compasses never pointed to true north; they pointed to the north magnetic pole.

At sea, a navigator estimated his latitude—his distance north of the equator—by measuring the angle of the North Star above the horizon. With rude instruments, this was not easy, and a mistake of only one degree would cause him to misjudge his position by as much as 60 miles. None of the early navigators had an accurate way of measuring distance east and west. This is why very old charts of North America, for instance, sometimes appear out of proportion; they show some points a couple of hundred miles east or west of where they actually are.

A step toward making navigation an exact art was taken in 1730 when Thomas Godfrey, of Philadelphia, invented a fairly

On previous page: Lighthouses and lightships required men to take care of them, but the new monster buoys, such as this one at the entrance to New York Harbor, need servicing only once a year. Radio signals from ashore control their operations. Photo: John M. Lehman.

accurate quadrant, the ancestor of the sextant used now by all navigators for taking star sights. But accurate measurements of the altitude of stars were of little use until they could be timed exactly. The invention of the chronometer by John Harrison, of England, in 1762, made it possible for a navigator to time his celestial observations and work out his position at sea.

The secret of the chronometer, which kept time to within a few seconds' accuracy in the course of a long voyage, was that it enabled a navigator to compare the time of his observation with the known time at one point on earth—the prime meridian in Greenwich, England. By reducing "local" time to that at Greenwich, the angle of a star with the horizon, no matter where the observation was made, could be computed on a common basis. But the complicated mathematical computations required to convert a star sight to a pinpoint on a chart were beyond the ability of most men.

The man who simplified the art of navigation to the point where any sailor who understood arithmetic could become a navigator was Nathaniel Bowditch. Bowditch was born in Salem, Massachusetts, in 1773, into such a poor family that he became a school "drop out" at the age of 10 and went to work for a ship chandler.

A few years later there came an incident that had far-reaching effects on seafarers, even down to the present time. An American privateer captured a British merchant vessel which carried, among other items, a fine library belonging to an Irishman, Doctor Richard Kirwan. The books were bought by Salem merchants who founded the Salem Atheneum, and Bowditch was given the job of caring for them. From then on he read everything he could, especially in mathematics.

At the age of 22 Bowditch went to sea as captain's clerk in the Salem merchantman *Henry*, bound for Mauritius in the Indian Ocean. He spent the next nine years at sea, working his way up until he became master of a ship. He continued to study mathematics, and applied his knowledge to the practical problems of navigation. He also learned several foreign languages and, when time permitted, taught celestial navigation aboard ship.

In 1801, he finished writing *The New American Practical Navigator*, the work that made him world-famous. It was not an original effort; an Englishman, John Hamilton Moore, had earlier written a handbook for navigators, but Bowditch found 8,000 errors in it. Consequently the American version was an entirely new work. After its publication in 1802, few American or British vessels went to sea without it. Soon it was used by the Russians, the French, and the Swedes.

The book contained methods for determining latitude; information on winds, currents, and navigational and plotting procedures; the duties of a master; the responsibilities of a shipowner; information on marine insurance and business; a glossary of sea terminology; and a large section on the principles of mathematics, from simple arithmetic through calculus.

Bowditch constantly revised his book to include new information; it went through ten editions during his lifetime. His son Jonathan carried the book through twenty-two more editions. After the Civil War, the Navy's Hydrographic Office took it over and published another thirty editions.

When Nathaniel Bowditch died, the East India Marine Society observed that "as long as ships shall sail, the needle points to the north, and the stars go through their appointed course in the Heavens, the name of Dr. Bowditch will be revered."

The usefulness of Bowditch's book is best described by seafarers themselves. Boston shipmaster Robert Bennet Formes wrote: "Beginning in 1817, with a capital consisting of a Testament, a 'Bowditch,' a chest of sea clothes and a mother's blessings, I left the paternal home full of hope and good resolutions."

The Hydrographic Office which took over Bowditch's book started out as an observatory. In 1809 Congress was petitioned by William Lambert, an amateur astronomer, to establish a national astronomical observatory. What resulted was a congressional appropriation for a center to provide information about coasts and waters "where public vessels sailed."

On 6 December 1830 the Depot of Charts and Instruments, as the center came to be called, began collecting all the nautical charts and instruments that had been gathering dust at various navy yards. Lieutenant Louis M. Goldsborough was put in charge and the depot moved into a rented house on G Street, between 17th and 18th streets, in Washington, D.C. Chart production began in May 1835, when the depot acquired a lithographic press. The first four charts, published in 1837, were of George's Shoal and Bank—the fishing ground east of Cape Cod that had been surveyed by Lieutenant Charles Wilkes.

When Lieutenant James M. Gilliss took over the depot in 1836, he finally succeeded in acquiring the instruments to set up the astronomical observatory Lambert had wanted. That activity has now become the Naval Observatory, which furnishes standard time to the entire United States. Time was once computed by observing the transit of certain stars over the meridian, but now it is determined by the oscillation of a cesium atom, and is accurate to one-tenth of a micro-second.

Matthew F. Maury   Next after Bowditch, the American whose name will long be revered by mariners of all nations is Matthew Fontaine Maury. Maury was born near Fredericksburg, Virginia, in 1806. Influenced by an older brother who was in the Navy, he became a midshipman in 1825. During the next nine years he made three cruises, one of them in the *Vincennes* as she circumnavigated the globe from 1826 to 1830. While serving as sailing master aboard the sloop of war *Falmouth*, Maury became intensely interested in winds and ocean currents, and gained considerable reputation because of his articles in *The American Journal of Science*. In 1836 he published *A New Theoretical and Practical Treatise on Navigation*, a classic textbook for students of navigation.

In 1839, as the result of a stagecoach accident, Maury received a permanent leg injury which made him unfit for duty aboard men-of-war. Three years later he was put in charge of the Navy's Depot of Charts and Instruments.

There he set about studying the old logbooks of naval vessels— most of which had been piled up like junk, and forgotten. With a few dedicated helpers he culled through them for facts on the oceans' currents and winds. He published his findings in 1847 in a book called, *Wind and Current Chart of the North Atlantic*. He than began supplying ship captains with specially prepared logs in which they were urged to record daily "all observable facts relating to winds, currents and other phenomena." The first taker was the skipper of the bark *W. H. D. C. Wright*, who followed Maury's suggested route to Rio de Janeiro. Three other vessels followed suit, and all shaved ten days from the average passage.

Maury's charts showed where the equatorial doldrums would be narrowest and how to navigate them; where to lose the northeast trade winds, and where to pick up the southeast trades. He published the first textbook of modern oceanography, *The Physical Geography of the Sea*, and began it with a poetic description of the Gulf Stream: "There is a river in the ocean. In the severest droughts it never fails and in the mightiest floods it never overflows. . . . The Gulf of Mexico is its fountain, and its mouth is the Arctic Ocean."

In 1853, he attended a conference in Brussels, at which representatives from all the principal maritime nations joined in a plan for establishing a system of meteorological observations at sea and of observations of the winds and currents of the ocean. Soon, in most of the nations of the world, naval and merchant vessels were able to gather the information they required.

Maury instituted a system for deep-sea sounding, and was among the first to suggest telegraphic communication between continents by submarine cables. The first transatlantic cable was laid in 1858 on the line indicated by him. He was the first scientist to foresee the possibility of daily weather reports, and as early as 1855 he laid down the steamer lanes in the North Atlantic—the most essential features of which were adopted 36 years later.

Because of his work in charting and piloting, Matthew Fontaine Maury is known as the Pathfinder of the Seas.

Lighthouses   In olden times, many a ship was navigated safely across the ocean, only to be wrecked as it tried to make port. The most dangerous part of an ocean trip was the last few miles, as a ship approached and finally sighted land. In storms, and at night, even the sharp eyes of a lookout could not always discern rocks and shoals in time to save his ship from disaster. The solution was to mark dangerous spots, or harbor entrances, with lights. This was first done in Egypt, about 300 B.C., where the entrance to Alexandria Harbor was marked by a tower on which priests kept a fire burning at night.

The first lighthouse in America was built on Little Brewster Island in Boston Harbor and went into operation in 1716. The light cost about £2,400 and was supported by a tax of a penny per ton on all vessels entering or leaving the port. A lighthouse-keeper was ordered to "diligently attend the light from sunset to sunrise," for which he was to be paid £30 a year.

George Worthylake, the first keeper, was drowned when heavy seas swept over the island. Benjamin Franklin, then a young printer in Boston, described Worthylake's death in a ballad entitled "The Lighthouse Tragedy" which was printed and sold all over Boston. The light was rebuilt after the Revolutionary War, and again in 1856. In 1964 it was designated a National Historical Landmark.

Other lights were soon established and, by 1789, there were 25 of them, strung out all the way from Maine to Georgia. The early lights were privately built, but in 1789 they were all placed under the control of the Secretary of the Treasury. In 1852 there were 325 lighthouses and 42 lightships, at which time they were turned over to a Lighthouse Board. All lighthouses, lightships, and other aids to navigation are now maintained by the Coast Guard.

The first lights were iron baskets in which a fire was kept burning. Later, lanterns were used; they burned melted lard, fish oil, whale oil, and, finally, mineral oil or kerosene. Such lights were weak, undependable, and required constant care. The development of acetylene gas, which could be compressed and stored in steel flasks, made it possible for lights to operate for months without any attention. Most lights are now electrically powered; and some are very powerful; the light on Little Brewster Island at Boston is rated at 2,000,000 candlepower, while the one at the entrance to Buzzards Bay is rated at a dazzling 9,000,000 candlepower.

Most lighthouses were in lonely, desolate places, and the men who took care of the lights sometimes did not see another person for months on end. Eventually, for one reason or another, some of the lights were taken over by women, whose devotion to their job earned them a lasting place in the hearts of seagoing men. One such woman was Ida Lewis, keeper of the Lime Rock Light off Newport, Rhode Island. She took over the light after her father and mother died, and was made official keeper by a special act of Congress in 1879. When she died in 1911, at the age of 69, the light-house was discontinued, but in her memory a 60-candlepower light still shows on Lewis Rock, the name given to it in the official Coast Guard list. The flag of the Ida Lewis Yacht Club of Newport shows a lighthouse, surrounded by 18 stars to mark the 18 lives Ida Lewis saved while taking care of her light.

Katherine Walker went to Robbins Reef Light, which stands on a rock at the entrance to New York Harbor, as a young bride soon after the Civil War. When her husband died in 1886 she carried on as keeper, and rowed her children to Staten Island each day for school. She died in 1918, at the age of 73, and was credited with saving the lives of 75 persons. The light at Michigan City, Indiana, was cared for by Harriet Colfax until she was 80 years old. Winter Island Light in San Francisco Bay was cared for by Kate Nevins who, during heavy fog, warned ships off by beating on her dishpan with a stove poker. The Turkey Point Light in Chesapeake Bay was cared for by Fanny Salters, who was appointed a permanent keeper by President Coolidge. She maintained the light for more than 40 years. Such dedicated people led lonesome lives and worked for very small wages, considering their invaluable service to mariners.

Lightships

In places where it was impossible to build lighthouses, lightships were used. The first American lightship was established near Norfolk, in the Chesapeake Bay, in 1820. The approach to New York Harbor was first guarded by a lightship in 1823. At first, open barges were used, and a man rowed out daily to take care of the light and pump out the barge's hull. Later, small sailing vessels were used, and they were eventually replaced by steam vessels. Lightships anchored near a harbor or a channel entrance and used lights or sound signals to warn ships. Many lightships are now being replaced by buoys or towers.

Buoys

The first floating buoys used in the United States were wooden barrels, or spars made of logs, placed in the Delaware River about 1756. The arrangement, shape, and color of these markers were usually the choice of the local customs man. For instance, a black one might indicate a wreck, a red one a channel, and a white one a reef. In 1850, Salem Harbor had 34 black buoys, 7 white ones, and 4 red ones; unless the seafarer was familiar with Salem Harbor he had no way of knowing which meant what. Now the system of buoys is standardized throughout the United States, as to shape, color, and use. The Coast Guard maintains about 22,000 buoys, of which about 3,500 are lighted. This buoy system was originated by the British, and is now international in use. Red buoys mark the right-hand side of a channel leading into a port from the sea and black buoys mark the left-hand side.

The first buoy to burn acetylene gas was used to mark a wreck in New York Harbor in 1882. When they were first used, electric lights were not effective because ice and storms knocked them out. Dependable batteries eventually replaced gas as a power source for almost all lights. Lighted buoys are of two types: a flashing light, which is off longer than it is on, and an occulting light, which is on longer than it is off.

Principal types of buoys maintained by the Coast Guard are:

Nun buoy—a cone, usually marking the right-hand side of a channel.

Can buoy—a cylinder, usually marking the left-hand side of a channel.

Spar buoy—a tapering pole or spar floating nearly vertically, used to mark the sides of a channel.

Bell buoy—a float topped by a framework in which a bell is sounded by the motion of the sea.

Gong buoy—similar to a bell buoy, but with four gongs, each sounding a different note.

Whistle buoy—usually a cone, with a whistle sounded by the motion of the sea.

Lighted buoy—no standard shape, with light powered either by electricity or compressed gas.

Combination buoy—no standard shape, with combinations of light and sound, a lighted bell buoy, a lighted gong buoy, and so forth.

Monster buoys   Super navigational sea buoys are now replacing some lightships. For example, Scotland Sea Buoy, which replaced the Scotland Lightship off Sandy Hook, New Jersey, in 1967, is 40 feet in diameter and displaces 100 tons. It carries a 5,000-candlepower light on a 33-foot mast, a fog horn, and a radio beacon. The buoy is powered by propane-fueled engine generators and nickel cadmium batteries; all its operations are controlled from shore by radio, and it is serviced only once a year.

All lighted buoys, whistle buoys, lighthouses, and lightships are marked on navigational charts, and each one has its own characteristics, so that once a navigator has identified such a navigational aid, he can locate himself on the chart. It is no longer necessary to see such aids. In the thickest fog or on the darkest night, buoys can now be picked up by radar; a radarscope shows a line of buoys marking the channel entrance to a port as a definite path through the sea which the ship can safely follow.

Many lighthouses are backed up by loran transmitting stations, which enable a navigator to pinpoint his position with great accuracy. The light at Cape Hatteras, for instance, is 193 feet above sea level and visible for 20 miles under good conditions, but its loran transmitter can be picked up hundreds of miles at sea.

Hydrographic Office

In 1866 Congress established the Hydrographic Office* as an activity apart from the Naval Observatory. "Hydro" began publishing pilot charts in their present form in 1883, with the first Pilot Chart of the North Atlantic Ocean. This was followed over the years by charts for the Pacific, the South Atlantic, the South Pacific, the Indian Ocean, and Central American waters. Now, more than 32 million charts are produced every year for use by ships of all nations in all the seven seas. These charts still carry the note: "Founded upon the researches made in the early part of the nineteenth century by Matthew Fontaine Maury while serving as a Lieutenant in the United States Navy."

Seagoing traffic routes

In the days of sail, the track a ship followed from Liverpool, England, to Baltimore was different from that followed by a steamship now. A sailing ship had to take advantage of prevailing winds, so it did not necessarily follow the shortest route. All traffic between the Atlantic and the Pacific oceans converged at the tip of South America as ships went either through the Strait of Magellan or around Cape Horn. Traffic from the Atlantic to the Indian Ocean all went around the Cape of Good Hope.

When the Suez Canal was opened in 1869, steamers no longer went around Africa, but instead cut through the Mediterranean and the Red Sea to the Gulf of Aden; the long route around the Cape of Good Hope was followed only by sailing ships. The opening of the Panama Canal in 1914 eliminated the steamer traffic around South America; again, the shipping lanes changed, and traffic between the Atlantic and Pacific funneled into the Caribbean Sea. Now, an immense amount of the traffic that moves between Mediterranean ports and northern Europe flows through the English Channel; there is a similar concentration of shipping in the Strait of Malacca, near Singapore. Steamship traffic between the Orient and the west coast of the United States swings across the Pacific as far north as the Aleutian Islands.

All these routes are definite paths across the various oceans; they are nearly as well defined as are highways US 66 and US 101 on land. A navigator planning a voyage from Baltimore to Gibral-

* The Hydrographic Office (HYDRO) is now part of the U.S. Naval Oceanographic Office (NAVOCEANO).

tar knows exactly where he will intersect the traffic route from Panama to New York and that from Rio de Janeiro to Rotterdam.

World trade routes from U.S. ports are actually numbered, like highways; the U.S. Department of Commerce lists 31 of them. Number 13, for example, runs from Gulf ports to the Mediterranean and the Black Sea; Number 23 runs from Pacific coast ports to the Caribbean and the east coast of Mexico; and Number 29 runs from Pacific ports, via Hawaii, to ports in the Far East.

Ships at sea, as a matter of routine, report their positions at regular periods; their locations are always known. When one considers that there are thousands of ships on the high seas at any one time, such information becomes important; when a ship is in danger, the ships nearest to her can be quickly routed to her assistance.

After steam came into common use, the tracks ships followed from point to point across the oceans were usually great-circle routes. A great circle is the shortest distance between two points, as seen on a globe. Modern electronics, however, have made it possible for ships sometimes to take a more advantageous route than the great circle, and still save time. Weather satellites now pinpoint storms that may be days ahead of a ship, and shore-based computer centers keep track of ships and weather. With computer input of a ship's speed, loaded condition, and destination, all the variables of wind and current can be considered and she can then be given a track to follow which should enable her to reach her destination in the least time possible. The system for providing this service is called Optimum Track Ship Routing (OTSR); besides saving time, it minimizes damage to ships and their cargo and cuts fuel consumption. Next to Bowditch and Maury, OTSR is a sailor's best friend.

CHAPTER 9
CLIPPERS TO CALIFORNIA

By the time the United States was 50 years old, it had endured several wars. The country was growing, economically and industrially. In particular, merchant shipping on the high seas was beginning to expand marvelously.

The Industrial Revolution not only pushed that expansion along, but was helped by it. In the 1850s American farms, thanks partly to the McCormick mower-reaper, produced huge grain crops for export. The repeal in 1846 of the restrictive British corn laws put England on a free-trade basis and enabled Americans to export large quantities of grain to the British Isles. Shippers needed cargo space.

Also of great importance in this thrilling saga was the Mexican War, which gave the United States a vast new empire in the West. With the sensational discovery of gold in California in 1848 and in Australia in 1851, there developed a frantic demand for rapid passage to the goldfields. Along with this was the repeal of the British navigation laws in 1849; Yankee clippers could outsail the British in rushing the new tea crop from China to London.

Before repeal of the British navigation laws in 1849, all goods bound for England had to be carried in British ships or in ships of the country in which the goods originated. Once these restrictions were removed, the British found that their own shipping had fallen far behind that of other countries.

Their first shock came when the American-built *Oriental* carried a cargo of tea from Hong Kong to London in 97 days. She was commanded on that run by Theodore Palmer, brother of Nathaniel Palmer, the Antarctic explorer.

On previous page: The intricate maze of masts and spars and standing and running rigging required to handle a square-rigged ship fills the sky in this view of the *Balclutha,* on display at Pier 43, in San Francisco. The ship, wrecked in 1903, was subsequently salvaged and restored to her original condition under the auspices of the San Francisco Maritime Museum. Photo: Karl Kortum.

The British had never seen anything like the *Oriental*. Low, lean, and with black-painted hull, she had masts taller than those of any other ships in the harbor. Other objects of British admiration were the *Challenge* and the *Architect*, both of which beat all the other tea ships from China by a full week. British merchants were quite willing to pay £8 per ton for tea shipped on American vessels instead of the usual £4, because faster passage meant less danger of spoilage and better sales.

A further spurt to the growth of trade was provided in 1847, when Matthew Fontaine Maury published his book *Wind and Current Chart of the North Atlantic*. This, along with his sailing directions, made profits greater and more certain for the shipowner.

Americans first went to California in the course of the Northwest trade (*see* Chapter 5). Later, Boston vessels traded with Spanish settlements in California, setting up shop on board ship and bartering shoes, wine, furniture, sugar, combs, and hardware for hides, called "California bank notes," leather bags, and tallow.

The California gold rush

In 1848, James Wilson Marshall, in partnership with Captain John A. Sutter, built a mill on the American River, about 100 miles northeast of San Francisco. Soon, Marshall unexpectedly found some yellow-colored metal that looked like gold. They sent it to San Francisco to see if it was the real thing. It was!

The news spread like wildfire; pandemonium broke loose. Everyone wanted to get to the goldfields first and make a fortune overnight. No longer did covered-wagon caravans head for Oregon; everybody wanted to go to California. In New York, men crowded the piers waiting for standing room on southbound vessels. In the Pacific, whalemen, pirates, and merchantmen left the sea for the beach. Even the North Atlantic packet rats jumped ship in New York and headed west.

There were three ways to get to California. The first was the overland route, by covered wagon. It meant embarking on a journey that lasted months, while one faced blizzards, floods, blazing heat, rattlesnakes, and hostile Indians.

Those who had the money to spend could go by ship. There were two sea routes. The first was a 14,000-mile trip around South America. Rounding Cape Horn, or "Cape Stiff," as the sailors called it, meant fighting mountainous waves, fierce gales, and sometimes icebergs. The average sailing time on that route was nearly seven months. Many ships that left the East Coast for California never arrived there. A somewhat quicker route was to sail to the Isthmus of Panama, then cross overland through jungles infested with malaria, snakes, and yellow fever. On the Pacific side, one bought passage aboard a ship sailing for San Francisco.

In spite of the hazards, between December 1848 and February

1849, 136 vessels sailed from Atlantic ports for San Francisco. Almost all of the 775 ships that reached California in 1849 were sailing ships.

The first paddle-wheeler   One of the exceptions to the sailing ships was the wooden-hulled steam-and-sail *California*. She was one of three paddle-wheel steamers built for the new Pacific Mail Steamship Company. The other two, the *Oregon* and *Panama*, carried mail between Panama and Oregon; such mail was taken by steamer from New York to Chagres, on the eastern shore of the Isthmus, and carried across to Panama City.

The sturdy little *California* cleared from New York in October 1848, bound for California. She made it to Rio de Janeiro in twenty-six days where she took on coal and food. She was the first steamer through the Strait of Magellan, a passage that took six days, much of which time was spent at anchor waiting for fair winds and weather. On 27 December, she reached Callao, Peru, where she took on 17 cabin and 80 steerage passengers. It was here that the captain and crew learned of the gold discovery in California.

At Panama City, she found no less than 1,500 eager gold-seekers wanting passage to the goldfields. In all, 365 people crowded onto the little steamer that was built to carry 75. A few held tickets purchased in New York, but others got aboard by paying up to $300 for their fare. Food, mostly salt beef and wormy bread, was scarce; the firemen mutinied so the captain put into Mazatlán, in Mexico, where he had the culprits jailed, and replaced them with Mexicans. Next, the coal gave out, so the sails were raised. Finally 100 bags of hidden coal were discovered and the fires were relighted. At last, on 28 February 1849, the *California* steamed into San Francisco.

Clippers   Prices in California soon skyrocketed: butter, $1.50 a pound; hens, $4 each; one egg, $1; flour, $40 a barrel. Lumber sold for $14 per thousand feet in New York, but that same measure brought $500 in San Francisco. Eastern merchants were offering $60 a ton to anyone who could get their goods to California in a hurry.

Shipbuilders in Boston, Baltimore, and New York realized that fortunes could be made by shipping cargoes to California—fast! A fast vessel could pay for itself in just one trip. The answer to the demand for speed was—the clipper ships, sometimes called the "greyhounds of the sea."

The word *clipper* means "that which moves or flies swiftly." With reference to ships, it meant a vessel that could "clip" through the waves.

The first "clippers," so-called, were used as privateers in the War of 1812, as illegal slavers, as pirate vessels, and as opium-smugglers in the China trade. Mostly schooner-rigged, they were seldom more than 200 tons; they were long, low, flush-decked, and had sharper lines and longer spars than conventional vessels.

In 1832, Isaac McKim, a wealthy Baltimore shipowner and merchant, decided he wanted a ship that had the lines of a Baltimore schooner but was twice as large. Kennard and Williamson, of Baltimore, built the *Ann McKim* (his wife's name) and spared no expense in her construction. She was 493 tons, 143 feet long, and had a 31-foot beam, a copper bottom, live-oak frames, and mahogany deck fittings; she mounted 12 brass guns.

There were other early examples of the classic Baltimore clippers. In 1839 the *Akbar*, built in Boston for the China trade, made the voyage from New York to Canton in 109 days. Other fast clippers of the era were the *Helena* and the *Paul Jones*. In 1844, the *Houqua* (named for the senior Hong merchant at Canton) made it to Hong Kong from New York in 90 days, logging an average speed of 158.6 miles per day. The *Rainbow*, launched in 1845, made it home from Canton in only 88 days. She was the fastest ship in the world at that time.

In 1850, shipbuilders Donald McKay, William Webb, Samuel Hall, and others began turning out magnificent ships with long, knifelike bows, slender hulls and tall, raking masts. All had a vast spread of lofty white canvas; the *Sea Witch* carried an acre and a half of sail—more than enough to cover a football field. Of the 433 clippers built, 35 could properly be called extreme clippers.

Clippers were built of the best oak, Southern pine, and hackmatack, copper-fastened and sheathed with yellow metal. Many had elegant staterooms and cabins for passengers: the *Mastiff* had a library that cost $1,200. Historian Samuel Eliot Morison wrote of them: "Scamping or skimping never occurred to a clipper-shipbuilder, and if it had, no Yankee workman would have stayed in his yard. In finish the clipper ships surpassed anything previously attempted in marine art. Those built in Newburyport, in particular, were noted for the evenness of their seams and the perfection of their joiner-work. The topsides, planed and sandpapered smooth as a mackerel, were painted a dull black that brought out their lines like a black velvet dress on a beautiful woman. . . ."

All had beautiful figureheads. At the bow of the *Sea Serpent* a golden eagle spread its wings, and sea serpents were carved across her stern. The *Flying Fish* had a fish on the wing at her bow. The *James Baines*, named for her Liverpool owners and called by the English "the most perfect sailing ship that ever entered the River Mersey," had as her figurehead a bust of James Baines, bewhiskered and top-hatted.

The clippers also had romantic or colorful names. Donald McKay in Boston produced ships named *Staghound, Flying Cloud, Witch of the Waves, Shooting Star, Lightning, Gamecock, Great Republic*, and *Sovereign of the Seas.*

Perfectly proportioned, the California clippers were breathtaking in their gracefulness. To quote Morison again: "Never in these United States, has the brain of man conceived, or the hand of man fashioned, so perfect a thing as the clipper ship. In her, the long-suppressed artistic impulse of a practical, hardworked race burst into flower. The *Flying Cloud* was our Rheims, the *Sovereign of the Seas* our Parthenon, the *Lightning* our Amiens. . . ." So swift that in a fair breeze they could outrun any steamer, they were America's great art form. It was said that a clipper went after the wind instead of waiting for the wind to come to her.

Stately as churches, swift as gulls,
They trod the oceans, then—
No man had seen such ships before
And none will see again.*

And the people loved them. On the waterfronts of New York and San Francisco, people thrilled to the sight of the great tall ships. Every clipper that sailed and every clipper that arrived was reported in the newspapers. Ships made port to the welcome of weeping, cheering, and singing admirers; their captains and crews were followed around the streets by adoring crowds. Even waterfront loafers who cared about little else knew and loved the majestic clippers.

It was even more exciting when the clippers began to race one another halfway around the world. The first great race in 1850 was backed by thousands of dollars and attracted worldwide attention, as seven clippers slipped out of New York for San Francisco. The winner, the *Sea Witch*, met dirty weather below the Horn, fought darkness, ice, bitter head winds, ice floes, and sleet, and still set a record by making the passage in 97 days. The next year, the *Sea Witch*, racing two others, struggled for two weeks in stormy blackness just to work around the Horn.

In 1851, the *Flying Cloud* made the passage from New York to San Francisco in 89 days and 2 hours. This record was never bet-

* Rosemary and Stephen Vincent Benét, *A Book of Americans* (New York: Rinehart and Company, 1933), p. 75. Reprinted by permission.

This three-quarter-sized replica of the famous clipper ship *Flying Cloud* was recently overhauled for use as a waterfront restaurant in Boston Harbor. The 256-foot dock, built in 1853, is believed to have handled the original *Flying Cloud*, which was built in Boston in 1851 under the direction of the famed Donald McKay. Courtesy: Bethlehem Steel Corporation.

tered, but she repeated the feat six years later and the *Andrew Jackson* tied the record that same year.

By the mid 1850s the whole East Coast was living from one clipper race to another. Aside from the excitement and glamor there was always the overriding profit motive. The *Sovereign of the Seas*, at 2,241 tons, was the most radically designed of the McKay clippers. She was the largest, most graceful ship in the world at that time. Despite skepticism from critics, McKay had faith in her and sank all his own money into the venture. In 1852, he sent her off to San Francisco under the command of his brother, Lauchlan McKay, with a crew of 105 men and boys and 2,950 tons of cargo. Lauchlan sailed her to San Francisco in 107 days—then on to the Hawaiian islands in ballast where he loaded sperm oil for New York. Homeward bound, the ship covered 2,114 nautical miles in a 10-day period, arriving in New York 82 days out of Honolulu, for a good record and a tidy profit.

The clippers had their year of glory in 1853—145 of them sailed for the Golden Gate. There was, however, one memorable day in August 1855 when, one after another, seven clippers sailed through the Golden Gate. San Francisco had never seen such a breathtaking sight. It would never be seen again.

In all, 161 clippers were launched between 1850 and 1855. After that clipper-building diminished. Only eight were built in 1856 and four the next year. Some of the decline in business was caused by the completion of the railroad across the Isthmus in 1855. But, in any case, there were just too many ships and too many people trying to make a lot of money quickly.

From queen to drudge   Clippers were expensive to build, operate, and repair. When rates tumbled from $60 a ton in 1850 to $28 a ton four years later, they could not carry enough cargo to make them worthwhile. They were built to serve a purpose and they did it well. When that purpose no longer existed they were put to work in the detested guano and coolie trades.

Guano is a natural fertilizer found in the Chincha Islands, off the coast of Peru. Here, millions of sea birds nested, and over the centuries their excrement piled up, in some places it was as much as 150 feet deep.

During the late 1850s, dozens of clippers waited offshore, sometimes for months, for their turn to load guano. When a ship's turn at last came, she drew up close to the cliff and Chinese coolies, with faces wrapped in rags and bandages, shoveled the powdery guano through a chute to the ship's hold. Loading covered the whole ship with an acrid dust that fouled the brass, silver, and everything else.

The coolies came from China to work for the Peruvian government on a five-year work contract under promises of good working conditions, proper housing, and food. Instead, they lived in primitive cane huts and were given a bundle of rags for clothes. Brutal overseers worked them from sunrise to sunset. Many died from starvation, sickness, exhaustion, and from breathing the guano dust. Some committed suicide by jumping off the cliffs.

Transporting coolies from China to the Chinchas, Australia, or Cuba was the most shameful use to which the beautiful clippers were put. Shipowners collected from $50 to $80 for each coolie carried, so a load of 700 of them could be worth $35,000. The business was not illegal and the British had been doing it right along, so the profitable but cruel practice continued.

The unfortunate Chinese shipped to Australia and Cuba fared little better than cattle or slaves and there were many instances of mutinies and suicides. By 1857, public opinion was aroused by stories of coolies being flogged and mistreated. When shipping companies were finally forced to give up the business, Peru responded by buying the clippers and transporting the coolies herself.

The end of the clippers   The life-span of the wooden clippers, particularly those driven hard in the California trade, was not long. Of the ones put to other uses, some were wrecked, some just disappeared at sea. A few were left to rot in dirty backwaters. The *John Gilpin* struck an iceberg and went down, the *John Milton* was driven ashore near Montauk, Long Island, with all hands lost, the *Flying Dutchman* was lost on Brigantine Beach, New Jersey, and the *Wild Wave* piled up on a coral island near Pitcairn Island, in the South Pacific, with all hands presumed lost. The *Flying Fish*, coming out of Foochow with a load of tea, was wrecked. The beautiful *Sea Witch* met a sad fate. In 1856, with 500 coolies on board, she piled up on a reef near Havana and was a complete loss.

When steam overtook sail as the preferred means of power, some clippers became drab workhorses. During the Civil War they served in the Union Navy; some were captured and burned by the Confederates.

The English were anxious to buy American clippers at bargain prices. They put them to work on the Australia run, flying the house flags of the White Star Line and the Black Ball Line (no connection with the American line of the same name).

Clippers were sold and resold, sailing under different flags and names. They went from one job to another carrying various kinds of freight. The *Flying Cloud* hauled lumber in the North Atlantic; the *Red Jacket* finished her days as a coal hulk, as did the *Donald McKay*. The *N. P. Palmer* and the *Nightingale* sailed under the Norwegian flag.

The clippers have gone now. In the poignant words of John Masefield, "Earth will not see such ships as those again." They live only in paintings and in ship models.

Clipper captains   Although design and fine shipbuilding had much to do with the success of the swift clippers, their records would probably not have been so dramatic had it not been for their captains. Without exception they were unique among sailors—men who had been brought up close to the sea and had worked their way to positions of command after spending years as foremast hands and mates.

Like the packet skippers, they had to be physically powerful and able to be on deck for days and nights at a time in foul stormy weather. Not only were they required to have superb seamanship but they also had to be gifted with a strange clairvoyance, a "wind sense." Their judgment would tell them how much sail they dared spread in any kind of weather without having their yards and sails carried away.

At the same time, a clipper captain was expected to be a gentleman in the drawing room, showing proper style and manners in the social and business world ashore. He was, after all, a celebrity.

Topping all these qualities was a spirit of competition—an urge to outrace all rivals and shave days off previous records. Since no foreigners had anything with which to compete, Yankee captains raced one another.

After offloading in San Francisco, clippers would either return to New York in ballast, or sail on across the Pacific to load tea for London, New York, or Boston. From China, they returned by way of the Cape of Good Hope. Almost all clipper captains went completely around the world at least five or six times.

Clipper crews   By 1851 there was a chronic shortage of qualified seamen. For wages that ranged from $8 to $15 a month, not many men wanted to sign on for such dangerous and hard work. Although clipper crews had fine accommodations and ate the same food as officers, they also had to handle huge sails and heavy yards. Too, no one liked the clippers' way of taking green water over their narrow bows and drenching anyone working on deck.

The gold mines of California drained seaports of thousands of able seamen. In San Francisco, the men jumped ship and headed for the goldfields. The ships lay idle until a new crew could be gotten together—some ships were abandoned and rotted away. On small vessels it did not matter so much because a few good sailors could handle things, but on the huge over-sparred clippers it was a critical problem. And sailors are not made overnight.

Rounding up crews involved "land sharks" going to the keepers of seamen's boarding houses. For a fee, these seedy characters would collect an assortment of bums, thugs, and ex-convicts one way or another (sometimes by drugging and kidnapping) and pass them off as able-bodied seamen. One trick was to put a horn on the ground and instruct the bum to stagger around it. From then on, he had technically "been around the horn."

Women aboard the clippers   As with the whalers and the packets, captains' wives and families sometimes sailed aboard the clippers. The "old women," as they were called, were a brave, resourceful lot. However, most of them were young women; some were only teenagers.

In the winter of 1856, nineteen-year-old Mary Patten sailed with her husband, Joshua, who was captain of *Neptune's Car*. Their first mate had to be put under arrest for insubordination, and Joshua became sick, lost his hearing, and developed a raging fever. He probably had meningitis.

Mary had learned some navigation on a previous voyage and, with the help of an illiterate but well-meaning second mate, she took over the duties of command. For 120 days, she fought the big clipper all the way around the Horn, then piloted her safely up the West Coast to San Francisco. Her feat, which included caring for a sick husband all the way, earned her the title of "Florence Nightingale of the Ocean." The hospital at the U.S. Merchant Marine Academy, Kings Point, New York, is named Patten in her memory.

The down easters

The shipbuilders of New York and Boston had built the swift, glamorous clippers, but it was the men of Maine who, in the 1870s, built the strong grain ships. Just after the Civil War, these wooden, full-rigged, so-called "down easters," *were* America's merchant marine.

Down easters were three-masted and squared-rigged; they looked somewhat like the California clippers, but their lines were less sharp. Their job was to carry Californian wheat to England, France, Germany, and other countries of Europe. Between 1870 and 1890 they were considered the finest ships afloat.

They were fast sailers, often going around the Horn from California and reaching England in less than four months, whereas earlier trips had lasted six months. The captains were invariably from Maine: 100 deep-water captains came from one small town alone. They took their wives and families on their voyages. Captain Dave Rivers, of the *A. G. Ropes*, even let his daughter keep her pony aboard ship.

By 1890, San Francisco was the third most important sailing port in the world. Only Liverpool in England and Newcastle in Australia had more ship traffic. As many as 100 down easters could be loading grain in San Francisco within a few months of each other.

Down easters around the world   The down easters carried grain, but they carried other products as well. Sometimes they hauled fertilizer from South America to Europe; sometimes they packed chunks of Maine ice in sawdust and sailed it to India. Ice was a big business (up to 30 million tons a year) before mechanized refrigeration was invented. Many down easters carried tins of kerosene (called case oil) for use in lanterns in China and Japan. One down easter hauled a locomotive to Hong Kong.

Down easters returned with silks and tea from Asiatic ports and sugar from Hawaii. Their great days at sea came to an end when English and Scottish shipowners began sending iron ships, so-called "lime-juicers," to compete for the California grain trade. Many of these lime-juicers eventually went into service with the "Star" fleet of the Alaska Packers Association: *Star of England, Star of India, Star of Alaska* were three of the original nineteen. They spent their last years hauling canned salmon to San Francisco. Many of them finally rotted away on the mudflats of San Francisco Bay.

The *Star of Alaska* had her name changed back to the original *Balclutha* and can be seen at the San Francisco Maritime Museum. The *Star of India* is on display at the Maritime Museum Association of San Diego.

America's maritime power on the decline

In 1858, the first transcontinental stagecoach made the trip from St. Louis to San Francisco and brought a complete change of attitude in America. In the past the brightest and most energetic young Americans and far-sighted businessmen had been attracted to ships and shipping, now they turned toward developing the West. There were fortunes to be made on land where living was easier and less risky than at sea.

There were many who mourned the passing of America's great sailing ships. Lincoln Colcord, who was born aboard his father's down easter, wrote in 1924: "One by one the few remaining deepwater sailing ships are disappearing. They drop away, and are heard of no more. With them goes much that is incalculable. It passes like a high squall sinking beyond the horizon, wind and sea, motion and color—all vanishing to leeward with the tall ship in their midst. The rigorous discipline, the peerless craftsmanship, the full life that was part and parcel of a close tradition, these belonged to the days of sail and to no other. A natural means of propulsion made natural seamen."

There was this in favor of the clipper ships—they never polluted the atmosphere by burning hydrocarbons, and they never fouled up harbors and beaches with oil slicks. The smoke-belching steamers that took over the merchant trade in the last part of the nineteenth century, and the jumbo tankers that wallow along the ocean highways now, are all alike in one respect—the fuel they burn, or haul to where it can be burned, can never be replaced. The square-riggers and clippers—the "wind ships"—used the wind and left it for anyone else who needed it.

Bark *Star of India* at San Diego, California. Courtesy: The Maritime
Museum Association of San Diego.

Top: Boston Harbor, as seen from Constitution Wharf (early 1800s). Courtesy: The U.S. Naval Academy Museum. Painting by Robert Salmon. *Bottom:* Celebration of George Washington's Birthday at Malta on board the USS *Constitution* (1837). Courtesy: The U.S. Naval Academy Museum. Painting by J. G. Evans.

Top: The extreme clipper *Young America.* Courtesy: The Fine Arts
Collection of The Seamen's Bank for Savings. Painting by Charles
Robert Patterson. *Bottom:* The steam frigate USS *Wabash* leaving New
York Harbor (1861). Courtesy: The U.S. Naval Academy Museum.
Painting by Edward Moran.

Top: The schooner yacht *America.* U.S. Naval Institute. Painting by
C. G. Evers. *Bottom:* The guided-missile cruiser USS *Leahy* replenishing
from the oiler USS *Pawcatuck.* Photo: Frank Uhlig, Jr.

Top: The guided-missile destroyer USS *Coontz*, the guided-missile cruiser *Josephus Daniels,* and the attack transport USS *Francis Marion. Photo:* Frank Uhlig, Jr. *Bottom:* The container ship *Panama.* Photo: Frank Uhlig, Jr.

The cargo ship *Pioneer Crusader*. Photo: Frank Uhlig, Jr.

The guided-missile cruiser USS *Leahy*. Photo: Frank Uhlig, Jr.

A Terrier-missile launcher aboard a guided-missile cruiser. Courtesy:
Vitro Laboratories, Silver Spring, Maryland.

CHAPTER 10
PIRACY AND SLAVERY

The annals of history are filled with accounts of men who would rather steal from others than earn their own living in an honest way. They were called robbers and highwaymen when they operated on land; at sea they were pirates.

Piracy reached its heyday in the early eighteenth century and was an evolution from the semilawful privateering of earlier times. There was little difference between the two "enterprises," except in purpose and division of booty. A privateer was commissioned by his country's government to raid and capture the commercial ships of unfriendly or enemy countries. When a "prize" was sold, the privateer's captain shared the profit with his government and his crew. Pirates, on the other hand, recognized no government and obeyed no laws; they divided the spoils among themselves. In peacetime, it was easy to make the switch from legal privateering to outright piracy.

Known as *marooners* because of their habit of leaving their victims marooned, the pirates sometimes flew their country's flag until they found a victim. When they did so, they lowered the flag, hoisted the Jolly Roger, a white skull and crossbones on a black background, and attacked.

At first, the pirates hunted Spanish ships in the Caribbean. These ships carried precious damask, raw silks, velvets, sheer linens, laces, pistols and other arms, spices, candlesticks, articles inlaid with gold and silver, religious statues, and all manner of treasure. Later they expanded operations to Madagascar and the Indian Ocean where they raided native vessels for treasure and for victims to be held for ransom. Cargo captured by pirates was

On previous page: Hogsheads of molasses were shipped from the West Indies to New England distilleries. The windmill in the distance ground the sugar cane to make it into molasses. This drawing was made by William Clark on the estates of Admiral Tallemach in Antigua, and first published in London in 1823. Courtesy: Kenneth M. Newman, The Old Print Shop, New York City.

sometimes brought to New York for sale at auction. In 1818, a ship reached Baltimore with eight wagonloads of gold and silver.

During the seventeenth century, when England was at war with Spain and France, the British happily endorsed piracy against their enemies' colonies and ships in the West Indies. Then, as more and more of the islands came under British control and tobacco and sugar plantations became sources of wealth, the British realized they had much to lose to the swashbuckling sea rovers. The Earl of Bellomont, who was sent in 1697 to suppress piracy in North America, reported that it was going on all along the coast, from Maine to Maryland. He wrote, "they not only wink at, but Imbrace Pirats, men and shippers. . . ." Even ships of the British East India Company had to sail with escorts.

In 1699, the British parliament made piracy a capital offense. The effect of this law was that bribes increased and the pirates were more careful in their activities. Officials were paid "protection" fees of £700 for a ship and £100 apiece for members of her crew. On moonless nights with a favorable tide, pirate ships could get rid of their cargoes without fear of the law.

Captain Kidd   In 1695, the Earl of Bellomont made a deal with a Scottish shipmaster, William Kidd, to suppress pirate trade in Madagascar. Through a mysterious set of circumstances, Kidd wound up being accused of piracy. At his London trial in 1701 he repeatedly asked that the king's commission under which he sailed be produced in court. It was not. Kidd, having been betrayed by Bellomont and his associates, was hanged. It was not until 200 years later that the king's commission, which would have saved Kidd, was found in the Public Records Office.

The Lafitte brothers   After 1808, when it became illegal to carry slaves in American ships, it was almost impossible to distinguish between pirates, slavers, and privateers. Smugglers often became pirates, taking slaves from ships belonging to other countries and smuggling them into the Southern states.

Two of the more famous privateers-turned-slave-smugglers were the brothers Jean and Pierre Lafitte. They were blacksmiths in New Orleans until 1809 when they decided slave-smuggling was a more profitable business. At Barataria, their hideout in the bayous southwest of the city, they gathered together a band of cutthroats, and began preying on merchantmen and slavers bound for the West Indies. By selling the blacks to Louisiana planters, the brothers became rich. They were popular and influential, frequenting the fashionable homes and restaurants of the old city. Finally the governor managed to bring them to trial but, with expensive legal defense, both were acquitted.

During the War of 1812, the brothers became heroes. The British tried to bribe them to fight against the Americans, but instead they lent their services to General Andrew Jackson and helped win the Battle of New Orleans in 1815. When peace was restored, the remnants of the Lafitte pirates moved from Barataria to the island off the Texas coast which is now Galveston. From there they moved in 1817 to Matagorda and Amelia Island, in Spanish Florida. Amelia Island was probably the biggest depot for slaves smuggled in by pirates and slavers the world has ever known. Between 1815 and 1818, about 20,000 blacks per year were landed on Amelia, each having been bought for prices ranging from $175 to $250. They were sold to planters for $500 to $1,000 apiece.

Pierre Lafitte eventually disappeared and Jean and 60 of his men are supposed to have died in a battle with a British warship.

Gasparilla   The Spaniard, José Gaspar, known as Gasparilla, operated from Gasparilla Island, on the Gulf coast of Florida, near Fort Myers. In 1821, he captured an American ship named *Orleans* with a cargo worth $40,000. The following year, he attacked what he thought was an unarmed British merchantman but was actually a U.S. warship in disguise, out hunting pirates. Gasparilla, realizing he would be caught and executed, wrapped a heavy anchor chain around his waist and jumped overboard. In Tampa, Florida, there is still an annual celebration for him.

South American privateers and pirates   There was peace in Europe after the Napoleonic Wars, and in America after 1815, but the Spanish colonies of South America were still fighting for their independence. Most South American countries were born between the years 1800 and 1825. Mexico had been in revolt since 1810 and declared herself an independent monarchy in 1821. The United States bought Florida from Spain in 1819.

As colonies revolted, their governments wanted to strike against Spanish shipping but they were powerless to do so because they had no navies. Their solution was to commission as privateers small, fast brigs, schooners, and sloops manned by crews of 25 to 100 foreign sailors. Many of these men were tough veterans of Trafalgar, New Orleans, and other sea battles. Others came from captured unarmed merchantmen whose crews were given the choice between being put to death or joining their captors. At one time, more than 10,000 cutthroats were sailing as privateers or as pirates, changing roles at whim or convenience. In five years they attacked nearly 3,000 merchant ships and boldly sailed in sight of Vera Cruz, Havana, San Juan, and St. Thomas—areas supposedly loyal to Spain but secretly sympathetic to the pirates and privateers.

So serious was the problem that ship captains refused to sail unless their vessels were heavily armed and provided with experienced gunners. Horror stories of murder, robbery, and violence at sea were recounted almost daily in American newspapers.

The public demanded that something be done and Congress finally gave President Monroe the power to suppress piracy. The U.S. Navy was authorized to halt and search suspicious vessels and all men found guilty of piracy were to be hanged. In 1822, Congress appropriated $500,000 to fit out a naval squadron to be commanded by Commodore David Porter. The government of Spain allowed the squadron to operate in Spanish territorial waters, and the British cooperated by instructing their vessels to chase and destroy lawless sea rovers in the West Indies.

Commodore Porter's West India Squadron consisted of the sloop of war *Hornet,* the brig *Enterprize,* the schooners *Spark, Shark, Porpoise,* and *Grampus,* and the little steam ferryboat *Sea Gull.* It was the duty of the *Sea Gull* to tow other craft into inlets in pursuit of pirates who, until then, had counted on being able to escape because of the shallow draft of their vessels. Each schooner carried a large rowing barge equipped with a brass swivel gun with which the pirates could be chased among the reefs and shoals.

Porter's squadron hunted pirates for two years along the coasts of Cuba, Hispaniola (Santo Domingo/Haiti), Puerto Rico, and the Lesser Antilles. Many heroic hand-to-hand battles were fought during the long weeks it took the U.S. Navy to clean the islands of pirates. Among the fearless young American officers who took part in such combat were James Biddle, Matthew Calbraith Perry, and David Glasgow Farragut.

Although Porter's squadron captured many pirates, the U.S. courts were slow and cautious in trying them. A few were put to death, many served prison terms, but some were acquitted. British and Spanish authorities were not so kindhearted with pirates; they simply hung them all. For expediency's sake, it became the practice for Americans to get as many pirates into British and Spanish courts as possible.

An example of this was the pirate Cofrece (or Cofrecina) who captured a Spanish vessel in the Virgin Islands, killed all the men, and left the women marooned on a barren islet called Sail Rock.* He then sailed away to bury his treasure. When he came back for the women he found they had all committed suicide by jumping into the sea.

Cofrece was captured in March 1825 by Midshipman Hull Foote, commanding a U.S. armed schooner, who took the pirate and his crew to Puerto Rico where Spanish authorities tried, convicted, and executed them.

The United States got into political trouble over pirates when, on 27 October 1824, Commodore David Porter sent Lieutenant Charles T. Platt in the schooner *Beagle* into Fajardo, Puerto Rico, to claim property stolen by pirates from an American firm in St. Thomas. Lieutenant Platt was jailed by local authorities who,

* The islet was so named because it looks like a sailing ship. It is visible from planes hopping between San Juan and Charlotte Amalie.

because of the loss of Florida, were anti-American and sympathetic to the pirates. Released a few hours later, Platt reported to the Commodore what had happened.

Angered, Porter landed at Fajardo with 200 sailors and demanded an apology—which he got. But in Washington what became known as the "Foxardo affair" was regarded as a diplomatic insult to the Spanish. Porter was recalled and given a court-martial. He was replaced by Lewis Warrington, a man of deeds and few words, who seldom took prisoners and, in the face of such treatment, piracy soon ended. The last known pirate in the United States, Charles Gibb, was hanged in New York in 1831. From 1818 to 1824, he had captured forty ships and murdered the crews of twenty of them.

Pirate literature   In a few years, the cruelty, the preying on defenseless vessels, the murder, and the robbery were all but forgotten. Grimy, ferocious cutthroats were romanticized by writers who portrayed them as colorful "good guys at heart," seagoing Robin Hoods, or perhaps the James Bonds of their day. The play *The Successful Pirate* produced at Drury Lane Theater in London in 1712 was strongly criticized for its glorification of sea robbers. American writers Washington Irving and Edgar Allan Poe made Captain William Kidd famous; even Harriet Beecher Stowe of *Uncle Tom's Cabin* fame wrote an adventure story in 1870 called *Captain Kidd's Money.* The greatest pirate yarn of all time, *Treasure Island,* was written by Robert Louis Stevenson to entertain a young stepson. Numberless armchair adventurers have thrilled to the words of the pirate chant:

> Fifteen men on the Dead Man's Chest*—
>   Yo-ho-ho and a bottle of rum!
> Drink and the devil had done for the rest—
>   Yo-ho-ho and a bottle of rum!

The slave trade   When slavery in America is mentioned, the usual impression is that of a group of blacks picking cotton on a Southern plantation. Actually, there were slaves in the southern colonies long before cotton became a crop there and there were also slaves in the North. The *importation* of slaves was not a southern practice; the first blacks sold in America came on a Dutch ship in 1619. Southern plantation owners *bought* slaves, but many of them arrived in the United States as part of profit-making ventures by some of the most respected names in New England.

The colonists who built the first ironworks at Saugus, Massachu-

---

* Probably a reference to the island called Dead Chest.

setts in 1644, and the men who later built smelters in New Hampshire and Connecticut found themselves in need of large amounts of cash with which to import tools and machinery from Europe. There were others who needed to raise money, and there was a simple way to do it.

Distilleries turned molasses from the Sugar Islands (the West Indies) into rum; the rum was shipped to West Africa and exchanged for slaves, and the slaves were taken to the West Indies and sold. Then another cargo of molasses would be carried to New England. The practice was known as the Triangular, or Three-Cornered, Trade, and it became the foundation of much of New England's prosperity in the eighteenth and early nineteenth centuries. Later, when abolitionists began protesting the cruel slave trade, New Englanders openly condemned slavery but continued to build the fast ships that carried their cargoes of "black ivory."

Curiously, the rich businessmen, shipowners, and their families never saw the loads of human misery for which they were responsible. Ships left New England with respectable merchandise and returned with molasses. How they acquired it was something else.

Rum, misery, and molasses   Most American slave ships sailed from Bristol, Rhode Island, loaded with rum and such trade goods as cloth and weapons. Their departure looked innocent enough, since a ship's carpenter did not begin cutting planks and arranging for the human cargo until the trade goods had been offloaded. Their return with cargoes of molasses looked equally innocent.

The first land sighted was the Cape Verde Islands, 300 miles west of the African coast. There, ships refilled water casks, took on fresh food supplies, and gathered the latest news. Then it was off to the African coast along the Gulf of Guinea where trading posts, or "factories," as they were called, were set up. What was then called the Grain Coast is now the Republic of Liberia, the Ivory Coast is the Ivory Coast Republic, the Gold Coast is Ghana, and the Slave Coast is Togo.

Often there would be as many as eight or ten slave ships at a trading post at the same time; British, French, Portuguese, and others, along with the Yankees. Because of the dangerous surf along the coast, vessels anchored well offshore. Transportation and loading had to be done in small boats, maneuvered by skilled black tribesmen who were familiar with the treacherous surf.

When the ship anchored, her cargo was hauled out on deck and her carpenter installed the 'tween decks, which consisted of two sets of platformlike shelves along each side of the ship, halfway between the floor and the underside of the main deck. These shelves extended toward the middle of the vessel, with a space between them. When the floor was filled, more slaves were put on the shelves. The arrangement allowed each slave a space 5½ feet long, a little less than 3 feet high, and 16 inches wide.

Double iron leg shackles with padlocks were riveted to the floors and the platforms and, on deck, a high netting was stretched along the sides to prevent anyone from jumping overboard. A stout wooden barricade, with a gate that could be locked, was installed to shut off the quarterdeck and cabin at the after end from any attempt by slaves to take over the ship.

A sloop could carry up to 120 slaves below deck; larger ships, such as the Baltimore clipper *Napoleon*, carried 350—a load that yielded a profit of $100,000. It often took five or six months to collect that many people, including replacing those who died in the process, and bargain for their purchase. It was a tedious, dangerous, and loathsome life for the crew, who normally stayed aboard ship while their captain was ashore making his purchases. The weather was stifling hot and humid, the stench was almost unbearable, disease was common, and the men, with nothing much to do but wait, were restless.

At the palaver house   In West Africa, the word *palaver* meant talk or argument, and it was at the palaver houses that ship captains spent weeks bartering for the slaves that were kept in nearby stockades—or barracoons.

Before any deals were made, "merchandise" was inspected for age, strength, and ability to work and to survive the voyage. Most of the slaves were young, strong males, but females were included for the purpose of reproducing slaves at no extra cost to plantation-owners. Those suffering from contagious diseases were discarded because they might infect everyone aboard ship.

After they had been bought, the slaves were branded with a red-hot iron, chained together, and marched to the beach. The sight of the ocean and the roar of the surf terrified villagers from the interior; they thought they were going to be eaten alive by a huge monster. Some of them jumped overboard from the rowboats and were drowned or eaten by sharks.

Once aboard ship, they were stacked 'tween decks like logs, and shackled. As each one lay down, the padlock on the shackle was snapped shut so that one of his legs was held fast. Most of the New England slave ships were so small that their captains used "tight packs," which meant that the slaves were squeezed in, spoon-fashion. Those who died were dumped overboard and replaced at the next factory.

Usually, it was necessary to make several stops in order to get a full load. Stopping was a dangerous and hated chore. With land in sight, the slaves were apt to revolt. Sometimes, when that happened, an entire white crew was killed.

The Middle Passage   The Middle Passage was the name given to the equatorial route over which 15 to 20 million black Africans were transported into slavery in the Americas. Although slavers tried to make the fastest time possible to the West Indies, some trips lasted as long as three months. In clear weather, the slaves were taken on deck, where the men were shackled to the bulwarks and made to "dance"—forced to jump up and down for exercise.

Slaves were given a cupful of water each day and meager rations of food. Some were fed horse beans—big beans boiled to a pulp, then covered with a mixture of palm oil, flour, water, and red pepper. Those who tried to starve themselves to death had their mouths forced open so that food could be shoved down.

In bad weather, conditions were unbearable. Slaves suffocated or went insane; some were clubbed to death and dumped overboard; others managed to commit suicide by holding their breath.

The voyage itself was hazardous. There was always the danger of French privateers chasing down a slave ship. British and American warships were after them too. Approaching the West Indies there were not only dangerous reefs to contend with, but "wreckers" who set up lights along the shore to lure ships onto the rocks. In Barbados, a man named Sam Lord tied lights to the horns of the deer on his plantation to make ship captains think they were approaching the island's capital of Bridgetown. When a ship was wrecked, she was robbed. The magnificent mansion Sam Lord built with the proceeds of this practice has been restored and can be seen today.

At the height of the Triangular Trade, in the last half of the eighteenth century, American slavers liked to sell their cargoes in Barbados and Jamaica, because the British paid the highest prices. Sometimes they traded at Cuba to supply southern plantations. Smuggling slaves was a big business. Fast ships picked them up in the islands and ran into southern ports; as mentioned earlier, as many as 20,000 a year were first landed on Amelia Island before the final dash to the United States.

Abolishing the slave trade   Great Britain was the first to abolish the trade in slaves. British ships and business interests had been the worst offenders; British-owned castles, forts, and factories were strewn all along the coast of Guinea. In 1806 Parliament passed a law forbidding slave-trading by any British vessel. In 1808 the U.S. Congress passed a law prohibiting American vessels from trading in slaves. Unfortunately, this law was not enforced.

Although British naval squadrons were sent to patrol the coast of Guinea and capture slavers, the War of 1812 ended the stop and search of American vessels. The English negotiated treaties with Portugal, Spain, The Netherlands, Sweden, and France; all agreed to give up slave-trading and allow the British to search their vessels. The United States refused to sign the treaty. The result was that other nations' slavers would often hoist the Stars and Stripes when the Royal Navy was snooping around.

In 1819, the United States authorized anti-slave patrols off the slave ports in Africa and along the American coast. The following year, a federal law equated the carrying of slaves with piracy, making it punishable by death.

Finally, in 1842, the Webster-Ashburton Treaty between the United States and Britain settled certain boundary disputes and pledged U.S. cooperation with Britain in abolishing the slave trade. After that it became harder for American slavers to stay in business, but they kept at it, nevertheless. Shipbuilders turned out fast, sleek topsail schooners and brigs that could usually outsail naval cruisers burdened with guns, provisions, and stores.

Not only were the slavers fast, they were tricky too. On arrival off the African coast, they would discharge their light cargo along with the manacles they planned to use later. Then they would innocently cruise along the coast taking in local cloth, ivory, some gold dust, and other cargo. One way or another they would contrive to be searched by the Americans or the British in order to establish as fact that they were indeed lawful traders. When the timing was right, they would make a second sweep along the coast to pick up the slaves they had earlier arranged to buy. The fate of these slaves was the worst yet. Slavers facing a death penalty if they were caught, did not hesitate to dump their entire cargo overboard when a warship was in pursuit.

Between the years 1843 and 1847 there were never more than seven U.S. Navy ships patrolling the coast of Guinea; the British never had less than 12. American cruisers made a dent in the vicious traffic—but only a small one.

Last of the slavers   The slave market in the West Indies began to slacken, partly because importing slaves was forbidden but also because enough children had been born into slavery to satisfy the need for workers. The one exception was Spanish-held Cuba. Its expanding sugar-cane crops required more labor, and plantation-owners were willing to pay high prices for slaves. In 1847, an able-bodied male bought on the Gold Coast for $10 sold in Cuba for as much as $625. On the eve of the Civil War, slaves smuggled into the Southern states sold for $2,500 apiece.

The last big attempt to haul slaves was made in 1860 by Captain Nathaniel Gordon of Portland, Maine. At the mouth of the Congo River, he crammed the *Erie* with 890 slaves, including 106 women and 612 children, then sailed for the Middle Passage and Cuba. Seemingly out of nowhere, the U.S. Navy's steam sloop *Mohican* bore down on the *Erie* and captured her. The slaves were set free on the coast of Liberia, and the *Erie* was taken to New York where Captain Gordon was tried. His first trial ended in a "hung jury," so he was tried again. Captain Gordon continued to refuse to reveal the names of the owners of the *Erie*, and the trial became even more sensational as threatening mobs gathered. A detachment of Marines was sent to protect him; then some strychnine was smuggled into his jail cell. Gordon swallowed it, but the prison doctor managed to save his life so that he could be hanged instead.

From that time on, the slave trade dropped off to almost nothing.

CHAPTER 11
TRADE, TREATIES, AND EXPLORATION

In the first century or so after Colonial America put to sea, ships set out on long voyages with such poor charts and incomplete information that they were lucky to reach their destination without having to spend some time looking for it. Many islands in the Pacific were discovered purely by accident—a ship's captain sailing along where his chart showed only water would suddenly be startled by the lookout's cry of "Breakers ahead!"

As commerce grew and naval operations began to cover all the seas, it was necessary not only to chart the best routes to known ports and existing markets, but to seek out new routes and markets, if possible. Whalers did a lot of unofficial exploring while hunting whales; however, they were at sea to turn a profit, and obviously could not waste time just looking for new islands. As ships of the Navy were in public service, supported by the government, it was only logical for them to perform such a vital service as exploration. There was also a need for government protection of American merchant shipping on the trade routes of the world; this too was a job for the Navy.

In the 25 years preceding the Civil War, the peacetime Navy conducted at least 11 major exploring expeditions in various areas of the world. Funds for such endeavors were sometimes absurdly small, considering the vital and historic missions the men tried to accomplish. As a result, many of the expeditions were poorly equipped, and the men endured suffering and tragedy.

On previous page: The first U.S. mission to Japan met with success when the Emperor finally agreed to accept a letter from the President of the United States. The ceremony took place as pictured here by W. Heine, who accompanied Commodore Matthew C. Perry's party when it landed at the village of Kurihama on 14 July 1853. The first two Americans to step ashore were Commodore Franklin Buchanan and Marine Major Jacob Zeilin. The ships *Susquehanna* and *Mississippi* lie offshore. Courtesy: The Office of Naval History.

Most early voyages for charting, surveying, exploration, and discovery were made in slow sailing ships. Such ships were cheaper and in some ways simpler to maintain than steam-powered vessels, but they required fine seamanship, courage, and determination from the men who sailed them.

In the early 1820s, a former U.S. Army captain, John Cleves Symmes, propounded the theory that the earth was hollow, with openings at the north pole and the south pole through which ships could enter. Oddly enough, the hollow-earth theory had quite a respectable following, and the Secretary of the Navy gave approval for a three-ship expedition to sail inside. Fortunately, that plan was abandoned.

Wilkes' Exploring Expedition, 1838–1842

When plans for the exploration of the South Pacific and Antarctic were revised, the hollow-earth theory was dropped. Instead, the Antarctic, Pacific Ocean islands, and Oregon coast would be charted for the benefit of merchantmen, whalers, and men-of-war, and scientific investigations would be made.

In 1836 Congress approved the idea for a U.S. Exploring Expedition—the first scientific expedition ever fitted out by the U.S. government—and appropriated $300,000 for its use. It later came to be known as the Wilkes Expedition of 1838–1842.

For two years there was disagreement as to the organization and leadership of the expedition. Finally, in 1838, the command was offered to Lieutenant Charles Wilkes, head of the Navy's Depot of Charts and Instruments. He had a strong background in astronomy, meteorology, terrestrial magnetism, and hydrography and was considered especially qualified for the command because of his experience in surveying off the coast of New England. Wilkes had entered the Navy as a midshipman on 1 January 1818, and, as a lieutenant, was extremely junior for such a command. Chosen for second in command was Lieutenant William Hudson, two years senior to Wilkes. Secretary of the Navy Mahlon Dickerson ordered that the expedition was to be purely scientific and without any military character at all—if war broke out, it was to come home immediately.

Originally the expedition consisted of the flagship *Vincennes* and the *Peacock*, both sloops of war; the schooners *Porpoise* and *Flying Fish*; the ferryboat *Sea Gull*; and the supply ship *Relief*. None of these ships was equipped for heavy weather, nor were their hulls reinforced against the ice they were sure to encounter. Even their stores were inadequate—provisions for twelve months and fuel for seven. Similar expeditions fitted out by the British and Russians carried supplies for two to three years. When Wilkes' pitiful armada sailed from Hampton Roads, Virginia, on 18 August 1838, it was the worst-equipped polar expedition in history.

As soon as the expedition got under way the six civilian scientists began grumbling about not being allowed to notify anyone outside the Navy Department of discoveries they might make. Many of the 82 officers and 342 seamen developed an early dislike for their tactless, bad-tempered commander whose tight discipline aggravated his subordinates. Wilkes wrote in his journal that he felt like one "doomed to destruction."

Despite these problems, slow ships, leaks, and balky pumps, they arrived in Orange Harbor, Tierra del Fuego, in less than six months. There, Wilkes assigned various missions to his ships. The *Porpoise*, with himself on board, and the *Sea Gull* sailed for the eastern shore of Palmer Land, which they sighted, but were unable to land because of ice. Wilkes wrote: "I have rarely seen a finer sight. The sea was literally studded with these beautiful masses, some of them pure white, and others showing shades of opal, others emerald green, and occasionally here and there some would be black. . . ."

The decks of the ships were soon covered with ice; fog, mist, and fierce gales were constant. The men were suffering from scurvy and, although their cold-weather gear had been "purchased by the government at great expense, it was found to be entirely unworthy of service and inferior in every way to the samples exhibited." Both ships headed back to Orange Harbor. Before they managed to beat through the Magellan Strait, the *Sea Gull* disappeared— she probably capsized in a gale.

Charting the South Pacific islands   Wilkes then took his ships into the South Pacific where they followed different routes to explore and survey the Tuamotu Archipelago, the Society Islands, Samoa, the Fijis, the New Hebrides, and New Caledonia. The *Relief* was ordered to Hawaii, and Sydney, Australia, for provisions and then headed home. After a 19-month voyage, she arrived in New York on 28 March 1840.

The expedition spent seven months charting the South Pacific atolls and islands, then sailed for Sydney, Australia, to prepare for another Antarctic voyage. Wilkes wrote of the Australians' doubts about the wisdom of such a trip: "they inquired whether we had compartments in our ships to prevent them from sinking. How we intended to keep ourselves warm. What kind of antiscorbutic [preventative for scurvy] we were to use. And where were our great ice-saws?"

Wilkes agreed with them that it was unwise to attempt the trip, "but we had been ordered to go, and that was enough. . . ." The *Peacock*'s captain pointed out the deplorable condition of his ship, but it would have been impossible to continue the expedition without her. Wilkes wrote: "The necessity I felt of subjecting so many lives in so unworthy a ship caused me great anxiety during the whole cruise."

Discovering the Antarctic Continent   On the day after Christmas 1839 the four ships set sail from Sydney. They were soon scattered. On New Year's Day the *Flying Fish* lost sight of the others; the *Peacock* lost the *Vincennes* and the *Porpoise* on 3 January. On 15 January, the *Vincennes* first sighted Antarctic land and followed the ice barrier through the thick fog, storms, and pack ice, hour after hour, day after day. On 30 January, she entered a small indentation and observed black rocks on a snow-covered hill about a mile and a half from the ship. Wilkes recorded: "Antarctic Land discovered beyond cavil." Later he wrote that he "gave the land the name of the Antarctic Continent."

The next day 15 seamen were ill, but Wilkes was determined to go on so long as his ship was not totally disabled. As the *Vincennes* continued to push westward, evidence of land was seen every day. On 12 February, Wilkes climbed the mainmast to observe what appeared to be a snow-covered mountain range: "The . . . land clearly determines or settles the question of our having discovered the Antarctic Continent."

By the time the weather forced a return to Sydney, Wilkes had charted 1,500 miles of the Antarctic coast. The squadron somehow remained intact. The *Peacock* was ordered to make repairs and join the squadron at the Tonga, or Friendly, Islands. By 7 October 1840, the ships were all together at Honolulu.

Charting the Oregon Territory   After several months in Hawaii, the expedition set out to explore the Oregon Territory and map the Columbia River region. The Strait of Juan de Fuca, Puget Sound, and Hood Canal were carefully surveyed. Land parties, accompanied by men of the Hudson's Bay Company and Indians, mapped the area east of the Cascades and the Columbia River as far east as Walla Walla.

The *Peacock* was wrecked on a bar at the entrance to the Columbia River. The *Vincennes* and *Porpoise* sailed to her rescue and luckily no lives were lost. The place where the ship was wrecked is still called Peacock Spit.

Homecoming   In June 1842 the Wilkes expedition returned to New York after a voyage of nearly four years. It had sailed about 85,000 miles, surveyed some 280 islands, 800 miles of streams and coastline in the Oregon Territory, and 1,500 miles of the Antarctic coastal region. Hundreds of new species of fish, reptiles, and insects were brought back for study.

Expedition members who had hoped to receive a cordial welcome and commendatory words from the government were met with cold, insulting silence. President John Tyler was cool and indifferent, as was Secretary of the Navy Abel P. Upshur. Wilkes' claim to have discovered the Antarctic Continent was challenged by the British explorer, Captain Sir James Clark Ross, who said Wilkes was either incompetent or was lying. Ross claimed to have sailed over areas that Wilkes said were land.

Two disgruntled officers charged Wilkes with brutality because 127 men had deserted during the cruise. The charges led to court-martial proceedings. Wilkes was found not guilty, but received a letter of reprimand for ordering illegal punishment for seamen.

Over the next 30 years, the results of the expedition were published in nineteen volumes; those on hydrography and meteorology were written by Wilkes himself, who also wrote the *Narrative of the United States Exploring Expedition*, after Congress finally realized what a stupendous task had been accomplished and appropriated the necessary funds.

There is little doubt that Wilkes was a stern, even a savage, commander, but it was this same determination and inflexibility that made possible the very real accomplishments of his poorly equipped expedition. The best monument to Wilkes' determination and ability is the fact that a hundreds-of-miles-long sector of the Antarctic Continent, south from Australia, is now named Wilkes Land.

Exploring the Dead Sea and the River Jordan, 1847–1849

In 1837, the scientific world learned that the surface of the Dead Sea was below that of the Mediterranean. Ten years later, Lieutenant William F. Lynch led a naval expedition to find out just exactly what the difference was. In addition, he was to gather pertinent information about the commercial situation and potential of the area. The Secretary of State described the objective as being to "promote the cause of science, and advance the character of the naval service."

The expedition sailed in the USS *Supply*, which was transporting provisions to the Mediterranean Squadron. They were to disembark at Smyrna for their overland journey, then meet the ship at Beirut.

Careful preparations included the provision for the first time of "prefabricated" boats that could be knocked down for shipping and later reassembled, and four-wheeled carriages for hauling the boats. With Lynch were 10 seamen, "young, muscular Americans . . . of sober habits." All of them were well armed with "a blunderbuss, 14 carbines with long bayonets and 14 pistols, four revolving and ten with bowie-knife blades attached."

Their adventures were often hair-raising, as they traveled over country that had no roads and hauled boats across mountainous terrain, over narrow gorges, and wet and rocky ground. Besides Lynch, his officers, and the 10 seamen, the party consisted of some dragomen (guides), all on horseback, 29 camels to pull the carriages, about 15 mounted Arabs, and various camel-drivers.

On 10 April 1848 the expedition split up. One party set out to observe the country and collect specimens of plants, while the boat party, under Lynch, traveled down the River Jordan. The latter made a topographical sketch of the river and recorded its course, rapidity, color, depth, and tributaries, as well as the nature of the bank and the country through which it flowed. At selected points, Lynch also measured how far below the surface of the Mediterranean the Jordan was.

The expedition discovered that there were in the river at least 27 threatening rapids, "besides a great many of lesser magnitude," and that "between Lake Tiberias and the Dead Sea, the Jordan River wandered at least 200 miles in a straight line distance of 60 miles."

It was said that the Dead Sea Expedition's astronomical, meteorological, hydrographical, and other observations "became the foundation on which all subsequent knowledge of the river and its valley was built and until the 1930's remained the main source of technical information on both the Jordan and the Dead Sea." The total cost of the expedition was slightly more than $700.

Lieutenant Matthew Fontaine Maury, a Virginian and a Southern sympathizer, felt that a commercial development in Brazil would benefit the Southern states, and beginning in the late 1840s, he began pushing for a naval expedition to the Amazon.

Expedition to the Amazon, 1851–1852

An expedition was eventually organized. It was led by Maury's brother-in-law, Lieutenant William Lewis Herndon, assisted by Passed Midshipman Lardner Gibbon. They reached Lima, Peru, on 20 January 1851. Herndon had orders to travel from Peru to the Brazilian seacoast by way of the Amazon, exploring the great river from its source to its mouth. He was to gather information "with regard to the navigability of its streams; to the number and condition, both industrial and social, of its inhabitants, their trade and products; its climate, soil, and production; but also to its capacities for cultivation, and to the . . . undeveloped commercial resources. . . ." He was also to examine the silver mines of Peru and Bolivia.

The Navy agent at Lima furnished funds "not to exceed $5,000 which were to be used only for *necessary* expenses." In the party that left Lima on 21 May 1851 to begin the long, arduous journey were an interpreter, a master's mate, a muleteer, and an Indian guide.

On 4 December 1851, the explorers reached the Brazilian frontier. By then, most of their live specimens had eaten or otherwise killed one another, jumped overboard and swum ashore, or managed to choke themselves to death.

To get around a long-standing law forbidding foreign vessels to navigate Brazilian waters, the local Brazilian commandant loaned the explorers his boat, and they went on their way. On 11 April 1852, after nearly a year of exploring, Herndon arrived in Pará, Brazil.

In 1857, Herndon, on leave of absence from the Navy and in command of a mail steamer, the *Central America*, was lost along with 426 others when his ship went down in a storm off Cape Hatteras. In his memory, the Herndon Monument was later placed on the grounds of the U.S. Naval Academy. A small historical marker on Cape Hatteras marks the spot where the *Central America* sank.

When Herndon returned from the Amazon expedition to the States, Gibbon stayed behind and continued his extensive exploration of Bolivia. He was the first white man to descend the Madeira River from its source to the Amazon and to give a full report on the region. His only monument is Volume 2 of *Exploration of the Valley of the Amazon*, a report that so impressed a young man named Samuel Clemens that he became a steamboat pilot and a writer, better known as Mark Twain.

Expedition to the Southern Hemisphere, 1849–1852
In August 1849 James M. Gilliss, a naval lieutenant, left New York City, bound for Valparaiso, Chile, with three assistants: Passed Midshipmen Archibald Macrae and Henry C. Hunter, and a captain's clerk, Edmond Revel Smith. Their objective was to erect the buildings necessary to conduct a series of observations of Mars and Venus.

Gilliss had an excellent scientific background. He was responsible for establishing in 1844 the Naval Observatory in Washington, D.C., of which he later became superintendent. His *Astronomical Observations made at the Naval Observatory* was the first such document to be published in the United States.

Convincing the authorities of the importance of the venture to South America was complicated and often frustrating. Certainly $5,000 was not enough money for the necessary equipment, so Gilliss sought private financing. He wrote to instrument-makers, merchants, and scientists in America and England. The British volunteered to furnish magnetic instruments and some of the meteorological equipment. Eventually, Congress appropriated $6,400 to pay for instruments, including an equatorial telescope.

A temporary observatory was set up near Santiago de Chile, where, in addition to making astronomical observations, Gilliss gave practical instruction in astronomy to three young Chilean students. Because he was sure government funds would not cover such expenses, he spent $650 of his own money to enable his staff to collect birds, mammals, fish, reptiles, shells, fossils, minerals, botanical specimens, and artifacts.

Gilliss helped establish a long and fruitful exchange of materials and specimens between the Smithsonian Institution and institutions in Chile, and persuaded the director of the National Agricultural School in Chile to send a collection of 133 plants, including strawberry seeds, to Washington.

Later, Gilliss found that the series of observations supposed to have been made in Washington in conjunction with his work in the Southern Hemisphere had, in fact, not been made. From this point of view, the expedition was a failure. However, the independent astronomical and other scientific observations made by the expedition were of importance, and its natural history collections were of lasting value.

The paddle-wheel steamer USS *Water Witch* departed Baltimore on 19 January 1853 for South America under the command of Lieutenant Thomas J. Page, whose mission was to "explore and survey the river La Plata and its tributaries." The 150-foot-long ship carried 11 officers and engineers, an assistant surgeon, and 50 men.

Exploring the River La Plata, 1853–1856

The *Water Witch* carried a "Daguerrean apparatus," the camera invented by Daguerre in 1839, as well as books, weapons, camping equipment, instruments, and materials for preserving natural history specimens. Page sent ahead to Paraguay materials for building a small steamer capable of navigating shallow waters. He also sent two metal lifeboats for exploring small streams.

At all times, great tact and diplomacy were required of the Americans because of the friction between Brazil, Argentina, and Paraguay.

Page's expedition was extremely successful. His reports of the geographical features and economic resources of the region were superior to those of any nineteenth-century expedition to South America. The public gained knowledge of regions that had previously been little known; travel was made easier and safer. Charts of La Plata and its tributaries were of great help to ship captains. The expedition produced the best natural history collections of that region, improved relations with the Argentine Confederation, and opened La Plata and its tributaries to commercial shipping.

In 1853, Commodore Matthew Calbraith Perry set forth on America's first major diplomatic overseas venture. His mission was to open up Japan, a country that had been closed to the rest of the world for centuries.

Commodore Perry's mission to Japan, 1853

It was a logical move for America to make, but a daring step that would require the utmost skill, tact, and toughness. The rewards for success could be phenomenal; trade with China was already worth $19 million a year. The trade potential with Japan was estimated at $200 million. And certainly trade with Japan fitted in with America's land expansion westward and on across the Pacific.

It was a period when politicians happily mixed religion with national and commercial goals. "God's will," entered into many a debate, as did "divine task," "immortal mission," and "teaching old nations a new civilization." Commerce and the Gospel went hand-in-hand when it was learned that there was coal in Japan. Secretary of State Daniel Webster referred to "a gift of Providence, deposited by the Creator of all things in the depths of the Japanese islands for the benefit of the human family."

Yankee whalers had been sailing western Pacific waters since 1820, but they had been less than welcome in Japan. Sailors unlucky enough to be wrecked along the treacherous shore were imprisoned and otherwise mistreated. If bases and shelters close to the whaling grounds could be provided, American castaways would be assured humane treatment.

But aside from human kindness, profitable commerce, and religious zeal, there was a real need for coaling stations in Japan. The new steam frigates burned enormous amounts of coal, all of which had to be transported from the United States. Coaling stations in Japan, particularly if coal could be mined there, would be a boon to America's globe-circling fleet.

Knocking on the closed door   Earlier American efforts to make friends with Japan had all failed. The Boston sloop *Lady Washington* and the *Grace* of New York were met with rebuffs in 1791, as were their successors. In 1837, Charles King in the *Morrison* should have been greeted with friendliness when he tried to land with seven Japanese sailors rescued at sea, along with gifts and American trade goods such as textiles and tools. After two futile attempts, he was forced to leave with everybody and everything still aboard ship.

In 1844, the American whaler *Manhattan* anchored at Edo (Tokyo). She, too, had a group of Japanese castaways. Captain Mercator Cooper requested, but was denied, permission to land. Small boats surrounded the *Manhattan*, attached lines to her, and pulled her out to sea.

But the Americans still had hope. In June 1845, Alexander Everett was sent to China to replace Caleb Cushing as U.S. Commissioner. He was given additional authority to negotiate a treaty with Japan. En route, aboard the *Vincennes*, Everett became ill and left the ship at Rio de Janeiro, so Commodore James Biddle continued the mission. He concluded the Treaty of Wanghia with the Chinese on 31 December 1845, then the following April sailed for Tokyo Bay with the *Columbus* and the *Vincennes*. After writing out his proposals, he boarded a Japanese patrol boat to receive the official reply.

Commodore Biddle was no ordinary merchant skipper but a duly authorized representative of the U.S. government; his ships belonged to the U.S. Navy. The circumstances being what they were, he was anxious not to provoke ill will, so when a Japanese guard pushed him, he decided not to press the matter by demanding that the offender be punished. He was not aware that this caused him to "lose face"—a major mistake in the Orient. His proposals were rejected and both his ships were unceremoniously towed out to sea. However, his insight and recommendations paved the way for Perry's trip eight years later.

More humiliation came in 1849 when the sloop of war *Preble* arrived in Japanese waters to demand the release of some American sailors. After much blustering and threatening, the prisoners were released but the *Preble* was forced to leave promptly.

Japan's isolation   No one was allowed to leave or enter Japan. The Japanese built no ships large enough to be used on the open sea. Anyone who dared leave would be put to death if he returned.

In 1542, three Portuguese were shipwrecked on the Japanese coast. They were followed by the usual influx of traders and Portuguese Jesuits. In 1549 the Spanish-born Jesuit, Francis Xavier, was cordially greeted by the Japanese and allowed to teach and establish a seminary there. By 1582 there were 150,000 Christians. Eventually it was decreed that all missionaries should leave because they were undermining the godhood of the emperor. In 1614, all foreign priests, Jesuits, Franciscans, Dominicans, and Augustinians were rounded up and shipped to Macao, where they could board ships bound for their homes. In Japan, the converts were hunted down and slaughtered. Tens of thousands of them lost their lives. After 1637, there were no foreigners left in Japan and for 215 years, it stayed that way.

Only the Dutch were allowed to stay on the tiny island of Deshima in the harbor of Nagasaki, the only western foothold in Japan.

Once a year, a Dutch envoy was given a so-called audience at the emperor's palace. He had to crawl into the audience chamber on his hands and knees, bow his forehead to the ground, present his gifts, then crawl out backwards, never looking up or saying a word.

Sometimes a book from the outside world would get through. Japanese students were greatly interested in what was happening in the West. They knew, for instance, about the American Revolution and drew sketches of their versions of various world events.

Three Russian expeditions had approached Japan—in 1792, 1804, and 1811. A British warship sailed into the harbor at Nagasaki in 1808 and other British ships tried to establish trade and to survey the coastal areas. The French were there in 1846. But none of these efforts succeeded in penetrating Japan's self-imposed isolation. The Japanese authorities decreed in 1825 that local authorities were to destroy any foreign ship that attempted to anchor. Any sailors coming ashore were to be arrested or killed.

Perry sails for Japan Matthew Perry was an ideal choice for the job of negotiating with Japan. As the younger brother of Oliver Hazard Perry, the naval hero of the War of 1812, he was conscious of his great responsibility in representing his country. A naval veteran with 44 years of service, he had a reputation for leadership and was an outspoken advocate of rigid training. One of his officers described him as "bluff, positive and stern on duty, and a terror to the ignorant and lazy. But the faithful ones who performed their duties . . . held him in the highest estimation."

In November 1852, Perry's squadron sailed from the United States. It consisted of the steam frigates *Mississippi*, the flagship, *Susquehanna*, and *Powhatan*; the corvette *Macedonian*; the three sloops *Saratoga*, *Plymouth*, and *Vandalia*; and the three storeships *Southampton*, *Supply*, and *Lexington*.

The ships assembled at Hong Kong and moved to Okinawa in the spring of 1853. From there on 2 July, the *Susquehanna*, *Mississippi*, *Plymouth*, and *Saratoga*, sailed for Japan, using Dutch charts for which Perry had paid $30,000.

On 8 July they anchored off the entrance to Tokyo Bay, just 27 miles from Tokyo. Perry then put into practice all the lessons he had learned from his studies of earlier voyages and put on a show of aloofness that rivaled even that of Japan's high authorities. He ordered away the Japanese guard boats and refused to deal personally with anyone whose rank was lower than his own. His officers made it quite clear that the letter from the American president would be delivered only to Japan's highest official.

Finally, Perry's demand for an audience with the Japanese royal commissioners was accepted. On 14 July, amid great ceremony, he landed with 400 officers, seamen, and Marines. Perry announced he would leave his request for a treaty in the hands of the commissioners and return for an answer in the spring. Then he sailed for Okinawa.

When Perry heard that, at the end of November, a French frigate at Macao had suddenly put to sea under sealed orders and a Russian admiral with a fleet of four vessels had appeared at Nagasaki, he became suspicious. He had no intention of letting the French or the Russians beat him in the race for Japan's trade. In February, he set out for Tokyo Bay with the steamers *Susquehanna*, *Powhatan*, *Mississippi*, and sail-ships *Madeconian*, *Lexington*, *Vandalia*, *Southampton*, and *Saratoga*. He had 120 guns and 1,800 men.

This time Perry insisted the ceremonies take place closer to Tokyo. When the Japanese protested, he waged a war of nerves by ordering his ships to move closer to the capital in slow stages. The Japanese finally consented to the meeting and on 8 March Perry went ashore with an escort of 500 men, all fully armed.

On Monday, 13 March, gifts from the United States were taken ashore for presentation to the Japanese. They were a cross section of American products—copies of John James Audubon's drawings of American birds, Noah Webster's American dictionaries, maps of North America and the individual states, garden seeds and tools, perfumes, Irish potatoes, champagnes, and whiskies.

The two most exciting gifts were a mile-long telegraph system and a quarter-size steam train—complete with engine, tender, one car, and 370 feet of track. The railroad was run in a circle. The car was so small that it could hardly carry a six-year-old child, but the Japanese were not to be cheated out of a ride, and "as they were unable to reduce themselves to the capacity inside the carriage, they betook themselves to the roof. It was a spectacle not a little ludicrous to behold a dignified mandarin whirling around the circular road . . . with his loose robes flying in the wind."

The negotiations lasted three weeks, and on 31 March 1854 the Treaty of Kanagawa was signed. By its terms, two ports, Hakodate and Shimoda, were opened to American ships to serve as trading centers and coaling stations; American castaways were guaranteed kind treatment, American consular agents were permitted to live in one of the ports, and the United States was promised rights equal to those granted other nations.

When it became known that Perry's expedition had been successful, newspapers and periodicals were filled with stories and praise of America's accomplishments. Perry was honored at social functions, including a state dinner in Washington, and Congress granted him a bonus of $20,000. He was not able to enjoy his honors for long because his health was failing; he died on 4 March 1858. By that time nine citizens had visited Japan under the protection of the treaty he had made. The first American consul, Townsend Harris, negotiated a commercial treaty which was the basis for Japanese-American relations until World War II.

Expeditions to the Isthmus of Darien, 1854–1857

On 17 January 1854, Lieutenant Isaac Strain, aboard the sloop of war *Cyane*, arrived on the Atlantic side of the Isthmus of Darien (now the Isthmus of Panama). His mission was to explore the area and find the best possible canal route for interoceanic shipping. With him were 12 officers and 13 seamen. They had provisions for ten days: blankets, clothing, arms and ammunition, food, and toilet articles. The Indians who came aboard ship were not friendly but did permit the group to travel through their country.

Strain's expedition was the result of the formation of the Atlantic and Pacific Junction Company, which planned to build a sea-level canal at a cost of $60 million. Strain's enthusiasm for his own venture was based partly on the reports of Edward Cullen, an Irish doctor, who in 1850 said he had found a gap no more than 150 feet above sea level.

The British were the first to send an exploring party. They stationed the brig *Espiegle* and the schooner *Scorpion* on the Atlantic side, and the steam sloop *Virago* on the Pacific side, for supply and support. On 19 December 1853, a group from the *Virago* set out on foot to cross the Isthmus. It took them fifteen days to cover 26 miles of jungle. At this point, the commander divided his party up, leaving four seamen to guard the camp, while the others tried to get through to the Atlantic side. When the latter, having been forced to turn back, returned to the camp they found the seamen—dead. They were probably killed by Indians.

Strain and his party, unaware of the British tragedy, were completely confident, as they set out with their ten days' supplies. They soon got lost and were wandering aimlessly. Insects and mosquitoes attacked them and hostile Indians were a constant threat. Their food ran out; they ate iguanas, hawks, cranes, a few "turkeys," bananas, palmetto leaves, and seeds from the trees. While they had the strength, they sang to keep up their spirits. Strain, who went on ahead in search of provisions, eventually reached a station run by the Atlantic and Pacific Junction Company, where arrangements were made for a rescue party from the *Virago*, to be sent in to save his men.

As a result of Strain's terrible experiences and of several deaths in the party, it was reported that the canal could not be built in the area he had explored. Sixty years after Lieutenant Strain landed in Darien, a canal was opened—in Panama (*see* Chapter 14).

Exploring Liberia, 1852–1853

On 13 November 1852, William F. Lynch, who, in the late 1840s, had led the naval expedition to the Jordan River, sailed from New York aboard a merchantman bound for Liberia, the African colony founded in 1822 by Negro freedmen from the United States. In 1839, they had united to form the Commonwealth of Liberia, which in 1847 became an independent republic, the first in Africa. Captain Lynch's mission was to find another area that could be settled by former black slaves.

At the capital city of Monrovia (named for President James Monroe), Lynch began his exploration of the St. Paul River. Traveling in a canoe manned by natives, he made careful notes along the way. From time to time he landed to explore villages and study the people, their dwellings, and their methods of farming. Part of the journey was through the dense forest, inhabited by elephants and other wild animals. Probably Lynch's most interesting and important contributions were his discussions of the people and the African way of life.

Captain Lynch had many harrowing adventures, particularly since the white man was justifiably considered an enemy in those parts. He recommended that future exploring parties should land at Monrovia, but keep contact with the "seashore." For establishing a colony, he advised that a "party should consist of as few whites as possible: the commander; an officer to take his place, should he perish; a physician who should also be a naturalist; and some 12 to 15 colonists."

Officially, he recommended that commercial treaties be drawn up with the principal independent tribes along the coast. Steamers, he said, should replace the sailing ships of the African Squadron. The recommendations he made were shelved when the Civil War broke out.

In May 1845 a seventh British expedition, this one under the command of Sir John Franklin, set out to search for the Northwest Passage to the Indies. It was not known at the time that no such passage existed in North America.

Arctic exploration, 1850–1855

Franklin's ships—HMS *Erebus* and HMS *Terror*—were caught in the ice off King William Island where, on 11 June 1847, Franklin died. The ships, which had been provisioned for three years, waited another year. Then all hands abandoned their ships and marched south, hoping to get to a Hudson's Bay Company post. Every one of the 105 men died before reaching safety.

Three British expeditions searched in vain for the lost explorers. Lady Jane Franklin wrote to President Zachary Taylor of the United States, pleading for help in finding her lost husband. In 1850, a wealthy New York merchant, Henry Grinnell, financed a search expedition with two ships, the brigs *Advance* and *Rescue*. Lieutenant Edwin J. De Haven was designated commander of the expedition.

The mission had a scientific as well as a humane aspect. While looking for the lost explorers, the Americans were to chart, take soundings, collect natural history specimens, and observe arctic conditions. In the party was Dr. Elisha Kent Kane, who proved to be an ardent enthusiast of the area. The voyage lasted 16 months. Sir John Franklin was not found, but De Haven's geographical findings were published by the Naval Observatory; short scientific papers dealing with botanical specimens were also published.

In May 1853, with help from private contributors, Dr. Kane went on a more extensive exploratory voyage. His observations about Eskimo life and conditions on the polar sea were of great importance. Most of the work done by that expedition was conducted with the help of the Navy.

Between 1855 and the late 1870s, the Arctic was explored, with minor help from the Navy, by Dr. Isaac Israel Hayes, the surgeon of the Kane expedition, Charles Francis Hall, and Lieutenant George Washington De Long.

North Pacific,
Bering Strait, and
China Seas,
1852–1863

Just before the Civil War, the Navy sent a four-year expedition to survey the western Pacific, all the way from Australia to the Bering Strait. Congress appropriated $125,000 for the enormous task of "survey and reconnaissance for naval and commercial purposes, of such parts of Behrings Straits, of the North Pacific Ocean and of the China Seas, as are frequented by American whaleships and by trading vessels in their routes between the United States and China." Scientific work was to be carried on, and arrangements were made to have specimens carried by the Navy directly to the Smithsonian Institution.

A squadron consisting of the sloop of war *Vincennes* (flagship), the schooners *Porpoise* and *Fenimore Cooper*, the steamer *John Hancock*, and the storeship *John P. Kennedy* was placed under the command of Commander Cadwalader Ringgold, who was later replaced by Lieutenant John Rodgers.

Civilian scientists were appointed as naturalists at $1,000 per year and "one ration per day. . . ." An artist was hired to take charge of the photographic apparatus for $800 a year. Two assistant draftsmen, and one maker and repairer of mathematical instruments went aboard at $500 per year. To help with the astronomical work, a Harvard graduate was appointed at $800 per year. There were also a bandmaster and four musicians on the voyage because it was reasoned that a naval band was important for morale and for ceremony abroad.

On 11 June 1853, the squadron sailed from Hampton Roads, Virginia. At the Cape of Good Hope, they split up, with three ships heading for Batavia, and the *Vincennes* and *Porpoise* crossing the Indian Ocean, rounding the tip of Australia, to the Caroline Islands and Guam and, finally, to Hong Kong.

The ships examined the China coast, sailed to Formosa, Japan, and Okinawa, then headed north for the Bering Strait. They charted, studied, took soundings and collected specimens everywhere they went.

From the standpoint of shipping and commerce, the expedition had extremely valuable results. Many navigational hazards were accurately charted; information was gathered about the winds, currents, and depths of the world's oceans and shorelines. The scientific achievements were considered highly significant. Many new specimens were sent to the Smithsonian Institution for study.

Naval exploration has, of course, continued. The most unusual specimens delivered to the Smithsonian Institution in the past hundred years were some small stones picked up by a naval officer in July 1969, when he became the first man on the moon.

CHAPTER 12
THE CIVIL WAR

In the presidential election of November 1860, the Republican Party nominated Abraham Lincoln on a platform opposing further slavery in the territories. The Democrats split on the question of slavery, after they had failed to get Jefferson Davis nominated for president. Lincoln received only 26,000 votes in all the Southern states, and he actually received about 1,000,000 fewer popular votes than the other three candidates combined. But the popular votes were so distributed among the states that he won a majority of the electoral votes.

On 8 February 1861 the Confederate States of America were formed, and the next day Jefferson Davis was elected president. The first shots of the war had already been fired: on 9 January 1861 the steamer *Star of the West*, chartered to carry supplies to Union troops at Fort Sumter, in Charleston, South Carolina, was fired on as she entered the harbor.

Abraham Lincoln was inaugurated as the sixteenth president of the United States on 4 March 1861. In his inaugural speech he said: "I shall take care, as the Constitution itself expressly enjoins upon me, that the laws of the Union be faithfully executed in all the States. . . ." He had three choices: let the Southern states go, peacefully; compromise with them; or fight them to preserve the Union. To Lincoln, the preservation of the Union was most important, and his chief aim was to keep it intact; he had no desire either to save or destroy the practice of slavery. In August 1862, he told Horace Greeley that if the Union could be saved without freeing any slaves, he would make that choice; if it was necessary

On previous page: This little wooden paddle boat, the *Thomas Freeborn*, fired the first shots by the Navy in the Civil War, using the muzzle-loading bow gun shown here. The action, against Confederate shore batteries, took place at Aquia Creek, Virginia, on the Potomac River, below Washington. Note the rough wooden wheels on the gun carriage and the ship's mascot. Courtesy: The Office of Naval History.

to free all slaves to save the Union, he would do that; and if the Union could be saved by freeing some slaves and leaving others alone, he would do that.

The Civil War began because conflicting interests between the slave and free states could no longer be settled peacefully. For several reasons, the Northern states had developed an industrial economy, while the Southern states had developed an agricultural economy, based on plantations.

In the north there were numerous fast-flowing rivers on which the early settlers built water mills. Water power served to grind meal, saw wood, and run spinning mills. Coal and iron-ore deposits were discovered and mined, making possible the development of steam power and the machines that resulted in an industrial economy.

South of the Potomac River, the country east of the Appalachians rolled seaward across meadow lands and then turned into flat coastal plains. Much of the land was filled with marshes and swamps. Generally, the South was suitable only for agriculture. Tobacco was the first crop, followed by rice, indigo, and cotton. All such crops had to be cultivated and harvested by hand. To grow enough of any crop to make a profit, a planter needed a large amount of land and plenty of cheap labor. The problem of finding cheap labor was solved in 1619 when a Dutch ship came in to Virginia with a load of Africans to be sold as slaves.

By 1790, there were nearly 700,000 slaves in the United States. Cotton was by then the chief crop in the Southern states—3,000 bales were exported that year. Until 1793, when Eli Whitney invented the cotton gin, a mechanical device for removing the seeds from the cotton fiber, a man could clean about 10 pounds of cotton a month—it took two years to produce one 500-pound bale. The hand-cranked cotton gin made it possible for a man to clean a bale of cotton in ten days. The sudden economic growth of the South— and its great reliance on slave labor—are indicated by these figures: in 1820 the South produced 335,000 bales of cotton, and held 1,538,022 slaves; in 1840 cotton production was up to 1,348,000 bales, and the slave population had reached 2,487,355; in 1860, cotton production reached 3,841,000 bales, and there were 3,953,760 slaves.

Not all Southerners were slaveholders. Of the more than 8,000,000 whites in the Southern states in 1860, less than 400,000 owned slaves.

One of the burning issues over slavery was whether or not, as new territories and states were admitted to the Union, they were to be allowed to continue the practice of slavery. Some states formed after the Louisiana Purchase—Louisiana, Mississippi, Missouri, and Alabama—came into the Union as slave states. But Ohio, Indiana, and Illinois came in as free states.

After the war with Mexico, there was more argument over

slavery in the newly acquired territory, as well as in California, which came in as a free state. Later there was a bitter struggle over slavery in the Kansas Territory. Federal troops were sent in to preserve order, and Kansas was finally admitted as a free state.

Four of the slave states, Delaware, Maryland, Kentucky, and Missouri, remained in the Union. After the surrender of Fort Sumter, the states of Arkansas, Tennessee, and North Carolina left the Union. Virginia was split—its western counties were so opposed to leaving the Union that they left Virginia and came back into the Union as West Virginia. Although Maryland and Kentucky were officially loyal, their people were so divided that about as many men from those states fought on one side as fought on the other. In fact, the Civil War has been called the "brothers war" because in many cases men from the same family fought on opposite sides.

In April Confederate forces seized federal property in the South and demanded the evacuation of Fort Sumter. When the Union commander refused, Confederates bombarded the fort on 12 and 13 April. On 15 April President Lincoln called for 75,000 volunteers to serve for three months. He was optimistic. The war went on for nearly four years. Federal and Confederate armies fought in six major battles and perhaps fifty lesser actions. Yet, despite the fact that the land battles of that war are usually given the most attention in history books, the Civil War was in many ways a naval war, and one of the greatest naval wars ever fought.

Preparation for war

As the United States moved toward civil war, the U.S. Army had about 16,000 regulars in uniform. General Winfield Scott told Lincoln he would need 300,000 men and three years to subdue the Confederacy.

The Union Army was, for the most part, volunteer state militiamen. Some state units were more or less semi-social groups with fancy uniforms and not too many guns. Anyone who could talk the governor of his state into issuing a commission could raise his own regiment of volunteers. Many boys no older than fifteen enlisted; probably more than half of all the men on both sides were under twenty-one years of age.

When the war began, the entire United States had a population of about 31 million people. Before it ended, the Union had over 2,606,000 volunteers and militiamen in uniform. This included more than 200,000 black soldiers. In the Navy, almost every third man was black.

The Confederates started raising an army of 100,000 men in March of 1861. Eventually, the total Confederate Army numbered about 1,000,000 men, but because of sickness and wounds, probably no more than 700,000 were effective at any one time.

Many officers in the Southern army, as in the Southern navy, were professionals who had been trained in the north and "went South" when their states left the Union. Southern soldiers were considered better marksmen than their northern opponents because most of them were used to hunting. Many northern soldiers came from factories and had never handled a rifle before, but better training in the northern armies paid off. Discipline in both armies was sometimes lax; a private who had known his colonel on a first-name basis before the war was not always convinced that his colonel knew any more about fighting than he did. Military duties were taken lightly and, when opposing armies were not actually fighting, men might be out between the lines, talking and making friendly exchanges. Southern soldiers had plenty of tobacco but not much coffee, while northern soldiers had coffee but no tobacco.

There were no standard weapons in either army. Union soldiers used over 80 different types of rifles, all muzzle-loaders. The best of them could fire no more than three shots a minute and were ineffective beyond 800 yards. Breech-loading rifles were available by that time, but senior officers objected to them. The artillery used bronze or cast-iron cannons of many kinds. Confederate troops used whatever they could get their hands on, imports from Europe or loot from Union forces. All the gunpowder used by both sides produced thick smoke, so that as soon as a battle got hot no one on either side had a very good idea of what was happening.

Naval operations

Because most accounts of the Civil War stress the great land battles, such as Bull Run, Antietam, and Gettysburg, it is easy to overlook the fact that the war was an outstanding example of the use of sea power. There were no great fleet engagements, and very few ship-to-ship battles. Yet, without a navy and the exercise of sea command, the Union could have lost the war.

One of the most important naval aspects of the war was the use of the Union Navy to discourage foreign intervention. England, especially, had a vast shipping business and her extensive cotton-spinning industry depended on imports from the South. The English had considerable reason for being sympathetic to the Southern cause, and if the Royal Navy had come to the support of the Confederacy, things might have been different. The Union Navy established a blockade and maintained it against all efforts by neutral nations to evade it on one legal technicality or another.

The Union Navy also exercised the principle of command of the sea by capturing, with the assistance of the Army in some cases, many Southern strongholds and ports. Once a port was captured, the blockading ships could be diverted to other tasks, incoming supplies to the South were cut off, and the place became a base for Union forces.

Union naval forces also served in the land campaign to divide the South. From the beginning of the war, one of their primary objectives was control of the Mississippi River system because it would cut off Arkansas, Texas, and most of Louisiana, the big food-producing states, from the rest of the South. Army troops could not assault heavy fortifications unaided, and in some cases they needed water transport to move them rapidly to front lines. The answer was combined operations—Army and Navy—and in some cases, amphibious operations. The campaigns for control of the rivers were staged by gunboats going down to Memphis, and seagoing forces coming in from the Gulf of Mexico to fight past New Orleans, Port Hudson, and Vicksburg. Army troops marched to attack some forts, and were moved by river boats to attack others.

The great naval effort of the Confederate Navy was to make attacks on Union commerce. This commerce-raiding campaign did not require large forces; it was a hit-and-run operation, the kind of tactic effectively used by a smaller, weaker power in cutting off supplies to a larger power.

Cotton was the base of the economy of the South. Southern leaders were confident that England and France would come to their aid because those nations needed cotton to keep their spinning mills running. The South even delayed shipping out the 1860 cotton crop, hoping to force England to come into the conflict on its side. It seemed impossible that the Union would be able completely to blockade the southern coast, 3,500 miles long, with eight major ports and many small harbors.

Yet, Gideon Welles, who replaced Isaac Toucey as Secretary of the Navy on 7 March 1861, had an effective blockade working within a few months. This was an amazing feat. There were only three ships suitable for blockade duty in northern ports when the war began, and many of the Navy's best officers—more than 250 of them—resigned to join the Confederate Navy. The Union Navy began buying or leasing almost anything that floated, including ferryboats, so long as it could carry a gun. In nine months, the Navy bought 136 ships, constructed 52, and repaired and recommissioned another 76. Finding crews for so many new vessels was a problem; in a year some 14,000 enlisted men and 1,000 officers joined the Navy. Many of them came out of merchant sailing ships and were not experienced in handling steam engines. At least once, a ship came into port stern-first because her engineers had stopped the engines and then could not figure out how to get them going ahead again.

Not all the new ships were seagoing types. Much of the Civil War fleet was a "shallow-water navy." Water in the rivers was in some places only six feet deep. A good deal of Yankee ingenuity went into the ships used on rivers, and it produced a weird fleet. The "Pook turtles" were ugly flat-topped things sometimes called "90-day gunboats" because the contract for them called for them to be completed in 90 days. Designed by Samuel M. Pook and built under the direction of James B. Eads, they were 175 feet long, weighed about 500 tons, and were driven by two high-pressure steam engines. By careful planning and simplified construction, Eads was able to launch the first one in 48 days. The Pook turtles could not make much speed upstream against the mighty Mississippi, but that did not matter—their mission was to go downstream and fight the Confederates.

Some river gunboats were side-wheelers, some were stern-wheelers—the water was not always deep enough for boats with propellers. The rivers were so narrow in some places that boats could not turn around, so the Union Navy used double-enders—boats with a pilot house at each end. It didn't really matter whether they were going or coming; they worked the same either way.

When iron plate could be obtained for armor, the boats were called ironclads. When the iron plates were very thin, they were called "tinclads." If no iron could be obtained, heavy oak timbers were used all around—boats so protected were "timberclads." Eventually someone discovered that bales of cotton stopped a cannonball fairly well, so the Navy used boats whose main decks were completely walled in with bales of cotton. These were called "cottonclads."

Three Union blockading squadrons were organized: one to operate in the Atlantic, one in the Gulf of Mexico, and a third to protect merchant ships from Southern privateers and commerce-raiders. In 1860, 6,000 ships arrived in Southern ports. After the blockade had been in effect for a year, only 800 got in. Southern imports of such critical materials as guns, ammunition, iron, and steel were almost completely stopped, and the export of cotton was seriously reduced. Blockade-running became a big business, much of it being done by British ships and officers. Fast ships sailed from Bermuda, Havana, and Nassau so as to reach the Southern coasts at night in the hope of being able to slip through the blockade. They carried guns, ammunition, and essential drugs, as well as such expensive luxuries as perfume, silk, wine, coffee, tea, and the latest hats and dresses from Paris. The importance of the blockade-runners lay not only in the vital supplies that they brought in, but in enabling the South to have its cotton carried to foreign markets. The freight rate varied from $300 to $1,000 a ton. By 1864, nearly 100 fast steamers were operating as blockade-runners. Lucky ones could clear $1,000,000 a year—until they were caught or were lost by running aground. During the war the Union Navy captured nearly 300 steamers and about 1,100 smaller ships.

But as the blockade reduced the supply of many items and Confederate money lost its value, prices in the South rose. Before the war ended, shoes cost up to $150 a pair and flour went for $1,000 a barrel. Eventually, the export of cotton was so reduced that Southern finances were ruined. Approximately $1,000,000,000 worth of banking capital was wiped out.

Commerce-raiders   In an effort to weaken the blockade of their ports, the Confederates sent out fast steamships to raid Northern shipping. It was hoped that this action would force the Union Navy to withdraw ships from the blockading squadrons to protect oceangoing commerce, and that the Confederacy would benefit by capturing cargoes or selling captured ships. About a dozen fast steamships were used as commerce-raiders: some of them were purchased abroad and some were specially built abroad. They captured numerous Union ships, but found there was little profit in the business. The blockade prevented them from bringing captured ships into Southern ports and many foreign countries refused to allow privateers to bring ships into their ports.

In most cases, when a commerce-raider stopped a Union merchant ship, she merely removed passengers and crew and set fire to the ship. One of the most successful raider captains was Raphael Semmes. His first ship, the *Sumter*, captured 18 Union ships before being cornered in Gibraltar by ships of the Union Navy, whereupon Semmes sold her. Later he took command of a new ship built in England and commissioned as the CSS *Alabama* on 24 August 1862. In the next two months the *Alabama* captured and burned 20 Union ships in the North Atlantic. She then sank the USS *Hatteras* in a short battle off the coast of Texas. On 11 June 1864, after raids in the East Indies, the *Alabama* reached Cherbourg, France, where the USS *Kearsarge* caught up with her. The *Alabama* was not allowed to remain in the French port, so on 19 June she sailed out to meet the *Kearsarge* in a battle watched by thousands of people. A special train brought sightseers from Paris for the event. In an hour the *Kearsarge*, under Captain John A. Winslow, sent the *Alabama* to the bottom.

The *Alabama* was a good example of what a fast ship with a determined captain could do in disrupting commerce and keeping an opposing navy busy. In twenty-one months she captured or burned more than 60 ships worth nearly $6,000,000. Union shipowners delayed sailings, paid increased insurance, and in some cases transferred their ships to foreign registry to avoid possible capture. Because the *Alabama* had been built and outfitted in England for use as a merchant-raider, the United States claimed that England was responsible for the damages done by her. In 1872, England agreed to pay the sum of $15,500,000 as an indemnity.

Another famous Confederate raider was the CSS *Shenandoah*, which put to sea following the loss of the *Alabama*. Much of her time was spent in the North Pacific, where she destroyed 38 ships, most of them whalers.

Confederate raiders sank about 5 percent of all Union merchant ships, but in no way affected the outcome of the war. In fact, commerce out of northern ports increased, as more and more of it was carried by neutral ships which were safe from attack by the Confederates.

When the war began the Union Navy had some one hundred ships. Nearly half of that fleet was tied up, out of commission, in order to cut expenses. Only about a dozen serviceable ships were in U.S. ports; this was because Isaac Toucey, the Secretary of the Navy, was a Southern sympathizer and had arranged for the others to be on distant stations overseas. Since all naval action against the Confederate States could be expected to take place in shallow coastal waters or on rivers, where sailing ships were practically useless, it was plainly apparent that the Navy had to convert to steam.

Union fleet expansion

Many problems, both offensive and defensive, faced the Union Navy. It had to be strong enough to prevent any foreign intervention in the war. There was the chance that England or France might come in on the Southern side; England, especially, needed southern cotton to keep her mills running.

A first task, as has been noted, was to establish a blockade of the Confederate coastline. Another was to capture the many coastal and river ports that were needed for military or naval bases, and to eliminate or defeat Southern forts.

American shipping had to be protected on sea routes to Europe and South America, in order to maintain the continuous flow of exports and imports essential to economic prosperity and to the war effort. This meant that warships had to hunt down and defeat or capture Confederate raiders and privateers.

Cooperation with the Army was required in many land campaigns, and naval forces were essential in moving troops and supplies on inland waters. This was an especially difficult problem. Much of the economic life of the Southern states depended on steamboat traffic on the Mississippi and its tributaries. Control of the entire river system was necessary to prevent Confederate troop and supply movements. But the Navy could not come up the Mississippi because Confederate forces controlled its lower reaches, and in order to go down the river, an entire fleet of shallow-draft gunboats had to be built inland.

The Confederate Navy started with practically nothing. At first it had more officers than it did ships. Merchant ships were converted to naval use by mounting on them whatever guns could be found.

Confederate fleet expansion

The war really began on 15 April, when Lincoln called for 75,000 volunteers for the Union Army. On 19 April he ordered a blockade of Southern ports. The following day Confederate forces prepared to attack the Norfolk Navy Yard. This was a large Union naval base; it had a dry dock, ship-repair shops, storehouses, and held some 1,100 guns, including 300 of the new Dahlgren guns. The big 50-gun steam frigate *Merrimack* was under repair there, along with the line-of-battle ships *Pennsylvania,*

Delaware, Columbus, the frigates *Raritan* and *United States,* the sloops *Germantown* and *Plymouth,* and the brig *Dolphin.*

To save them from capture, the commandant of the yard ordered the ships burned and scuttled. The loss of the ships was a great blow, but the loss of 300 Dahlgren guns was a greater one. The Confederates captured the guns and turned them against their former owners at many strategic points before the war was over. Only the *Merrimack* was salvageable. The Confederates raised her, repaired her engines, and converted her to an ironclad by cutting away her superstructure and covering her hull with iron plates anywhere from two to four inches thick. They armed her with ten of the captured Dahlgren guns. They also renamed her the CSS *Virginia,* but most history books ignore that and call her by her original name.

This conversion was not made overnight; it took some 1,500 men about eight months to do the job. There was no secret about it, either. Newspapers in Richmond described the new ship, and Secretary of the Navy Gideon Welles set about finding a ship to oppose the Confederate monster.

The answer was the *Monitor,* described as a "cheesebox on a raft." She was 172 feet long and 41 feet wide. She was so low in the water that, while at sea, fish were washed up on her armored deck. John Ericsson designed her and she was built at Greenpoint, Long Island. Work on the ship began in October of 1861 and she was launched at the end of January 1862. Ericsson did not have time to draw completed plans. He sketched out details as workmen put the ship together. The sides of the craft were 30-inch white oak protected by 6-inch iron plates and her deck was double-plated, 1-inch iron over 8 inches of oak. The sides of her turret, which could be revolved by steam machinery, had 8-inch iron plate. Her guns could be pointed by slowly rotating the turret to the desired position. Only one gun could be fired at a time.

There was almost a race to see which ship would be ready for action first. The Confederates hoped that, if they won, they would be able to smash the Union blockade of Hampton Roads and open Norfolk Harbor to European commerce. The *Merrimack* was ready first, and about noon on 8 March 1862 she steamed out to attack Union shipping.

There was considerable excitement and confusion, as ships maneuvered to meet the strange craft, and surprised gunners saw their cannonballs bounce off her sides. The *Merrimack* rammed the USS *Cumberland,* which later sank. Then she set fire to the USS *Congress.* A couple of Union ships ran aground in the battle. The *Merrimack* withdrew after several hours, with 21 men dead. The old wooden ships of the Union Navy took a severe beating and lost 250 men.

Early the next morning the *Merrimack* came back to finish off the USS *Minnesota,* still aground. She was met by the USS

Monitor, which, having been towed down from New York, had arrived in Hampton Roads late the night before.

For four hours the two strange ships circled around each other, like a couple of dogs. They were so slow they could hardly get out of their own way. They banged away at each other at such close range that sometimes they were nearly touching. Neither one could hurt the other. Shells bounced off the sloping sides of the *Merrimack* and skipped across the flat deck of the *Monitor*. Neither ship lost a man.

It was a slow fight. The *Merrimack* had to swing herself broadside to the *Monitor* in order to get a hit and could fire only four guns on a side. Although the *Monitor* had only two guns, she did better in gunnery. She could fire only one gun at a time, but she could turn her turret instead of having to turn the whole ship. Loading the guns was a hard, slow job. Old prints that show the two ships in a cloud of smoke and bursting shells are in error. The *Monitor* fired only 40 shells during the entire battle; sometimes it took seven minutes to load and fire a gun.

When the two ships finally gave up the fight and went home, neither had won. They never fought again. But all naval warfare was changed from that day on. Steam engines, iron hulls, and turret-fired guns replaced wooden-hulled square-riggers loaded with broadside guns. The days of "iron men and wooden ships" had gone forever.

Port Royal, South Carolina

Port Royal Sound was needed as a base for Union blockading vessels. The operation to acquire it began late in October 1861, when 13,000 troops embarked in transports at Annapolis and sailed for Hampton Roads. The entire force of about three dozen transports, eleven warships, and several smaller craft sailed from Hampton Roads on 28 and 29 October and arrived off Port Royal on 4 November. They began a bombardment on 7 November, and the forts in the area surrendered or were abandoned. The port was occupied without landing troops.

New Orleans

Below New Orleans, the Mississippi River was guarded by Fort St. Philip and Fort Jackson, and a floating barrier of hulks and logs chained together. A first attempt by Union ships to pass these defenses in October 1861 failed when fire rafts forced them to retreat. Captain David G. Farragut was selected to make the second attack with a force of about three dozen ships. After they entered the mouth of the Mississippi, it took about a month to get the heavier ships over a shallow bar. They started up the river early in April 1862. Mortar schooners, under Commander David

Dixon Porter, bombarded the forts with more than a thousand shells a day. This went on for six days and nights before Farragut took his larger ships up to bombard the forts. When a Confederate force came out to meet the attackers, most of its ships were burned, sunk, or put out of action. The forts surrendered, and on 1 May 2,500 troops were landed to occupy New Orleans.

Fort Henry and Fort Donelson Fort Henry on the Tennessee River and Fort Donelson on the Cumberland River, in northern Tennessee, guarded the Confederate States' northwestern border. The Union attacks on them took place in February 1862, with four ironclads and three timberclads under Flag Officer Andrew H. Foote. Some 18,000 Union troops under General Ulysses S. Grant were unloaded from transports and marched the last four miles to attack Fort Henry from the land, while the ships were bombarding it from the river. Although three of the Union ships were disabled by the Confederate gunners, most of the fort's guns were knocked out and it surrendered before the land force arrived. General Grant then led his troops overland to Fort Donelson, where the Union ships began another attack on 14 February. Again the Confederate gunners did considerable damage to the ships, which withdrew. However, two days later the fort surrendered to Grant.

Charleston Because Charleston was known as "the cradle of secession," its occupation or capture was a major objective of the Union forces. A long-drawn-out campaign against that port began on 7 April 1863, when Rear Admiral Samuel F. Du Pont led nine ironclads in to bombard its fortifications. His force was badly mauled: the *Keokuk*, hit ninety times in the two-hour battle, sank the next day.

In July, when a Union force under Rear Admiral John A. Dahlgren made a second attack, 11,000 troops were landed on Morris Island. During much of July and August, Confederate positions on that island were bombarded almost daily. In the first week of September, Confederate forces evacuated the island. Thereafter, captured Confederate guns joined the Union guns in bombarding Fort Sumter and Charleston from Morris Island. Another attack on the fort, on 26 October, still failed to knock it out.

Vicksburg Situated at the point where the Yazoo River joins the Mississippi, Vicksburg was a Confederate strongpoint. One hundred and seventy miles down the Mississippi was the well-fortified village of Port Hudson. The Red River, on which supplies came in from Texas, entered the Mississippi between Vicksburg and Port Hudson, and while the Confederates held those two points, they not only blocked the Mississippi, but kept open the route for essential provisions to reach them from the west.

After the capture of New Orleans, Farragut took his force up the Mississippi for an attack on Vicksburg. The passage took weeks, as ships ran aground, collided, or were snagged on underwater obstructions, but on 28 June 1862 Farragut's vessels shot their way past Vicksburg. A few days later they met Captain Charles H. Davis' force that was steaming down from Memphis to attack Vicksburg. On 15 July the new Confederate ironclad *Arkansas*, which for safety had been towed from Memphis to Yazoo City, came down the Yazoo River on her way to Vicksburg: it was intended that thereafter she should help liberate New Orleans. In an episode that Union Secretary of the Navy Gideon Welles described as "the most disreputable naval affair of the war," the *Arkansas* ran through the Union force and reached Vicksburg. A few days later, Farragut received permission to withdraw downstream and, fearing that his ships would be caught by low water, he did so.

Another move on Vicksburg came late in the year. It involved complicated movements of armies, troop transports, gunboats, and ironclads over great distances, an operation that required months of planning and execution. A Union army of 30,000 men under General Ulysses S. Grant began marching overland from a point about 15 miles northwest of Vicksburg near the end of March, 1863. Building bridges and roads as they went, they took about a month to cover that distance. Grant's troops were supplied by the Navy; gunboats and ironclads under Admiral David Dixon Porter ran past Vicksburg towing bargeloads of stores. Grant's army made two attacks on Vicksburg and was repulsed both times. Finally the troops dug in and began a steady siege of the city. For weeks, artillery, assisted by gunboats on the river, pounded the city into rubble; her citizens hid out in caves to avoid the shells.

Finally, on 3 July 1863, Vicksburg surrendered to General Grant. Four days later Port Hudson, downstream, surrendered, and the Mississippi was open. "The Father of Waters," said Lincoln, "now rolls unvexed to the sea."

The Union victory had several immediate results. Midwest harvests had piled up in granaries for two years because rail traffic was too limited to move much of it to the East Coast; grain could now move down the river for export to overseas markets that were eagerly awaiting it, and the first ship to enter the Mississippi trade again, the *Imperial*, reached New Orleans on 16 July. More important, Union control of the river meant that the Confederate states east of the river could no longer bring in vital supplies from the states west of the river.

Mobile Bay   Mobile was an active port for blockade-runners, and as at New Orleans, the channels into it were protected by strong forts. Union plans to take the port included four ironclads and fourteen wooden steamers under Farragut, and 2,400 Army troops. The ships went in early on the morning of 5 August 1864, and began to exchange shots with Confederate batteries at Fort Morgan. About the same time, they moved into an area where mines ("torpedoes") were suspected and, fearful of these new weapons, they began to slow down. It was then that Farragut snapped out, "Damn the torpedoes!" Almost immediately a mine blew up under the monitor *Tecumseh*, which sank with heavy loss of life. In what turned into a general melee, the Confederate ironclad *Tennessee* ran in among the remaining seventeen Union ships and was heavily damaged before being forced to surrender. On 7 August Fort Gaines surrendered; Fort Morgan was starved into submission before the end of the month. However, the city of Mobile was not finally occupied until three days after General Robert E. Lee had surrendered at Appomattox.

Land campaigns   Many of the land battles took place in Virginia, one of the
and battles   border states between North and South. One reason for this was that when the Confederate capital was moved from Montgomery, Alabama, to Richmond, Virginia, it was less than a hundred miles from Washington, D.C., the Union capital. Both Confederate and Union armies made repeated attempts on the opposing seats of government. In the First Battle of Bull Run, 21 July 1861, some 50,000 troops of the two armies fought in northern Virginia, not far from Washington, and the Union army was badly defeated.

In 1862, Union forces attempted to advance on Richmond, in what was called the Peninsula Campaign because it was fought between the James and York rivers. The Confederate forces under General Robert E. Lee were at first driven back, but in heavy fighting around Richmond frm 25 June to 1 July, they forced the Union armies to withdraw from the peninsula. In August, Union forces were again defeated at Bull Run and the Confederates crossed the Potomac into Maryland. At the Battle of Antietam on 17 September they were repulsed by Union troops.

The Union forces spent several months reorganizing and training, but in the Battle of Chancellorsville, 1-4 May 1863, they were again defeated. The Confederate forces under General Lee then moved north through the Shenandoah Valley and invaded southern Pennsylvania.

The turning point in the war came when Confederate forces, under General Robert E. Lee, and Union forces, under General George G. Meade, met at the decisive Battle of Gettysburg, which took place during the first three days of July. Casualties were heavy on both sides. The Confederates were forced to retreat across the Potomac, and were thereafter on the defensive.

In the west, Union forces took Vicksburg, Mississippi, on 4 July 1863, after siege and a naval bombardment. This cut off Texas, Arkansas, and Louisiana from the rest of the Confederate states. The Battle of Chattanooga, 23-25 November, gave the Union forces control of Tennessee and made it possible for them to advance into Georgia.

In 1864 General Ulysses S. Grant was made commander in chief of all Union armies, and at the same time General William T. Sherman was given command of the armies in the west.

General Grant led the Union forces into the Battle of the Wilderness (near Fredericksburg, Virginia), which took place on 5 and 6 May, 1864. In several engagements, Grant's forces were unable to defeat Lee, but laid siege to Petersburg, 20 miles south of Richmond. Confederate raids into Maryland and Pennsylvania were driven back by Union forces under General Philip H. Sheridan. Then in May 1864, Union forces under General Sherman began a march through Georgia to Atlanta. On 2 September Confederate forces retreated from that city. Sherman's army reached

The USS *Hartford*, Farragut's flagship at the Battle of Mobile Bay, shows the transition from sail to steam. She had a steam engine and propeller, but still carried masts and spars with which to spread a suit of sails. The objects hanging in the rigging are sailors uniforms, washed and strung up to dry. Courtesy: The Naval Historical Foundation.

the sea on 12 December and forced Confederate withdrawal from Savannah on the 20th. As Sherman's army started north, Grant's army started south. The Confederates gave up Petersburg on 2 April 1865 and surrendered Richmond the next day. Finally, on 9 April, General Lee surrendered the Confederate forces to General Grant at Appomattox, Virginia. Jefferson Davis, the only president of the Confederacy, was captured in Georgia on 10 May. The final surrender took place at Shreveport, Louisiana, on 26 May.

Unofficially, the Civil War will probably go on forever. Some historians have spent their entire lives delving into its origins, operations, and results. Literally hundreds of books have been written about every conceivable aspect of the war. Innumerable novels have been based on the Civil War, the most famous being the Pulitzer Prize winner, *Gone with the Wind*, by Margaret Mitchell. First published in 1936, it was filmed in 1940, and is still going strong. Civil War monuments and memorials stand in hundreds of towns throughout the United States, and many of the great battlegrounds of that war are now national parks. The names of its naval and military leaders on both sides have been given to streets, parks, and schools throughout the country. And the spirited marching songs of that war have always been popular; no matter on which side his ancestors fought, everyone likes "Dixie!"

Wartime developments

Iron ships and gun turrets, along with advances in steam engineering, are usually noted as being the chief developments of the Civil War. Such technical advancements greatly changed naval warfare, but the Civil War brought other changes, some of them minor, and others that had long-lasting effect.

Before the war, people sat around a kitchen or parlor table at night, reading or sewing in the light of candles or whale-oil lamps. As Confederate commerce-raiders began cutting down the Union whaling fleet, whale oil became scarce. There was a substitute for whale oil, but until the Civil War no one really knew about it. For years, people in Pennsylvania had been mystified by some strange black stuff that oozed out of the ground and burned if a flame reached it. The substance was petroleum, and a well from which it could be pumped was put down at Titusville, Pennsylvania, in 1859. By 1862 millions of gallons of it were being produced and distilled into kerosene. Cheap glass lamps were making brighter light in many homes by the time the war ended.

Another change came in food. Dried and salted foods used by both the Army and the Navy were pretty much the same before the war—awful. The art of preserving food in cans originated in France late in the eighteenth century, but there had been little advancement in the process, and none in the United States until about 1860. Then, in Indianapolis, Gilbert Van Camp began a process of cooking pork and beans and packing the result in tin cans. The

Army liked it. Soon, canned tomatoes and canned meats were available; Union soldiers ate canned foods by the case. Canned foods have improved greatly since then, but Van Camp's name is still on the shelves at the supermarket.

Railroads and the telegraph were in use before the Civil War. They offered great military advantages in moving troops and transmitting orders to troop commanders in the field. Both sides soon noted that broken lines of communication created great confusion, and put considerable effort into tearing up each other's railroad tracks and bridges, and pulling down telegraph wires.

Being the weaker naval power, the Confederate States tried to offset their weakness by developing new weapons. Underwater explosive devices called "torpedoes" were tried, and proved effective in more than one case. These were the ancestors of what are now called mines, and might be anything from a beer keg to a locomotive boiler, filled with gunpowder. When Admiral Farragut said "Damn the torpedoes! Full speed ahead," in the Battle of Mobile Bay, he was talking about mines. Farragut and the USS *Hartford* were lucky that day; during the entire war 35 Union ships were sunk or damaged by mines.

The Confederates also tried submarines, but had limited success with this device. Small steam-powered craft called "Davids" carried four men and had a very limited range. One of them damaged the USS *New Ironsides* in Charleston, but was swamped and two of her crew were captured. A hand-powered craft, the CSS *Hunley*, sank five times and drowned five crews before she did sink the USS *Housatonic*—but she and her crew went down with their victim.

A few 30-foot surface craft called torpedo boats, because they carried a "torpedo" on a spar at their bow, were tried by the Union Navy. Three of them attacked Confederate ships off Roanoke on 27 October 1864. One sank and one ran aground and was captured. The third, under Lieutenant William B. Cushing, managed to sink the CSS *Albemarle*, but not before she herself sank.

Union forces took to the air during the Civil War, but only briefly, and no one went very high. Balloons tethered to steamers were used in attempts to spy out blockade-runners and to observe enemy batteries. They were not successful, and the Army Aeronautics Corps was abolished in 1863.

Medical care of wounded men was given greater attention than in previous wars. A U.S. Sanitary Commission was organized to fit out hospital units, and sent both men and women to perform nursing duties at the battle fronts. Two women prominent in this work were Mary A. Livermore and Annie Wotenburg. Nurses for Army hospitals were recruited by Dorothea Dix and Clara Barton, who later organized the American Red Cross. Even wounded and injured sailors were given attention; the Navy fitted out the *Red Rover* as a hospital ship. A side-wheeler, she was put in service at St. Louis in 1862 and served on the Mississippi River; she had not only operating rooms, elevators, bathtubs, ice vaults, but *women nurses!*

Along with the books and songs that have kept the Civil War fresh in memory, there is yet another remarkable record of that war, in photography. Cameras went to war for the first time, and although primitive and bulky, they produced thousands of photographs of men, ships, and weapons.

Matthew Brady was the most noted photographer of the Civil War, but many men were busy with their awkward black boxes, making a visual record of the conflict. It is possible to read a book about the Civil War and forget it, but it is very difficult to look at the faces of mere boys, proud in their uniforms, standing beside their guns, and not wonder what happened to them.

"When somebody wins, somebody loses," Carl Sandburg once wrote. But when the Civil War ended, everyone lost. The war cost the Union about $4,000,000,000, and the Confederate states about $1,000,000,000. Military destruction of buildings, railroads, and equipment in the South was devastating. Total destruction could be a relative thing; if a poor planter's only team of mules was killed and he could not plow his fields, he was as badly off as a man whose factory burned down.

About 540,000 people died between 1861 and 1865, on both sides. The Confederate armies lost about 250,000 men, nearly a fifth of the productive male population of the South. Not all deaths were in combat; poor sanitation and lack of proper medical facilities resulted in twice as many deaths as were caused by battle.

After "the war to free the slaves," the slaves were indeed free, but their new freedom did not automatically provide them with a job, home, or food. Many poor whites in the South, who had lost what little they did have, were as badly off as the ex-slaves. The Emancipation Proclamation of 22 September 1863 freed all slaves in the Confederate States as of 1 January 1863. The Thirteenth Amendment abolished slavery everywhere in the United States. The Fourteenth Amendment provided in part that no state could "abridge the privileges or immunities of citizens of the United States . . . nor deprive any person of life, liberty, or property, without due process of law; nor deny to any person . . . the equal protection of the laws." But even the best-intentioned law could not make up for the intense poverty and misery that followed the war. Congress set up a "Freedman's Bureau" and the relief efforts of various states did their best, but funds were limited and all such efforts were overwhelmed by the immensity of the problem.

There had been famine in the South in 1862, little farming during the war years, and a crop failure in 1865. The whole South was stricken with poverty, and the spirit of defeat held the people down for many years. As late as 1873, a visitor to New Orleans noted that people's faces were filled with "the expression of entire despair."

CHAPTER 13
INLAND WATERWAYS

In the late 1700s, ship after ship sailed from New England ports to carry on a rich trade with the Orient. Their owners dealt in furs, tea, silk, porcelain, and spice, and although the voyages were long and dangerous, many great fortunes were made. However, not all seagoing Americans sailed as far as China. A brave and hardy man in a 30-foot fishing boat could make a living and never get out of sight of land. A few men in a fast schooner could do better taking codfish off the Grand Banks. Others—the seagoing truck-drivers of their time—hauled cargo up and down the coast; they would take anything from pigs to pots to passengers, so long as there was a profit to be made.

Still other Americans, some of whom might never have seen salt water, were pushing off on trips that took them hundreds of miles on the canals, lakes, and rivers of America. Over the years, these fresh-water sailors built up a commerce worth more than all the tea in China.

The canals came first, even before the packets, clippers, and steamboats. Early canals were built to help boats get around water-falls at Richmond, Virginia, and Hadley, Massachusetts, and were very short. By 1804 the Middlesex Canal in Massachusetts was carrying passengers 31 miles from Lowell to Charlestown.

American canal boats were not as romantic as the packets and clippers. After all, a canal boat was nothing more than a barge towed by a team of horses. But the growing nation had to get its crops and produce to market; transportation was essential and the canals provided it at low cost.

On previous page: A steamboat race, with flags flying and whistles tooting, was always exciting. Sometimes the boats were within shouting distance of each other, nose to nose all the way. This race could have taken place a hundred years ago; the fact that it is a modern reenactment is given away by the automobile on the boiler deck of the *Delta Queen*. Photo: Lin Caufield.

George Washington, while he was building Mount Vernon, was also planning a canal along the Potomac River. That canal was commenced in 1829 and completed in 1850. It ran 184 miles from the Potomac waterfront of Washington, D.C., to Cumberland, Maryland. A series of 85 locks raised the boats a total of 613 feet. Boats on the Chesapeake and Ohio Canal, as it was called, were nearly as standard as freight cars were later. The average canal boat, towed by a mule, carried about 120 tons of freight, and had a bunkhouse on deck for the captain and his family and a small stable at the bow for the mules. The mules took turns; one rode and one towed, and every six hours they traded places.

The canal became a principal coal-carrying route and, at the height of its operation, more than 800 boats were busy hauling the "black gold" to Washington. Railroads eventually took over the coal traffic, and the canal was abandoned in 1924. However, parts of the canal and the old towpath still exist, and visitors can sometimes ride one of the old canal boats for a few miles through Georgetown.

The most famous, and probably the busiest, canal in the country, was the Erie Canal, which crossed New York State from Albany to Buffalo. Governor De Witt Clinton, of New York, worked hard and long to convince officials that it should be built. Construction commenced in 1817 and the entire 363-mile-long canal, with 84 locks, was finished in 1825. It set a standard for American canals; 40 feet wide at the waterline and tapering to 28 feet wide at the bottom, it was 4 feet deep. The entire canal was dug by men using picks, shovels, and horse-drawn scrapers. Most of the workers were newly arrived Irish.

People did not believe it would be possible to lift canal boats nearly 700 feet over the hills between Albany and Buffalo, and the estimated cost of some $7,000,000 was called fantastic. Scoffers nicknamed the project "Clinton's Ditch." Before the canal was opened, merchants were paying $120 a ton to move freight from Buffalo to New York by wagon and Hudson River sloops. The canal cut the cost to $14 a ton. It helped develop water traffic on the Great Lakes; wheat from farms in Illinois went from Chicago to Buffalo by lake schooner; there it was ground into flour and packed in barrels for the trip through the canal and down the Hudson to New York. From New York, it was shipped to Europe.

A branch canal to Lake Champlain, opened in 1823, brought border trade from Canada. The canal boats on that route were sloop-rigged for the sailing trip to Whitehall, at the lower end of the lake; there the masts were removed and left ashore, and boats were hauled the rest of the way by horses. On the return trip, they picked up their masts at Whitehall and sailed on home.

By 1882, when tolls on the canal were abolished, it had produced income of over $120,000,000. At the height of its operation, more than 25,000 people worked on it.* Many immigrants began their long trip into new western communities by a trip along the canal.

Canal boats moved quietly, sliding past green fields and along tree-lined banks where birds sang. Passengers could fish, swim, or get out and walk awhile. At night, the boats were tied up, the horses or mules were fed, and everyone went to bed. In comparison with American roads, which were miserable at best, travel by canal boat was pleasant, with no bumps or dust. A trip of about a hundred miles cost $4, and that included meals. Of course, the meals were poor and the bunks had bedbugs, but early railroads had the same drawbacks, plus the interesting possibility that sparks from the engine might set a coach on fire.

The United States had 3,326 miles of canals by 1840, before the country began building railroads. At one time, Pennsylvania had about a thousand miles of canals in operation. A canal from Evansville on the Ohio River, in southern Indiana, ran across that state and through Ohio to Cleveland on Lake Erie, a total of 460 miles. Most canals were quite narrow—just wide enough for two boats to pass—and very shallow. These factors limited speed to about four miles an hour. Greater speed would have worn away the banks, which meant that steam-powered craft were not practical. The rapid development of railroads about the middle of the century soon made most canals uneconomical, although some continued in use well into the twentieth century.

There are no complete records of the total amount of freight moved in small loads by slow-moving animals during the century that the canals were used. In New York State, over a million tons were hauled in 1837 alone. The peak was reached in 1872, when more than six and a half million tons of freight were handled. After that, tonnage gradually dropped off, the canal-boat horses were put out to pasture, and the new "iron horses" took over.

About the time canal boats began operating in the east, a new kind of water traffic was beginning across the mountains to the west. The men out there did not need horses; they harnessed the rivers.

These were the frontiersmen who began using the great inland rivers to move their crops to market. They were not sailors; most of them probably did not know a compass from a capstan, but they made long trips, sometimes thousands of miles, and endured many of the dangers of life at sea—fire, storm, wreck, plus attacks by Indians.

First, they used keelboats, which averaged 70 feet in length, 12 feet in width, and could carry up to 80 tons of freight. A crew of twenty or so men, rowing to make better time, took them down-

---

* For good accounts of life on the canals, see Rome Haul or Erie Waters, both by Walter Edmonds.

stream. Coming back upstream, the men walked along the bank, towing the boat at the end of a long line, or stood on deck and pushed against the river bottom with long poles. By 1794 keelboats were making regular trips up and down the Ohio River between Cincinnati and Pittsburgh. Some twenty-five years later there were at least 500 keelboats on the Ohio alone, and far more on the Mississippi.

Next came rafts or flatboats built strictly for a one-way trip. Big ones, open barges able to carry up to 100 tons, were called "broadhorns" because they were steered by long oars. Flatboats were simply big open wooden boxes, and they carried all kinds of produce down the rivers to market: grain, cotton, tobacco, lumber, cider, pork, fur, dried fruit, and rude furniture—anything a man could grow, make, or catch and sell to someone else. Many of them went all the way down the Mississippi to New Orleans. After their cargoes were sold, the owners sold the flatboats and began the long, slow walk back home. When Abraham Lincoln was young, he made a couple of trips down the Mississippi on a flatboat. Even after steamboats began running on the river, flatboats sailed in swarms because the trip was free—there was no freight charge. As late as 1847, more than 2,700 flatboats went down the Mississippi, and they continued long after that. Mark Twain describes flatboats in his *Life on the Mississippi*, and in *Huckleberry Finn* he recounts how Tom Sawyer and Huckleberry Finn sailed down the river on their own small raft.

Broadhorns were frequently used by people who were moving downriver to a new home: after they built the raft, they loaded it with everything they owned—tools, furniture, carts, horses, cows, pigs, chickens, dogs, cats, and food for all. When they reached their destination, they might well tear the raft apart and rebuild it into a house or barn.

As soon as Robert Fulton had proved his steamboat, the *Clermont*, a success on the Hudson River in 1807, other men saw that steamboats would be useful on the inland rivers. But before Nicholas J. Roosevelt ventured a steamboat on inland water, he first scouted out the situation. He built a flatboat at Pittsburgh, put his new wife aboard, and drifted all the way down the Ohio and the Mississippi to New Orleans. Then he returned to New York by steamer, through the Gulf of Mexico and the Atlantic, went back to Pittsburgh, and built his own steamboat. Named, naturally, *New Orleans*, she was 148 feet long, had a paddle wheel on each side, and carried masts and sails in case her engines failed.

Late in the fall of 1811 the *New Orleans* left Pittsburgh for New Orleans with her flags waving, black smoke pouring from her tall chimney, and her paddle wheels churning up the water. She carried Roosevelt, his wife, their big Newfoundland dog named Tiger, and four servants. The crew consisted of a captain, pilot, engineer, and six deckhands. It was a slow trip. Sometimes the boat was held up by low water; sometimes she was stopped while her crew went ashore to cut more wood for the fires under her boilers.

Just after the *New Orleans* entered the Mississippi, a great earthquake changed the bed of the river, and at times she sailed through what, when Roosevelt went down the river earlier on his raft, had been deep forests. The trip ended on 12 January 1812. Only two weeks of that long time had been spent in actual travel, so the *New Orleans* set no speed records. However, Mrs. Roosevelt became the first woman to give birth to a baby on a Mississippi River steamboat, and Tiger became the first dog ever to arrive in New Orleans on a steamboat.

Roosevelt, convinced there was a future on the river, put the *New Orleans* into service between New Orleans and Natchez, and went back to Pittsburgh to build more steamboats.

Until 1815, no steamboat went any farther up the Mississippi than Natchez. In that year Captain Henry M. Shreve took the *Enterprise* all the way up the Mississippi, the Ohio, and the Monongahela, past Pittsburgh to Brownsville, Pennsylvania, a 2,200-mile trip, in 54 days. Shreve immediately saw that boats such as Fulton built, with boilers and engines down inside the hull, as they were in seagoing ships, were not suitable for river operation. He designed a radical new type of boat for use in very shallow water: her hull was wide and flat; only the bottom section of her paddle wheels was in the water; her boilers and engines were on the main deck, where cargo was carried; her decks above contained staterooms, lounges, and dining rooms. Although there is a monument of a sort for him in Louisiana—the city of Shreveport is named for him—very few people know that Shreve was the real inventor of the Mississippi steamboats.

Steamboats were built mostly of wood and so decorated from stem to stern with fancy frills and scrollwork that some of them resembled wedding cakes. Typical of the age of splendor on the river was the *Great Republic*, which had a 300-foot-long grand saloon flanked by 54 elegant staterooms. Under gilded chandeliers and stained-glass skylights, white-coated stewards served meals of twelve courses. After dinner the passengers could stroll the promenade decks or rest in the "Gentlemen's Social Hall" or the "Ladies Cabin," visit the library, or drop postcards in to the post office.

Steamboats were of two types: side-wheelers, which had one big wheel on either side, each driven by its own steam engine; and stern-wheelers, which had one big wheel clear across the stern, usually driven by two engines. Side-wheelers were more maneuverable, because they could go ahead on one wheel and back down on the other. Stern-wheelers were less liable to wreck a wheel on a floating log, and were used almost exclusively on the Missouri River because it was very narrow and there was no room for side-wheelers in some channels.

The early steamboats provided travel and transportation in a growing country long before the railroads came. They were inexpensive compared to the cost of building miles of track and maintaining hundreds of freight cars, passenger coaches, and locomotives. The smallest river town could send freight or passengers to any other city in the country, so long as a steamboat could stop at its landing. The boats soon covered the entire Mis-

"Steamboat a'coming!" People in derby hats and long dresses crowded the river front to see the first boats pass through the new Davis Locks on the Ohio River, about five miles below Pittsburgh, in 1885. A few men are standing on the lock gate, at right. Six steamboats are waiting for the lock to open; several others are faintly visible in the distance. Courtesy: American Waterways Operators, Inc.

sissippi-Missouri river system. By 1823 a steamboat had reached St. Paul, Minnesota, and eight years later the *Yellowstone* had chugged into the upper Missouri. By the time of the Civil War it was possible to ride a steamboat 2,200 miles up the Missouri to Fort Benton in Montana.

In 1836 there were 381 steamboats on the western rivers. By 1840 New Orleans was the second largest port in the United States. Ten years later, there were more than 1,000 boats on the inland rivers, but only 9,000 miles of railroad track in all the United States. In 1850, it was common to see 50 steamboats lined up along the St. Louis waterfront at one time. That year, more than 8,000 boats arrived at and departed from the busy port of Cincinnati, an average of about one an hour for the entire year.

Some steamboats, especially those built for use in the small rivers, were mere "puddle jumpers." Steamboat men bragged that they could run across a pasture in a heavy dew. The *Iowa City* could run in water only 20 inches deep, and the *Chippewa*, when not loaded, could navigate in only 12 inches of water. The giants, built between 1850 and 1876, were the *Great Republic*, 350 feet long, and the *Eclipse*, 365 feet long. Their paddle wheels were as tall as a four-story building. Smaller boats puffed from one landing to another, picking up passengers and freight wherever they could. The big, fast boats ran regular schedules and made good time. In 1844 the *J. M. White* ran from New Orleans to St. Louis, a little more than 1,200 miles, in 95 hours and 51 minutes. On 30 June 1870 the famous *Robert E. Lee*, racing the *Natchez* from New Orleans, reached St. Louis in the record time of 90 hours and 30 minutes. She averaged 11.58 miles per hour.

Nevertheless, water transportation was slow, but it was cheap. It cost a merchant $8 to have 100 pounds of merchandise hauled overland from an Atlantic port to West Virginia. For the same money, he could ship 800 pounds of merchandise by sea to New Orleans and all the way back up the river by steamboat to the same destination.

About 1830 northern lumber companies began sending log rafts as long as 600 feet down the Mississippi. Traffic on the river was further increased when steamboats were used to control some of the rafts. Around 1880 Minnesota was sending more than 2,000 rafts a year on their way to river ports. By the early 1900s, when the last rafts were used, some of them were 1,600 feet long.

In 1911, one hundred years after the *New Orleans* first steamed down the river, a couple of dozen steamboats gathered at Pittsburgh to celebrate that event. But like buffaloes and passenger pigeons, they were growing scarcer. Now, only a dozen or so of the romantic old craft are still on the river. The 1898-vintage, 96-foot stern-wheeler *Julius C. Wilkie* is at Winona, Minnesota, and the *Blue Berry Belle* is at Brainerd, Minnesota. The *George M. Verity*, a towboat, is at Keokuk, Iowa. The *Delta Queen* and

Cotton Blossom are at St. Louis. The *Sprague*, largest stern-wheeler ever built, is at Vicksburg. The *River Queen*, a reconstructed boat, is a museum at Hannibal, Missouri, the home of Mark Twain. Hannibal was also the home of the most famous steamboat of all, the *Big Missouri*, which never sailed on the river at all but which, for a hundred years now, has played a big scene in the second chapter of Mark Twain's *Adventures of Tom Sawyer*.

American clipper ships and whalers sailed the seven seas, yet there is another sea on which no clipper or whaler ever appeared. That is the big American inland sea, 95,000 square miles of fresh water, stretching for a thousand miles across the United States from New York to Minnesota. The Great Lakes—Ontario, Erie, Huron, Michigan, and Superior—have carried American water-borne commerce for a century and a half. Traffic on the lakes was at first strictly a short-haul business, but canals connecting the lakes and the St. Lawrence River now make it possible for ocean-going ships to unload cargo in Duluth, Minnesota, 2,342 miles from salt water.

As soon as the first settlers reached the shores of Lake Erie and Lake Ontario, they began building sailing vessels. During the War of 1812, in a decisive naval engagement on Lake Erie, Commodore Perry defeated a British force off Put-in-Bay. The lakes were frozen over for part of each winter, but during the rest of the year commerce developed rapidly. Fast-sailing schooners soon dotted the lakes, hauling produce to Erie, Cleveland, Buffalo, Chicago, and other lake ports. By 1870, there were more than two thousand barks, brigs, and schooners on the five lakes. The first steamboat on the lakes was the *Michigan*, a 156-foot side-wheeler built in 1833. She was so successful that within 20 years there were sixteen fast boats running between Buffalo and Chicago on a regular schedule, two boats leaving each city every day.

At first, ships coming up the St. Lawrence could sail into Lake Erie, but no farther. In 1829 the opening of the Welland Ship Canal made it possible for them to reach Lake Huron and Lake Michigan. In 1855 the canal at Sault Sainte Marie opened the way into Lake Superior for ships up to 350 feet long. The canal at the "Soo," as it is called, was more of an engineering feat than it appeared to be because it opened up all the lakes to ocean commerce. The port of Chicago welcomed its first overseas visitor on 14 July 1857 when the steamship *Madeira Pet* docked after an 80-day voyage from London.

While some steamboats were making trips of thousands of miles up and down the rivers, or across the Great Lakes, a few of them, like ducks in a puddle, just paddled around and never went anywhere. The side-wheeler *Ticonderoga* did exactly that on Lake Champlain for 47 years, and she is still there, on display at the Shelburne Museum in Vermont.

In 1804, years before the first steamboat reached St. Louis, the explorers Meriwether Lewis and William Clark set out from that small town on a long journey up the Missouri River and across the mountains to Oregon. Sometimes they made only five miles a day. Now, as jet aircraft cross the continent at 10 miles a minute, their passengers can look down on the Mississippi from 35,000 feet above St. Louis, and see where the Missouri joins it, 17 miles upstream. Along the city's waterfront, they can see a tiny white object, the *Goldenrod* showboat, one of the biggest steamboats of its kind ever built. Out in the river, they may see what looks like a boat, four or five times longer than any steamboat ever built— a 5,000-horsepower, diesel towboat pushing a string of barges more than a quarter of a mile long, the new way to handle freight on the river.

The old steamboats made lots of smoke, but their freight capacity was small; a thousand of them averaged only 250 tons each. Many boats, of course, were of smaller tonnage than that. A record load of freight was hauled down to New Orleans by the *Henry Frank* in 1881, when she carried 2,300 tons—9,226 bales of cotton stacked so high no one could see the boat. Now one towboat on the lower river can handle up to 40,000 or 50,000 tons in one load. The *Delta Queen* and *River Queen* still haul tourists at 8 miles an hour, but they leave the freight to the towboats. Towboating is not as romantic as steamboating, but it is big business.

There are more than 25,000 miles of inland waterways in the United States. This does not include the Great Lakes, with a coastline of 8,300 miles and an area of 95,000 square miles. The inland-water transportation system provides shipping facilities to 38 of the 50 states. Of the 150 cities in the United States with a population of 100,000 or more, 131 are served by it. More than 20,000 barges are operated on it and, if they were all loaded at once, they would be able to carry over 27,000,000 tons. In 1971 the barge traffic on the Mississippi River alone amounted to more than 320,000,000 tons. Some 4,278 towboats and tugs move this traffic.

Cotton is no longer quite the king it was at the time of the Civil War. With all of America on wheels, petroleum now accounts for 44 percent of all water freight. Although grain accounts for only 2.0 percent of the waterborne freight, it makes a big mountain; in 1971 barges hauled 594,000,000 bushels down the Mississippi to Gulf ports for export. On all inland-water systems that year, more than 870,000,000 bushels of farm crops were moved. Even the Columbia River, once merely a happy home for salmon, carried more than 50,000,000 bushels of grain.

Most barge traffic is handled by towboats which, despite their name, push the barges. The disadvantage of a tug pulling barges at the end of a tow line is that it cannot stop its load quickly; no matter what the tug does, the load keeps coming. But a towboat, snubbed up tight to a string of barges and pushing them, can go astern on all engines and stop the whole load in its own length. Towboats range in length from 117 feet to 160 feet, and their horsepower varies from 1,000 to 6,000. A big towboat costs over $1,000,000. The largest diesel boats can handle up to 50,000 tons of freight in one tow, whereas the biggest diesel locomotives can pull a string of 120 loaded, 50-ton cars for a total of 6,000 tons.

Barges are as standardized as are the semi-trailer rigs hauled on the highways. Open hopper barges, from 175 feet to 290 feet long, can carry up to 3,000 tons of anything from lumber to locomotives. Covered, dry-cargo barges, not quite so large, carry up to 1,500 tons of anything that has to be protected from the weather. Tank barges come in various sizes and carry all kinds of liquids, from salad oil to grain alcohol to molasses. The biggest tank cargo, of course, is petroleum—better than 1,000,000 tons a year. Deck barges carry vehicles and machinery of all kinds. Car floats carry loaded railroad cars—from West Coast ports all the way to Alaska.

Towboats and their strings of barges move up and down the rivers through locks, exactly as the old canal boats did. The locks are huge, some as long as 1,200 feet, and a whole tow can go through at once. It takes about thirty minutes to raise or lower a tow from one level to another. Towboats do not make much speed —the run downriver from Pittsburgh to New Orleans takes ten days, and from St. Louis to New Orleans, four days—but because they haul such huge loads, the freight charge is very low. In 1971 the average cost of moving a ton of freight one mile in the United States was: by air, 22.5 cents; by truck, 8 cents; by rail, .16 cents; by barge, .03 cents.

Once a towboat makes up a string of barges, it runs night and day, and the crew works 12 hours out of every 24: the operating cost of such an outfit is about $100 an hour. Towboat men* have no time to sing sea chanteys or to carve scrimshaw, as the old clipper and whaler sailors did, but they have good meals, air-conditioned cabins, and television. No matter where they are, voice radio keeps them up to the minute with the home office.

In the late 1840s, men could make fortunes in the golden west if they were lucky, but many were not, and sailed 15,000 miles in vain. Among the gold-seekers heading west in 1848 were 38 people who paid $300 each for a trip to California in the brig *Eureka*, which began the trip in, of all unlikely places, Cleveland, Ohio. The Welland Ship Canal having been open for 20 years by then, it was indeed possible to sail from Cleveland to California, but it was necessary to head east to the Atlantic first. The *Eureka* made the long trip in 182 days. Whether any of her passengers made fortunes, no one knows. Their chances of striking it rich were

---

* For an entertaining, fictional account of towboat operations, *see High Water* by Richard Bissell.

probably better at home, but few people then recognized that the gold in the Great Lakes was in the unlikely forms of grain, iron ore, and coal.

The golden flow of grain through the lakes began in 1839 when the brig *Osceola* carried a load of 2,900 bushels to a mill near Buffalo. Four years later so much grain was being handled that steam-powered unloading gear was being used. By 1867 Buffalo had 25 grain elevators with bucket conveyers. Bigger and bigger ships were built for the grain trade: the *William M. Mills*, built after World War II, could carry more than 500,000 bushels in one load. Grain trade on the lakes amounted to more than 960,000,000 bushels in 1973.

Iron ore and coal, the essential raw materials for the production of steel, make up the bulk of Great Lakes traffic. As in the grain trade, the first shipment was small—the brig *Columbia* hauled 132 tons of ore from Marquette to Sandusky, Ohio, in 1842. The first boat built specifically to carry ore was a 211-foot steamer named *R. J. Hackett*. By 1900 iron ore was moving on the lakes at the rate of 22,000,000 tons a year.

Big ore boats made their appearance in 1906, when lake operators began building 600-footers. Over 200 of them were turned out in four years. Mechanical unloaders were developed and, by 1930, such devices could scoop 11,000 tons of ore out of a ship in two hours. Now, there are ships—the 1,000-foot *Stewart J. Cort*, for example—that can haul 50,000 tons of ore in one load, and unload it at the rate of 20,000 tons an hour.

Coal, used primarily in the production of steel but also for generating electric power, is another commodity that moves across the lakes in vast quantities. Most of it is shipped out of ports on Lake Erie. In 1973, more than 34,000,000 tons of coal were handled.

In the last century, a huge industrial empire, based on the combination of low-cost transportation and the ready availability of raw materials, grew up around the Great Lakes. Steel mills, flour mills, coal mines, stone quarries, factories, docks, railroad yards, and related businesses brought a vast flow of commerce to the lakes region. Soon America's industrial strength had moved from the Atlantic seaboard to the Midwest. The fresh-water ports of Milwaukee, Chicago, Gary, Detroit, Toledo, Cleveland, Pittsburgh, Youngstown, Erie, Duluth, and Buffalo, among others, comprise the greatest manufacturing region the world has ever known. None of it would have been possible without ships, and their hard-working crews.

There is one unusual feature about Great Lakes shipping; when winter comes, everyone goes home. The lakes freeze over solid and for about four months traffic stops, except where Coast Guard icebreakers can smash through the ice to keep ship channels open. Even so, the Great Lakes fleet of 200 ships carries about 15 percent of all waterborne commerce in the United States—approximately 162,000,000 tons. The value of such cargo is beyond calculation. A load of 100,000 tons of iron ore, coal, and limestone is not particularly valuable, but by the time it has been smelted into pig iron, refined into steel, and manufactured into machine tools, jet engines, or automobiles, its value has increased a thousand times.

As American ore boats and bulk carriers ply their trade on the lakes, they meet ships flying the flags of many other nations. The St. Lawrence Seaway, opened on 26 June 1959, allowed deep-draft, oceangoing ships to use the lakes for the first time. In its first year of operation, the Seaway cleared more than 2,100 ships, some of them 600-footers, into the lakes. At that time, depth restrictions in the locks barred lake boats bigger than 27,000 tons, and deep-sea ships bigger than 10,000 tons.

It is no longer necessary to journey to Boston or San Francisco to meet deep-water ships. Far from salt water, ships of the seven seas now sail past the corn fields of Indiana and the pine forests of Minnesota. Through engineering marvels De Witt Clinton and Robert Fulton never dreamed of, much of the country's waterborne commerce sails on a vast inland sea with a shoreline longer than either the Atlantic or the Pacific coast. Not all America's merchant sailors go down to the sea in ships any more; sailors on the Great Lakes go *up*—600 feet above sea level.

PART THREE
A CENTURY OF PROGRESS

In the seventy-five years of the twentieth century that have passed—within living memory—there have been more and greater changes than in all the recorded centuries of past history. The contrast between life as it was in 1900 and as it is now is so great that this seems to be another world. In fact, so much is new and so little of 1900 is left that this *is* a different world.

In the last years of the eighteenth century the United States entered the machine age with the development of the cotton gin and the steamboat. Although in the nineteenth century steamboats and steam locomotives gave immense impetus to industrial expansion, the country was still largely agricultural: there were more than 1,700 cities, but 1,300 of them had less than 10,000 residents.

One of the marked developments of this century has been the vastly increased use of energy, made possible by the invention of the internal combustion engine and the electric motor, and by the nationwide distribution of electrical power. Unlimited power, available at any time and any place, has changed agriculture, transportation, and building, and has made possible numberless new kinds of business and industry. At the same time, developments in industrial techniques—interchangeable parts, prefabrication, and sub-assembly—as well as technological advances in communications, electronics, and cybernetics, have opened new fields of endeavor. This progress goes on at a constantly increasing rate: some of the people who saw the Wright brothers fly the world's first successful airplane also saw the first man walk on the moon.

On previous pages: The United States became a highly industrialized nation in the twentieth century. By World War II, even shipbuilding had been put on an assembly-line basis. Here, the Permanente Yard at Richmond, California, works on more than a mile of Liberty ships. Four are fitting out, and eight are on the ways. The third and fourth ships from the left are almost ready for launching; the fifth does not yet have her engine. Courtesy: National Archives.

Concurrent with technological and industrial advances, there have been many changes in educational methods, sociological understanding, and scientific research. Because of the complicated structure of modern society, every one of these changes makes an impact on more than one small segment of society. Rapid dissemination of information through worldwide communication systems means that any change or new development, whether for better or worse, might have a strong influence on millions of people within a very short period.

The following chapters describe some noted changes and developments that have significantly affected this country in the past seventy-five years.

It should be remembered that nothing will ever again, not even tomorrow, be exactly the same as it is today. There will be at least some small change in every person, in every city, in every country—in the entire universe. After reviewing the history of the past seventy-five years, consider the exciting changes that might come in the next twenty-five. The past is history, and no one can change it. The future is open for active participation by anyone with imagination and new ideas, and the determination to carry them through. Think big.

CHAPTER 14
THE NAVY AND THE NATION

After the Civil War ended, the Navy faced the usual postwar demand for economy. Ships cost money. Tie them up and send the sailors back to the farm. The nation that had been a leading maritime and naval power turned away from seaports and rotting ships and concentrated on railroads and industries, which had little visible connection with the sea. Within a decade about the only people who could see any reason for maintaining a navy were a few senior officers who believed that a fighting fleet was as necessary in keeping the peace as in winning the war. The fleets that sailed to victory and fame under Porter and Farragut were steadily depleted by lack of maintenance funds, until by 1885 the Navy would have been hard pressed to fight its way out of a duck pond. The fleet that had numbered almost 700 ships in 1866 was cut down to 185 in 1871 and to 139 in 1881. By 1885 the Navy had no more than 90 ships, only 25 of which were at sea.

Once the nation had recovered from the shock of the Civil War, it entered an era of prosperity. There was a great increase in overseas trade, especially with South America. New, fast steamships—few of them flying the U.S. flag—awakened people to the fact that the wide Atlantic, which had once protected America from aggression by European nations, now made it possible for those nations to attack with very little warning. Those who remembered that British blockade of American ports had ruined commerce during the War of 1812 began to argue that the Navy should again be made strong enough to protect American commerce and the merchant marine should again be built up to the point where it could carry such commerce.

On previous page: This is the White Fleet at Hampton Roads, Virginia, in 1907, a few months before it set out on a cruise around the world. The ships are "dressed" with rainbows of flags, and are firing salutes as President Theodore Roosevelt reviews them from the yacht *Mayflower*. Courtesy: The Library of Congress.

Americans, wanting to have the biggest and best, were startled when the war between Chile, Bolivia, and Peru from 1879 to 1884 proved that South American navies were stronger and more modern than that of the United States. This revelation was especially disturbing to those who were familiar with the strong words of President James Monroe's annual message to Congress on 2 December 1823. Later referred to as the Monroe Doctrine, the message stated that "the American continents, by the free and independent condition which they have assumed and maintained, are henceforth not to be considered as subjects for future colonization by any European powers." Monroe also said that European intervention in the Western Hemisphere could not be viewed "in any other light than as the manifestation of an unfriendly disposition toward the United States." He had given the United States the task of defending the whole Western Hemisphere against the wave of imperialism then evident in Europe. But with what?

Naval expansion

Finally, in 1883 Congress authorized the building of four steam-powered, steel-hulled ships: the cruisers *Atlanta*, *Boston*, and *Chicago*, and the small despatch boat *Dolphin*. Painted white, these ships were known as the White Squadron and also as the ABCD ships. Annually, for the next ten years, Congress authorized more new ships. This shipbuilding program, which resulted in improved techniques for steel production and armor manufacture, reached its height in 1889 when Congress appropriated funds for the Navy's first true battleships, the 10,000-ton *Indiana*, *Massachusetts*, and *Oregon*.*

In 1890 Alfred Thayer Mahan published his book, *The Influence of Sea Power upon History*, and began advocating a big navy, not only as essential to national defense but as an element of national prosperity and greatness.

War with Spain

The expansion of the Navy brought a growing need for overseas bases where ships could be repaired and fueled. Furthermore, since the United States could not afford to maintain fleets in both the Atlantic Ocean and the Pacific Ocean, there was need for a canal across the Isthmus of Panama, to give ships rapid passage from one ocean to the other. Such a canal would have to be protected against enemy attack, and for that purpose also, island bases would be required—Cuba and the West Indies in the Atlantic; Hawaii and Samoa in the Pacific.

* The *New Jersey*, the last battleship in commission, was retired from service in 1969.

Hawaii was already closely tied to the United States; by 1890, 99 percent of all the sugar exported from Hawaii was going to the United States. Cuba was also producing sugar, with American financing. When sugar prices dropped in 1895, because Congress gave a bounty to producers of sugar in the United States, Cuba entered a depression. Cubans began an insurrection against Spain. Spain was too weak to restore order, and Americans feared that France, Germany, or Britain might take over the island.

As Spain made feeble attempts to quell the disturbances in Cuba, the *New York World* and the *New York Journal*, in an effort to increase their own circulation, began printing stories of Spanish atrocities in Cuba. The stories had the end result of convincing many Americans that they really wanted to go to war with Spain. In 1896 William McKinley was elected president on a platform calling for Cuban independence. One of his first acts was to order the four-year-old, 6,600-ton, second-class battleship *Maine* to Havana, where a riot threatened the safety of U.S. citizens. She arrived in Havana on 25 January 1898.

"Remember the Maine!"   At 9:40 on the evening of 15 February, an explosion completely wrecked the ship, and she sank in water so shallow that much of her wreckage was visible. Out of a crew of 355, 252 men were killed outright and eight died later. Captain Charles Sigsbee, the commanding officer of the ship, urged caution in handling news of the disaster until an investigation could be made, but American newspapers, still using the "yellow journalism" that built circulation totals, soon scared the public into near hysteria. "Remember the Maine!" became a battle cry, frequently combined with "To hell with Spain!"

The cause of the explosion has never been determined. General American opinion was that a submarine mine exploded beneath the ship and sank her. Spanish authorities held that she was sunk by an explosion in her own magazines. More than seventy-five years later, statements by a survivor of the *Maine* indicated that the Spanish may have been correct; sailors smoking below decks in unauthorized places very probably did cause the explosion. Actually, Spain had nothing to gain by forcing the United States into war, and stood a good chance of losing Cuba if she did so.

No matter who sank the *Maine*, Americans were convinced that they wanted to fight Spain. Commodore George Dewey, in command of the U.S. Asiatic Fleet, prepared for war after Acting Secretary of the Navy Theodore Roosevelt cabled him on 25 February: "Keep full of coal. In event of declaration of war Spain, your duty will be to see that the Spanish Squadron does not leave the Asiatic coast, and then offensive operations in the Philippine Islands." Dewey did exactly that. He bought a shipload of coal— and the ship that carried it. He started gunnery drills, had his white ships painted gray to make them less visible, and moved them from Yokohama to Hong Kong.

On 19 March the battleship *Oregon* was ordered to make a fast run from Bremerton, Washington, around South America to the East Coast. She made the 15,000-mile run in 66 days—and showed dramatically why the United States needed a canal in Panama: the voyage could have been made in half the time had the canal been in existence. While the *Oregon* was making her long end run around South America, Congress on 19 April declared Cuba to be free and independent, and on 24 and 25 April, the United States and Spain declared war on each other.

Action in the Pacific   Two days after war was declared, Dewey sailed his squadron to the Philippines. Despite warnings that the entrance to Manila Bay had been mined, he took his ships into the bay, then slowed them so as to arrive off Manila about dawn on 1 May.

Spanish ships—several old cruisers and a gunboat—were anchored across the bay from Manila. They fired on the Americans as soon as they appeared; long before they were within range. Dewey waited until his ships were less than three miles from the enemy, then gave Charles V. Gridley, captain of the *Olympia*, the famous order, "You may fire when you are ready, Gridley." Within a few hours the Spanish fleet had been sunk, the shore batteries destroyed, and a white flag of surrender raised. Nearly four hundred Spaniards were killed; only a few Americans were wounded.

By the time the *Oregon* reached the Key West Naval Base on 26 May, the naval side of the Spanish-American war was over in the far Pacific.

Action in the Caribbean   In the Caribbean, the naval war went on considerably longer. American forces were uncertain as to the exact location of a Spanish squadron that had been sent out from Spain. Two U.S. squadrons, one under Admiral William T. Sampson and the other under Commodore Winfield Scott Schley, wasted several days and a lot of coal chasing Spaniards where there were none, before it was definitely established that they were in Santiago Bay, on the south coast of Cuba. Finally, on 31 May, the Americans set up a blockade outside the harbor and waited for the Spaniards to come out. Meanwhile, a few U.S. Marines went ashore on 18 June and, in the first fighting on Cuban soil, took Guantanamo Bay. Four days later an Army expeditionary force of 16,000 men began landing east of Santiago, at a place called Daiquiri, remembered for the fact that the Americans named a drink after it.

Six Spanish ships, fearful that U.S. troops would trap them in the harbor, tried to break out on the morning of 3 July. Taken by surprise, blockading U.S. ships got off to a slow start in pursuit, but soon began making hits that set the enemy ships on fire. One by one, the Spanish ships ran ashore. In what became known as the Battle of Santiago, some 260 Spaniards were killed or drowned and another 1,800 were taken prisoner; one American sailor was killed and one wounded.

Spain was hopelessly outclassed. Her ships were claimed to be faster than U.S. ships, but lack of upkeep canceled out that advantage. Spanish guns were inferior to U.S. weapons; some of them could not be operated, none of the ships had fired target practice in over a year, and most of their ammunition was found to be defective.

With Spain's naval forces in the Pacific and Atlantic wiped out, the rest of the war was a one-sided proposition. The U.S. Army, assisted by naval bombardment, took Santiago, Cuba; Manila, in the Philippine Islands; and the principal cities of Puerto Rico. The island of Guam, then a Spanish possession, surrendered to the first American ship that arrived there. Hostilities ended on 12 August 1898. There were nine sailors among the almost 7,000 American casualties, most of whom were victims of disease, not combat.

The war ended officially on 10 December, when the United States and Spain signed a peace treaty in Paris. Under terms of the treaty, Spain withdrew from Cuba, and the former Spanish possessions of Guam, Puerto Rico, and the Philippine Islands were turned over to the United States. Spain was paid $20 million for the Philippines.

Four days after the Battle of Santiago, the United States annexed Hawaii, thereby eliminating any possibility that another nation might establish a base there. The next year Wake Island and Samoa were annexed. These annexations not only provided the desired overseas bases but set up a series of stepping-stones across the Pacific from California to the Philippines, and put the United States in a position to compete in the western Pacific with the rapidly growing naval power of Japan. The country was on its way to becoming a world power, and began building a navy strong enough to help establish that status.

Every year after the Spanish-American war ended, one or more new battleships were built. These were seagoing ships, not the old shallow-water monitors of Civil War fame, and to prove that they were, President Theodore Roosevelt sent sixteen of them— the White Fleet—on a 14-month cruise around the world. This was "showing the flag" on a scale never attempted before by any nation, and visible demonstration of Roosevelt's determination to "speak softly but carry a big stick."

The Panama Canal   Ever since Vasco de Balboa discovered the Pacific Ocean in 1513, sailors had been impressed, and baffled, by the fact that it was only 50 miles from the Atlantic to the Pacific if one walked— across the Isthmus at Panama—but thousands of miles if one went by water around South America. The two-month-long "dash" of the *Oregon* from the Pacific to the Atlantic in 1898 and the plodding cruise of the White Fleet from the Atlantic to the Pacific in 1907 emphasized the need for quick transit from one ocean to the other, not only in times of war, but as an aid to merchant marine operations.

There had been interest in a canal somewhere across Central America as early as 1823. The gold rush to California in 1849 proved that even the worst way across the Isthmus was faster than the best way around the Horn. In the 1880s a French firm called Compagnie Nouvelle made some highly expensive attempts to dig a canal, but were defeated by poor engineering and mosquitoes. Their plan for a sea-level canal involved the moving of an incredible amount of earth, given the primitive equipment then available. But poor sanitation and disease—particularly malaria and yellow fever, which no one yet knew were carried by mosquitoes—stopped the project. More than 22,000 workers died of disease between 1881 and 1889.

In 1870, the Navy sent the first of several survey expeditions to Central America to determine the best route for a canal. Negotiations between the United States and Colombia over the rights that would have to be acquired for the construction, operation, and control of a canal went on for several years. Finally, in January 1902, Congress appropriated $40 million to purchase the rights of the defunct French firm. The following year Panama revolted against Colombia, was soon recognized by the United States as an independent nation, and agreed to a treaty giving the United States control of a zone ten miles wide (now called the Canal Zone) in which to construct a canal across the Isthmus.

Before the canal could be built, disease had to be eliminated. Under the direction of Colonel William C. Gorgas, U.S. Army Medical Corps, swamps were drained in order to control mosquitoes, a sewer system was installed, and a safe water supply was made available for the cities of Panama and Colón. Without such efforts, the canal probably could not have been completed.

Preliminary construction began in 1904 and the canal was opened to traffic on 15 August 1914. During that time, an average of 39,000 men worked daily, and deaths from all causes were 6,630. In excavating for the canal and building dams, U.S. engineers using steam shovels and railroad dump cars moved over 400,000,000 cubic yards of earth. By the use of dams, Gatun Lake, with an area of 165 square miles, was created 85 feet above sea level. Ships are lifted up to the lake, and lowered again, through locks 1,000 feet long and 110 feet wide.* Electric locomotives,

---

* Those dimensions limited the length and beam of all U.S. battleships and aircraft carriers up through World War II. Large modern carriers with angled decks cannot use the canal.

called *mules*, tow ships into and out of the locks. Total cost of the canal, locks, dams, and equipment was $375 million.

Ten years after the canal was opened, ships were passing through at the rate of 6,000 a year. Since a ship sailing from New York to Los Angeles via the canal has to travel only about 4,900 miles, as compared to about 13,000 miles if she goes around South America, it can be seen that the saving in money and time is well worth the toll, which is based on cargo-carrying capacity. Besides the effect the canal had in reducing costs for merchant ships sailing between the East Coast and the West Coast, it greatly increased the mobility and effectiveness of the U.S. Navy. Instead of having to maintain two fleets, one in each ocean, the Navy could build one strong fleet and move it from ocean to ocean in comparatively short time.

World War I   In the same month that the Panama Canal opened, World War I began in Europe. The incident that precipitated a long and costly war took place on 28 June 1914, when Archduke Francis Ferdinand of Austria was assassinated in Sarajevo, Serbia. A month later Austria declared war on Serbia. During the month of August a dozen European nations became involved. American political and naval leaders did not expect the war to have much effect on the United States, and for the first couple of years the country remained neutral.

The land war soon turned into trench warfare, in which neither side made any extensive gains. But the story at sea was different. In June 1916, Germany's High Seas Fleet and England's Grand Fleet met in the Battle of Jutland. The German fleet, although greatly outnumbered, did considerable damage to the British fleet; the German ships were better built and German gunnery was better than that of the British. Shocked, Congress immediately approved an ambitious naval building program which was to augment the fleet by 10 battleships, 6 battle cruisers, 10 scout cruisers, 50 destroyers, and 67 submarines in three years.

Although the United States remained neutral, the war had a significant effect on its commerce. Trade with the Central Powers—Germany and her allies—which amounted to $170 million in 1914, had dropped to nearly nothing by 1916. But trade with the allied nations—England, France, Italy, and Russia—had increased four times to more than $3 billion by 1916.

Germany, in a move to starve England before the United States decided to send her aid, announced a policy of unrestricted warfare at sea, and used submarines to sink the merchant ships of any nation, belligerent or neutral. Although in May 1915, a German U-boat torpedoed the British liner *Lusitania*, which sank with the loss of 1,200 lives, including 128 Americans, the United States still remained neutral. "There is such a thing as a man being too proud to fight," declared President Woodrow Wilson. But two years later he had changed his mind and, on 6 April 1917, the United States declared war on Germany.

By that time Germany was turning out three submarines a week, and had already sunk one-fourth of all allied merchant shipping. In April 1917 alone, German submarines sank more than 900,000 tons of merchant shipping; England had enough grain to last only a month, and soon would either starve or be forced to surrender. Admiral William S. Sims was sent to London to work with the British and recommend how best to use U.S. naval forces. He arrived three days after the United States had declared war on Germany.

Antisubmarine warfare   Sims soon realized that the submarine war against merchant shipping could not be handled by battleships; what was needed were submarine-hunters and convoy escorts. Six U.S. destroyers were soon on their way to England, under the command of Commander Joseph K. Taussig. After a stormy Atlantic crossing, the ships steamed into Queenstown, Ireland, where the British admiral asked when they would be ready for duty at sea. Taussig was widely quoted as having replied, "We are ready now, sir," although he sensibly modified that by adding, "as soon as we have taken on fuel." By July nearly three dozen U.S. destroyers were on patrol out of Queenstown. German submarine "kills" of merchant shipping fell off rapidly thereafter.

The destroyers were soon joined by several dozen 110-foot sub-chasers, known as the "splinter fleet."

Despite British objections that convoys were limited to the speed of the slowest ships in the groups, few ships were lost out of convoys. The first U.S. convoy sailed for England on 24 May 1917. By the following year more than 400 ships in the Naval Overseas Transportation Service were operating out of Hampton Roads. Among the 45 troop transports operated by the U.S. Navy were 20 German liners that had been commandeered in U.S. ports. In all, 2,000,000 troops were transported overseas without the loss of a single man.

Mine warfare   Naval escorts kept the U-boats away from convoys, but lone merchant ships were still being sunk. Finally, in spite of British arguments that the plan was impractical, it was decided to try to pen the U-boats in their own bases by laying a vast minefield in the North Sea. The mines were built in Norfolk, Virginia, at the rate of 1,000 a day. Cargo steamers carried them to Scotland. Navy minelayers began planting the mines on 8 June 1918. By the time the war ended, nearly 70,000 mines had been put down. The exact number of submarines destroyed in the minefield has never been determined.

Naval aviation   When World War I began, the U.S. Navy had only 54 aircraft and 48 qualified aviators. The first naval aviation unit sent overseas arrived in France on 5 June 1917; it consisted of 7 officers and 122 men. By the time the war ended, Navy and Marine Corps units were operating from 27 bases in England, France, Ireland and Italy. Overseas aviation units numbered 16,300 officers and men, 500 aircraft, 50 kite balloons, and 3 dirigibles. Navy aircraft had attacked at least 25 U-boats, and sunk or damaged a dozen of them. Planes were either land-based or seaplane types; there were no aircraft carriers in the Navy at that time.

The U.S. battleships *Texas, New York,* and *Florida* operated for a while with the British Grand Fleet, but no ships of the U.S. Navy engaged in any surface action, other than scattered attacks on U-boats. The destroyer *Jacob Jones* was torpedoed and sunk by the U-53, and the cruiser *San Diego* was sunk off Fire Island, New York, by a mine laid by a submarine. U-boats torpedoed and sank seven Navy cargo vessels and transports and one small Coast Guard cutter. Six of them crossed the Atlantic to operate off the east coast of the United States: the U-151 damaged three small schooners off Cape Charles, and the U-53 torpedoed five vessels off Nantucket.

Submarine development   World War I was the proving ground for submarines. Before the war began most subs had a cruising range of about 300 miles. During the war Germany built craft with longer cruising endurance and used supply ships to fuel them at long distances from their bases. By 1915 U-boats were operating in the Mediterranean, and by 1916 a few had sunk vessels off the east coast of the United States. Before the war ended, U-boats had an operating radius of 10,000 miles.

The U-boat campaign against merchant shipping nearly won the war for Germany. Submarines were comparatively inexpensive, when it was considered that one of them could account for a dozen or more merchant ships in a few weeks at sea.

Germany began the war with only 28 active submarines. When the war ended, she surrendered 176 U-boats. Many more were under construction. It is estimated that during the war she lost 203 undersea craft from all causes. Despite such losses, Germany proved the submarine to be one of the most potent naval weapons ever devised.

Shipbuilding programs   When the United States declared war on Germany in 1917, a big naval expansion program began. The fleet received 396 new ships, for a total of 798,000 tons. The battleships, and most destroyers, were completed too late to serve in the war, but many of them took part in World War II. After World War I ended, the usual economy moves forced the Navy to put more than a hundred destroyers out of commission. Fortunately, they were still serviceable in 1940, and 50 of them were swapped to Great Britain for 99-year leases on bases in British possessions in the West Indies and the Caribbean.

The U.S. merchant fleet, in 1917, consisted of a little over 500,000 tons of steam and motor vessels, plus a considerable number of sailing craft. Congress immediately set up an emergency government agency whose mission was to build a "bridge to France" by purchasing and constructing merchant ships as fast as possible. The building program included cargo ships, tankers, refrigerator ships, and passenger ships. Large ships were built of steel, many small types were built of wood, and a few were built of concrete. Shipyards on the Great Lakes turned out 450 cargo ships of 2,000 tons each. Yards in California, Oregon, and Washington built merchant vessels of all types. A complete shipyard was built on Hog Island, near Philadelphia, where 35,000 men turned out 122 freighters, which were nicknamed "hogs."

During the entire merchant-ship building program, American yards delivered 2,311 seagoing ships of all types for a total of 13,627,311 tons. As a result of the building boom, in 1920 the merchant fleet was ten times as big as it had been in 1914. But, with the war over, there was no need for many of the ships. Hundreds of them were tied up in dead storage, then called "rotten row." Ships that had cost $200 a ton to build were sold for $5 a ton. Henry Ford bought 149 new "lake boats," cut them up, melted them down, and turned them into Ford cars.

World War I losses were comparatively light for the Navy and merchant marine, much heavier for the Army and Marine Corps. Merchant-ship losses from all causes totaled 199, with 1,553 lives lost. The Navy lost 48 ships, but only 10 to enemy torpedoes or mines; the rest were lost in collisions, fires, and accidents. Total loss of life in the Navy amounted to 1,142. The Army and Marine Corps had approximately 49,000 combat casualties, and a far larger number of deaths—57,000—from disease, mostly influenza and pneumonia.

The armistice that ended World War I was signed at the 11th hour of the 11th day of the 11th month of 1918. The Treaty of Versailles, signed on 28 June 1919, ceded some German territory to France, Belgium, and Poland, and established the League of Nations. The United States rejected the treaty but did cooperate with the League of Nations.

In the years following World War I, the country again leaned toward the idea of isolation. A large navy did not fit the theories of isolationists, and a demand for national economy forced a reduction in naval forces. A first move in this direction came in

After World War I

1922, when the Washington Conference was called to consider naval armament and policies in the Far East. The conference, which lasted from 12 November 1921 to 6 February 1922, ended in the Five-Power Treaty, signed by the United States, Great Britain, France, Italy, and Japan. Each signatory guaranteed the rights of all the others to insular possessions in the Pacific, and established a 10-year naval holiday during which no vessels larger than 10,000 tons with guns larger than 8 inches were to be built. The treaty also established a 5-5-3 ratio for capital ships, which meant that the United States and Great Britain were each allowed 525,000 tons of combatant types, while Japan was allowed only 315,000 tons. The United States had opened the conference by stating that she was about to scrap new construction on which $300 million had already been spent; in fact, she would scrap seven battleships and six battle cruisers, for a total of 400,000 tons.

The loss of the battleships was not as serious as it might have appeared. The Navy's first aircraft carrier, the *Langley*, was commissioned in 1922, and two of the unfinished battle cruisers which were to have been scrapped were completed as aircraft carriers, the *Lexington* and *Saratoga*, which joined the fleet in 1927. The big carriers marked a change in naval thinking; twenty years after the Washington Conference, they were replacing battleships as the first line of defense.

Another disarmament conference, held in Geneva in 1927, was a failure. France and Italy balked at attending, Great Britain said she needed more ships to protect her colonial interests. Congress decided to authorize the building of 15 heavy cruisers. The London Conference, held in 1930, further reduced naval strength, but the move was futile. Japan announced that, when the treaties expired in 1936, she would no longer abide by any limitations.

The result was to be expected. The United States was slowly recovering from the economic depression of 1929, and President Franklin D. Roosevelt, an ardent believer in the Navy, authorized a large shipbuilding program as a part of the National Industrial Recovery Act.

There was something about the situation that called for the well-worn expression "Here's where we came in." For the third time in the memory of many people, the country had tried without success to settle the question of when too few ships became too many ships. The Civil War, the Spanish-American War, and World War I had all caught the country with too few ships— and left it with too many.

Some of the Model T "Tin Lizzies" that Ford built out of ships back in the 1920s were going to complete the cycle. They were going to be cut up, melted down, and turned back into ships again.

CHAPTER 15
SOCIOLOGY AND EDUCATION

America's mariners have affected people's lives in many ways. In seeking to improve the welfare of men at sea, they have been directly responsible for improving many aspects of life ashore. This applies not only to the advancement of political freedom and the supply of material goods, but also to health, education, environmental conditions, conservation, and law enforcement.

The first changes were simple enough—slight improvements in food and some realization of the fact that sailors, like captains, were people deserving of consideration where the basic rights of humanity were concerned.

Flogging and punishments

In the old days, flogging was almost a way of life at sea. Many captains of old sailing ships, when making or taking in sail, had the habit of hurrying men into the rigging, in order to maintain a reputation as the captain of a smart ship. Boatswain's mates stood by the shrouds and urged the men aloft; it was common to flog a man merely for being the last into the rigging.

The practice of flogging, along with other harsh punishments aboard ship, was a carry-over from the British Navy. Such barbaric treatment of people probably reflected the cruelty of the times, and conditions aboard ship contributed to it. When as many as 500 men, some of them hardened characters, were packed into two decks of a ship for months on end, they were bound to fight out of sheer boredom. Even in port men were often kept on board for fear they would get in trouble ashore, or desert. Ships

On previous page: Coast Guard cutters *Morgenthau*, *Dallas*, and *Rockaway* nest at Governors Island with the skyline of Lower Manhattan as a backdrop. Just below the Brooklyn Bridge, at right, some old square-riggers of sailing-ship days are berthed at the South Street Seaport. Courtesy: John M. Lehman.

might cruise for months or years without a man getting ashore once. When they did get ashore—and sometimes even when they did not—they got into trouble. In the old Navy and merchant service, when a man got into trouble he was punished.

The severity of the punishment depended on the offense and the mood of the captain. "Doubling the tub"—going to the end of the food line for "seconds"—called for severe punishment. Slowness in obeying orders or being the last man aloft called for the whip. Fighting, insolence to officers, stealing, and murder were the obvious major crimes.

The commonest punishment was confinement in the ship's prison, or brig, with single or double irons on both hands and legs, and usually a diet of bread and water. In most cases the brig was a dark, dismal place on the berth deck, about 10 to 12 feet square, in which up to a dozen men might be confined.

An act passed by Congress in 1799 forbade a captain to order more than twelve lashes for any one offense. But a tyrannical officer could charge a man with several offenses and give him a dozen for each, so the regulation did little good.

When flogging was ordered, the man was stripped to his waist and spread-eagled against a grating; a boatswain's mate then "laid on with a will" up to ten dozen lashes with the cat-o'-nine-tails. The "cat" is a short wooden club, bound at one end with nine slender ropes, each terminating in a hard knot or a pellet of lead to make them bite more viciously into the man's flesh. Even a dozen lashes left a man's back bleeding; seven or eight dozen could be fatal. All hands were mustered to witness the punishment, and the surgeon was ordered to stand by to see if the results were threatening the man's life.

In the earlier days, the man to be flogged was lashed over the breech of a gun, a process referred to in the British Navy as being "married to the gunner's daughter."

Many people feared that, without flogging, discipline at sea would fail. Even old salts who prided themselves on the number of ugly scars across their backs were convinced that there would be no discipline without the threat of the cat-o'-nine tails.

In 1843 the frigate *United States*, in Hawaii, signed on a 24-year-old whaleman for the voyage home. The man was Herman Melville, an ordinary seaman, who was destined to become known as an extraordinary author of books about the sea. He became world-famous for his sea classic, *Moby Dick*, but his book *White Jacket*, an account of the 14-month cruise aboard the *United States*, had great and far-reaching effects, particularly in the U.S. Navy. His descriptions of the 163 floggings he witnessed saved innumerable men from unbelievable pain and suffering.

There had been some public demand for an end to flogging before *White Jacket* appeared, but the book was read by far more people than there were sailors who had been flogged, and it created great pressure to end the practice. Most naval officers agreed that flogging was inhuman, and in 1850 Congress abolished the practice.

Other brutal punishments continued in practice and a few new ones were contrived. Steam vessels brought the "sweatbox," a prison six feet high and three feet wide, with only tiny holes for ventilation. It was placed near the ship's boilers where the heat was most intense. Admiral Farenholt, who saw the sweatbox used on board ships during the Civil War, wrote: "There was no special crime to fit this punishment. I remember a case in which a man, for attempting to smuggle liquor on board, was confined in the sweatbox for 10 nights from 8:00 until midnight. In 1868, on board the steam sloop-of-war *Brooklyn*, a man died in the sweatbox. . . ." There was an investigation of the latter case and the captain was relieved of his command.

Worse than the sweatbox was "tricing up," where a man's hands were put in irons, raised in front, and triced up with a rope so that his feet barely touched the deck. Sometimes men were ironed with their hands behind them to the ringbolts on deck or to the gun carriages. At sea, with the ship in motion, it was a horrible punishment.

These and other such practices were finally brought to an end, largely through the efforts of those who had to witness them and then patch up the victims—ships' surgeons.

Machine age in the Navy

In square-rigger days, all a sailor needed to know was how to furl sails and tie a few knots. But by the time the nation was moving into the age of steam that came with the Civil War it had become obvious that the Navy needed more-skilled and better-educated men. Steam engines, screw propellers, and complicated ordnance required people who knew how to operate and maintain such machinery.

Until 1845, most midshipmen entered the Navy at fifteen or sixteen years of age and trained at sea as members of ships' crews. Later they could take a leave of absence to get further schooling on their own or attend the school for midshipmen that had been set up in Philadelphia in 1839. When they had passed the required exams, they became "passed midshipmen." It was a woefully inadequate system.

Morale and discipline were bad; midshipmen who were "passed" but not quite officers were often bored and discouraged as they waited for promotion. Since there was no system of retirement, the senior ranks were filled with officers from the War of 1812, many of whom blocked the promotion ladder by living a very long time. Energetic and ambitious young officers had little hope of moving up in rank.

The need for a change in training and administrative methods was dramatically demonstrated during a cruise to Africa by the brig *Somers* in 1842. The ship was under the command of Commander Alexander Slidell Mackenzie, an older man who belonged to the martinet school of thinking. As matters proved, he was a poor choice to deal with 130 new midshipmen and youthful apprentice seamen, the oldest of whom was 22 and the youngest about 14.

The *Somers* Mutiny

Among the midshipmen was a high-spirited, irresponsible young fellow named Philip Spencer, son of the Secretary of War. Spencer had been expelled from college, joined the Navy as a lark, was thrown out, then reinstated because of his father's influence.

The cruise to Africa was a disaster from the very beginning. Tempers boiled over in the tropical heat, orders were disobeyed, and the young crew members grumbled constantly. On the return trip, the purser's steward told Mackenzie that a mutiny was brewing. Spencer was said to be the leader, his accomplices being Boatswain's Mate Samuel Cromwell and Seaman Elisha Small. They supposedly planned to seize the ship, kill the officers, and head for the Spanish Main as pirates.

Mackenzie ordered Spencer clapped in irons. A search of Spencer's seabag revealed a scrap of paper with a list of officers and crew bearing the notation "to be killed." The following day there were demonstrations by the crew, who shouted, stomped, and gathered in ominous groups. This convinced Mackenzie that Cromwell and Small should also be put in irons. He then ordered that the three men be put on trial.

Evidence against Spencer included his reading pirate novels, having an odd gleam in his eye, and making music by squeezing his hands together. He was later said to have made some sort of confession. Cromwell professed his own innocence to the end.

The three were found guilty and hung from the yardarm in the presence of the entire ship's company. When the *Somers* reached home, there was a tremendous outcry and scandal. Newspapers carried the story of the Secretary of War's son. Questions were asked; were the young men really mutineers or merely pranksters? And why could they not have been brought back under close guard and tried in a calmer atmosphere?

Mackenzie was tried by a court-martial. He was exonerated on the grounds that, at sea, a captain's judgment is the law. The tragedy pointed up the awesome authority of officers at sea and the need for improving their caliber and training. Young midshipmen, too, needed to be carefully selected and educated.

The *Somers* incident occurred at the time James K. Polk became president. He appointed George Bancroft, a historian and philosopher, as Secretary of the Navy. Bancroft wanted to establish the

The U.S. Naval Academy

kind of naval academy proposed earlier by Matthew Fontaine Maury but, since Congress turned a deaf ear to the idea, he was forced to doctor his requests for funds with various ruses. He fired the old seagoing professors and replaced them with four academic instructors and a lieutenant to teach engineering and gunnery. The capable Commander Franklin Buchanan was put in charge. Bancroft borrowed from the Army old Fort Severn at Annapolis and the school opened on 10 October 1845. Classes were held in a wooden shed; three midshipmen made up the student body.

After that, as midshipmen returned from cruises, they entered the school in a steady stream. A new type of officer appeared. Being gentlemanly and brave was not enough any more; the Navy had to have educated professionals. During the academic year 1850–51, the school was renamed the Naval Academy and a four-year course of study was adopted.

A number of other important changes aimed at improving the quality of personnel were made. In 1842, naval boards were set up to determine by means of examinations the qualifications of officers for appointment or advancement. Bancroft ordered entrance exams for naval constructors, boatswains, carpenters, and sail-makers. For line officers, promotions were judged by an examining board or by efficiency reports. In 1855, the Naval Retiring Board was set up to determine the retired lists for officers.

Enlisted training

After the War of 1812, enlisted men were usually "shipped" for three years, then discharged. Men who enlisted for a second or third cruise were given no added pay or other considerations. Long-term training and career-planning were unknown. In 1852, a permanent corps of seamen was formed. Five years later, the ordnance ship *Plymouth*, commanded by John A. Dahlgren, began taking seamen on six-month cruises to learn management of the heavy ordnance that was coming into use.

It was the modest beginning of what has become one of the largest school systems in the world. The Navy now maintains hundreds of specialized schools for training men to handle its complicated ships, weapons, and systems.

When the Civil War ended, men were encouraged to remain in service and, eventually, increased pay for added service was an inducement to make the Navy a career. The Navy's present system of training and career-planning enables a person to complete a military career, acquire a technical or academic education, and, through promotion, attain a position of great responsibility.

Today, education for the Navy's enlisted men and women begins with recruit training and continues throughout their naval service, whether this be four years or thirty years. Every Navy enlisted person has the opportunity to acquire skills and knowledge, either through schools or through Navy training courses and on-the-job training. Young men and women who want to learn and improve themselves have unlimited opportunities in the Navy: they can take correspondence courses; attend several of more than 400 schools; earn a General Educational Development certificate (the equivalent of a high school diploma); take a four-year college course and gain a degree; or apply for officer training and gain a commission.

Naval reserve

The first step towards establishing a system of naval reserves came during the Civil War when the Union Navy set up a blockade of Confederate ports. Every available vessel, including ferryboats, was used. There were not enough regular officers for a large fleet. The blockade fleet was manned by volunteer civilian officers, most of whom came from the merchant marine.

In 1887 a bill was introduced in Congress to set up an official naval reserve, but it was not enacted. Another try was made during the Spanish-American War, but it too failed, and it was not until 1916 that the president approved a bill to establish a naval reserve force made up of former officers and civilian volunteers.

Today's naval reservists are an important part of the naval organization. The 129,000 selected reservists in all fifty states are qualified and trained for active duty in time of war or national emergency.

Naval Reserve Officers Training Corps (NROTC)

Colleges and universities participating in the NROTC program offer courses in naval science and related subjects, which prepare students for commissions in the Navy. About 30 percent of all junior officers enter the Navy through this program.

Candidates for NROTC training are carefully selected. They must make qualifying scores on their college aptitude tests and be interviewed by their state selection board, before that board can approve them. Each state has an annual quota.

Once an NROTC candidate is accepted, he receives a tuition-and-textbook subsidy from the government for four years. Graduates agree to serve as officers in the regular Navy, or the Naval Reserve, for a stated period.

The NROTC program helps the Navy to keep in close touch with local communities. People who live far inland learn to know and appreciate their Navy and what it is trying to accomplish.

Officer Candidate School (OCS)

The Officer Candidate School at Newport, Rhode Island, also provides numerous junior officers for the Navy. There, college graduates are given sixteen weeks of intensive study, after which they have a short term of obligated service. When released from active duty, men and women officers spend time in the Naval Reserve and often continue this association for many years.

Merchant marine training facilities

One of the institutions that train officers for the merchant fleet is the U.S. Merchant Marine Academy, at King's Point, New York. About 200 cadets graduate each year to become deck officers or engineer officers. Many of them go into related fields and become leaders in the maritime industry. For example, at the present time six steamship company presidents are graduates of the school. Up to now, it is the only federal academy that accepts women as students. The five-year course of study includes engineering, nuclear propulsion, chartering, management, and liberal arts.

Five states—California, Maine, Massachusetts, New York, and Texas—operate maritime academies, and maritime unions operate upgrading schools for unlicensed men. The National Maritime Union of America Upgrading and Retraining School in New York and the Marine Cooks and Stewards Training Program in San Francisco accept persons who have no seafaring experience. The Calhoon Engineering School in Baltimore provides two years of academic training and one year at sea, which leads to a Third Assistant Engineer license.

The Harry Lundeberg School of Seamanship at Piney Point, Maryland, trains young people for jobs as ordinary seamen, wipers, and stewards. Students who have taken one course can return for further training to upgrade their job classifications.

There are a number of labor management schools which, although not financed by the federal government, are operated within the guidelines established by the Coast Guard and the Maritime Administration.

Maritime medicine

Improved educational methods fitted men to handle the complicated machinery and work with the more involved organization of the new Navy, but, as always, it was apparent that a smart sailor was of no use if he was a sick sailor. And sickness was a scourge in sailing ship days; sometimes so many men in a crew were incapacitated by various ailments that the ship could not get under way.

Maintaining the health and well-being of seafarers has led to many improvements in the lives of people ashore. Nearly every field of medicine has been affected by early shipboard experiences; preventive medicine, epidemiology, sanitation, diet, and surgery are only a few of them. The ancient Greeks and Romans made short voyages, mostly in the Mediterranean, and sickness was not a serious problem. It was not until the long sea voyages of the sixteenth century that serious shipboard health problems arose. Columbus, Vasco da Gama, and Magellan made voyages that lasted for years and brought terrible scourges to sailors.

Scurvy, typhus fever, smallpox, and similar diseases relentlessly stalked every ship that set sail. Injuries, overcrowding, bad air and water supply, poor food, and lack of care for the sick made a healthy existence for sailors virtually impossible. Traditionally, the number-one nautical killer was scurvy, a deficiency disease caused by a lack of Vitamin C in the diet. After two weeks at sea without fresh fruits and vegetables, sailors would show signs of weakness, of swelling of legs and arms, and gums so soft that teeth would fall out. Victims were prone to pneumonia and heart failure. Sir John Hawkins, the sixteenth-century naval captain, reported that in his twenty years at sea scurvy killed 20,000 men in the British Navy. Of the many men who set out on Magellan's historic circumnavigation of the globe, only eighteen completed the voyage in 1522. Most of the losses were from scurvy. When Lord Anson's fleet sailed around the world, 1740–44, two-thirds of the 961 sailors who began the voyage died of the disease.

Although preventive measures for scurvy had been known years before, it was not until 1747 that a British physician, James Lind, proved the value of lime juice in treating and preventing the dread disease. Fifty years later, Sir Gilbert Blane succeeded in making lime juice a requirement for all vessels of the Royal Navy; hence the nickname "limeys" for British seamen. This dramatic milestone in maritime medicine led to other improvements; in time, smallpox inoculation for the entire fleet was given official sanction. These and other practices were adopted by the Americans.

The earliest clear record of there being surgeons and surgeons' mates in the Royal Navy is dated 1512, during the reign of Henry VIII. Reference is made to a commissioned officer who served as a ship's doctor. He had no regularly assigned assistant, but usually depended on a cabin boy, a cook, or a convalescent sailor to feed the sick and injured and to maintain cleanliness as best he could. Later naval regulations stated that, when a man was sick or injured, he was to be removed to the sick bay to swing his hammock there until he recovered.

Eventually, ships' boys were assigned the regular duty of assisting surgeons and caring for the sick. They became known as "waisters" because the sick were treated at the "waist" of the ship, or as "loblolly boys," because the gruel or porridge they fed to the sick was called *loblolly*.

Loblolly boys   The duties of a loblolly boy are described in the U.S. Naval Regulations of 1814: "He will announce sick call in the morning by ringing the bell about the decks. He will feed, wash and shave the sick, and provide a tub of sand to catch the blood during surgical operations to prevent the staining of the deck. . . ."

In early days the sick bay was an area set above the waterline on the gun deck or the berth deck, and it was often exposed to enemy fire. Before long it was realized that a more sheltered area was needed for the wounded, particularly in battle. An additional space, called the dressing station and operating room, was set up in large ships; but it also did duty as living space for the midshipmen, surgeon's mates, master's mates, purser, and the captain's clerk. Eventually a sheltered compartment below the waterline was set aside for the sick and was officially designated as the "sick berth" or the "sick bay."

In 1778 Congress passed an act that regulated the medical establishments of the Army and Navy. That act provided for a "suitable number" of hospital mates to assist the surgeons. It is well that it did, for, during an encounter with the enemy, there might be hand-to-hand combat with cutlasses, gun butts, clubs, chains, or any other improvised weapons. Such encounters, plus cannon balls, caused many fractured limbs, and the accepted treatment for compound fractures was amputation.

Before a battle, loblolly boys turned to with such chores as providing the sick bay with water and tubs of sand for amputated limbs, arranging braziers in which to heat searing irons for stumps caused by amputations, and heating tar for stopping hemorrhages.

With the establishment of the Bureau of Medicine and Surgery in 1842, the loblolly boy became the more dignified "surgeon's steward." His pay was listed as $18 a month and one ration. For the first time, surgeons' stewards were officially allowed at all naval hospitals, navy yards, and on board every vessel that had a medical officer. Doctors were to select their stewards from men "as have some knowledge of pharmacy and ordinary accounts and are of industrious and temperate habits. . . ."

At the beginning of the Civil War, male nurses were accepted for duty aboard receiving ships. The first hospital ship, the *Red Rover*, which served during the Civil War, had women as well as men on her medical staff. Later U.S. Navy hospital ships included the *Idaho, Solace, Relief, Mercy, Comfort, Hope,* and *Repose.* The *Repose* and *Sanctuary* served during the Vietnam War. The *Hope* later became famous as a civilian ship for the medical help and training she provided to people in developing countries.

The loblolly boy had come a long way when, near the end of the nineteenth century, he reached the rating of "ship's apothecary." True, he had had little instruction or training but he carried his responsibilities with pride and honor. He ran the dispensary, compounded and dispensed medications, and, since there were no typewriters on board ship, made out his daily, monthly, and quarterly reports in pen and ink. "Baymen" attended the sick, kept the dispensary storerooms clean, painted when necessary, and sand-scrubbed the stools and benches. On "scrub bag and hammock days" baymen scrubbed the bags and hammocks belonging to those who were too ill to do their own.

The Hospital Corps   During the Spanish-American War, the Hospital Corps was organized as a unit of the Medical Department. Twenty-five senior apothecaries of the Navy were appointed "pharmacists" and, in August 1902, a Hospital Corps school was established at Portsmouth Naval Hospital in Virginia. This hospital, the oldest one in the Navy, had been commissioned in 1830 and was used during the crucial yellow-fever epidemic of 1855 when, out of Portsmouth's 5,000 inhabitants, 1,000 died and 1,000 were seriously crippled by the disease.

Graduates of the school had their first duty under fire when they served with the Marines in Haiti in 1915. Because Navy medical personnel are responsible for the medical care of Marines, non-combatant hospital corpsmen are assigned as an integral part of the "Leatherneck" Corps. They were with the Marines on the battlefields of Europe in World War I, and during the fierce jungle battles in the Pacific in World War II. Of the seven Congressional Medals of Honor awarded Navy men in the Korean conflict, five went to hospital corpsmen.

Corpsmen serve aboard U.S. Navy ships, in submarines, airplanes, at dispensaries, hospitals, and research laboratories all over the world. In peacetime they are often called upon to aid victims of such natural disasters as earthquakes and floods. Because they are frequently required to make independent decisions without the help of physicians or nurses, their training is intensive and thorough. Throughout the country there are more than 30 schools for training corpsmen in various specialties. Since July 1948, women have been accepted in the Hospital Corps, which numbers today about 23,500.

Navy corpsmen are in great demand by the civilian community as pharmacists, laboratory and x-ray technicians, and in the myriad specialties for which they have been trained.

The Navy Nurse Corps

Navy nurses, male and female, have brought great distinction to their profession. The Navy Nurse Corps was formally established in October 1908 when 20 nurses, who later came to be called the "Sacred Twenty," donned their uniforms and white aprons to become a part of the U.S. Navy. The following year, their number doubled and, by 1910, they were serving outside the United States—in the Philippines, Guam, Honolulu, Samoa, Yokohama, Cuba, and the Virgin Islands. They established schools of nursing for the native women of Guam and Samoa, and during World War I served in France with the American Red Cross.

During World War II, Navy nurses served in twelve hospital ships, in air evacuation of the wounded, and in overseas establishments, as well as in forty hospitals in the United States. A number of them were captured by the Japanese on Guam and in the Philippines in the early days of World War II. In their years of captivity they cared for fellow prisoners and saved many lives. In 1944, the destroyer *Higbee* was named for Lenah S. Higbee, the second Superintendent of the Nurse Corps.

In peacetime Navy nurses assist in disaster-relief missions, both at home and abroad. An important contribution they make to other countries is the teaching of nursing skills.

In 1968, for the first time, a man was accepted as an officer in the Nurse Corps. Today about 2,600 Navy nurses are on active duty as commissioned officers.

Maritime medicine goes ashore

Through the years, the problems faced by doctors and their assistants at sea were also confronting people on land. The main difference was that, at sea, everything was exaggerated. When someone came aboard with a contagious disease, chances were that everybody would get it. There was no sending him off to the countryside for a leisurely recovery. If the drinking water was contaminated or the food was rotten, there would most likely be an epidemic of some sort because everyone ate and drank from the same source.

If the ship was dirty, damp, and poorly ventilated, as old sailing vessels invariably were, crews suffered from typhus fever (generally known as ship fever), dysentery, pneumonia, tuberculosis, and a host of other ailments. Sailing as they did into faraway ports, the vessels picked up venereal diseases, cholera, and yellow fever. It was up to the ship's surgeon to insist that health measures aimed at protecting everyone on board the ship be practiced on a mass scale. Many innovations came ashore and became public health practice and law; inventions and medical breakthroughs can trace their origins over the rolling waves.

For example, the Stokes stretcher, so common today, was first used in the Navy in 1904 for moving wounded men in confined or difficult spaces. In 1911, compulsory vaccination against typhoid fever eliminated that disease from the Navy and set an example for the general public. Between 1940 and 1943, the Navy had to develop portable hospital facilities for use in combat areas, and the civilian community soon adopted many applications of that principle.

Sulfonamides used in wounds to prevent infection and the use of penicillin in treating gas gangrene, pneumonia, and local infections were pioneered by the Navy. Apparatus for the desalination of water for use in lifeboats and life rafts was refined for civilian use. The use of blood plasma in field surgery and the closed method of treating open wounds and compound fractures, developed in 1943, are in common use today. The first bone and tissue bank was established at the National Naval Medical Center in Bethesda, Maryland; it preserves bones and tissues for future use in reconstructive surgery. In 1955, a laboratory process was developed for freezing whole blood, especially rare types, for future clinical use. In 1957 the first nuclear reactor for medical use began operation at the National Naval Medical Center. Navy researchers invented a refined method of recording changes in human body temperatures from the ear drum—helpful in treating medical and surgical cases. In 1963, the Navy developed an artificial kidney, and the following year successfully tested a fluoride treatment for preventing tooth decay. Experts in Navy submarine medicine developed a way to use 100 percent oxygen for treating various conditions such as carbon-monoxide poisoning. Recently, the Navy has developed a hooded jacket that guards against disease-carrying insects: the jacket will soon be on the commercial market.

These are only a few instances of how maritime medicine has come ashore to better the lives of everyone. The Navy has come a long way from the unhealthy life aboard old sailing ships.

In the first days of independence, it became apparent that the new country needed some way of enforcing laws, particularly to ensure that import duties were honestly collected.

Law enforcement

Smuggling was rampant and, in order to suppress it, the first Secretary of the Treasury, Alexander Hamilton, requested several boats, "two for the coast of Massachusetts and New Hampshire, one for Long Island Sound, one for the Bay of Delaware (which would ply along the neighboring coasts) one for South Carolina and one for Georgia."

The first revenue cutters were small, swift schooners, capable of carrying plenty of sail aloft because their missions frequently called for speed; each was armed with a swivel gun. They were manned by crews of "respectable character."

Wages were quite good for those times. The master of a cutter received $30 a month, the first mate $20, the second mate $16, and the third mate $14. Crewmen got $8 a month, and cabin boys $4. All hands also received their food and a daily ration of brandy, whiskey, or rum.

Alexander Hamilton was killed in a duel with Aaron Burr in 1804 and did not see how successful his Revenue Marine became. For a while, smuggling ceased to be a popular and patriotic sport. But, as American and European shipping increased, running goods into the country without paying duty again became a highly profitable business. Stronger measures were required: between

1795 and 1801 the ten original cutters were replaced by thirteen bigger ones that carried heavier guns and larger crews and were capable of challenging the fast craft used by smugglers.

Since the U.S. Navy was not established until 1798, for eight years the Revenue Marine, which operated under the Treasury Department, was the country's only navy. Its descendant, the Coast Guard, operates under the Department of Transportation and, in wartime or at any time by direction of the President, becomes a part of the U.S. Navy.

Revenue cutters fought against the French raiders in the undeclared war of 1799. The *Eagle* captured five French vessels, recaptured seven American ships, and assisted in the taking of ten others. Cutters also fought in the War of 1812 and later against the pirates plying the East Coast and the Caribbean. In 1836, during the Seminole War in Florida, the crews of eight cutters made their first amphibious landing, thereby saving Fort Brook from destruction. During the rest of the war, cutters helped blockade rivers, carried dispatches, transported troops and ammunition, and provided landing parties to defend white settlements. When peace was restored n 1842, all hands were rewarded by being given a quarter square mile of public property in Florida.

In 1843 came a reorganization of the greatly extended service. Under Secretary of the Treasury John Spencer, the Revenue Marine Bureau was set up and consisted of many departments— legal, accounting, engineering, personnel, operations, and intelligence. Forty-six cutters took part in the Civil War; the *Miami* carried President Lincoln up and down the Potomac River and the Chesapeake Bay for firsthand views of Confederate forces; the *Hercules* captured a schooner in the Chesapeake.

Saga of the *Bear* Through the years, the service, which in 1915 came to be called the U.S. Coast Guard, used many cutters, side-wheelers, and a great variety of odd-looking craft experimenting with early steam engines. The most famous "cutter" of all was the former whaling ship *Bear*. Her career epitomizes the many sociological roles played by the seagoing service.

The *Bear* was designed for work in polar seas. Built in 1873 by Alexander Stephen and Sons, in Dundee, Scotland, her massive beams, heavy oak frame, and reinforced bow, as well as her Australian ironbark sheathing gave her a toughness unmatched by other vessels of her time. For 10 years, as a merchant ship, she was a seal-hunter off Newfoundland.

The Greely Expedition   Worldwide fame came to the *Bear* in the early 1880s, shortly after the historic Greely Expedition to the Arctic came to a disastrous end. The expedition, under the command of Lieutenant Adolphus Washington Greely, was one of two groups sent to the Arctic to set up a chain of observation stations. Despite elaborate plans, a series of misfortunes left Greely and his men stranded in the pitiless Arctic winter without adequate food and clothing.

To assist the Greely party, the Navy organized a rescue fleet of three ships: the *Bear, Thetis*, and *Alert*. On 22 June 1884, less than two months after her departure from the Brooklyn Navy Yard, the *Bear* found the survivors of the expedition. She returned triumphant from her rescue mission only to have the Navy declare her unfit for further service. In 1885 she was transferred to the Treasury Department for use in the Alaska area. In all, the *Bear* spent 41 years patrolling Alaskan waters.

The *Bear*'s many duties   The *Bear* had many duties not usually thought of as seagoing jobs. She carried to Alaska mail that had accumulated at Seattle during the winter, as well as government agents and supplies. On her trip south from Alaska, she transported federal prisoners and other questionable characters. Her deck often served as a court where justice was meted out. The *Bear*'s personnel also conducted investigations and undertook crime prevention and law enforcement. She and other cutters like her were often the only representatives of the law in Alaska.

When at sea, she took soundings so that charts of Alaskan waters could be made more useful. The *Bear*'s surgeon was often the only medical man within hundreds of miles. He looked after Eskimos, gold prospectors, missionaries, and whalers; his medical practice included pulling teeth, delivering babies, performing amputations, and curing stomach aches.

Help for Alaskan natives   Alaska swarmed with ruthless adventurers and it was often the law-enforcement powers of the Revenue Marine that protected the Alaskan Indians and Eskimos from abuse. One unusual practice, begun by the *Bear*, was the hauling of the entire Eskimo population, including dogs, from King Island to Nome, 80 miles away. There they spent each summer, camped in tents or under their upside down open boats, known as umiaks. At summer's end, the *Bear* returned for them and carried them back to King Island. The sojourn at Nome was the only real contact these people had with the world beyond their island—and they loved it.

Reindeer for Alaska   Among the *Bear*'s accomplishments was the importation of reindeer from Siberia to provide food for the Alaskans, who were frequently on the verge of starvation. Her first skipper, Mike Healy, reasoned that reindeer would also be an excellent source of clothing and transportation.

Healy took the *Bear* along the Siberian coast, arranging with native leaders for the purchase of reindeer, which he would pick up the following year. To make sure the animals would survive in captivity, he penned sixteen of them on board ship for three weeks. They were landed in good condition at Unalaska, after a sea voyage of more than 1,000 miles.

The *Bear* made five trips to Siberia and hauled 175 reindeer to Port Clarence, on the American side of the Bering Strait.

Rescuing the whalers   Another famous *Bear* exploit was her overland rescue of 1897. In the fall of that year, eight whaling vessels became trapped in the ice pack off remote Point Barrow, Alaska. Their crews, totaling about 275 men, faced almost certain starvation, unless they could be saved by the *Bear* on the first Arctic voyage ever attempted during the winter season.

By 14 December 1897, when she was approximately 85 miles off Cape Nome, the *Bear* was stopped by heavy ice but, before she turned back, she landed a volunteer shore party consisting of First Lieutenant David H. Jarvis, Second Lieutenant E. P. Bertholf, and Surgeon S. J. Call.

With dog teams, sleds, and guides, Jarvis and his companions made a 1,600-mile journey of three and a half months through frozen, trackless wilderness to Point Barrow. En route they collected a herd of nearly 450 reindeer. To the despairing whalers, the arrival of the relief party, complete with provender, was nothing short of a miracle. Healy's foresight had paid off.

The *Bear*, which had been rejected by the Navy in 1885, was still around in 1917 when the United States entered World War I, during which she served with the Navy. In 1929 she was decommissioned and turned over to the city of Oakland, California, for use as a maritime museum. It was at this time that she served as the set for the filming of a movie based on Jack London's *The Sea Wolf*.

To the Antarctic   In the early 1930s, Admiral Richard E. Byrd selected the *Bear* for his second Antarctic expedition. Said the Admiral of her then, "She was respectably old when the *Oregon* raced around the Horn, but there was a fine and indestructible courage in her oak timbering with its sheathing of iron bark which age and rot could not corrupt. . . ." The *Bear* reached Little America in the latter part of January 1934.

For the Antarctic expedition that began in 1939, Admiral Byrd again called upon the *Bear*. By this time, however, her boiler and engine had been replaced by a diesel drive, and her auxiliary equipment had been electrified. By 16 May 1941, she had completed her work in the Antarctic and was back at Boston.

Later that year, the *Bear* was assigned to the Greenland Patrol, which was operated by the U.S. Coast Guard. She took part in the capture of the Norwegian trawler *Buskoe*, a ship that had been fitted out by the Germans to transmit weather reports and information on Allied ship movements. In June 1944, the *Bear* was turned over to the Maritime Commission for sale. She remained in Nova Scotia until 1963 when she was bought for use as a floating museum and restaurant in Philadelphia.

As she was being towed south, she ran into a late winter storm, capsized, and went down. Her legendary career, spanning several generations, had finally ended, and the *Bear* took her resting place at the bottom of the sea, where most brave ships end. Men who had known her felt sad at the loss of the old ship, yet relieved—a dull existence as a restaurant was not proper for her, and it was better that she should end as she did.

In 1912 the service, which at that time was known as the Revenue Cutter Service, took over the job of being seagoing cowboys—riding herd on the fur-bearing seals of the North Pacific. In the Bering Sea, where the Aleutian Islands sweep southwest in a long arc from the southern coast of Alaska, their job was to apprehend poachers, who were ruthlessly slaughtering the seals for their furs.

Conservation

The Pribilof Islands and the seal herds congregating there were discovered by the Russians in 1787. For twenty years thereafter the animals, without regard for age or sex, were killed for their valuable furs. When the herds were near extinction the Russian government forbade such carnage for a time but when it was resumed, it was worse than ever. In 1868 when the United States took possession of the islands as part of the purchase of Alaska, it leased them to the Alaska Commercial Company, and fishing and hunting were free to all. As a result, in a single year an estimated 250,000 seals were killed. Finally, an agreement reached with the Alaska Commercial Company limited sealing to young bachelor animals only. But this did nothing for pelagic sealing, that is the killing of seals at sea as they migrated to California. Seals were about to go the way of passenger pigeons, buffalo, sage hens, and other wildlife wiped out by commercial greed.

Facing that fact, Japan, Russia, Britain, and the United States agreed to halt sealing in the North Pacific and the Bering Sea every year during the months of May, June, and July, when the pups were born, but sealers managed to evade all agreements.

In 1894 an officer of the Revenue Cutter Service and a few crew members camped on two of the Pribilof Islands to make a two-month survey of the situation. The following year an armed guard was landed to protect the seal rookeries. Recommendations were made for the seals' protection, but the killing continued. The great herds, which had been 5,000,000 strong when Alaska was purchased by the United States, had dwindled to less than 100,000. In 1911 Britain, Russia, the United States, and Japan signed a treaty for the "Protection of Fur Seals and Sea Otters." The Pribilofs became a seal sanctuary and were not to be used for private interests.

In 1868, the Revenue Marine was given the job of searching for and arresting anyone hunting fur-bearing animals without a license. Bird sanctuaries also came under its control and, in 1889, the salmon industry was also placed under its protection. Seventeen years later, the law was extended to all fisheries; the patrol was authorized to prevent aliens from fishing for anything, including whales, in Alaskan waters.

Ice patrol In April 1912 the *Titanic,* one of the largest passenger liners built to that date, sailed from England for the United States on her maiden voyage. The 66,000-ton ship, declared unsinkable, carried 2,201 passengers and crew members. About midnight on Sunday, 14 April, at a point some 900 miles off Newfoundland, while the ship was making better than 22 knots in thick fog, despite radio warnings from five other ships about ice, she plowed into an iceberg that ripped a 300-foot gash in her hull. In less than three hours the "unsinkable" ship was at the bottom of the Atlantic. About seven hundred survivors were picked out of lifeboats the next morning by the *Carpathia,* which had heard the frantic distress calls sent out by the *Titanic* and made a 58-mile run through the night on her rescue mission. Another ship, the *Californian,* was less than 10 miles from the *Titanic* when she sank, and her bridge watch saw the lights of the sinking ship, but because her radioman had shut down his set and gone to bed, no one on the *Californian* knew about the disaster until the next morning.

As one result of that tragedy, the U.S. Coast Guard started an ice patrol along the steamship route across the north Atlantic, and in 1914 the principal maritime nations, meeting in London, inaugurated the International Ice Patrol, which the Coast Guard has maintained ever since. The slow-moving cutters have now been replaced by four-engine C-130 type aircraft, which can cover hundreds of miles in a day and, with onboard radar, can spot icebergs even when they are hidden by fog.

From February to August, the season in which ice moves south from Greenland, an average of 400 bergs drift across the steamer lanes. The area patrolled by the Coast Guard—some 45,000 square miles—is about the size of Pennsylvania and is crossed by dozens of ships every day. Only once since 1913, when the *Seneca* and *Miami* became the first cutters to go on station, has a ship hit an iceberg.

Rescue at sea

Far out in the Atlantic and Pacific, the United States keeps ocean station vessels and ocean weather ships constantly on station—stations Bravo, Charlie, Delta, and Echo in the Atlantic, and Victor and November in the Pacific. Each ship cruises continuously in a square of ocean 210 miles on a side, sends hourly weather reports to continental stations, and stands by to perform rescue missions.

One of the best-known rescues performed by an ocean station vessel took place on 16 October 1956, when the Pan American Airways stratocruiser *Sovereign of the Seas* had to ditch. The plane was en route from Honolulu to San Francisco when two of its engines failed. The Coast Guard cutter *Pontchartrain* was alerted, set out flares to mark the ditching area, and had boats in the water when the plane came down. All the passengers and the crew were picked up and aboard the cutter fifteen minutes later.

The Coast Guard also handles Atlantic Merchant Vessel Emergency Rescue (AMVER), a system initiated in 1958. The ships of more than 60 nations are constantly at sea in the Atlantic, and AMVER takes care of them. Ships north of the equator and west of the prime meridian of Greenwich can make daily position reports to AMVER which keeps computer plots on about 800 of them. When a ship in the plot reports trouble of any kind, AMVER can alert nearby vessels to go to the rescue in a matter of minutes.

More than half-a-century after an iceberg sank the SS *Titanic*, the U.S. Coast Guard still patrols the North Atlantic sea-lanes to warn ships of monsters such as this. The USCGC *Acushnet*, 213 feet long, gives an idea of the size of this mountain of ice. Photo: U.S. Coast Guard.

AMVER handles an average of three alerts daily. When a Flying Tiger plane ditched in the Atlantic in 1962, ships sent to the spot rescued 48 survivors. When the American tanker *Pine Ridge* broke in two off Cape Hatteras, her own radio operator did not have time even to get off a call for help. But another tanker saw the ship sinking, alerted AMVER, and helicopters from the *Valley Forge* soon showed up to rescue all hands.

You have to go out!   The unofficial motto of the Coast Guard is "You have to go out; you don't have to come back." In other words, the people in the Coast Guard are pledged always to go to the rescue, no matter how great the danger and risk of life entailed.

Since 1871 the Coast Guard has saved 304,000 lives and more than $400 billion in property. Coast Guardsmen flying helicopters and fixed-wing amphibians and patrolling in cutters and small boats go into flood areas, fight fires along waterfronts, and rescue passengers and crews from distressed ships on the high seas. Their high-endurance and medium cutters—capable of operating far from shore—escorted convoys across the Atlantic during World War II.

Law enforcement remains a primary duty, with particular emphasis being placed on preventing aliens from entering the country illegally and on breaking up traffic in illegal drugs.

On the Great Lakes, the icebreaker *Mackinaw* breaks up ice in main ship channels, thus lengthening the season during which lake commerce can operate. An important Coast Guard mission everywhere is the prevention of oil pollution. Even as this was being written, Coast Guard crews were cleaning up oil spills in the Potomac River, in San Francisco Bay, and in New York Harbor, in a continuing effort to keep our waters clean and safe.

CHAPTER 16
TECHNOLOGY

Progress is never an orderly process. This is especially true in maritime affairs. For a century after steam engines went to sea, American yards were still turning out sailing ships. Coal-burning ships were smoking up the sea-lanes long after diesels went to sea, and ships powered by nuclear reactors may still meet old-timers with "up and down" reciprocating engines. The new twin-hulled oceanographic research vessels, such as the Naval Research Laboratory's *Hayes*, are big catamarans, a type Magellan saw the Malays using over four hundred years ago.

A few facts extracted from the American record of shipbuilding history show this helter-skelter progress. The *Clermont*, the first steamboat in the United States, began operating in 1807, yet big sailing ships were still being built in 1917. The *Demologos*, the first steam warship in any navy, was built in 1814, yet the U.S. Navy's last wooden combat ship, the *Trenton*, was built in 1875. Coal was first used as a fuel in 1834, yet many ships still burned wood during the Civil War. And, although oil was being produced in Pennsylvania in 1859, the first ship in the Navy to burn oil was the *Cheyenne*, which converted from coal in 1908.

By the opening of the twentieth century, there had been great advances in the shipbuilding art. Ships as big as 15,000 tons were being built of steel, twin screws were common, reciprocating engines had been improved, a few ships were powered by steam turbines, and a very few ships had electric lights. But in one respect, all ships were still as primitive as those Magellan took around the world in the sixteenth century. When a ship left port and disappeared over the horizon, she was literally out of this world for

On previous page: The use of radar aboard naval vessels was one of the best-guarded secrets of World War II. Now even private yachts and fishing vessels carry radar. The oceanographic research vessel USNS *Eltanin* displays several radar antennas, along with many other types of electronic equipment. Courtesy: The National Science Foundation.

weeks or months, until she reached her destination or at least exchanged signals with a passing ship.

Long after submarine cables began carrying messages from continent to continent, ships at sea were cut off from the rest of the world. In case of distress, they could not call for help—not even to a ship that had passed only a couple of hours earlier and was just over the horizon. Hundreds of ships, caught in such a predicament, disappeared as completely as if they had sailed over the edge of the world. The invention of radio changed this. However, many shipowners were slow in adopting something that did not appear to *do* anything, except cost money to install and to operate.

The first permanent radio installation—or wireless, as it was then called—is credited to the Italian, Guglielmo Marconi, who set up a station on the Isle of Wight in Hampshire, England, in November of 1896. But Marconi merely ran with the ball, as it were. Several other people had made it possible for him. About 1830, Michael Faraday, an Englishman, used a mechanical generator to produce electricity—the same kind of electricity Benjamin Franklin managed to pull out of a thunderstorm through a kite string without killing himself. Soon afterwards, Joseph Henry, an American physicist, developed an electromagnet that could lift a ton of iron, and a year later he produced a simple electric motor. In 1888 Heinrich Hertz, a German, produced simple radio waves by jumping a high-voltage electric spark across a short gap. By that time Thomas Alva Edison, the American inventor of the phonograph, had produced the incandescent electric light which, with some later development by Lee De Forest, turned into the vacuum tube. Samuel F. B. Morse had perfected the telegraph, and Alexander Graham Bell had produced the telephone. All these inventions were the ancestors of modern communication and of many other technical and scientific developments which have made it possible, not only to cross the oceans in safety, but to voyage all the way to the moon.

Telegraph

The telegraph came first. Samuel Morse, working with primitive equipment, set up a telegraph line running from Baltimore to Washington, D.C. Congress appropriated $30,000 to build the entire system. He also devised a system of dots and dashes—Morse code—by which letters of the alphabet could be turned into a series of "dits" and "dahs" for transmission by wire or radio. The first telegraph message in the world was sent from the Supreme Court room in the Capitol to Baltimore on 24 May 1844. The message was short but full of portent, "What hath God wrought?" After that, telegraph lines spread across the country rapidly. The Atlantic and Pacific Telegraph Company had a line all the way to California by October of 1861, but messages then cost fifty cents a word. When Captain David McDougal, at the Mare Island Navy Yard, sent sev-

eral messages to the Navy Department in Washington—collect—
the Secretary wired back: Telegraph only in case of absolute
necessity.

Morse proposed that a submarine cable be laid across the Atlantic to carry messages to England, but the problems involved in
fabricating a cable 2,500 miles long, making it waterproof, laying
it, and generating enough current to go all the way across, were not
easily solved.

The first step was to establish a route. In 1853 and 1856, the
Navy sent the steamers *Dolphin* and *Arctic* to survey a route. Deep-
sea soundings were simplified by a device developed by Lieutenant
John M. Brooke, but they were far from being the type of soundings now made by sonar. It took six hours to drop a line to the bottom and recover it from 12,000 feet of water, and soundings were
made only at points 200 miles apart. The soundings showed that
between Newfoundland and Ireland there was a vast submarine
plain that would make a fine site for the cable. Accordingly, the
area was named Telegraph Plateau.

The first cable was completed, all the way across, in 1858, with
the USS *Niagara,* then the largest steam frigate in the world, assisting HMS *Agamemnon.* The cable opened for business on 27 September when Queen Victoria sent a 90-word message to President
Buchanan. The signals were so weak it took over an hour to get the
message through, but the system worked! There was a great celebration in New York, with fireworks that set the town hall on fire.
After the initial completion, the cable broke and had to be spliced
several times, but by 1866 it was in fairly continuous operation. For
a long while, submarine cables were far more efficient than radio,
which had limited range. By the end of World War I, nearly 300,000
miles of submarine cable had been laid across all the oceans of the
world. Not everyone approved of the invention. After the first
cable had been laid across the Pacific, an old admiral complained:
"The laying of the cable to Hong Kong spoiled the old China Station; before that, one really was somebody; after that he became
merely a damned errand boy at the end of a telegraph wire."

Radio   Although Marconi had a wireless station set up in England in 1896,
his first transatlantic transmission was not made until 11 December
1901, when the letter *S* (· · · in Morse code) was picked up by a
receiver at St. John's, Newfoundland. Actually, Marconi came in
second to Lieutenant Bradley Fiske of the U.S. Navy, who in 1888
had managed to transmit signals from the USS *Atlanta* to a nearby
ship by wrapping several turns of insulated wire around both ships,
sending flashes of current through the coil on one, and listening in
on the other with telephone receivers. Fiske made the earlier transmission, but Marconi made the longer one.

An early use of radio in the United States was the reporting for the *New York Herald* of the America Cup race in 1899 between the English *Shamrock* and the American *Columbia*. The radio signals were transmitted from the SS *Ponce*, of the Puerto Rico Line. Average speed was about 15 words a minute.

That same year the Navy began experimenting with shipboard radio, when installations were made aboard the battleships *New York* and *Massachusetts*. The ships were anchored in the North River at New York, about 500 yards apart, and handled messages at 12 words a minute. Later they went to sea and sent messages over a distance of 36.5 miles.

In 1903 the Navy purchased 30 German-made radio sets and installed them in ships of the Atlantic Fleet. Very few people understood the principle of radio at that time. One officer said he "didn't give a damn about wireless," but he did care about the appearance of his ship: he had the antenna wires changed around to make them look neater. People then and later believed that it was impossible to receive a radio transmission unless both the transmitter and receiver were made by the same manufacturer. A man who played the piano was considered a likely radio operator because he "knew how to tune a set."

By 1906 U.S. Navy shore radio stations were broadcasting storm warnings, and merchant ships equipped with radio were making daily weather reports to the Weather Bureau. The SS *Cartago*, off the coast of Yucatán on 26 August 1906, sent the first hurricane warnings. By that time the Naval Observatory in Washington had commenced sending out daily time signals by telegraph, and the radio station at the Boston Navy Yard began broadcasting them to ships at sea. Range at that time was 50 miles.

A first use of radio in time of disaster came after the great San Francisco earthquake and fire of 17 April 1906. Because the telegraph wires belonging to Postal Telegraph and Western Union were all down, the cruiser *Chicago* docked near the Ferry Building, and for a few days Midshipman Stanley Hooper handled all communications between San Francisco and the rest of the country. The messages went to a station on Yerba Buena Island, which relayed them to Mare Island, about 25 miles up the bay; and from there they went out across the country by telegraph.

When the White Star liner SS *Republic* collided with the SS *Florida* off Nantucket on 22 January 1908, the radio operator of the *Florida*, Jack Binns, got off a message that resulted in rescue ships saving more than 1,600 lives. But merchant ships were still not required to carry radio, and a bill requiring it in ships carrying more than 50 people or sailing more than 200 miles was fought by the steamship companies because they feared it would result in a monopoly. Next the new White Star liner *Titanic*, one of the biggest ships in the world, hit an iceberg around midnight of 15 April 1912. Her radio operator got off distress signals, but at least one ship, which was only a few miles away, never heard them because she carried only one operator and he was asleep. As a result, over 1,500 lives were lost. Congress then passed the bill that had been turned down in 1908 and made it compulsory for ships to carry two or more radio operators.

Radio proved itself as a great lifesaving device as soon as it was installed in ships. The first distress signal sent out in the United States was made by the Nantucket Shoals Lightship when she was forced to leave her station during a heavy storm in December 1905. Radio-equipped ships went to her rescue; she sank ten minutes after her crew got off. The well-known sos signal was first used by an American ship on 11 August 1909 when the SS *Arapahoe* broke her propeller shaft off Cape Hatteras. Before that time, the usual distress signal had been the Morse code for cQD. The signal sos has no real meaning, although people think it stands for "Save Our Ship" or "Save Our Souls." It was chosen because the series of three dots, three dashes, and three dots is unmistakable. The same sequence of dots and dashes can be made by sending in Morse the letters v t b or the letters i j s.

All modern ships, even the smallest recreational craft, now carry radio equipment. The original continuous-wave (cw) equipment that sent Morse code with a key, or bug—the familiar dit-dit-dit-dah sound heard in old movies or television shows—is still used, but voice radio is used on conventional marine radiotelephone bands. Small portable radios—walkie-talkies—were first used in World War II. They are now used for bridge-to-bridge talk between merchant ships. The Navy uses a similar system called tbs (talk-between-ships): this system offers better security than does low-frequency radio, because it operates in the vhf band on line-of-sight and is not liable to be intercepted by enemy or other unauthorized receivers.

Large Navy combatant ships have dozens of radio transmitters and receivers. Every aircraft, military, commercial, or private, also carries radio. Early cw radio could be heard "all over the dial," but modern vhf radio, with crystal-controlled frequency, packs hundreds of communication channels into a narrow band. Even a light aircraft must be able to work a hundred different channels.

Modern radio communication demands ultrahigh speed, impossible with cw or voice. Submarines, in particular, have to cut their transmissions short in order to prevent an enemy from taking bearings on them. This is done by pre-recording a message, in code, then transmitting it in a "squirt" of very high speed. At the receiving end, the "squirt" is recorded, then played back at the proper speed. The system was refined for use in deep-space probes such as those that surveyed Venus, Mars, and Jupiter. As these probes fly around a planet, they collect many kinds of information which they store in a computer and transmit on a trigger signal from earth.

Airborne radio　　In 1911 the Navy moved its Curtiss flying machines, the A-1 and the A-2, to Annapolis. By June of 1912 Lieutenant T. G. Ellyson had managed to climb the A-1 to an altitude of 900 feet in three minutes and thirty seconds. At the same time experiments with radio began. The plane, a 32-horsepower pusher with chain-driven, center-rotating wooden propellers, was called the *Flying Windmill*. A generator bolted to the lower wing was driven by a leather belt that ran around the flywheel of the engine. The antenna wires were rigged under the wings, bamboo poles bought at the local fish market being used for spreaders. The operator, who sat beside the pilot, had a telegraph key and ammeter strapped to his legs. He also carried a screwdriver and a monkey wrench for tightening various nuts, bolts, and screws when they worked loose on the engine. When he was not using the wrench, he laid it on the wing—the plane could not fly fast enough for the wind to blow it off.

With this outfit, which is better described by the sailor's term "lash up," Ensign Charles Maddox, the operator, and Lieutenant John Rodgers, the pilot, managed to get 300 feet into the air and, on 26 July, to send a message to the destroyer *Stringham*, three miles away. Captain Washington I. Chambers, the director of naval aviation, was impressed enough to think that eventually they might be able to send signals as far as fifty miles, and would no longer have to depend on homing pigeons.*

Pilots were not enthusiastic about using radio. They had enough to do flying the airplane, without trying to use a telegraph key at the same time. By 1928, radiotelephones had been developed and tested out aboard the carrier *Saratoga*. They soon became just another piece of cockpit equipment and no pilot would consider getting into a plane without radio. Now, even a private pilot uses voice radio as readily as he would his home telephone.

With widespread use of radiotelephones, there is no need for Morse. Around the world now, ships, commercial aircraft, pleasure boats, and fishermen use the word "Mayday" as a distress signal. "Mayday" has no hidden political meaning, it is merely a simplified spelling of the French *m'aidez*—help me. Someone who is not yet in trouble but thinks he soon will be—perhaps a private pilot running low on gas with no field in sight—goes on the air with "Pan Pan Pan," meaning he has an urgent transmission to make.

---

* Nevertheless, for many years after that, seaplanes did carry homing pigeons. When a plane was forced down, the pilot guessed where he might be, gave the pigeon a note, and sent him home. Sometimes it worked. But when the Navy's first aircraft carrier, the *Langley*, began fitting out at Norfolk in 1922, the pigeon-trainer sent his birds out every day for exercise. Later the ship moved up the Chesapeake for training, and the pigeons were sent out as usual, but they failed to return. After several weeks, the *Langley* went back to Norfolk, where all the pigeons were on the dock waiting for her. No one had told them the ship was going to be moving around.

The range and clarity of radiotelephone transmissions have been improved. It is no longer surprising to enter a cab and hear the driver telephone his dispatcher to tell where he is taking you, just as it was hardly surprising one night in July of 1969 to hear Neil Armstrong, wearing a helmet with built-in radio, say, "The Eagle has landed," just before he stepped down onto the moon—240,000 miles away.

Remote control by radio   In 1921 special radio equipment was installed in the battleships *Ohio* and *Iowa* that allowed the *Iowa* to be radio-controlled from the *Ohio*, at a distance of four miles. The experiment worked so well that when the *Iowa* was used as a bombing target for Army planes there was not one man aboard her. The experiments were not continued because there did not appear to be any great need for a radio-controlled ship, except as a bombing target. There did appear to be use for a radio-controlled aircraft that could speed in and drop bombs on a combatant vessel. By 1923 an automatic pilot and radio-control equipment had been developed. A year later it was possible for a ground control station to put a plane into the air, maneuver it for forty minutes, and land it. Unfortunately, the gear required for these operations weighed about as much as the two pilots it replaced.

Radio control of pilotless planes offered an excellent chance for antiaircraft practice by ships of the fleet, and in 1938 a high-speed drone was first used as an aerial target by the aircraft carrier *Ranger*. Control of the drone was handled by a man riding in another aircraft. Drones soon became standard for antiaircraft gunnery training, their only drawback being that the man "flying" a drone had to be able to see it. Since the war in Vietnam, a new type of remote control has been used—television. A glide bomb is steered to its target by an operator in a control plane who "watches" its progress through a television screen which, in turn, is fed by a camera in the bomb.

It is not necessary to go to war in order to fly a radio-controlled plane. Hobby shops now sell model planes equipped with radio controls; a hand-held transmitter enables anyone to be a pilot.

Ocean depths   Before the development of electronic depth-finders, the only way to measure water depth was to drop a weighted line to the bottom. In shallow waters, a man dropped a line marked with bits of cloth and leather, noted when it grew slack, then sang out the marking at the water level. "By the deep six!" meant 6 fathoms, or 36 feet. The same system was used on the shallow Mississippi River and frequently gave "Mark twain!" which meant 2 fathoms, or 12 feet —and gave Samuel Clemens his pen name.

When Columbus crossed the Atlantic for the first time, his men dropped a lead line on 20 September 1492 and found no bottom at 200 fathoms, which convinced them they were over the deepest part of the ocean. Actually, soundings at that spot now show 2,292 fathoms—nearly 14,000 feet. Some three centuries later the system was still much the same—Maury used a cannonball on a wire 10,000 fathoms long, which permitted deeper soundings, but was not highly accurate. It was difficult to keep a ship in exactly the same spot for a long time—in water three miles deep, it took an hour to lower a sounding line and haul it in again. The line might not be vertical, and it was difficult to tell exactly when the weight hit bottom.

By 1922 the Navy had perfected a sonic depth-finder, which gave continuous readings at hundreds of fathoms. In June of that year the destroyer *Stewart* sailed from Norfolk to China, making continuous soundings for 6,500 miles. In the following years, ships equipped with sounding devices that produced inked tracings on paper began charting the ocean bottoms. Such charts led to the discovery of submarine canyons and underwater mountains called *guyots*. With ships making thousands of such charts as they cross and recross the seas, oceanographers can now map the bottoms of the oceans in great detail.

The air is filled with sound waves of many kinds, all moving at approximately 1,100 feet per second. It was not known until recent times that the sea is also filled with sound. Water is a better conductor of sound waves than is air—sound moves at about 5,500 feet per second in water and travels much farther than it does in the atmosphere. Superstitious sailors in old whaling ships were sometimes spooked by strange sounds; no one knew then that whales chirped, sang, and bellowed, and that the wooden hull of a ship amplified sound.

Underwater sound

Experiments made early in the twentieth century showed that bells ringing underwater could be heard at greater distances than could foghorns, and by 1912 submarine bells had been installed as navigational aids at dangerous places along the coasts of the United States and many other countries. A simple underwater microphone picked up not only the sound of the bells but many other sounds, such as the engines and screws of ships.

When the Navy became involved in submarine-hunting in World War I, it developed simple underwater listening devices, which were the ancestors of modern sonar. Two or more ships "listening" for a submarine could pinpoint its location, and at least six U-boats were sunk after being tracked down by sound, a fact that considerably lowered the morale of German submarine crews.

All such equipment was "passive"—it merely listened. After the war ended, the Navy began working with sonic depth-finding devices that were "active,"—they sent out an impulse and measured the time for the echo to return. This experimental work went two ways; it resulted in the Fathometer, which measures depths in the ocean, and in sonar, which measures distances in a horizontal plane.

Sonar Research in acoustical sound systems continued after World War I and by 1927 simple echo-ranging devices had been installed in a few ships. Four years later some submarines were equipped with echo-ranging sonar. Development was slow because the way in which sound was transmitted through water was not understood until Woods Hole Oceanographic Institution discovered that there were in the sea different layers of water whose temperatures varied. Sometimes sound was bounced back by these so-called "thermoclines." Eventually the Navy learned that submarines could "hide" under such a layer, so that surface-search sonar signals would bounce back from it and not detect them.

As World War II developed, both the British and Americans worked on underwater sound research. When the United States actually entered the war, only 170 U.S. destroyers were equipped with sonar. Soon all vessels—even submarines—were so equipped. With sonar, surface ships could track down a submarine no matter how quietly it operated; on occasion, a sonar-equipped U.S. submarine attacked and sank a Japanese submarine before the latter had any inkling that another submarine was in the area.

Although developed as a military necessity, sonar has many peaceful uses. Fishing boats use sonar to detect schools of fish. Side-looking sonar was used to locate an H-bomb lost off the coast of Spain when two Air Force planes collided in 1966. Sonar is also extensively used in oceanographic research. Deep-submergence vehicles (DSVS)—such as *Alvin* and *Deepstar*—use sonar. One of the most mysterious features of the ocean, the deep scattering layer (DSL), was first detected by Navy sonar operators. It appears to be composed of multitudes of minute ocean creatures which rise toward the surface at night and drop into the depths in the daytime, but oceanographers are still not exactly certain what they are.

Gyrocompass For hundreds of years ships were steered by magnetic compasses which sometimes pointed east of north, sometimes west of north, and, once in a great while, directly north, and if a forgetful seaman came near such a compass with a steel knife in his belt, it was liable to forget its business and point at him. That was because the north magnetic pole is hundreds of miles from the north geographic pole; the difference between where the compass points (magnetic) and where it should point (geographic) is called *variation*. A navigator had to know the local variation and allow for it in his computations. A seaman's knife, or any other iron or steel object near the compass, produced an effect called *deviation*. Iron ships had their own magnetic field, which affected the compass.

For all these reasons, plotting courses by magnetic compass could be a highly inaccurate affair. Every navigator *knew* where north was—the North Star was right there or, at most, a degree or so off. But on cloudy nights the North Star was no help. Navigators needed to know all the time which way was north.

The answer was found in a simple toy, the gyroscopic top, probably invented in Germany or France late in the eighteenth century. Set spinning at high speed, a gyro tended to keep spinning in its original position, but experimenters later discovered that if a gyroscope was free to move in any direction, it eventually moved so that its axis lined up with the axis of the earth. The gyro flywheel was kept spinning by an electric motor—a high-speed descendant of that invented by Joseph Henry in about 1831. All the pieces were put together by Elmer A. Sperry, and sea trials of his gyrocompass began on 21 April 1911 on the Old Dominion Line steamer *Princess Anne*, running from New York to Hampton Roads. Next, the gyrocompass was tried out on the destroyer *Drayton*, where it kept pointing exactly north for five days, no matter in what direction the ship went.

There were, of course, a few bugs in the gyro, but they were worked out over the following years. The development of the gyro also made possible automatic pilots, first for ships and soon afterwards for aircraft. The first commercial ship to be equipped with an automatic pilot, which seamen soon nicknamed "Metal Mike" or "Iron Mike," was the Standard Oil Company's tanker *John O. Archibald*, in 1922. Ten years later a thousand ships had automatic pilots; now almost anything that floats is so equipped.

The artificial horizon used by all aircraft for instrument flight is actuated by a gyro, and the Ship's Inertial Navigation System (SINS), by which nuclear submarines can navigate underwater indefinitely, is also based on gyroscopic principles. Another device that has a gyro as its basic element is the automatic stabilizer, with which modern cruise liners keep an even keel—no rolling from side to side to spill soup in the dining room. When the astronauts went to the moon, highly sophisticated gyros went along to help in navigation and flight evolutions.

Radar

One day in 1922, Dr. A. Hoyt Taylor and Mr. Leo Young, who were employed by the Naval Aircraft Radio Laboratory in Washington, D.C., were working on experimental radio equipment when they noticed that some of their signals were being bounced back by the *Dorchester*, an old wooden steamer on the Potomac River. They reported that they thought something could be made of the fact; perhaps destroyers sending signals to each other at night could tell if another ship passed between them.

Nothing came of this. But in 1930, another experimenter, Mr. L. A. Hyland, noticed that signals from a radio direction-finder were deflected by a passing aircraft. This discovery was described in a report titled "Radio-Echo Signals From Moving Objects." Someone in the Navy Department recommended that the idea be developed. From that simple beginning came the radar that now guides airliners to safe landings on fog-shrouded runways, helps astronauts on their flights to the moon, and enables traffic-control officers to set up the gadget that detects a driver going at 40 miles an hour in a 35-mile zone.

Radar works on the principle of sending out a tight beam of electronic impulses and measuring the time it takes for any echoes to return from an object in the beam. There are many types of radar in use; a large warship might have as many as two dozen different radar installations. The most common is a surface-search type, which reproduces on a Plan Position Indicator (PPI) a bird's-eye view of the area covered by the search beam, showing ships, buoys, shorelines, and other geographical features. A similar type of radar is used at large airports to show all air traffic in the area.

The first radar set used in the Navy, which was installed on the destroyer *Leary* in 1938, could detect planes fifteen miles away. By late 1941, radar was being installed on a few battleships and cruisers, and some destroyers. The large antennae then in use were called "bed springs," and not many people really knew what they were. Radar was one of the best-kept secrets of World War II. Although the Japanese also developed it, their equipment never matched that of the United States. Fire-control radar enabled American ships in night battles to fire on targets they could not see. Later, carrier planes equipped with radar operated at night, guiding other aircraft to targets.

Since World War II, radar has been constantly improved. By 1946 the Army Signal Corps Research Laboratory at Fort Monmouth, New Jersey, had bounced radar echoes off the moon. In 1966 the Naval Research Laboratory, using radar, began mapping the moon. Closer to home, nearly a hundred radar tracking stations maintained by the Weather Bureau can spot hurricanes up to a distance of 250 miles, which makes it possible for warnings to be given before a storm becomes dangerous. Radar also helps in weather predictions; by tracking high-altitude balloons, it provides wind speed and direction at various levels.

The Navy uses planes with huge horizontal radomes built above them for tracking enemy forces by radar. When an uninformed civilian saw such a plane take off for the first time, he called the air station in great excitement to report that "one of them flying saucers just came down and flew off with one of your airplanes."

Even a small private plane can benefit from radar. When a pilot is lost, or in trouble, or when his radio goes out, he can still call for help by flying short legs to form a triangle. When that pattern shows up on a radar screen anywhere, a plane is sent to investigate.

Loran

Loran, or Long-Range Navigation, is an electronic navigational system which in many ways replaces old-fashioned lighthouses. But where a lighthouse was visible for no more than 20 miles or so, loran gives fixes at distances of hundreds or thousands of miles, and it is available for use by either ships or aircraft. In fact, the first U.S. loran stations were established by the Coast Guard in the western Pacific during World War II in order to guide planes on bombing missions over Japan.

A loran system depends on transmissions from a master station and a slave station. A ship making a loran fix uses a receiver in which an oscilloscope displays pulses transmitted by both stations. The time difference between receipt of the two pulses is established electronically, and an operator refers to loran charts for the data which establish the ship's position.

Determining position by loran is much quicker than it is by use of star sights and the computations required in celestial navigation. It is also far more accurate and much easier to learn. The system can be used at any time, day or night, no matter what the weather may be.

Shoran

Shoran, or Short-Range Navigation, was developed during World War II to allow planes that were above the clouds to bomb land targets accurately. It works in somewhat the same fashion as loran, and can be used by either ships or aircraft. A radio signal sent by a ship or aircraft that needs a fix automatically triggers two beacon transmitters ashore; the signals emitted by the transmitters are displayed on a receiving unit which electronically calculates the distance to each beacon. A plot of the two ranges and their bearings establishes a fix.

Nuclear power

The world entered the atomic age when an Army Air Force plane dropped the first A-bomb on Hiroshima, Japan, on 6 August 1945. Another A-bomb was dropped on Nagasaki three days later. The bombs were more powerful than anything ever known before; both cities were virtually wiped out. Since then the United States and other nations have developed nuclear weapons far more destructive than the A-bombs. Yet nuclear reaction need not always be destructive; it can supply power, heat, and light, and the Navy was the first to develop such uses.

In 1939, when it was first learned that energy could be produced by splitting a uranium atom—a process called *atomic fission*—Ross Gunn, a scientist at the Naval Research Laboratory, decided that it might be possible to use such energy to drive an engine. This was long before the United States had started work on the highly secret and expensive Manhattan Project that produced the A-bombs, and the Navy did not have vast funds for research and development As a starter, Gunn got $1,500 with which to commence studying atomic fission.

Over the next several years, the Navy worked on the idea of nuclear power, particularly as propulsion for a true submarine. In 1946 a contract was given to the General Electric Company to design a nuclear-propulsion plant. The project was set up at Oak Ridge, Tennessee, where the Manhattan Project had been developed, and one of the officers assigned to it was Hyman G. Rickover, a navy captain with a degree in electrical engineering. The following year Fleet Admiral Chester W. Nimitz recommended the development of a nuclear submarine.

Eight years later, on 17 January 1955, the USS *Nautilus* pulled clear from a pier in New London, Connecticut, for her trial runs, and her skipper, Commander Eugene P. Wilkinson, sent the historic message, "Underway on nuclear power." A full account of what transpired in those eight years when Hyman Rickover would allow nothing to stand in the way of his developing the atomic submarine, could fill several books—and probably will.

Less than 30 years after a contract was first issued for the building of a nuclear-propulsion plant, the Navy had more than a hundred nuclear-powered submarines at sea, plus nuclear-powered, guided-missile frigates, nuclear-powered cruisers, and nuclear-powered aircraft carriers. The program took more than money.

The space age   A satellite weighing 184 pounds, Sputnik I, was put into orbit around the earth by the Russians on 4 October 1957, marking the first time a man-made object ever lifted above the stratosphere. On 5 May 1961 Commander Alan B. Shepard, Jr., U.S. Navy, became the first American to go into space, as he made a 302-mile flight in the *Freedom 7* which was picked up by the carrier *Lake Champlain*. The following year Lieutenant Colonel John H. Glenn, Jr., U.S. Marine Corps, in a space capsule named *Friendship 7*, made three orbits of the earth, was picked up by the destroyer *Noa*, and later airlifted to the carrier *Randolph*. And in July of 1969 *Apollo 11* flew to the moon: Neil A. Armstrong, a former Navy pilot, and Edwin E. Aldrin, an Air Force officer, became the first men to walk on the moon. On their return to earth, they were picked up by the carrier *Hornet*.

American space flights depend on the Navy for recovery vessels, whereas the Russians land their space vehicles in the vast interior of their country. All space flights and many of the advances in astronomy, physics, and other sciences were made possible by the experiments of Albert A. Michelson, who graduated from the Naval Academy in 1873 and in 1907 became the first American in history to win the Nobel Prize. Michelson became a physicist, and accomplished two things that had lasting effects on science: he invented an apparatus called an "interferometer" for measuring the wavelength of light; and, following the experiments of Jean Foucault, determined the speed of light to be exactly 186,284 miles per second. That figure is as important as Pythagoras' theorem ($h^2 = a^2 + b^2$), because it is a mathematical constant. It entered into Alfred Einstein's development of the theory of relativity, which is expressed as $E = mc^2$, where c is the speed of light, as determined by Michelson.

All forms of energy—light, ultraviolet, infrared, high-frequency and low-frequency radio waves—move at the same speed, and exact determination of that speed has provided a basis for radio communication, radar, loran, shoran, and the involved computations necessary in space travel.

However, although radio waves move at the speed of light, they do not always move in a straight line, as light does. When Marconi's signals were first heard 2,100 miles away, experts were surprised. They assumed the waves went out in a straight line, and would soon be so far above the earth no one could pick them up. In 1920 the Kennelly-Heaviside layer, an area of charged particles about 65 miles high, was discovered. The layer reflects long waves, which is why long-distance radio is possible, but it absorbs short waves—FM and TV—which is why TV broadcasts were generally limited to line-of-sight—as far as one could see the transmitting tower—until satellites were put into orbit to bounce them back.

The U.S. Naval Research Laboratory (NRL) pioneered space research in America when it launched some ex-German V2 rockets in 1946. Since then NRL has worked on the detection of x rays from the sun and has recorded ultraviolet solar images by satellite. Working with huge radio telescopes, NRL has measured the exact distance between the earth and the moon, the temperature of Venus, and lately it has detected magnetic fields far out in intergalactic space.

During the 1957 International Geophysical Year (IGY), in which 67 nations participated, the Navy launched *Vanguard*, the country's first orbiting scientific satellite. It is a 6-inch sphere, which the Russians described as nothing more than a "grapefruit," but it is still in orbit, and will probably continue to beep its way around the world for the next 2,000 years.

In order to track such satellites, NRL built Minitrack, a system that can track an object 200 miles high at speeds up to 18,000 miles an hour. The Minitrack computer can collect all the readings taken by the system for a period of eight days, and in two minutes compute the orbit of the object being tracked.

Satellite navigation   Not all satellite development is for purely military purposes. The Navy's satellite navigation system, completed in 1958, is now being used by hundreds of merchant ships, including some belonging to England, Japan, Sweden, France, Canada, Belgium, and the Soviet Union. The satellites orbit at a height of 600 miles and continuously broadcast their positions: the position for any moment in a 12-hour period is computed by a ground station and transmitted to the satellite for its broadcast. Any ship with a receiving unit has only to tune in the satellite broadcast and feed it into a computer that instantly gives a readout of latitude, longitude, and time. The system has all but eliminated the traditional instruments of celestial navigation, and the navigator as well.

Men on the moon   Before manned rockets could be sent into orbit around the earth, an around-the-world system of tracking, monitoring, and command stations was needed. Shore stations in Houston, Hawaii, and Australia were not spaced to permit full coverage of orbital flight, so three "moon ships," named *Vanguard, Redstone,* and *Mercury,* were equipped. One of them took station about a thousand miles downrange from Cape Kennedy, one held a position between Australia and Hawaii, and one was located in the far western Pacific, near the equator.

These ships were World-War-II-type tankers. Their bows and their after-machinery sections were cut out, and new 380-foot midsections were welded in. Each ship was given nearly 500 tons of sensitive electronic equipment, an operations control center, a satellite communications center, a command control room, a mission control room, and a data-processing center, as well as inertial-navigation and laser-tracking systems. Their radar tracking systems were able to track a six-foot object at 32,000 miles.

Soon after Russia put Sputnik I into orbit, the Navy proposed building a surveillance system to keep track of whatever man-made objects might be orbiting in space across the United States. This was designed as a huge electronic fence, stretching across the country from Fort Stewart, Georgia, to San Diego, California, with installations at about a dozen points on that line.

Space and Surveillance (SPASUR) installations resemble mile-long fences laid on the ground. There are no big sweeping radar antennae, but the fences can detect, track, and compute an orbit for any unannounced, radio-silent satellite passing over the country. SPASUR feeds its information into the even more sophisticated Space Detection and Tracking System (SPADATS), a global system of radar, radio, and optical sensors, which detects, tracks, and catalogs all man-made objects in space and feeds the results into the North American Air Defense Command (NORAD). The computers NORAD uses are capable of handling up to 160,000 computations a second and a printout of 21,000 words a minute.

Some of the radars used in space-tracking operations are fan types called "football fields," 400 by 168 feet in size, which can track objects 2,000 miles out in space. Another type, housed in 140-foot radomes that look like huge golf balls, can detect objects 40,000,000 miles out in space. That is a big step from the 15-mile range of the first radar in 1938.

Oceanographic research probably began several thousand years ago when some Phoenician seaman poked an oar over the side of his ship to see if the water was shallow enough for him to wade ashore. It began in this country, in a very simple way, when merchant skippers first noted the difference between blue Atlantic water and green Gulf Stream water, and found that they made good time going east in the green water but had better keep out of it when they were going west.

Oceanographic research

Benjamin Franklin expressed an interest in this current. He might have liked a ride in the deep-sea research vessel named in his honor *Ben Franklin*, which is designed to drift silently at a depth of 2,000 feet, while technicians on board spend up to six weeks on a slow trip from Miami to Nova Scotia, charting the Gulf Stream.

Serious charting of ocean currents began with Matthew Fontaine Maury, a lieutenant in the navy. Maury founded the Hydrographic Office, which has now become the Naval Oceanographic Office with a couple of dozen ships at sea engaged in various types of research.

The discovery of ocean currents, and their effect on climate, is one important result of oceanographic research. The Gulf Stream carries warm water across the Atlantic and provides a gentle climate for France, Portugal, and Spain. The Japan Current, sweeping across the North Pacific and down the West Coast of the United States, does the same for Washington, Oregon, and California.

SOFAR   During World War II, oceanographic research revealed a definite layer of water, varying from 500 to 5,000 feet down, that would transmit sounds as far as 10,000 miles. This discovery resulted in Sound Fixing and Ranging (SOFAR), a system first used to rescue aviators downed at sea. A downed pilot would drop a small explosive charge, which detonated at a predetermined depth; SOFAR stations scattered around the rim of the ocean would hear the explosion and could take a bearing on it.

Besides the Navy, many universities and research institutions send oceanographic vessels to sea. Any one of these ships, such as those that put to sea from the Woods Hole Oceanographic Institution or the Scripps Institution of Oceanography, is a floating laboratory, carrying a multitude of instruments and equipment designed for many tasks. This may include buoys of various types, either to float on the surface and record information on weather, currents, and temperature, or to be anchored on the floor of the sea to measure subsurface currents; echo-sounding devices, side-scan sonar, underwater cameras; Nansen bottles to obtain water samples while recording temperatures at particular depths; nets and dredges for collecting biological samples; bathythermographs that plot temperature and depth; coring devices to pull plugs from the floor of the sea; magnetometers to measure the earth's magnetic field; heat probes that measure heat coming through the earth's crust from its interior; and hydrophones which are towed to receive signals from seismic reflection and refraction operations for the study of the ocean floor.

Deep-submergence vehicles   Although the Navy does not disclose how deep a nuclear ballistic-missile submarine can go, it is a well-known fact that many civilian research craft can go deeper than anything the Navy has.

Starting with the basic submarine concept, the sort of craft operated by John Holland in the late 1890s, the Navy and industry have produced a whole fleet of exotic undersea craft generally classed as deep-submergence vehicles (DSVs). One of the biggest, *Aluminaut*, can dive to 15,000 feet, roll around the bottom on tricycle gear, and, with its hydraulic arms, pick up a golf ball or a two-ton weight.

Smaller craft, such as *Perry Cubmarines*, work depths to 600 feet, which is satisfactory for surveys on the continental shelf. The small deep-diving submarine *Alvin* carries equipment for drilling in rock, measuring magnetic fields and gravitational influence, and recording the presence and amount of plankton, the minute sea life on which larger fish feed. The deepest-diving craft of all is the *Trieste*, developed by Auguste Piccard and owned by the U.S. Navy. In 1960 Jacques Piccard and Navy Lieutenant Don Walsh reached the very bottom of the sea, in the Challenger Deep, off Guam—35,800 feet down. In between those two extremes of depth, a whole world remains to be explored, and a series of bottom-dwelling submarines capable of operating at 20,000 feet is being developed for rescue work and exploration in that part of the world called "inner space."

CHAPTER 17
SHIPBUILDING

Shipbuilding in colonial times was a fairly simple matter. Timber was readily available, and the only other requirement, besides a sharp axe, was plenty of time. The men of the Popham colony, in Maine, who in 1607 were the first to build a ship in America—the little 30-foot *Virginia of Sagadahock*—needed no blueprints. Some of them probably could not read. They would not have been able to comprehend that in 350 years shipbuilding would become so complicated that the nuclear-powered aircraft carrier *Enterprise* required more than 16,000 plans and 2,400 miles of blueprints—enough paper to outweigh the *Virginia* and her crew.

The *Virginia* was an open boat. When rain or snow fell during her several Atlantic crossings, everyone in the crew knew it. The first decked-over vessel built in America was the *Onrush*, launched at New Amsterdam in 1614. A 300-ton vessel was launched in 1641 at Salem, Massachusetts. She was a large ship for the time—the *Mayflower* was only 180 tons—and, for the next 150 years, American-built craft averaged about 50 tons.

Early shipbuilding   Boston entered the shipbuilding business in 1630 with a small vessel named *Blessing of the Bay*. Other seaport towns followed, until by the end of the seventeenth century there were shipyards all the way from Maine to the Delaware River. Massachusetts soon became a leading shipbuilding colony; by 1676 some 700 Massachusetts-built ships were at work in coastal waters. Between 1674 and 1714

On previous page: A welder can do better work when he is bending down than he can when reaching up, so the Avondale Shipyards, near New Orleans, build the hulls of the Navy's new destroyer escorts upside down. They are turned right side up for completion. The circular frames on the hull at left will be removed after the ship has been turned over. Courtesy: Avondale Shipyards, Inc.

the colony built more than 1,200 ships, and by 1770 it was building half of all the ships turned out in America.

The American merchant marine—coasters, fishermen, and overseas trading vessels—reached a total of 476,274 tons in 1798. In 1800, shipyards launched 995 ships, for a total of 106,000 tons. In 1855, American yards built more than 2,000 ships, but thereafter shipbuilding declined. The government turned over to British ships the business of carrying the U.S. mail and, without such government support of transatlantic shipping, there was reduced demand for large oceangoing ships.

Shipyards   In every colonial seaport, the shipyard was the center of activity, where shipwrights turned out sloops and brigantines for the coastal trade, and pinks, ketches, and other small craft for the fisheries. Around the shipyard were related businesses: workshops making sails, pumps, ironwork, anchors, masts, and spars; and stores selling provisions, watches, charts, nautical books, and nautical clothing.

Shipyard workers lived within sight of the building ways, walked to work, and spent long hours on the job—literally from dawn to dark. On clear moonlit nights they sometimes worked a couple of hours more. In 1701 a carpenter made from 50 to 58 cents a day. Twice a day all hands knocked off work when the foreman called "Grog O!" It was estimated that for every ton a ship displaced, the men who built her drank a gallon of rum. Records on the Navy brig *Oneida*, built on Lake Ontario in 1809, show that she cost $20,505, and her builders drank 110 gallons of rum.

Where possible, building ways were laid out in a north and south direction, so that the sun would beat down equally on both sides of a new hull and provide even weathering. Shipbuilding involved no complicated design work and no elaborate construction gear or heavy-lift equipment. Beams and timbers were sawed and shaped by hand. The first water-powered saws went into operation in 1710; steam-powered saws went into use in 1830. A big step in ship design came in 1794, when Orlando B. Merrill, of Newburyport, Massachusetts, developed the half model; after a small model of a new hull was carved out, measurements of the model were taken to determine the dimensions of the actual ship. Then the model was sawed in two, from one end to the other, and the owner and the builder each took one half.

Wooden ships   The first period of wooden-ship construction in America began in 1607 with the building of the aforementioned *Virginia of Sagadahock* and lasted until the Revolutionary War. In that time, ships ranged from 20 tons to 400 tons. Anything larger than 50 tons was considered oceangoing, and a 400-ton ship was considered very big. By 1771 the colonies were turning out about 35,000 tons of shipping annually, and selling so many ships to

England that American-built ships accounted for nearly one-third of all British tonnage.

The second period in shipbuilding history began with the Revolutionary War and extended to about 1820. There was a depression immediately following peace with England, and American builders concentrated on selling their ships at home instead of overseas. Building costs were still low; a ship could be built in the United States for $34 per ton, whereas the same ship would cost from $55 to $60 a ton in Europe. Not only were wages higher there, but shipbuilding timber was in very short supply.

New ship types Shipbuilding requirements changed with the times. After the Revolutionary War, yards turned out small, clumsy trading ships. However, while European nations were at war, bigger craft of 300 to 600 tons were in demand for transatlantic use. After the War of 1812, Americans were building brigs and schooners, but they also began building more efficient warships and fast merchant ships designed for carrying passengers. The port of New York specialized in passenger ships and built most of the fast Atlantic packets. On the Chesapeake Bay, builders began designing small, fast ships which were used as privateers, slavers, and blockade-runners. From such rather tawdry beginnings, these sharp-built craft evolved in a few decades into the graceful clippers of gold-rush days.

In the first part of the nineteenth century sailing ships were still simple and inexpensive. In 1800 an average ship cost about $12,000. The clipper ships ran from $75,000 to around $90,000. Later in the century, steam freighters cost $250,000. (In 1974, a modern container ship costs as much as $40 million.)

Full-rigged ships The golden age of American wooden-ship construction began about 1830 and lasted until the end of the Civil War. By then, steamships were being built in America but they were far from efficient and trustworthy. Sailing ships, however, had gone through some two centuries of development and designers and builders were not only making technical improvements in hull construction, but were creating new types of craft—packets, clippers, and freighters.

Full-rigged ships built before 1830 were short and chunky; they had literally to smash their way through the seas. The fast Chesapeake Bay craft, first the Baltimore clipper schooners and then the true clippers, had sharp lines forward and tapered after bodies that eliminated the old sawed-off, square stern, which created underwater drag. Ship designers had not yet heard the term *streamlined* but Longfellow, in his classic poem "Building of the Ship," described exactly such a hull form:

Broad in the beam, but sloping aft
With graceful curve and slow degrees,
That she might be docile to the helm,
And that the current of parted seas,
Closing behind, with mighty force,
Might aid and not impede her course.

In the few years immediately following the California gold rush, the country produced over 2,500 ships. Not more than a couple of hundred of these could be classed as clipper types. Most new ships were full-rigged craft built to replace ships that had sailed to the Pacific during the gold rush and never returned; it was estimated that some 600 ships had been abandoned in California.

New England shipyards still led the nation in shipbuilding. The Bath area of Maine, in 1862 alone, turned out more ships than all the southern states from North Carolina to Texas. Southerners, unfortunately for their cause, were willing to let someone else haul the cotton they produced. As a result, when the Civil War began, New England was able to provide 2,000 masters and 40,000 sailors for the Union Navy, while all the southern states together furnished less than 600 seafaring men for the Confederate Navy.

The clipper ships, famed for their speed and beauty, won a much larger place in maritime history than they really deserved. They were not efficient cargo carriers, but they did fill a need for transportation at a time when hundreds of treasure-seekers were willing to pay for a fast trip to the goldfields. In 1849 alone, 90,000 such men sailed for California from Boston and New York. Aside from the technical details of hull and rigging that identified a clipper type, a ship qualified as a real clipper only by sailing from New York to San Francisco in 110 days or less, and only 100 clipper-type ships performed that feat.

Nevertheless, the clippers were imposing ships. The *Staghound*, 209 feet long, had masts as tall as a 25-story building. Their big attraction was speed. The *Lightning* once sailed 3,722 miles in 10 days, and set an all-time record of 490 miles in 24 hours, for an average of 18.2 knots. The only ship ever to sail faster was the *James Baines*, which in 1856 logged 21 knots for a short time.

The clippers were soon gone, if not forgotten, and fast packet ships beating their way across the Atlantic on regular schedules replaced them as news items. But it was the thousands of full-riggers, the prosaic contemporaries of the clippers, that carried American commerce—and the flag—to the far corners of the world. They sailed everywhere and carried anything.

Down easters   After the Civil War, the clippers began to disappear and their places were taken by the 500 or so ships and barks built in New England yards between 1870 and 1902 and known as "down easters." These craft were neither fast nor big, but they were smart sailers and they were the American foreign-going merchant marine during the last quarter of the nineteenth century. During those years, Americans were building and sailing steamers, but they had not made as much progress as had the British. Sailing-ship tonnage in the United States reached its peak in 1907, just a hundred years after Robert Fulton launched his first steamboat. It was only five years before that, in 1902, that steamship tonnage finally exceeded sailing-ship tonnage.

Schooners   Because the clippers, packets, and even whalers had an air of adventure and excitement about them, they are well known and remembered, whereas the most versatile of all American sailing ships, the schooners, are practically forgotten. It was the schooners that continued the age of sail in America down into the twentieth century and through the period of World War I.

Schooners were simple to build and inexpensive to operate. Their fore-and-aft rig was less complicated than that of the square-riggers and they required only a small crew. Large clippers used to carry nearly a hundred men; by 1900, schooners larger than most square-riggers had ever been were going to sea with about ten men.

Over the years, schooners were undoubtedly the most important of all American sailing craft. About 1716 colonial shipbuilders began building small schooners, which, through the years, were used as privateers, slavers, revenue cutters, naval vessels, pilot boats, fishing boats, in the West Indies fruit trade, and on the Great Lakes. In the last part of the nineteenth century schooners carried lumber, coal, and ice out of New England ports. Three-masted schooners came into general use about 1850, and from then until the end of World War I more than 1,500 of them were built on the Atlantic coast. On the Pacific coast, where 122 of them were built, they were primarily lumber carriers.

The three-masters reached their practical limit on size at about 1,000 tons, with cargo capacity of some 1,500 tons of coal. Many larger schooners were built with four and five masts, a few with six, and one with seven. The first four-master, the 996-ton *William L. White,* was launched at Bath, Maine, in 1880. The first five-master, was the 1,788-ton *Governor Ames.* The first six-master was the 4,000-ton *George W. Wells,* launched in 1900. The first, last, and only seven-masted schooner in the world was the 5,218-ton *Thomas W. Lawson,* built by the Fore River Shipbuilding Company at Quincy, Massachusetts. She had a steel hull—one of only seven steel schooners ever built in the United States.

By tradition, the masts of a three-masted ship, whether schooner or square-rigger, were designated fore, main, and mizzen, but more masts needed more names. The *Lawson* went on with jigger, driver, pusher, and spanker. For the benefit of landlubbers who could not remember whether jigger, driver, or pusher came first, her masts were also named Sunday, Monday, Tuesday, Wednesday, Thursday, Friday, and Saturday. The *Lawson* was a dinosaur among ships, more interesting to look at than useful. She was too big for easy handling, and soon wrecked herself.

Log rafts   Not all West Coast lumber was hauled in schooners. Oceangoing log rafts, similar to those first used on the Mississippi and later on the Great Lakes, frequently moved south along the coast like huge bark-covered whales. Hundreds of redwood logs would be chained together on the Columbia River, then a tugboat would haul them to San Diego—a trip that might take as long as three weeks. The first raft, 600 feet long, made the trip in 1906. Sometimes as many as five rafts would be towed south during the summer season. Eventually, rafts as long as 1,000 feet would contain up to 5,000,000 board feet of lumber, and maneuvering one of them through a harbor filled with cruisers, submarines, and destroyers could require real seamanship. The last big raft entered San Diego Bay in 1941.

Steamships

Early in the twentieth century schooners began giving way to steam. They lasted through World War I, when anything that floated could make money. During that war, they sailed in the coastal trade, both in the Atlantic and the Pacific, and some sailed as far as the West Indies and South America. A few crossed the Atlantic, but the way an old wooden ship fell apart when hit by a torpedo soon discouraged that. After World War I, shippers demanded that their cargoes depart and arrive on time. While sailing ships had to wait days for a favorable wind, steamboats could maintain a schedule and soon put the last of them out of business.

The history of steamships in America is not as long or as colorful as that of the age of sail, but it is a story of much more rapid progress and of much greater variety in size, configuration and use. Fulton's *Clermont* made her first trip up the Hudson River in 1807 at the rate of 5 miles an hour. In 1952 the liner *United States* set a world record on her first Atlantic crossing with an average speed of 40.98 miles an hour.

Paddle wheelers   The *Fulton* and the boats that immediately followed her were paddle-wheel types with weak engines and copper boilers that frequently blew up. They were merely sailboats into which someone dropped an engine and a boiler; most of their metal fittings were hammered out by blacksmiths. It was such a boat—the *Savannah*—that, in 1819, claimed the distinction of being the first steamboat to cross the Atlantic. Actually, her paddle wheels and engine were used for only three days during the 29-day trip, and were later removed. Fast sailing ships made much better time.

It was not until 1845 that another American steamboat, the *Massachusetts*, crossed the Atlantic, and she was no faster than the *Savannah*.

Oceangoing steamers   Beginning in 1847, wooden-hulled paddle-wheel, oceangoing steamships were built for the Collins Line and they, in competition with the ships of the British Cunard Line, provided the first real test of American steamship operations. These were the 2,700-tonners *Arctic, Atlantic, Baltic,* and *Pacific*. Similar ships were soon built for runs from the East Coast to Panama and from Panama to San Francisco.

By 1860, about two dozen such ships had been built and were already obsolete. Their huge paddle wheels, alternately digging deep into the water and rattling around in the air as the ship rolled, set up vibrations that wooden hulls could not withstand. Of course, the risk of fire in a wooden hull was something not mentioned in advertisements for transatlantic passenger service.

Technical developments   Although the first successful American ship built of iron and using propellers instead of paddle wheels, the *R. B. Forbes*, had been launched in 1844, American shipbuilders were slow to adopt iron hulls and screw propellers. The technique of producing iron plates and beams was not as advanced as it was in England, and timber was plentiful and cheap. As for the screw propeller, its vibrations shook wooden hulls apart just as fast as did those of paddle wheels. Some engineers preferred paddle wheels because they were mounted high on the hull, where they could be easily repaired. A propeller, on the other hand, was underwater and could be worked on only by putting the ship in dry dock. The Navy objected to paddle wheels because a couple of lucky hits on them could easily put a ship out of action.

By the time of the Civil War in the United States, England was building iron ships with screw propellers in the conviction that they were better than wooden ships with paddle wheels. As the U.S. Navy expanded during that war, it moved rapidly from sail to steam. Ironclad monitors with screws and various types of river gunboats with paddle wheels took over in shallow waters where sailing ships could not operate. A first example of quantity production was the building of seven ironclad gunboats on the Mississippi River. All were built to the same plans and the first one, the *St. Louis*, was launched 45 days after the contract was signed.

After the Civil War there was the usual postwar slump in both merchant and naval shipbuilding. Labor costs were high; iron was expensive. The United States had no steel industry. Despite the success of the ironclads, wooden ships were still being built; the Navy's last wooden steam frigate, the *Trenton*, was launched in 1875.

Steel shipbuilding   A new era in shipbuilding began in 1883 when the Navy ordered its first steel ships, the *Atlanta, Boston, Chicago,* and *Dolphin.* In the next six years, 38 steel ships were either building or on order. Some ships were being fitted with twin screws, and the new triple-expansion steam engines gave better fuel economy. But they still burned coal. The first Navy ship to steam on oil-fired boilers was the monitor *Cheyenne,* which sailed from Mare Island, California, in 1908, burning oil that cost one dollar a barrel.

The year 1892 was the first in which the United States built more steamships than sailing ships, and by 1901 the country was building more ships of iron and steel than of wood. The old yards that, knee-deep in wood chips and sawdust, had turned out whalers and clippers, could not handle modern construction techniques and materials, and big industrial yards were being built. These included the Newport News Shipbuilding and Dry Dock Company; the Fore River Ship and Engine Company at Quincy, Massachusetts; the Union Iron Works at San Francisco; and, about the time of World War I, the Bethlehem Shipbuilding Corporation.

Electric power   A big advance in shipbuilding came with the introduction of electrical power, which permitted more efficient plant layout and greater safety in the yards. Long overhead drive shafts and dozens of flapping belts made working hazardous in shops powered by steam. With electric motors, each machine had its own power source. Electricity also made possible heavy-lift equipment; the old steam cranes that could lift perhaps as much as five tons were replaced by traveling cranes that could lift as much as 150 tons.

Prefabrication   When the gunboat *Michigan* was built on Lake Erie in 1843, her iron plates were rolled out and shaped at Pittsburgh, then hauled by canal boat and wagon to the launching ways where the ship was erected. This was one of the first instances of prefabrication, a process used for many types of ships in World War I, and for ships, aircraft, tanks, and vehicles in World War II. Another early American development that greatly influenced not only shipbuilding but all assembly processes was the use of interchangeable parts, which had been introduced by Eli Whitney in 1789 in the manufacture of parts for guns.

Prefabrication, off-site subassemblies, and interchangeable parts made possible the large-scale production of standardized designs. Without those techniques it would have been impossible to build the destroyers, submarines, patrol craft, and merchants ships needed in World War I or the thousands of merchant ships, tens of thousands of aircraft, and the dozens of aircraft carriers, destroyers, other combatant ships, and amphibious craft needed by the Navy in World War II.

World War I   When the United States entered World War I, some 70,000 men were working in 142 U.S. shipyards. In 1918, a year later, 500,000 men were building ships; by then the country had 243 shipyards with 1,202 building ways in use. On 4 July of that year, 100 ships of many types were launched.

One of the most remarkable of the new yards was the Hog Island Yard, outside Philadelphia, which in 1917 was a swamp and in 1918 had 50 shipways, all in use. It was the first shipyard built especially for the mass production of a single type of ship. The island had once been called Quistconck, a Delaware Indian name meaning "place for hogs." The first ship launched there was christened *Quistconck*, and obviously all the ships built there were called "hogs." The war ended before any of the 122 "hogs" were completed, but eventually they were turned out at the rate of one every five days. The fastest time between keel-laying and delivery was just under eight months.

"Hogs" were 380 feet long, had a 54-foot beam, and a 2,500 horsepower steam turbine. Many of them were active in the merchant marine during World War II, when 58 were sunk by submarines or lost in other ways. The *Wright, Chaumont,* and *Argonne* were Navy "hogs."

Standard types   In general, each shipyard built one or two standard types of freighter of its own design. Naval ships that were produced to a standard design included destroyers, submarines, subchasers, and Eagle boats—the last-named being small patrol craft built by the Ford Motor Company. World War I destroyers, which were also called flush-deckers, four-pipers, tin cans, and, as they grew older, rust buckets, were built by several different commercial and Navy yards, but they all looked exactly alike except for the numbers painted on their bows. More than one sailor, returning late at night to a nest of destroyers, went down to the bunkroom and tried to throw some stranger out of his bunk, only to discover that he was in the wrong ship. The four-pipers were only 314 feet long and displaced but 1,200 tons, but their steam turbines produced 25,000 horsepower—more than contemporary battleships—and could drive them at 32 knots and better.

In the years from 1917 through the end of the building boom in 1921, American shipyards produced 6 battleships, 225 destroyers, 107 submarines, and enough other naval craft to total 472, for a combined tonnage of 798,301. In the same period, U.S. shipyards turned out 1,724 merchant ships of 2,000 tons and larger, for a total of 8,000,000 tons.

Postwar development   Between the two world wars, although shipbuilding was at a low ebb, American builders and designers continued to make technical developments in ship design and construction. Turbo-electric drive was improved, and for naval vessels steam plants were designed to operate under temperatures and pressures far exceeding those that the plants of other nations could sustain. Vessel performance, fuel consumption, cargo-handling, speed, carrying capacity, navigating equipment, refrigeration, and crew accommodations were all studied continuously. With the decline of tramp shipping (ships that sailed from port to port with no firm schedule or route), vessels became highly specialized for particular operations.

Diesel engines, which had first appeared in freighters before World War I, were made more reliable and more powerful and were installed in passenger ships. Although diesel engines are heavier than steam engines of equal power, they burn much less fuel, take up less space, and can be ready to move in much less time than it takes to light fires under a boiler and work up steam pressure.

During the period of World War II, from 1940 through 1945, the United States built more naval vessels than it had done in its whole previous history. Vessels added to the fleet in that time included 349 destroyers, 137 aircraft carriers, 203 submarines, and many other types in large numbers. In addition, the Navy received several thousand small craft and nearly a hundred thousand amphibious craft of all types.

World War II

Naval construction   Combatant vessels were built in the eight U.S. Navy Yards, in about sixty large commercial yards, and in hundreds of smaller yards, which sprang up wherever flat ground and some water were available, including on the rivers and the Great Lakes. A new yard in Manitowoc, Wisconsin, built submarines, which were ferried down the Mississippi to New Orleans to complete outfitting. A unique shipbuilding operation took place in Denver, Colorado, where plants that had built irrigation pumps and sugar-beet loaders prefabricated sections of destroyer escorts; the sections were hauled across the mountains by rail to California and assembled at the Mare Island Navy Yard. More than 300 ships launched in California were built in the mile-high yards of Colorado.

Work force   The fact that a ship could be assembled in a few days, or weeks, fails to show how many people worked on all the pieces before they were put together. On an average it took 592,000 man-hours to build a Liberty ship, and 873,000 man-hours to build a destroyer escort. A battleship or aircraft carrier, fifty times bigger than an escort, took far more than fifty times as much work because it was so much more complicated. All together, the merchant shipbuilding program of World War II turned out over 51,000,000 tons of ships. The entire U.S. Navy in the War of 1812 did not displace as much as did one Liberty ship.

There were 120,000 men—and women—at work in American shipyards in 1939. By December 1943, the labor force numbered 1,722,500. In 1942, women made up 4 percent of all shipyard work forces; two years later, in some yards they comprised 20 percent of the force. Women worked as blacksmiths, welders, shipfitters, crane operators, and truck drivers; such women were collectively honored by Norman Rockwell's painting of "Rosie the Riveter" on a cover of *The Saturday Evening Post*.

Liberty ships   Merchant ships were built in comparable numbers. Commercial shipyards turned out 5,600 cargo ships, tankers, and other types. The majority of these were Liberty ships, simple cargo ships, designated EC 2 by the Maritime Commission. The 2,710 wartime "Liberties" constituted the largest single-ship-type fleet the world had ever known. They were all built from the same plans in 19 shipyards on both coasts, and, to a large extent, built by unskilled labor—former salesmen, transplanted farmers, part-time students, ex-millworkers, and liberated housewives.

A Liberty was 441 feet and 6 inches long, had a beam of 56 feet, and displaced about 7,500 tons. It could carry 9,146 tons of cargo with a full load of fuel. Most Liberties carried more than that; it was a common sight to see them leave port with a deckload of aircraft, tanks, trucks, or locomotives. Their five holds could stow enough cargo to fill 300 railroad freight cars.

The ships were designed for mass production; their lines were simple, so their steel hull plates were easily shaped. They had simple reciprocating engines that could be built in almost any machine shop and maintained by almost any monkey-wrench mechanic; they produced 2,500 horsepower and drove the ship at 10 or 11 knots. The first Liberty, the *Patrick Henry*, was launched on 27 September 1941 by the Bethlehem Shipbuilding Company at Baltimore, Maryland. Ships were turned out so fast that the Maritime Commission actually had trouble finding names for them.

Parts for the Liberties were made in nearly every city in the United States, using mass-production techniques. At the shipyards, subassemblies weighing up to hundreds of tons—complete with wiring, piping, and even built-in furniture—were put together in special areas, then transported to the ways and welded together to complete the ship. Average time for the whole operation, from keel-laying to launching, ran from a few months at the beginning of the program to a few days near the end of it; a yard in Oakland, California, built the *Robert E. Peary*, complete, in 4 days, 15 hours, and 30 minutes.

Liberty ships were fairly simple compared to combatant ships with their extensive electronic equipment, super-heated steam plants, and high-speed turbines, but even so, a single ship contained more than 250,000 different items, which included:

". . . a three cylinder reciprocating engine, standing all of three stories high and weighing 135 tons, a propeller shaft, two water-tube boilers, one condenser, one steering engine, two anchors, two propellers (each ship carried an emergency spare), at least ten anti-aircraft guns, six generators, and six steam pumps. Each ship also required booms, winches, fans, beds, ventilators, hatch covers, life rafts, lockers, compasses, chairs, gauges, ladders, stoves and other equipment, thousands of miles of wiring and pipe (from ¼″ to 12″ in diameter), hundreds of valves, and a storeroom full of spare parts and fittings. The construction of one Liberty ship required 3,425 tons of hull steel, 2,725 tons of plate, and 700 tons of shapes, which included 50,000 castings."*

Liberty ships carried millions of tons of supplies, ammunition, vehicles, and provisions to all the war zones. The Navy used more than a hundred of them as cargo vessels and repair ships. Some 200 of them were either bombed, torpedoed, mined, burned, blown up, wrecked in collisions, or otherwise lost, but some of those that survived were still sailing 25 years later. One Liberty, the *John W. Brown*, was being used in 1974 by the New York City Board of Education as a maritime training school.

Amphibious ships   Besides letting women into the shipyards, World War II had another unusual result—a completely new type of ship, classified as "amphibious." Before the war, ships were designed to stay in the water; a captain who ran his ship on the beach would be looking for a new job. In World War II, thousands of Navy ships were built for only one purpose—to run high and dry on the beach. A captain who could not "beach" his ship and keep her there until she was unloaded might be looking for a new job. Amphibious ships were the first really new type of craft since Fulton put a boiler and some paddle wheels on a boat. "Amphibs" were big, empty cargo holds that had their engines at the stern and doors and ramps at the bow, which allowed them to unload troops and motorized equipment directly onto the beach.

The concept of beaching an oceangoing ship in order to unload it originated with the British, who had learned in the disastrous Gallipoli landings of World War I that it was impossible to put troops onto a hostile beach by the traditional method of sending them ashore in small boats. The landing-ship building program began in April 1942; before the year ended the United States had obligated $1 billion for amphibs, which included:

LST—Landing Ship, Tank;
LCI—Landing Craft, Infantry;
LSM—Landing Ship, Medium;
LCT—Landing Craft, Tank;
LCM—Landing Craft, Mechanized; and
LCVP—Landing Craft, Vehicle and Personnel.

* From *Liberty Ships, The Ugly Ducklings of World War II*, by John Bunker.

An LST was 328 feet long and could carry 4,000 tons, an LCVP was small and could carry a couple of vehicles or 36 troops. LCM and LCVP types were carried to landing areas on larger ships.

The amphibs put millions of men ashore on enemy beaches in Africa, Europe, and all across the Pacific, with amazing speed. When the Allies invaded Normandy on 6 June 1944, more than 100,000 troops with their guns, tanks, and other vehicles were put ashore that first day.

Special types of ships   The first American ships built for a special purpose were whalers: they were designed and built for whaling and were of little use in any other business. Schooners were a definite type of ship, but they could carry fish, slaves, or rum, as the traffic demanded. The Great Lakes ore boats were built to carry ore and nothing else. The rapidly increasing use of petroleum in the late-nineteenth century resulted in another special type of ship, the tanker.

Tankers   The first tanker in the world was the 794-ton *Charles*, of Antwerp, whose 59 iron tanks could carry 7,000 barrels of oil. The first American tanker was the 175-foot *George Loomis*, built in 1895. By 1900 there were 100 tankers afloat, and by 1939 the Standard Oil Company's tanker fleet alone amounted to 600,000 tons. Between 1923 and 1939, 77 tankers were built in the United States. In World War II, thousands of ships burned oil, and the thousands of aircraft and millions of automotive vehicles used by the military forces burned gasoline. Most 10-knot merchant ships carried enough fuel to cross an ocean and return, but combatant ships operating at high speed needed fuel frequently, and tankers had to be available in the war zones in order to supply them. To handle that logistic problem, American shipyards delivered hundreds of tankers during the war years. They ranged from 10,000 tons to 18,000 tons in size.

In 1948 the Bethlehem Steel Corporation at Quincy, Massachusetts, built a 28,000-ton tanker, and in 1962 launched one of 106,500 tons. The largest tanker built in the United States up to 1974 was the *Brooklyn*, displacing 225,000 tons. Shipyards are now building tankers as big as 600,000 tons, designated VLCC (very large crude carriers).

Not all tankers carry petroleum. Some carry such cargoes as molasses, tar, and chemicals. The 7,000-ton *Tropicana* made her first run from Florida to New York in 1957, her stainless-steel tanks filled with 650,000 gallons of orange juice; and the same year the *Angelo Petri* sailed from California to the East Coast, carrying 2,500,000 gallons of wine. Giant, 960-foot tankers now building at the Newport News shipyards, in Virginia, will carry liquid natural gas (LNG) at a temperature of 260 degrees below zero. Each ship will carry 125,000 cubic meters of LNG, which will convert to 2,645,600,000 cubic feet of gas—enough to heat the entire city of New York for a week in 25-degree weather.

Roll-on, roll-off   A ship type used in World War II amphibious operations has been greatly developed by the merchant marine since then. The LST, which the Navy still uses, has been followed by "roll-on, roll-off" (RORO) cargo ships, which are fitted with bow or stern doors and ramps that lead from one deck to another. Such a ship can load or unload several hundred truck-sized containers in a couple of hours. RORO is a special form of containerization. It is a door-to-door shipping system that has built-in security against pilferage and amazing flexibility for handling almost any cargo.

Container ships   The container system of handling freight involves complete integration of road, rail, and sea cargo-handling facilities; it is built around a standard-sized container that serves as a truck body, a railroad car, or a storage unit in a ship's hold. A container ship can carry hundreds of containers, stacked as much as six deep and ten wide in her hold and in three or more layers on deck. Some ships have huge cranes which travel along the main deck to handle containers; others are dependent on dockside cranes.

Some containers are insulated, some are refrigerated, Most of them open at one end, but they can be fitted to open at the top or sides for special cargo. Containers can be used to carry liquids, automobiles, grain or other bulk materials, fruit—in fact, just about anything. Once a box has been sealed at the loading dock of a producer or manufacturer, it is not opened until it arrives at its destination.

The Sea-Land Service of New Jersey uses container ships that are 946 feet long and can carry more than a thousand 35-foot and 40-foot containers. Their ships displace over 51,000 tons and operate at a speed of 33 knots—faster than a World War II aircraft carrier or destroyer—yet need a crew of only 49 men. Sea-Land Service's main terminal, which can park more than 6,600 containers at one time, uses color-coding labels, optical scanners, and computers to keep an inventory of containers at the terminal. Sea-Land has more than 35,000 containers in use by a fleet of 46 container ships which can unload cargo at the rate of 45 tons in four minutes.

LASH system   A newer form of containerization is the LASH system—an acronym for Lighter Aboard Ship. A LASH ship, which can carry loaded barges as well as containers, can operate completely independently of port or terminal cargo-handling facilities, because it carries its own cranes. The barges can be loaded in shallow water anywhere—even on rivers hundreds of miles inland; they are then towed to a seaport, where the ship's big barge crane picks them up and stows them, two deep, on the main deck. Smaller containers, which can carry any type of cargo, bulk or liquid, are picked up and stowed by a 30-ton crane that runs on the same rails used by the barge crane. LASH container vessels operated by the Delta Steamship Lines are 893 feet long and can carry 74 loaded barges plus 288 containers, or a total of 1,740 containers. LASH ships of the Prudential Grace Lines are 820 feet long and carry 76 barges, or as many as 1,500 containers. The two LASH ships operated by the Central Gulf Lines carry 83 barges each.

Barge ships   The newest, and most sophisticated cargo-handling system of all is provided by the new Sea Barge ships (Seabees), now operated by the Lykes Bros. Steamship Company. A Seabee combines features of the container ship, RORO, LASH, and the old-fashioned break-bulk ships, which stowed any kind of cargo, one sling-load at a time. The unit load carried by a Seabee is a barge with a capacity of 832 tons—about the same as twenty 20-foot containers. Seabee ships are 875 feet long with a 106-foot beam, and a speed of 21 knots; each ship has a stern crane able to lift 2,000 tons.

Barges are carried on three decks and are rolled into position on wheeled dollies. A full load of 38 barges amounts to about 24,000 tons. Because Seabee ships can carry about twice as much cargo as a regular break-bulk ship and can load or unload a full cargo in only a few hours, one such ship will, in a year, transport about five times as much cargo as a regular ship. The barges are integrated by size into the standard American and European inland barge systems, so they can be handled anywhere. It is possible for a Seabee barge to be loaded in Basel, Switzerland, hauled through canals to Rotterdam for pickup by ship, transported to New Orleans, and then towed up the Mississippi River to Minneapolis, without the contents ever being disturbed.

In only a few years the modular concept of cargo-handling has grown to an immense business. As of 1973, fifteen U.S. shipping companies and eight leasing companies maintained an inventory of more than 408,000 containers—enough to make a railroad train 185 miles long. These companies operated 175 ships (including RORO types.) The 23 LASH and Seabee ships in operation or under construction will have a total lift capacity of about half a million tons.

All the ships built in America in the first 150 years of the country's history would displace about as much as two of the latest VLCC tankers. The little *Virginia*, which started it all more than 350 years ago, could be stowed away in one of the containers handled by a modern container ship.

CHAPTER 18
GLOBAL WAR

"When peace has been broken anywhere, peace of all the countries everywhere is in danger," President Franklin D. Roosevelt said in a nationwide radio broadcast on 1 September 1939, the day Germany invaded Poland. And so it was. Two days later England and France declared war on Germany. The following year Germany invaded Denmark, Norway, Belgium, and The Netherlands. Italy declared war on England and France. Japan occupied French Indochina.

Diplomatic negotiations between the United States and Japan grew tense in 1940 and 1941. In May of 1940 Roosevelt ordered the Pacific Fleet to Hawaii from West Coast bases. Japan considered this a hostile act. In following months, the United States first limited and then virtually stopped the export of scrap iron, aircraft engines, and aviation gasoline to Japan. In July of 1941 Japan ordered all her merchant ships out of the Atlantic; in October the United States ordered all American merchant ships in Asiatic waters into friendly ports. Japanese aircraft bombed the U.S. river gunboat *Tutuila* at Chungking, China, in September.

The American war at sea had already begun, insofar as Germany was concerned. A German cruiser, the *Deutschland,* had captured the SS *City of Flint* in the Atlantic in October 1939, and in November 1940, the SS *City of Bayview* was sunk by a German mine off Australia. German submarines sank the SS *Robin Moor* in the South Atlantic in May 1941, and the SS *Lehigh* off West Africa in October. In September German bombers sank the SS *Steel Seafarer* in the Gulf of Suez. The U.S. destroyers *Greer* and *Kearny* were attacked by U-boats off Iceland, but not sunk; on 31 October the destroyer *Reuben James* was torpedoed and sank with the loss of a hundred men.

On previous page: Kamikaze! On 11 May 1945 two Japanese suicide planes crashed into the carrier *Bunker Hill,* setting off a raging fire of gasoline, burning aircraft, and exploding rockets and bombs. While men fought fire, gun crews stood by to repel further enemy attacks. The ship was kept afloat and returned to the United States for repairs. Photo: U.S. Navy.

Many other moves toward a wartime condition had been made by the United States. A neutrality patrol had been ordered in the Atlantic by the President on 5 September 1939. Early in September of 1940 the United States traded 50 old destroyers to Great Britain in exchange for 99-year leases on bases in British possessions in the Caribbean and West Indies. In 1941 the Lend-Lease Act authorized the United States to transfer many kinds of munitions to the Allies. Marines were landed in Iceland in July, to release British troops for service, and the Coast Guard began operating patrols in the Iceland-Greenland area.

War plans were made by Japan long before the 7 December attack on Pearl Harbor; in fact, the details of that attack had been worked out months earlier. In the days just before the Pearl Harbor attack, Japan had many ships moving to attack positions near the Philippines and in the South China Sea, as well as in the Pacific north of Hawaii.

As soon as the United States entered World War II, she was at war in two oceans at once. The Atlantic war against Germany involved convoy escort and submarine-hunting; the Pacific war against Japan involved surface battles, carrier attacks on bases and shipping, submarine warfare against merchant shipping, and a long campaign of invasion, conquest, and occupation of island bases all the way from the South Pacific to Japan. During that war, American troops and air forces fought in Africa, in Europe, and all the way across the Pacific. Merchant ships operated in all the oceans of the world. The Navy fought in the Atlantic, the Pacific, the Mediterranean, and the Sea of Japan.

Accounts of many World War II naval battles must of necessity be impersonal and statistical. Naval battles in the War of 1812 might be fought by two ships so close that men could swear at each other; perhaps only a couple of hundred people would be involved, and when the fight was over the winners would frequently take care of the losers. But naval battles in World War II were fought by ships sometimes 10 miles apart, sometimes two hundred miles apart. Men fired guns or torpedoes without ever seeing an enemy— merely a green pip on a radar screen. When a submarine sank an enemy ship, it was submerged at the time, and usually left the scene fast to avoid enemy air attack. And when a submarine was sunk there was usually no one left to tell about it.

The surprise attack on Pearl Harbor and on Army installations in Hawaii began at 7:55 a.m. on Sunday, 7 December 1941. About 60 torpedo planes and bombers first hit ships in the harbor. There were more attacks, by horizontal bombers and dive bombers; an estimated 354 aircraft took part in the raid, which lasted less than three hours.

Pearl Harbor attack

The Japanese had planned the attack in great detail, over a period of several months. Their strike force was organized around six aircraft carriers, which were escorted from Japan by two battleships, four cruisers, and a dozen destroyers. More than two dozen submarines scouted ahead or lay in wait off Hawaii. All the ships sailed from a remote harbor in the Kurile Islands and steamed at a speed that would bring them to the launching point for aircraft (about 200 miles north of Hawaii) just at dawn on the morning of the attack. Some of the submarines carried, piggyback fashion, little two-man subs, which were launched very early that morning so as to be in position to torpedo any U.S. ships that might try to escape from the harbor.

The U.S. Pacific Fleet had been based in Pearl Harbor, instead of in its usual West Coast ports of San Diego and San Pedro, since early May of 1940, at the direction of President Roosevelt. The commander in chief of the Pacific Fleet objected to this move, on the grounds that the ships could be better protected on the West Coast, but had been overruled by the President.

Protection of the fleet while in port was a duty of the U.S. Army, but the Army had neither enough big guns to fight off possible battleship attacks, nor enough antiaircraft guns to fight off enemy air attack. This was proved at Manila, when Japanese planes flew leisurely back and forth on bombing runs, at an altitude where the Army guns could not reach them. There was some air patrol around the Hawaiian and Philippine islands—Navy patrol planes searched certain sectors out to about 600 miles, but the Navy did not have enough planes to maintain a constant patrol all around the islands.

Radar was not much past the experimental stage then. Some ships had radar, but they could not use their sets in Pearl Harbor because the surrounding mountains blocked the radar waves. An Army radar post did actually detect the incoming Japanese raid on 7 December, but as some Army planes were expected to arrive from California that morning, no one was alarmed by the fact that more planes were coming than had been expected.

The first indication of an attack came early on that Sunday morning when the minesweeper *Condor*, patrolling outside the harbor entrance, spotted one of the two-man submarines heading in. She reported the submarine to the destroyer *Ward*. Nearly three hours later, as she hunted around the harbor entrance, the *Ward* also spotted the submarine, fired on it, and sank it. She thus acquired the distinction of firing the first shots of World War II in the Pacific (the gun that sank the submarine is now in Minneapolis, Minnesota), and the submarine became the first Japanese ship sunk in World War II. The skipper of the *Ward*, Lieutenant Commander William W. Outerbridge, became the first man to win a Navy Cross in World War II. Another of the little two-man submarines ran aground that morning; one member of its crew drowned trying to get ashore, the other was captured by an Army sergeant and became the first Japanese prisoner of war.

If the fleet had been at sea when the submarine was sighted, the *Ward* would have hoisted a flag signal and every ship would have been alerted instantly. As it was, the message reporting the sinking of the submarine was put in code, sent to Pearl Harbor by radio, decoded, and then routed around to the senior commanders. All this took time. The Japanese aircraft had started taking off from their carriers at six o'clock that morning and they were getting nearer every minute. Only one ship in the harbor, the destroyer *Helm*, was under way. A plane flew by, low and fast, and a man on the *Helm* waved at the pilot, who waved back. Not until he had passed did anyone realize that he was flying a Japanese plane.

At five minutes to eight, all ships in the harbor prepared to "make colors," hoist the flag at eight. The band on the *Nevada* was playing "The Star-Spangled Banner." Planes suddenly appeared all over the harbor. They were seen almost simultaneously by literally hundreds of men, and because they had pre-selected targets, which they hit at almost the same time, the war actually started all over the place all at once. Some sailors had machine guns firing within a couple of minutes—the Japanese later said they were startled at how soon the Americans began fighting back. Planes bombed and strafed the battleships, machine guns and antiaircraft batteries raised an increasing roar of defiance, planes began burning and blowing up at the Naval Air Station, and sailors, still too startled or stunned to believe their own words, kept yelling anyway "The Japs are here!" Many men, already in dress uniform and ready to go ashore for a day at Waikiki Beach, were killed before they left the quarterdeck.

A Japanese bomb set off the ammunition magazines in the battleship *Arizona* and she blew up, killing more than 1,100 men in the first minutes of the battle. The battleship *Oklahoma* and the old target ship *Utah* were torpedoed, rolled over, and came to rest bottom up. Before the attack was over, a few ships got under way to run out of the harbor. The battleship *Nevada* started out, but so many Japanese planes attacked her—if they could sink her in the channel, the whole harbor would be bottled up—that she was deliberately run aground to avoid any chance that she might sink.

In the couple of hours the attack lasted, many men performed feats of bravery that won them a Navy Cross or Medal of Honor. One winner of the Medal of Honor was Peter Tomich, a chief watertender, who stayed in the engineroom of the *Utah* to make certain his men got out, and went down with his ship. Chief Boatswain E. J. Hill was blown overboard and drowned, as he tried to get the *Nevada* under way. Dorie Miller, a mess attendant on the *West Virginia*, fought fires, helped rescue people, and manned a machine gun. He was awarded the Navy Cross, was killed later in the war when another ship went down, and became one of the first black people in the Navy to have a ship named in his honor.

But only 75 men got medals that day. Hundreds more earned them but never mentioned it; they were only doing their job. Ensign

Stanley Caplan had just reported aboard the destroyer *Aylwin;* when the attack started he took the ship to sea, with the help of another ensign, although his skipper and other officers were still ashore. And on the cruiser *New Orleans,* Chaplain Howell Forgy, who, as an ordained minister, was not supposed to fight, cheered on those who could with "Praise the Lord and pass the ammunition," a minor battle cry that became a song hit of the early war.

In order to satisfy the requirement of international law that a nation must not open hostilities without first declaring war, Japan planned to deliver a declaration of war to the U.S. government in Washington at 1:00 p.m. on 7 December, which would be 7:30 a.m. in Hawaii—an advance notice of 30 minutes. However, Japanese officials in Washington had trouble decoding their last "war message" (U.S. officials had already read it) and so met with the U.S. Secretary of State to announce a war that had been going on for half an hour or so.

As the first terse radio announcements of the attack flashed across the United States, they were received with disbelief, shock, and amazement. Only later did people begin to feel outrage, turn fighting mad, and go off to recruiting stations to sign up for the duration of the war. It was months before anyone learned the full details of what happened in Pearl Harbor.

The Japanese made several errors in executing their surprise attack. If they had bombed the dry docks and repair yard at Pearl Harbor, *no* badly damaged ship could have been put into operation for many months; and if they had blown up the tank farm where millions of gallons of fuel oil were stored, undamaged ships in Hawaii would have soon been forced to cease operations for lack of oil. They also underestimated the American people; the "sneak" aspect of the attack infuriated and united the country as nothing else could have done.

Nevertheless, in the few weeks immediately following their attack on Pearl Harbor, the Japanese had the ball and were off and running with it. They bombed the Cavite Navy Yard in the Philippines on 10 December, and occupied the island of Guam that same day. Japanese troops landed on Luzon, in the Philippines, on 11 December, and made a second landing in the area on 22 December. Wake Island's Marine defenders held out as long as they could but surrendered to the Japanese on 23 December. The Asiatic Fleet began pulling out of the Philippines.

Admiral H. E. Kimmel, who had been Pacific Fleet commander when the war began, was relieved of his command on 17 December. On 31 December, Admiral Chester W. Nimitz, in a brief ceremony aboard a submarine at Pearl Harbor, took command of the Pacific Fleet. It was up to "Uncle Chester," as he became known, to win the biggest naval war the United States had ever got herself into.

Japan was a "have not" nation. She had to import 90 percent of all her oil, 88 percent of all her iron, 24 percent of her coal supplies, and 25 percent of all her food. To take care of rapid industrial expansion and to support large military forces based in Asia for her war on China, Japan had to keep the imports moving in from southwest Asia. When the United States cut off fuel oil, gasoline, iron, and other critical materials she urgently needed, Japan had to invade the Philippines and southeast Asia to get raw materials.

Japan's plan for conquest included setting up a ring of defensive bases, extending from the Aleutian Islands, down across the Pacific to the Solomons, and westward to the Indies. Japan believed that, with most of the U.S. fleet knocked out in the opening days of the war, she would be able to beat off any U.S. attacks and induce the United States to negotiate for peace, leaving her with all her newly conquered land in the East Indies.

Being an island nation, Japan was dependent on sea transport. The country had thousands of large seagoing ships and unnumbered smaller craft when the war began. Yet despite her frantic ship-building program, her merchant fleet had been whittled down to 231 large ships when the war ended.

The war on Japanese merchant shipping began in 1942 as submarines patrolled in the Malay Barrier: by midyear submarines were hunting in "the Empire," lying in wait for merchant ships on the crowded sea-lanes from the Indies. As more submarines joined the fleet in 1943, operations spread wide across both the Southwest Pacific and the Central Pacific. By that time, the Submarine Force, Pacific Fleet, had been turned over to Vice Admiral Charles A. Lockwood, who had been a submariner since 1914 and knew how to use his boats.

Submarines gave up hunting on "lone wolf" missions and were organized into groups, most of which were known by the name of the senior officer, as, for example, "Blair's Blaster's," "Fenno's Ferrets," "Banister's Beagles," and so on. Fifty-two submarines were lost during the war. The number would have been fifty-three, had the *Growler* not been saved by her skipper, Commander Howard W. Gilmore, the only submarine man ever to win the Medal of Honor. As the *Growler* attacked a Japanese gunboat on 7 February 1943, the enemy suddenly changed course and swept the bridge of the submarine with machine-gun fire. Two men were killed instantly and Gilmore was too badly wounded to climb down into the conning tower. "Take her down!" he ordered. There was no time to lose; if the hatch were not closed instantly and the submarine taken down, she would be lost. Training and discipline paid off; the *Growler* submerged and escaped. Commander Gilmore was left behind in the sea.

Wolf packs began operating along main Japanese convoy routes and picking off ships all along the Asiatic mainland from Indochina up through the Japanese islands. Other submarines supported various fleet operations and performed such special missions as landing supplies for guerrillas and standing by during island air strikes to rescue aviators who were shot down.

By early 1945, there were so many submarines on patrol and

so few Japanese ships left that hunting was becoming difficult. The only Japanese merchant ships still afloat were those that crept along the Japanese coast from port to port. Shortly before the atomic bomb was dropped on Hiroshima, leading industrialists warned the military leaders that, if the war went on another year, 7,000,000 Japanese would die of starvation.

In the last months of the war, U.S. submarines laid mines in Japanese waters and along shipping routes. Army B-29 planes dropped thousands of mines in such areas. The mines dropped by bombers sank 670 ships, while only 15 bombers were lost—45 ships sunk for each bomber lost, which was far better than bombers could do by dropping bombs. Submarine-laid and air-dropped mines were responsible for sinking 2,289,416 tons of Japanese shipping. Nearly 9,000,000 more tons of shipping—2,398 ships—were sunk by U.S. submarines, surface ships, and aircraft. More than 300 of these lost ships were combatant types, knocked out in the battle zones. Of the merchant ships—those on which Japan depended for oil, rice, rubber, iron, and coal—U.S. submarines sank more than 1,100, for a total of 4,700,000 tons.

The United States had 51 submarines in the Pacific when the war began, and 203 more joined the fleet during the war. All together, submarines sank more than 1,300 Japanese ships; they proved a most effective and relatively inexpensive weapon.

Atlantic war   Months before the war officially began in the Pacific, the Navy was on a close-to-wartime footing in the Atlantic. Germany invaded Poland on 1 September 1939 and four days later President Roosevelt ordered the Navy to establish a Neutrality Patrol in a 300-mile-wide zone along the Atlantic coast of the United States. In March 1941 the Lend-Lease Act was passed, making it legal to transfer war materials to other nations; that same month the United States seized all German, Italian, and Danish ships in American ports. On 10 April, in the first action of the yet undeclared war, the destroyer *Niblack* depth-charged a German submarine off Iceland. By that time the Neutrality Patrol had been extended to take in almost the whole Atlantic Ocean.

After the outbreak of war, Atlantic operations centered on escorting convoys to Great Britain, Russia, and the Near East. A base that was established in Iceland for American combatant ships also served as a gathering point for convoys to Russia. American battleships and cruisers operated with the British fleet at various times but, except for antisubmarine operations, the U.S. Navy was not involved in any sea battles in the Atlantic.

Antisubmarine warfare   Allied naval forces soon drove U-boats off the U.S. east coast, but some time elapsed before surface and air antisubmarine forces were effective enough to keep them away from all shipping lanes. The use of radar for spotting surfaced submarines and of sonar for locating them when submerged gave submarine-hunters a great advantage. In 1942 Allied forces sank 85 German submarines in the Atlantic; in 1943 the figure jumped to 237; and in 1944, to 241. In the last four months of the war 153 U-boats were sunk. American submarine-hunters were so effective that, in May 1944, one team consisting of the escort carrier *Guadalcanal* and five destroyer escorts sank two U-boats in two days. The skipper of the carrier, Captain Daniel V. Gallery, and his officers then decided that they would capture the next U-boat that was forced to the surface. On 4 June, the *U-505* was tracked down, depth-charged, and forced to surface. As her crew was trying to sink her, men from the *Guadalcanal's* destroyer escorts boarded her, disarmed her explosive charges, and captured her and her entire crew. She was towed back to the United States, and may now be seen at the Museum of Science and Industry in Chicago, Illinois.

North African landings   The Allies opened a second front against the Axis on 8 November 1942 when an Allied Expeditionary Force under the supreme command of Lieutenant General Dwight D. Eisenhower landed troops at Casablanca, Oran, and Algiers, in Operation TORCH. The U.S. Navy's Task Force 34 was commanded by Rear Admiral H. Kent Hewitt and included about 100 ships and 70,000 men. There was some resistance by French naval forces, and several French ships were sunk. Three U.S. Navy transports were torpedoed by U-boats. The land campaign in Africa ended on 13 May 1943; some 275,000 Axis soldiers were taken prisoner, and 433,000 tons of Axis shipping were sunk by Allied air, surface, and submarine forces.

Invasion of Sicily   Operation HUSKY, the invasion of Sicily, was also under the command of General Eisenhower. The over-all naval commander was Admiral of the Fleet Sir Andrew Cunningham, Royal Navy. D-Day was 9 July 1943. A British fleet landed the British Eighth Army; a U.S. task force under Admiral Hewitt landed the U.S. Seventh Army at Gela, Licata, and Scoglitti, all on the southern side of the island. More than 500 U.S. ships were involved. The approaches to the island were mined and had to be swept before amphibious craft could beach. Enemy air opposition was heavy; a U.S. destroyer and a couple of amphibs were sunk and many more ships were damaged, most of them by air attack. Sicily was completely under Allied control by 17 August.

Invasion of Italy   D-Day for Operation AVALANCHE, the invasion of Italy, was 9 September 1943. On the 8th, as the invasion force approached its objective, Italy signed an armistice with the Allies— but the country was still full of Germans. The operation was again headed up by General Eisenhower, with Admiral Hewitt leading one naval task force, and Rear Admiral John L. Hall leading another. The landings at Salerno met fierce German resistance; the Navy lost three destroyers and many smaller craft, and had far more ships damaged. The Salerno campaign was officially declared closed on 11 October, and two days later Italy declared war on her former ally, Germany.

Landings at Anzio   Operation SHINGLE, landings at Anzio, in central Italy, was set for 22 January 1944. It was designed as an end run to cut off the German forces that were holding up the Allies at Salerno. Some 250 U.S. ships under Rear Admiral Frank J. Lowry landed about 50,000 U.S. and British troops, who met fierce resistance. Before Anzio was secured, U.S. losses amounted to 5,000 men and 20 ships, mostly minesweepers and amphibs. Allied troops finally entered Rome on 4 June 1944—just two days before the Allied invasion of Normandy.

Invasion of Normandy   Operation OVERLORD, the invasion of Normandy under the supreme command of General Eisenhower, was the greatest amphibious operation in all history. It involved transporting 100,000 troops and their equipment across the English Channel and landing them on the coast of France on D-Day—6 June 1944. More than 4,000 ships loaded in a dozen English ports, assembled off the Isle of Wight, moved across the Channel in darkness, and simultaneously hit five landing sites on the French coast. Most of the American ships were in the Western Task Force, under the command of Rear Admiral Alan G. Kirk, which put the First Army, under Lieutenant General Omar N. Bradley, ashore on "Omaha" and "Utah" beaches. Battleships (some of which had been sunk at Pearl Harbor, raised, and repaired) headed the invasion fleet and, along with numerous cruisers and destroyers, provided shore bombardment.

Because the landings had to be made over open beaches, instead of in protected harbors, the Allies built artificial harbors. They did this by sending in with the D-Day force some 30 merchant ships manned by 1,000 merchant sailors and so rigged that, after they were in position off Normandy, they could be blown up and sunk to form a breakwater behind which other ships could safely unload troops and equipment. Following D-Day, some 150 American merchant ships formed a cross-channel supply run from England to France to support the Allied forces as they drove for Germany. Many of them were damaged, or sunk, by mines.

Mines were especially dangerous weapons, and the Germans had planted hundreds of them. There were contact mines, which had to be struck by a ship before they would detonate; magnetic mines, which were set off by the magnetic field surrounding a ship; and pressure or "oyster" mines, which were set off by the slight increase in water pressure created as a ship passed over them. The last two types were called *influence mines:* they lay on the bottom and it was very difficult for a minesweeper to clear them out. It took 385 minesweepers to clear paths for the invasion fleet to follow.

Ships most likely to be sunk by mines were minesweepers, and Ira Wolfert, a news correspondent, was watching when the USS *Tide* was virtually blown out of the water by a magnetic mine.

"There was a big explosion, and gray smoke and white water all mingled," wrote Wolfert. "We saw first those who had been blown farthest by the explosion. They were all dead. . . . And then from all over the sea around us, sounding small and childlike in the wild world of waters, came cries of 'Help! Help!' and one startling plea of 'Please help me!' We fished six men out of the water, two un-

This view of a beach in the early stages of the 1944 Normandy landings gives an idea of the huge numbers of cargo ships required to carry the equipment for an invasion force. The LSTs on the beach have their bow doors open and ramps down to unload vehicles. The captive balloons, anchored by steel cables, were put aloft to discourage enemy dive bombers. Photo: U.S. Navy.

injured. Other craft had come to the rescue and we searched among them, taking only the living and leaving the dead bobbing and ebbing awash like derelicts in an unwitting sea. One of the men we got was naked. Every stitch of clothing had been blown off him."

More than 30 U.S. ships were sunk by German mines during the Normandy campaign, and many more were damaged. The largest ships lost were destroyers. Many merchant ships ferrying supplies across the Channel were sunk in the weeks following the initial landings, but supplies continued to pour into France. In the first month, the Allies landed 929,000 men, 586,000 tons of supplies, 177,000 vehicles, and vast amounts of armament. Despite strong German resistance, Allied troops broke out of the beachhead and by 18 June had surrounded Cherbourg. Another large Allied landing was made in southern France on 15 August, under the command of Vice Admiral H. Kent Hewitt; ground forces were under the command of Lieutenant General Alexander M. Patch, U.S. Army. Again, extensive minesweeping was required before large ships could move in, and there were heavy naval gunfire and aircraft attacks on enemy positions before the landing. Once the troops were ashore, naval vessels engaged German shore batteries, as they had done at Normandy.

Three months after the first landings in France, American troops entered Germany. However, the war was far from over. Fighting went on all through the winter; Germany finally surrendered on 7 May 1945.

Pacific war   After the attack on Pearl Harbor, the Japanese Navy confined its operations to actions in the Philippine Islands and the Netherlands East Indies. For several months the U.S. Navy was on the defensive. The Asiatic Fleet withdrew from the Philippines to Java, and from there took part in three actions with superior Japanese forces: the Battle of Makassar Strait on 24 January 1942; the Battle of Badoeng Strait on 19–20 February; and the Battle of the Java Sea on 27 February. The action in the Java Sea ended organized resistance to the Japanese fleet and, as American, Australian, and Netherlands ships retreated, several destroyers were sunk. Surviving ships withdrew to Australia.

Manila had been declared an open city late in December 1941, but Japanese bombing continued and met little resistance because the U.S. air bases had been wiped out in the first few days of the war. The Japanese took Manila and Cavite on 2 January 1942. However, Corregidor and Bataan were still being defended. A few U.S. submarines sneaked in at night with ammunition and food, but it was not enough to help. When the USS *Trout* brought in 3,500 rounds of 3-inch ammunition on 20 February 1942, her skipper asked for 25 tons of sandbags to ballast his boat before she left, but no sandbags could be spared. Instead, officials loaded the submarine with $10 million worth of gold bars and silver pesos—22 tons of the stuff. The crew had to walk over the treasure until they could unload it in Pearl Harbor. The cruiser *Detroit* took the gold and silver on to San Francisco, locked up in the ship's barber shop.

President Quezon, of the Philippines, and the American High Commissioner, Francis B. Sayre, were taken off Corregidor in the submarine *Swordfish* on 20 February. General Douglas MacArthur, Commander of U.S. Army Forces in the Far East, and some members of his staff were evacuated on 11 March. They rode Navy PT boats to Mindanao, where Army bombers picked them up and took them to Australia. There General MacArthur established new headquarters. Eventually naval forces in the southwest Pacific area were organized as the Seventh Fleet, which operated under MacArthur's command on the long drive back to the Philippines.

Corregidor surrendered on 6 May. The last Americans to escape were 18 sailors and officers from the minesweeper *Quail*, who called themselves the "Quail liberty party." The night before the surrender, they loaded a 26-foot motor whaleboat with drums of diesel fuel and a few guns, and slipped out of the harbor. They ran only at night—island-hopping to hide in swamps during daytime—and in 30 days sailed 2,000 miles, to reach Darwin, Australia.

Air raid on Japan   The first U.S. strike against Japan herself came on 18 April 1942 in a daring operation. Sixteen Army B-25 bombers, launched by the aircraft carrier *Hornet* about 650 miles from Japan, hit targets in several Japanese cities before flying on to China and Russia. Only one plane landed safely; the crews of the others either bailed out or made crash landings, but 70 out of the 80 airmen survived. The raid did little damage in Japan, but it greatly mystified the Japanese, who knew that the United States had no base near enough to Japan from which to make such a raid. President Roosevelt said the planes flew from Shangri-La, a mythical Asiatic land featured in a novel by James Hilton, and the Navy later commissioned a carrier with that name. The American public was not told where the planes were launched, but the fact that Japan had been bombed did a great deal to boost morale at a time when it was very low.

It would be more than two and a half years before another Army bomber flew over Japan. The next raids were by heavy B-29s, which made the 1,500-mile hop from Saipan, in the Marianas.

Drive across the Pacific   The Navy opened the war in the central Pacific with raids by cruisers and carriers on Japanese bases and fleet anchorages in the Gilbert and Marshall islands on 1 February 1942, Salamaua and Lae in New Guinea on 10 March, and Tulagi on 4 May. That was followed by the Battle of the Coral Sea, on 7 and 8 May. The U.S. carriers *Lexington* and *Yorktown* and the

Japanese carriers *Shoho*, *Shokaku*, and *Zuikaku* were the principal
opponents, yet no carrier ever got within sight of an opposing carrier. It was the first naval battle in history in which opposing warships did not exchange a shot—all the fighting was done by torpedo
planes, dive bombers, and fighters. Some half-dozen U.S. and
Australian cruisers and a dozen U.S. destroyers, which were supporting the U.S. carriers, fought off the Japanese air attacks; the
destroyer *Sims* and the oiler *Neosho* were sunk by air attack.

Planes from the *Lexington* and *Yorktown* sank the *Shoho*, and
the next day damaged the *Shokaku*, forcing her to withdraw from
the battle. But on that day fierce enemy attack left the *Lexington* a
burning wreck. She took five bombs and two torpedoes about noon,
and her crew fought fires for several hours before her skipper,
Captain Frederick C. Sherman, finally had to order them to abandon
ship. Destroyers picked up hundreds of men; some slid down lines
to ships alongside the carrier, others went into the water and swam
to rescue boats. While men waited on the flight deck to leave the
ship, some of them went down to the ship's service store and filled
their helmets with free ice cream. Techniques for abandoning ship
called for men to remove their shoes before they went into the
water, so hundreds of men took off their shoes and lined them up
in neat rows on the flight deck, as if they expected to come back for
them later.

Had the Japanese drive toward island bases in the South Pacific
been successful, it would have cut Allied supply lines to Australia.
The Coral Sea battle not only ended that drive but it terminated the
purely defensive operations of the U.S. Navy. It also left the Navy
with only a couple of undamaged carriers in all the Pacific. The
Yorktown had been damaged but made it back to Pearl Harbor,
where it was estimated that it would take a hundred days to repair
her. However, the Navy Yard at Pearl Harbor worked on a crash
basis and had her ready for service in only three days.

The loss of the *Lexington* and all her planes was a real blow.
Dozens of new carriers joined the fleet in 1942 and 1943, but when
the "Lex" went down, the Navy had only eight carriers in commission and some of them were in the Atlantic. The *Yorktown* and
the *Saratoga* (sister ship of the *Lexington*) had been damaged.
Besides, the "Lex" and "Sara" had been with the fleet for 14 years
and were like old friends.

When a ship sank, men lost everything they owned, except for
the clothes they wore. A war correspondent who escaped from the
Lexington returned to Washington, D.C., a few weeks later. When
he tried to buy a tube of toothpaste, the clerk refused to sell him
one unless he brought in the old tube, which was at the bottom of
the Coral Sea.

Battle of Midway   About halfway between North America and
Japan, Midway Island would have made a good base for attacks
eastward, and the Japanese determined to take it. They planned a

vast operation, for early June, with a carrier strike on the Aleutians intended to draw the U.S. fleet out of the Hawaii-Midway area. Then a larger carrier force was to bomb Midway, after which an invasion force of 5,000 men would take it over. The Japanese believed that they had sunk the *Yorktown*, as well as the *Lexington*, in the Coral Sea battle and, as they had sighted the *Enterprise* and *Hornet* in the South Pacific only a few days before their planned attack date, they thought it likely that the United States had no carriers in the central Pacific. However, American code-breakers had read enough Japanese messages to have a fair idea of what was planned, and Admiral Nimitz managed to move his three available carriers into the Midway area. As a result, the *Enterprise* and *Yorktown* intercepted the Japanese force.

In a two-day air battle that began on 3 June, four of the Japanese carriers that had raided Pearl Harbor six months earlier—the *Akagi*, *Kaga*, *Soryu*, and *Hiryu*—were sunk. The *Yorktown* was bombed and torpedoed on 4 June, but remained afloat. Odd things happen in battle; one of the bombs blew a man overboard, and when a chief petty officer saw him in the water he bellowed, "Who gave you permission to leave this ship?" The crew, assisted by men from as many as six destroyers, fought fire for two days in an effort to save the ship. On 6 June a Japanese submarine torpedoed the destroyer *Hammann* and she sank instantly. More torpedoes in the *Yorktown* added to the salvage problems, and she sank on the morning of 7 June. Among the *Yorktown*'s survivors was a pet rabbit.

The first air attack on the Japanese carriers was made by 41 torpedo planes from the *Enterprise*, *Yorktown*, and *Hornet*, flying low over the water. Torpedo Squadron 8—fifteen planes from the *Hornet*—was wiped out completely. The only survivor, Ensign George Gay, floated around all day in the middle of the battle, waiting to be rescued. By flying in low, the planes had forced the Japanese to keep their fighters down low; as a result, the next waves of dive bombers came in high, were unopposed, and were able to make hits on all the Japanese carriers.

Midway marked the first defeat for the Japanese Navy in 350 years, and ended its offensive in the Pacific. Having lost four aircraft carriers with all their aircraft and trained pilots, Japan never made another major offensive move.

South Pacific campaigns   In July 1942 the Japanese began building an airfield on Guadalcanal, which would enable them to strike ships supporting U.S. bases in the New Hebrides and cut U.S. supply lines to Australia. The offensive-defensive phase of the war began on 7 August 1942, when a navy task force of 77 ships under Vice Admiral Frank J. Fletcher landed the 1st Marine Division on Guadalcanal. After fierce fighting, Guadalcanal was secured on 9 February 1943.

Naval action in the Solomon Islands began with the invasion of

Guadalcanal and lasted for several months. There were frequent battles between U.S. surface forces and the "Tokyo Express," a group of fast Japanese cruisers and destroyers that ran down at night from a base farther up in the Solomons. Nine major naval actions were fought in the Solomons in 1942 and 1943. They were the battles of Savo Island, 9 August; Eastern Solomons, 23–25 August; Cape Esperance, 11–12 October; Santa Cruz Islands, 26 October; Guadalcanal, 13–15 November; Tassafaronga, 30 November; Kula Gulf, 6 July 1943; Kolombangara, 13 July; Vella Gulf, 6 August; and Empress Augusta Bay, 1 November. During the entire campaign, the Japanese lost two battleships, a carrier, five cruisers, twenty-four destroyers, and many smaller craft; the United States lost two carriers, eight cruisers, twenty destroyers, and a number of smaller craft.

Most of the action in the Solomons involved surface and air war but Japanese submarines were also active. An all-time record for sub-hunting was set by the destroyer escort *England*, which arrived in the Solomon Islands for her first combat operations in May 1944. About that time the Japanese sent a group of six submarines to patrol between Truk and Manus to detect any U.S. fleet movements to the westward. On 19 May the *England* was patrolling off Bougainville, along with the escorts *George* and *Raby*, when she made a sound contact. Submarine! Five times the *England* made an attack run over the submarine, firing hedgehogs (small weapons that exploded if they hit something). The last run brought up oil, wood, and a bag of rice. Scratch one submarine.

On 22 May the same three escorts made another sound contact, and all made hedgehog attacks. The *England* attacked last and, on her second firing run, she set off a tremendous underwater explosion. Wreckage floating to the surface showed that she had sunk her second submarine.

Another sound contact on 23 May was worked over by the escorts, and again the *England* brought up submarine wreckage. An hour later, still another submarine was tracked down; the *England* got that one, too. Her score was then four submarines in five days. However, the Japanese had sent out six scouting submarines. On 26 May the *England* got her fifth submarine, and on 31 May she sank her sixth, for an all-time record—six enemy submarines in twelve days. For their one-time-only performance, the *England* and her crew were awarded a Presidential Unit Citation.

Central Pacific campaign   By 1943 the Navy had built up combatant power in the Pacific, with many new carriers, cruisers, destroyers, and battleships, and began the offensive phase of the war against Japan by hitting islands on the eastern rim of Japan's defensive barrier. These operations were built around fast carrier task forces. Carrier bombers, fighters, and torpedo planes took the war to the enemy; battleships, cruisers, and destroyers escorted and guarded the carriers. At the same time, strong amphibious forces began island-hopping from New Guinea toward the Philippines.

After preliminary air strikes, the Gilbert Islands were invaded on 20 November 1943. Although the U.S. Marines met especially bitter resistance on Tarawa, in three days the islands were secured. The Marshall Islands were hit next, commencing with air strikes in November of 1943 and landings by Army and Marine forces on 31 January 1944. The various islands and atolls of the group, Roi, Namur, Kwajalein, and Majuro were all secured by 20 February. Meanwhile, carrier task forces had hit Truk in the Caroline Islands and commenced preliminary raids on the Mariana Islands.

Northern Pacific campaign   The Aleutian Islands, reaching down from Alaska across the North Pacific toward Asia, were a logical route for Japanese forces launching an attack on the American mainland. Japanese bombers raided Dutch Harbor at the time of the Battle of Midway in June 1942, and a few days later enemy forces occupied Kiska and Attu, at the far western end of the Aleutians. American forces bombarded Kiska on 7 August and, when they occupied Adak later that month, they used it as a base for continuous air raids on Kiska. A Japanese surface force moving to reinforce Kiska and Attu was turned back by ships of the North Pacific Force in the Battle of the Komandorski Islands on 26 March 1943. American forces landed on Attu on 11 May and all Japanese resistance there ended on 29 May. Ships and planes then hit Kiska for several weeks, but when troops landed there on 15 August it was discovered that the Japanese had withdrawn.

Southwest Pacific operations   The U.S. advance across the Pacific followed two routes: from Hawaii through the Gilberts, Marshalls, and Marianas; and from Australia along New Guinea and the East Indies to the Philippines. The advance from Australia to the Philippines was under the command of General of the Army Douglas MacArthur and consisted of numerous amphibious landings, beginning with one on Kiriwina Island, at the eastern tip of New Guinea, on 30 June 1942. In short hops of from 60 to 900 miles, amphibious craft of the Seventh Amphibious Force, under Rear Admiral Daniel E. Barbey, hauled Army troops to one beachhead after another. The seventeenth landing was made at Morotai, in the Celebes Sea, in September 1944.

Marianas operation   The Mariana Islands, which include Saipan, Tinian, and Guam, were needed as bases for U.S. long-range bomber attacks on the Japanese homeland. Fast carrier task forces began bombing the islands on 12 June 1944. Three days later, Marines landed on Saipan, and organized resistance there ended on 9 July. More Marines landed on the island of Guam on 21 July and on Tinian on 24 July.

While pre-invasion bombardment of Guam was going on, the destroyer *McCall* spotted flashes of light on a jungle hill—someone on the island was signalling in English. A boatload of armed men went in to the beach and met a wild-looking man in filthy clothes, who asked to be rescued. Taking no chances, the sailors made him take off his clothes and swim out to the boat. As he pulled off his pants, someone said "He looks like a white man!" And so he was. Radioman, First Class, George R. Tweed had hidden from the Japanese when they took the island on 10 December 1941, and had managed to keep away from them for over two and a half years, living in a cave in the jungle.

With the Mariana Islands again under U.S. control, Guam was built up as one of the largest advance bases in the Pacific. Air bases built on Saipan served as hopping-off places for long-range bombers staging raids on Japan.

Battle of the Philippine Sea   A strong Japanese force attempting to cut off U.S. landing forces at Guam was met by U.S. carrier aircraft on 19 June. In a two-day battle, the Japanese lost two aircraft carriers and over 400 airplanes; no U.S. ships were lost. Total U.S. losses were 130 aircraft and 78 pilots and crewmen. The United States might have lost many more planes and men, but for the compassion of Admiral Marc A. Mitscher, the task force commander.

Late in the afternoon of 19 June, two hundred planes were launched for a strike on the Japanese and flew out 300 miles to meet the enemy. By the time they returned to the carriers, night was falling and they were running out of gas. It was standard wartime procedure for all ships to run darkened at night—no lights at all topside. Without lights to guide them down to the flight decks, all those planes would be lost.

Aware of the predicament, Admiral Mitscher made what was probably the shortest and most wildly cheered speech of World War II, "Turn on the lights." The whole fleet lit up, sailors cheered, and dozens of weary, frightened pilots brought their planes in. A lot of men spent that night in their bunks instead of at the bottom of the sea, thanks to Marc Mitscher.

Return to the Philippines   The invasion of the Philippines began on 18 October 1944, as more than 1,400 ships, 50,000 sailors, and 165,000 troops moved into Leyte Gulf. After the initial landing at Leyte on the 20th, seventeen more were made in the Philippines, including one at Zamboanga on 10 March and one at Panay on 18 March 1945.

Japanese and U.S. forces met in the biggest surface engagement of the war during the Philippine campaign. In the battle for Leyte Gulf, 23–26 October, the Japanese sank three U.S. carriers, one submarine, and three destroyers; the Americans sank four Japanese carriers, three battleships, ten cruisers, and nine destroyers.

Another huge U.S. invasion force landed in Lingayen Gulf on 9 January 1945, at which time the Navy met the first concentrated suicide attacks by Japanese aircraft—the kamikazes. Many ships were damaged there, but only two were sunk.

Assault on inner defenses of Japan   The occupation of the Marianas provided bases from which heavy bombers could attack Japan, and also hit the island of Iwo Jima, which was only 750 miles from Japan. It was a small island, about five miles long, but of great importance in staging air raids on Japan. Planes flying from U.S. bases in the Marianas had to make a 3,000-mile round trip; if Iwo could be taken, it would provide an interim landing field for planes that had been shot up or were running low on fuel.

The immense Fifth Fleet, under Admiral Raymond A. Spruance, was given the job of taking Iwo. In spite of the fact that the island was bombed several times in the months before the Marines landed there on 19 February 1945, strong resistance was expected, and the invasion force was ready for it. More than 800 ships moved in to take Iwo; 60,000 Marines made the landing; they met all the resis-

Little ships with a big punch. These LSMRs (Landing Ship Medium, Rocket) blast Japanese installations on the island of Okinawa. Rockets were fired from simple launching racks on deck, which were less expensive and easier to handle than heavy guns. Photo: U.S. Navy.

tance that had been expected, and then some. The highest point on the island, Mount Suribachi, had been given the code name of "Hot Rocks," but the Marines soon nicknamed it "Mount Plasma" because so many men were wounded there. On 23 February, a 40-man patrol rushed the peak and took it. They carried an American flag with them, and used a piece of Japanese pipe as a flagpole from which to fly it. A news photographer, Joe Rosenthal, took a picture of the men raising the flag and produced one of the most noted photographs of World War II. The scene was later reproduced in a heroic piece of statuary, the Iwo Jima Memorial, which was erected in Washington, D.C., overlooking the Potomac River. The Memorial honors all Marines and names every battle in which they took part. Of the Marines at Iwo Jima, Admiral Nimitz said they made "uncommon valor a common virtue."

Iwo Jima was a costly battle for both sides. More than 13,000 enemy bodies were counted and buried, and it was estimated that another 8,000 were sealed up in caves or buried by the Japanese. There were more than 20,000 Marine casualties, nearly 5,000 of whom were killed. Yet, in the long run, the score at Iwo came out even. From first to last, more than 2,000 heavy bombers landed there, too crippled or too low on fuel to make it back to Saipan. Each plane carried 11 men, so at least 22,000 members of the 20th Air Force may well have owed their lives to the Marines who took Iwo Jima.

Planes from the fast carrier task forces began bombing Japan on 16 February 1945. A second raid was made on 25 February. Heavier raids were made frequently after that. On 14 July battleships, cruisers, and destroyers joined in with shore bombardments of mills and factories in Japan. Carrier raids were made until the war ended; in fact, planes were en route to Tokyo on 15 August when the "cease fire" order caught up with them before they had dropped their bombs.

Invasion of Okinawa   The Japanese island of Okinawa was only 350 miles from Japan proper. With air bases there, U.S. planes would be able to commence the bombing of Japan required to wipe out resistance on the home islands before they were invaded. Okinawa was defended by about 120,000 Japanese troops, and was within easy flying distance of air bases in Japan. The invasion of Okinawa—Operation ICEBERG—involved 1,475 U.S. ships and about 548,000 Army, Navy, and Marine Corps personnel. Initial landings were made on 1 April 1945, when 50,000 troops went ashore. The island was secured in 81 days of hard fighting.

Operation ICEBERG was planned as a prelude to Operation OLYMPIC, the landing on the Japanese home island of Kyushu. As events turned out, the atomic bombs cut the war short, and Okinawa became the last battle of World War II. For many ships, and many of the men in them, Okinawa had a more fateful meaning—

it was simply the last battle. Some small portent of this may have influenced Ernie Pyle, the famous war correspondent. "No action is minor to the man who loses his life," he had written as he sailed across the Mediterranean with the invasion fleet on Operation AVALANCHE, the landings in Italy. The war in Okinawa was not like anything he had seen before. "If I come through this one, I'll never go on another," he wrote to his wife. On 18 April, as he rode with an Army officer across the little island of Ie Shima, a burst of Japanese machine-gun fire ended the chance that Ernie Pyle might "go on another."

By the time Operation ICEBERG got under way, the Japanese Navy had been so nearly wiped out that it offered little resistance. A week after the invasion began, the new Japanese battleship *Yamato*, the biggest in the world, headed for Okinawa with an escort of one cruiser and eight destroyers. Carrier planes sank the battleship, the cruiser, and four of the destroyers.

The greatest menace to the U.S. Navy at Okinawa was the Japanese use of suicide planes (kamikazes) in mass attacks. The kamikazes made their first attacks on 1 April, and continued them through 29 July. It was a costly battle on both sides. The Japanese sank 36 U.S. ships—none larger than a destroyer—and damaged 250 more, including carriers, battleships, and all other types. In so doing, they lost 7,830 aircraft. The U.S. Navy lost 790 aircraft. The Japanese lost about 110,000 troops and some 24,000 Okinawan civilians; U.S. casualties were 49,000—about 12,000 killed and the rest injured; some 4,900 of these were Navy men.

Japanese surrender   By the end of 1944, Japan had been knocked out of the war. She had no aircraft carriers and few battleships or cruisers left. In the last six months of the war, while many cargo ships were sunk, only a dozen of them were as large as 10,000 tons. By the middle of July 1945, American planes were appearing over Japan in waves of 500 at a time. On 6 August an Army B-29 took off from Tinian and dropped an atomic bomb that flattened most of the city of Hiroshima. Three days later another atomic bomb wrecked the city of Nagasaki.

On 14 August Japan agreed to surrender. From the headquarters of the Commander in Chief, Pacific Fleet, Admiral Nimitz sent the message, "Cease offensive operations against Japan." On the battleship *Missouri*, off Japan, Admiral William F. "Bull" Halsey added, "And if any Japanese aircraft show up, shoot 'em down in a friendly manner."

The victorious U.S. fleet—at least, 368 ships of that fleet—entered Tokyo Bay on 28 August 1945. The surrender documents were signed on board the *Missouri* at 9:00 a.m. on 2 September 1945. General of the Army Douglas MacArthur signed for the Allied Powers, and Fleet Admiral Chester W. Nimitz signed for the United States. The flag that flew above the *Missouri* that day had flown in Washington, D.C., on 7 December 1941. It had flown in Rome when Italy surrendered, in Berlin when Germany surrendered, and it later flew in Tokyo. It is now at the U.S. Naval Academy at Annapolis.

Personnel   When the war began in December 1941, the Navy had a strength of about 330,000 officers and men, an enormous increase from the slightly more than 100,000 on duty when the President declared a limited national emergency on 8 September 1939. In the month of December 1941, more than 40,000 men joined the Navy. By the end of 1942, the Navy's strength was up to 1,259,167. Two years later, it was 3,227,525; and when the war ended, it was 3,408,347.

As soon as the war ended, demobilization released hundreds of thousands of men to return to civilian life. The following years took their toll of men and women who made a career of the Navy; one by one, they retired. Now, as this is being written, there are very few people in service who took part in World War II. It is interesting to note that in 1942, the Navy had four junior officers

General of the Army Douglas MacArthur (left) signed the Japanese surrender documents on behalf of the Allied Nations. Fleet Admiral Chester W. Nimitz (seated) signed on behalf of the United States. Officers standing behind Nimitz are Admiral William F. Halsey and Rear Admiral Forrest P. Sherman. Photo: U.S. Navy.

who were then unknown, but who became nationally known later. They were Lieutenant John Fitzgerald Kennedy, and Lieutenant Commanders Lyndon B. Johnson, Richard M. Nixon, and Gerald Ford, who served consecutively as the thirty-fifth, thirty-sixth, thirty-seventh and thirty-eighth presidents of the United States.

Early in 1942, in order to make many of the men holding shore jobs available for vital billets at sea, the Navy decided to take in 1,000 officer and 10,000 enlisted women. They were designated "Woman Accepted for Volunteer Emergency Service," from which they took the short title of WAVES. They proved so useful that the original quota was raised; by the end of 1943 there were over 6,000 officer and 40,000 enlisted WAVES on duty. When the war ended WAVES totaled 93,074. More than a fourth of them were assigned to aviation duties, which included servicing aircraft, repairing aircraft engines, handling air traffic control, and teaching air navigation.

Training in the Navy was a big job; by 1944 there were more than 900 training schools, with a daily population of more than 300,000 men and women. Officer-training was greatly expanded; the thousand or so officers the Naval Academy turned out annually were far too few, and several schools for Reserve Midshipmen put qualified candidates through accelerated courses to train them for commissioning. Thousands of senior petty officers were promoted to commissioned rank without taking any formal training whatsoever. About one-tenth of all naval personnel were officers.

The Navy and Marine Corps lost about 56,000 officers and men from all causes during World War II. Because modern medical techniques were available on all large ships and even close behind the front lines in shore operations, 98 percent of all wounded men who survived long enough to reach medical care recovered.

The Navy's enlisted medics, the hospital corpsmen, went ashore with the Marines, in every landing. Under the terms of the Geneva Convention, they were non-combatants, and the Geneva Cross (a red cross) they wore was supposed to protect them. But in the Pacific, enemy snipers deliberately picked them off—a dead corpsman meant a lot of wounded Marines would die. No one knows how many lives hospital corpsmen saved, but it is known that more than 1,700 corpsmen died in battle. Corpsmen aboard submarines were in a difficult position—two months at sea and no doctor within hundreds of miles. They were *not* surgeons, yet when a man came down with appendicitis, there was only one thing to do—operate. Corpsmen had been ordered not to perform operations aboard a submarine, but no one could order men not to get appendicitis. So when it was necessary, the corpsmen operated. Not one man in the submarine force died of such surgery.

In the Navy, feats of great bravery and courage are rewarded by decorations—the Medal of Honor, the Navy Cross, and the Silver Star. It is to be expected that submarine skippers and bomber pilots would be in situations that earn them decorations, but it is surprising to note how many non-combatants—non-fighting hospital corpsmen—won decorations. In World War II, 7 Navy medics won the Medal of Honor, 67 won the Navy Cross, and 464 won the Silver Star. In the Korean War, there were only seven awards of the Medal of Honor to the *entire Navy:* hospital corpsmen won five of them. During the Vietnam War, three corpsmen won that award.

Merchant marine   When the war began, the U.S. merchant marine had about 55,000 licensed officers and merchant seamen. At the peak of its wartime strength, it numbered 250,000 officers and men. As in the Navy, rapid expansion required a huge training program. The entire War Shipping Program turned out over 260,000 trained men, which included more than 30,000 officers, and thousands of radio operators, engineers, and deck ratings.

From 1939, when the immense wartime shipbuilding program began, to 1945, the United States built over 5,600 ships of more than 54,000,000 tons. Up to V-J day, 733 American merchant vessels of over 1,000 tons were lost from all causes, and 5,638 merchant seamen and officers were casualties. Up to the first part of 1943, casualties in the merchant marine were greater, in proportion, than in any of the armed services. In 1942 alone, at least 12 percent of all merchant ships carrying Lend-Lease cargoes to Russia were sunk on the hazardous Murmansk run.

Merchant vessels were not built to fight, but during the war they all carried naval personnel who, assisted by merchant sailors, tried to fight off air attack. They were not always successful. Convoy PQ-17 which sailed from the United States in July 1942, for Murmansk, had 22 of its 50 ships sunk and nearly all the others damaged in air attacks. In September of 1942 the Liberty ship *Stephen Hopkins* was intercepted off the coast of Africa by a German auxiliary cruiser, the *Stier,* and an armed blockade-runner, the *Tannenfels.* With only one 4-inch gun and a few machine guns, the *Stephen Hopkins* took on both enemy ships in a blazing gun battle that killed 41 of her crew of 60, and sent her to the bottom. However, she had set the *Stier* on fire and had caused severe damage to the *Tannenfels.* The *Hopkins'* survivors took to their boats and a few minutes later the *Stier* blew up and she, too, went to the bottom.

Accounts of merchant-ship operations in World War II would fill many books. The merchant ships provided the lifelines to our overseas allies, and they supported our military operations in all theaters of war. At the same time, they brought to the United States from overseas the millions of tons of critical materials, particularly petroleum and iron ore, without which the war effort would have been impossible.

Until World War II began, battleships were the backbone of the **Carrier operations**
fleet. A battleship could attack an enemy only within range of its
guns—a maximum of 20 miles. Aircraft carriers, on the other hand,
could send out bombers to hit a target a couple of hundred miles
away, and maintain an umbrella of fighters to protect themselves
from enemy air attack. The Battle of the Coral Sea and the Battle
of Midway pointed out the right way to use carriers—as floating air
bases from which to project war against a distant enemy.

Early in the war, carrier task forces consisted of one or two
carriers, some destroyers to scout for submarines, and some cruisers
whose antiaircraft batteries could drive off enemy planes. Prewar
battleships were too slow to operate with carriers, but as new fast
battleships joined the fleet, carrier task forces were beefed up with
much more antiaircraft defense. By 1944, a fast carrier task force
might contain as many as 15 carriers, 6 battleships, 12 cruisers, and
75 destroyers. Such a task force carried about 236 5-inch guns and
nearly 1,400 40-mm. and 20-mm. guns; its total fire power was
6,000 shots a second, or about 200 tons a minute. In addition, a
task force of that size carried more than 1,000 operational aircraft.

Rapid wartime development of that electronic marvel, radar,
enabled carriers to spot incoming enemy raids miles before they
were visible, and at night as well as in daytime. By 1945, radar-
equipped aircraft had made night operations possible; the *Enterprise* ("Big E") once kept planes continuously in the air in the
combat zone for 174 hours.

A typical carrier task force, late in World War II, sailed with a
weird menagerie. About 60 miles ahead of the carrier "Tomcats"
patrolled; these were destroyers, making a radar search for the
enemy. "Jackcaps" buzzed around the carrier at low altitude; these
were fighters. "Scocaps" searched far ahead of the "Tomcats";
these were scouting planes. Another group of aircraft were in the
air high above the carriers from dawn to dusk; these were "Dadcaps." At sundown, the "Dadcaps" were relieved by "Batcaps."
At all times, "Radcaps," radar picket planes, were in the air.

The Navy began the war with eight aircraft carriers. During the
war it commissioned twenty-three large carriers and about eighty
escort, or "jeep," carriers. Ten carriers were lost. Navy and Marine
pilots destroyed over 15,000 enemy aircraft, sank 174 Japanese
warships (including 13 submarines), and 447 Japanese merchant
ships. In the Atlantic they sank 63 German U-boats.

By law, the Coast Guard operates as a part of the Navy during **Coast Guard**
wartime. That service was rapidly built up during the war, until it
included 170,480 men and women (9,624 SPARS*), and had 1,677

* From the Coast Guard motto, "Semper Paratus"—Always Ready.

craft in service. In addition, the Coast Guard manned 326 Navy ships—most of them amphibious—and 254 Army vessels. As part of its wartime duties, the Coast Guard provided convoy escorts, took part in ASW operations and sank several U-boats, and instructed Navy boat crews in surf operations.

The Coast Guard maintained security and provided fire protection in many U.S. ports; many Navy fireboats in forward areas in the Pacific were manned by the Coast Guard. Thousands of ships were handled by Coast Guard pilots as they entered and left U.S. ports. The Coast Guard built and maintained many LORAN (Long-Range Navigation) and RACON (Radar Beacon) stations on both coasts, in Alaska, and as far west as Iwo Jima and Okinawa. LORAN stations in the combat zones guided U.S. planes on bombing missions over Japan.

Seabees   As the Navy began building advance bases in the Pacific, it employed hundreds of skilled construction workers. Since, as civilians, these workers could not carry arms and lacked what little protection a military uniform gave in wartime, the Navy Department organized construction battalions, which immediately became known as Seabees. Experienced men from some sixty trades were enlisted, rated according to their experience, given some military training, and formed into military groups. They were particularly trained for amphibious operations, but the Seabees could do almost anything—build a dock or a dam, erect a pier, set up a power or concrete plant, or build an airport.

The Seabees chose "Can Do" as their motto, and during World War II they demonstrated its validity: in the Pacific alone, they built 111 major airstrips, 441 piers, 2,558 ammunition magazines, 700 square blocks of warehouses, tanks for storing 100,000,000 gallons of gasoline, and housing for 1,500,000 men. Fifteen hours after landing at Tarawa, they had repaired a shell-cratered airfield. At Guadalcanal, they fought their way ashore, ducked Japanese bombs while they were at work, and had an airfield ready for flight operations in five days.

Top strength of the Seabees in World War II was about 240,000. All the armed services had many very young men, but the Seabees had lots of much older men because it took years to gain experience in some construction trades. The Marines, who admired the way a Seabee with a bulldozer could flatten a Japanese machine-gun nest, said, "Never hit a Seabee . . . he may be your grandfather."

Morale   In the old days of "iron men and wooden ships" the word *morale* was not known. Bulkheads on the gun decks were painted red, so that the blood would not show up so much during battle, and when someone had to have an arm or a leg cut off, the surgeon might heat his saw before he used it, to lessen the pain. For recreation, one could always count rats, bedbugs, or whatever else he shared his bunk with. Men were supposed to be happy with a shot of rum once a day.

In World War II, no one in the Navy had all the comforts of home, but a vast amount of effort was put into keeping men reasonably comfortable and contented. Most ships had laundries, almost every ship or shore station had movies, and mail was hauled to the far corners of the Pacific and transferred to ships along with ammunition and fuel oil. The American Red Cross and the United Services Organization (USO) maintained clubs and recreation centers in the United States and at many overseas bases. USO troupes went almost anywhere they could find a piece of ground big enough and flat enough for a stage.

Religious services were held aboard most ships larger than destroyers and submarines and at advance bases where the Seabees built some attractive chapels. Submarine crews were usually sent ashore after a war patrol—some of the hotels at Waikiki Beach in Honolulu were taken over for this purpose. Even at such advance bases as Ulithi, sailors could get ashore for an afternoon to swim, play ball, or just sit under a palm tree. The part of Ulithi reserved for recreation was Mogmog Island; when the war ended, Mogmog was rumored to be solidly covered with flattened beer cans.

Korea

When World War II ended, American and Russian occupation forces moved into Korea; the Russians north of the 38th parallel and the Americans south of it. Then, on 24 June 1950, Communist North Koreans moved across the dividing line. In two days they had taken Seoul, the capital of South Korea. Against the invasion force of about 100,000 men, the South Koreans were helpless. By 30 July the Communist army had taken almost the entire peninsula of South Korea; only a small area around Pusan, in the extreme south, remained free. Units of the U.S. Eighth Army and U.S. Marines, moved in to support the South Koreans, who were in danger of being overrun.

General Douglas MacArthur, the Commander in Chief of U.S. forces in the Far East, decided to cut off the Communist forces by making an amphibious landing at Inchon, far up the west coast of Korea. Most naval and military authorities were against the idea, believing that it was nearly impossible to move troopships through the Yellow Sea unobserved and make a surprise landing. Another problem was that the immense tides at Inchon—as much as 33 feet —required the landing be timed exactly. Ships had to get in on high water, which came only four times a month, and they had to land at the exact hour of high water. From the time it was decided to make the landing until the actual landing, only 23 days elapsed.

In that time 250 ships had to be loaded with troops, tanks, weapons, ammunition, and provisions, make the trip from Japan around Korea into the Yellow Sea, and arrive off the beachhead at Inchon at the proper times. Most amphibious landings during World War II were made in early morning, but at Inchon the tide determined the time—5:30 p.m. The gamble paid off. Troops landed as planned, and in three days were in Seoul, the capital of South Korea.

The Korean conflict was a United Nations action. Besides the forces of the Republic of Korea and of the United States, ships and men were sent into action primarily by Australia, Canada, Great Britain, and New Zealand. A total of 14 other nations, including Greece and Turkey, took some part in the action.

The U.N. forces drove the North Koreans back toward Manchuria until 25 November, when the Red Chinese army entered the conflict. Some 100,000 troops moved down from the north and met the First Marine Regiment at a place called Chosin Reservoir. Slowly the Marines fell back, while carrier planes bombed the enemy forces. In bitter winter weather, Marines pulled back to the east coast ports of Wonsan and Hungnam. There a vast reverse amphibious operation was carried out. In two weeks some 180 ships loaded 200,000 troops and civilian refugees, 35,000 tons of cargo, and 17,500 vehicles. Anything to escape from the Communists; one cargo ship packed in over 12,000 people.

All during the Korean war, carrier aircraft fought over the front lines, supporting troops and bombing enemy targets. All the battleships had been decommissioned after World War II, but some of them were called out of mothballs and used for shore bombardment. The 16-inch guns of the *Iowa, New Jersey, Wisconsin,* and *Missouri* had pinpoint accuracy and could knock out an enemy battery miles inland.

Mine warfare—on the part of the Communist forces—played a big role in the Korean war. Mines could be laid at night by native boats or sampans. The discovery of even one mine off an invasion beach meant that no large ships dared venture in until all the water had been cleared. In October of 1950, the U.N. landing force of 250 ships loaded with 50,000 troops had to mill around off Wonsan for eight days while minesweepers made certain it was safe for them to go in. The only U.S. ships sunk during the entire war were minesweepers, the *Magpie, Pirate,* and *Pledge,* which were blown up by Communist-laid mines.

The land war in Korea bogged down in a stalemate, with neither side making any direct gains. Truce talks were proposed in June of 1951, and the first meeting of main truce delegations took place on 10 July 1951. The talks dragged on for nearly two years, as representatives met at Panmunjom. A cease-fire agreement was finally reached on 27 July 1953. The war had cost the United States nearly 150,000 killed and wounded, and an expenditure estimated at $20 billion. President Truman wanted to fight a limited war, and in this he succeeded—Russia did not intervene. However, the Communist threat to peace in Korea was not eliminated. There are still minor clashes across the border between North Korea and South Korea.

Perhaps the best assessment was made by Vice Admiral C. Turner Joy, who was the naval theater commander for the first two years of the war and chief of the United Nations truce delegation: "Nothing can erase the tragedy that is Korea. But if Korea has taught us that in unity lies the strength that will preserve our freedom, then Korea has not been in vain. . . ."

Vietnam

When Japanese occupation forces pulled out of Indochina in 1945, there was a move toward nationalism in that part of Southeast Asia; in 1946 the Republic of Vietnam was recognized by France. Thereafter, the Communists, or Vietminh, became active and, when France recognized the new anticommunist provisional government of Vietnam in 1948, civil war broke out. This state of affairs has continued intermittently ever since, with the United States supporting the government of South Vietnam. North Vietnam was supplied with Soviet-made weapons, aircraft, and, eventually, missiles. When North Vietnamese patrol boats attacked the U.S. destroyer *Maddox* in the Gulf of Tonkin on 2 August 1964, aircraft from the carrier *Ticonderoga* drove them off. In retaliation for the North Vietnamese attack, aircraft from the carriers *Ticonderoga* and *Constellation* bombed targets in North Vietnam.

At first, U.S. military advisors were sent to help the South Vietnamese, but before long U.S. troops were ordered into combat. Eventually, U.S. Army troops, Marines, the U.S. Air Force, the Coast Guard, and units of the U.S. Seventh Fleet were committed to the longest war the United States has ever fought.

Partly because there were no definite battle lines in Vietnam, the war turned into a guerrilla action fought from rice paddy to rice paddy, village to village. The Seventh Fleet protected U.S. supply lines—most of the ammunition, food, fuel, and weapons were moved across the Pacific by the merchant marine. Carrier aircraft made air strikes on enemy supply dumps, industrial targets, and power plants, and mined harbors in North Vietnam. Cruisers and battleships used heavy guns in shore bombardment, and carrier aircraft worked with the U.S. Marines. The Navy also engaged extensively in "riverine warfare"—operations in coastal and river waters. Types of small boats used in these operations included a modified LCM called *Mike 6*, monitors fitted for shore bombardment and for gunfire support of troops ashore, armored troop carriers, command control boats, and *Swift* boats. Thousands of South Vietnamese men were trained for and thousands of small boats were turned over to the South Vietnamese Navy for use in river and inshore operations.

Ships from the Royal Australian Navy and from the Republic of Korea joined in some of these operations; troops of those two nations joined Vietnamese and U.S. forces ashore.

After lengthy peace negotiations, a cease-fire agreement between opposing forces finally went into effect on 27 January 1973, after which U.S. military forces began to withdraw. However, the war was far from over. North Vietnamese forces built up strength and drove south in 1974. By mid-April 1975 they were threatening the capital city of Saigon. In a massive airlift, some 7,500 Americans and about 50,000 Vietnamese were evacuated to the United States. Saigon fell to Communist forces on 29 April. The war in Vietnam cost some 55,000 American casualties; it was one of the most costly wars in U.S. history and was highly unpopular because of its "undeclared" status.

Logistics World War II was sometimes termed a war of production and a war of machines. For the United States, it was also a war of logistics. Troops fighting in Africa, Italy, France, Germany, and all across the Pacific from Guadalcanal to Okinawa had to be supplied with provisions, weapons, ammunition, vehicles, and fuel. Army Air Force bombers and fighters, in the many theaters of war, required vast quantities of gasoline, ammunition, bombs, and repair items. Ships operating in all the combat zones required the same items, in vast quantities, and they needed to be repaired at the front, where possible, to avoid time-consuming trips back to the United States. In addition, allied forces were supplied with millions of tons of equipment, ammunition, and fuel. Much of this war material had to move over thousands of miles, and it had to arrive at its destination when it was needed, not a month early or a few days late. This was logistics.

Statistics on the wartime sealift are staggering: total cargo lift from the United States amounted to 203,522,000 tons of dry cargo, 64,730,000 tons of petroleum products, and over 7,000,000 troops and civilians. Included in the sealift were more than 1,000,000 vehicles and over 24,000 aircraft.

The four major steps in any logistic process are: determination of requirements, procurement, transportation, and distribution. In World War II, the last two steps involved the Navy and the merchant marine. To supply forces afloat, the Navy had to build hundreds of overseas bases and establish a shipping system to carry material to those bases and to operating forces afloat. Certain material was shipped to supply bases overseas and stored until ships that needed it arrived to load it. But material for battle-damage repairs—complete units of pumps, turbines, boilers, generators, radar equipment, and guns, for example—was kept in the United States, ready for immediate delivery wherever needed. Thus, when a submarine arrived at a distant base with damaged main controls, the repair materials were loaded on a transport plane in the United States and were en route within 36 hours.

Advance bases, particularly in the Pacific, supplied ships on a 24-hour basis, and did repair work. Floating dry docks were towed to island bases where repair crews could patch up the hull of a torpedoed ship in a few days and save several weeks of travel to the mainland. But because it took time to build and equip an advance base, the Navy perfected a system of floating bases, called service squadrons (SerRon). A SerRon included repair ships, ammunition ships, oilers, refrigerator ships, supply ships, floating docks, aircraft-engine repair vessels—even post offices. Once an invasion force had taken over a Japanese island, a service squadron could move in and be handling all the supply duties of a regular shoreside supply base in a few hours.

When the fast carrier task forces were operating in the western Pacific, service force ships supplied them "on the run." Oilers, ammunition ships, and supply ships met them at sea and transferred oil, ammunition, food, mail, and officers and men, while the ships kept moving. A big ship could take on in less than an hour enough stores and provisions to last three weeks.

It is difficult to visualize the immense amount of material required to maintain a fleet in combat. During the latter part of World War II, 600,000 tons of cargo went to the western Pacific—about 60 shiploads—every month. This meant that two loaded ships had to leave West Coast ports every day. In the Okinawa campaign, ships fired over 50,000 tons of 5-inch and 6-inch projectiles alone. The advance base that was set up on Okinawa, in preparation for the final assault on Japan, was planned to support more than 3,000 ships. Building and supplying that base involved work equivalent to taking apart the city of Wichita, Kansas, as it was in 1945, moving it 6,000 miles, unpacking it, and setting it up for business.

The actions in Korea and Vietnam required fully as much logistic support as any other combat operation, and all involved long ocean hauls. It was estimated that for every soldier sent into action in those countries, five tons of equipment were needed; and it took 64 pounds of consumable supplies every day per man to maintain combat operations. Extremely urgent cargo was air-lifted into Korea and Vietnam, but for every ton of air freight delivered across the Pacific, four tons of gasoline had to be made available at the other end of the airlift in order to bring the planes back. The gasoline, of course, had to be transported in tankers.

A theoretical study on the efficiency of airlift and sealift, covering transportation of 20,000 tons of cargo from San Francisco to Manila, revealed that two cargo ships could make the entire lift in twenty days. Four C-141 cargo planes flying shuttle trips could make the same lift in 120 days. Of course, more planes could reduce the time—32 of them could make the lift in about 15 days.

But for every 6,000 tons of cargo carried by air, the planes would need a whole tanker load of gasoline—140,000 barrels—in Manila to refuel for their return trips. The conclusion was that airlift required more ships to support it than were required to make the sealift complete.

Brush-fire wars   Since World War II, there have been several incidents in foreign countries in which U.S. forces took some part in preserving peace. There have also been dozens of incidents that might well have developed into large-scale conflicts except for timely diplomatic negotiations. Such small disturbances are called "brush-fire" wars.

In 1955 Red China threatened to invade Formosa, and the U.S. Seventh Fleet was ordered to protect the island as necessary. There was no combat, but units of the Seventh Fleet evacuated 300,000 Nationalist Chinese from the Tachen Islands.

In 1958 a revolution in Lebanon was fomented by Communists and, on 14 July, the Lebanese President appealed to the United States for aid. Within less than two days U.S. Marines from the Sixth Fleet were landed and carriers were standing by offshore to provide air support, if required. This show of force enabled the Lebanese government to hold a peaceful election, the situation returned to normal, and all U.S. forces withdrew in October.

In 1962, after air observation showed that missile bases were being established in Cuba by Soviet Russia, the United States announced a naval quarantine of Cuba. Naval patrols stopped and inspected all Russian ships bound for Cuba and those carrying missiles were turned back. Missile installations on the island were dismounted and the missiles were shipped out of Cuba.

In all these incidents, the fact that naval forces were at sea, in the area or nearby, enabled the United States to take effective action before the situation got out of hand. As the United States is now directly committed to help defend some sixty nations against aggression, it can be seen that the country may at any time be called upon to make good such commitments. Peace, as well as war, can be waged by having a few ships in the right place at the right time.

CHAPTER 19
OUR CULTURAL HERITAGE

The sea is filled with more than fish and salt water. For centuries men have marveled at its mysteries. Explorers and scientists have searched out its secrets, yet it is still a vast unknown—more men have walked on the moon than have seen the deepest parts of the sea. Fascination with the sea is not limited to whalers, sailors, and surfers. People who have never seen salt water, as well as retired admirals and tattooed seamen, are still drawn by what John Masefield called "Sea Fever."

The reasons for this fascination are varied. For some people, going to sea and returning safely, whether from a few hours in a 20-foot sloop or from 14 days in a cruise ship, becomes a personal victory over an age-old enemy—the sea is dangerous; it is a killer. For thousands of people—merchant seamen, offshore drillers, and fishermen—the sea is merely a way to make a living. Some men hate it every minute they are out of sight of land, and as soon as they get ashore, they hurry back to sea. In some cases, going to sea offers an escape from the tedium of dull routine between four walls and a chance to live in a completely different world which, in some ways, is the same now as it was when the Phoenicians and Vikings went to sea.

The sea is filled with monotony, danger, and discomfort, but to some few men it offers beauty as fresh as when the world was young, the opportunity to find deep understanding of other men, great faith in the well-ordered scheme of all things natural, and time to work out their personal philosophies. Most men, of course, keep such thoughts to themselves; not many have the ability to put them into words. But over the years a few men have gone to sea

On previous page: On 22 May 1819 the 100-foot, 320-ton auxiliary steam packet *Savannah*, commanded by Moses Rogers and with her paddle wheels splashing merrily, set out to cross the Atlantic. Sails proved more effective than steam; she sailed most of the way and used steam power for only 80 hours. Painting by Charles R. Patterson. Courtesy: The Seamen's Bank for Savings.

and brought back riches worth more than pearls and ambergris; they have produced the literature of the sea—an immense library of adventure, history, romance, poetry, science, and philosophy.

The sea has also had great influence on such other creative disciplines as art, language, and music. Artists have spent their lives depicting the sea and the ships that sail it. Craftsmen have preserved for all time the grace and beauty of ships in intricate models. Plays and musical comedies have been based on nautical themes. An entire school of folk art was devoted to the carving of figureheads for ships. Scrimshaw, an art form based on carved whale teeth, was developed by sailors, as was marlinspike seamanship, the art of tying knots. Tattooing, a practice once considered more artistic than it is now, came from the sea. Much seagoing language has come ashore; many words and terms once used only by seafaring men are now used by everyone.

Even architecture and advertising have at times been flavored with salt water. The beautiful opera house in Sydney, Australia, very much resembles a sea shell, *Lopha cristagalli*, a kind of oyster. Another sea shell, the scallop, has become known worldwide as the symbol of the Shell Oil Company.

Literature

The literature of the sea might be said to have commenced with the stories of Noah's ark, Jonah in the whale, and the adventures of Ulysses and of Sindbad, the Sailor. It is such a vast area that discussion must be limited to American sources: even so, subjects run right through the alphabet, from admiralty law to zoology. Also, the discussion must be limited, in general, to books that describe life at sea. This is "escape" literature for both seagoing and shoreside people. Literature of the sea has one other quality; almost invariably it is written by people who have gone to sea. Anyone can research a book on a nautical subject in the stacks of a library, but the good books about the sea have been written by sailors. A sailor, to fit this category, is someone who went to sea, whether he was seaman, skipper, or admiral. Some writers have been all three.

As America, from colonial times, was a seagoing country, it was natural that books about the sea should find a ready audience. Some of the earliest American "sea stories" were written by James Fenimore Cooper, the first American novelist to gain real recognition outside the United States. Cooper was born in 1789, the year George Washington was inaugurated as our first president. He entered Yale University at the age of 13. In 1809 he joined the Navy as a midshipman, and for a while served in the USS *Wasp*, under James Lawrence. In 1822 he became annoyed by a book published anonymously in England under the title *The Pirate*. Cooper declared it was written by a landlubber and said he could do better. Two years later he published his first sea story *The Pilot*. The book was based on the exploits of John Paul Jones, and the critics agreed that it was better than *The Pirate*. By that time, it was known that the latter book had indeed been written by a landlubber, Sir Walter Scott.

Cooper wrote several other sea stories: *The Red Rover, The Two Admirals, The Wing-and-Wing, Miles Wallingford,* and *Afloat and Ashore*. He also produced the first history of our Navy, *History of the Navy of the United States*. Although nautical experts might catch Cooper in a technical error at times, his sailors were said to be well portrayed, and his books to be "full of the charm and mystery of the sea. . . . In other words . . . they lift the story of adventure into the realms of poetry."

The next American author after Cooper to gain great fame with a book about sea life was Richard Henry Dana, who entered Harvard in 1833, but had to drop out because of poor eyesight. In 1834 he shipped aboard the brig *Pilgrim* for a voyage to California, to load hides. He reached home two years later, and in 1840 published *Two Years Before the Mast*, a classic sea adventure story.

Another sailor-author was Herman Melville, born in 1818. He spent several years at sea in whalers, then enlisted in the Navy while in Hawaii. His cruise aboard the USS *United States* was the basis for *White-Jacket*, published in 1850, a moving account of the life of enlisted men that resulted in the abolition of flogging as a punishment. Melville is best known for *Moby Dick, or The White Whale*, first published in 1851 and considered one of the greatest novels in American literature, if not in the world. Only a man who had gone to sea and hunted whales could have written with the technical accuracy displayed by Melville. More than that, according to John Masefield, "Melville seems to have spoken the very secret of the sea, and to have drawn into his tale all the magic, all the sadness, all the wild joy of many waters." Between 1846 and 1849, Melville also wrote *Omoo, Israel Potter* (in part about John Paul Jones), *Typee, Mardi,* and *Redburn*. Most of these were based on life in the South Seas, but none of them could compare to *Moby Dick*. Oddly enough, Melville did not become highly popular until after World War I. When he died in 1891, in New York, his obituary consisted of the following six words, "Died, yesterday, Herman Melville, a writer."

Perhaps the very earliest American poet was Philip Freneau. Born in 1752, he began publishing poetry in 1771. During the Revolutionary War, he was captured by a British ship in the West Indies. His long poem, *The British Prison-Ship*, was based on his experience as a prisoner of war. A full book of his poetry was published in 1786. He later went to sea again, and was captain of a ship in the War of 1812.

Undoubtedly more sailors spent their time scribbling poetry than writing books. Very little of such poetry was ever printed, and probably much of it was unprintable. English poets, possibly because they were still closer to the sea than most Americans after 1815, produced much excellent poetry about the sea. Any anthology of sea poetry will list Robert Browning, Samuel Coleridge, Rudyard Kipling, John Masefield, Alfred Noyes, Percy Bysshe Shelley, Algernon Swinburne, Alfred Tennyson, and others.

Many Americans wrote poetry about the sea, but most of them, it seems, chose to write in a snug den ashore rather than in a creaking ship at sea. Aside from patriotic verses celebrating naval victories, those worth consideration were produced by Henry Wadsworth Longfellow, John Greenleaf Whittier, and Walt Whitman. Longfellow was named after his uncle, Henry Wadsworth, an officer killed aboard the USS *Intrepid* at Tripoli. He crossed the Atlantic several times and played around the waterfront in Portland, Maine, as a boy. In "My Lost Youth," there is a touch of that experience:

Spanish sailors with bearded lips,
And the beauty and mystery of the ships,
And the magic of the sea. . . .

Longfellow's most quoted poem is "The Building of the Ship."

Walt Whitman never went to sea, but he knew the waterfront in Brooklyn and New York, and many of his poems have a salty flavor: "Song for All Seas, All Ships," "The Dismantled Ship," "Passage to India." His most quoted poem is "O Captain, My Captain."

Along with Longfellow and Whittier, many other New England poets wrote sea poetry, among them James Russell Lowell, Ralph Waldo Emerson, and Henry David Thoreau.

Oliver Wendell Holmes wrote many poems about ships and the sea, but he is best known for "Old Ironsides." This was written in 1830, when Holmes learned that the USS *Constitution* was to be scrapped. The opening lines are:

Aye, tear her tattered ensign down!
Long has it waved on high,
And many an eye has danced to see
That banner in the sky. . . .

The poem was reprinted in almost every newspaper in the country and so aroused the American public that the ship was saved from the scrap heap. She may still be seen in Boston.

Another poet became famous for only one poem. Francis Scott Key, after watching the British bombardment of Fort McHenry in Baltimore on the night of 24 August 1814, hurriedly scribbled the words we have been singing ever since as "The Star-Spangled Banner."

As the American merchant marine declined in the middle of the last century with the disappearance of the clipper ships, there were fewer stories about the sea. Then, as the Spanish-American War made the United States a world power at the end of that century, there was renewed interest in the sea. Jack London, who was born in 1876 and grew up along the waterfront in Oakland, California, went to sea at the age of sixteen. He wrote many books about sea life, either in the North Pacific or the South Seas, from about 1900 to 1919. His best-known works are *The Sea Wolf, The Cruise of the Dazzler,* and *The Mutiny of the Elsinore.* Much like London, Morgan Robertson, born in 1861, ran away to sea when he was sixteen. He sailed around the world twice. He is best known for collections of short stories about the sea, published as *The Grain Ship, Spun Yarn, Where Angels Fear to Tread,* and *Futility.*

There may be something about the air in waterfront towns that sends men to sea. Frederick O'Brien, a contemporary of Jack London, who grew up in Baltimore instead of Oakland, learned about the sea before he wrote about it. He was a lawyer, reporter, and editor, but he was also a sailor and beachcomber. He learned enough about the South Seas to write *White Shadows in the South Seas,* which was published in 1919 and which Rupert Hughes, a noted American novelist, called the most fascinating book he had ever read in any language.

In basing a novel on John Paul Jones, James Fenimore Cooper began a practice picked up by Herman Melville and followed by many other writers for more than a century. The best of such stories is *Richard Carvel.* It was published in 1899 by Winston Churchill (not the British statesman), who had been a midshipman at the Naval Academy from 1890 to 1894. More recent novels based on the life of Jones are *Stars on the Sea* by F. van Wyck Mason and *Captain Paul* by Rear Admiral Edward Ellsberg.

Two Englishmen with long seagoing experience who qualify for inclusion here are Arthur Mason and William McFee. Both lived in the United States for many years. Mason, who was born in Ireland, became an American citizen in 1899. He spent forty years at sea and wrote many short stories about the sea, *The Ship That Waited, Ocean Echoes,* and *Wide Sea and Many Lands.* McFee was born aboard a ship named *The Erin's Isle* in 1881 and came to the United States in 1912. He spent seventeen years as an engineer in the British merchant service and produced many books about the sea. His best-known works are *Aliens, Casuals of the Sea, Harbourmaster, Watch Below, Beachcomber,* and *Derelict.*

A series of books that are very British in subject and flavor were written by two Americans many people have probably assumed to be British. Charles Nordhoff was born of American parentage in London, England; James Norman Hall was born in Iowa, and they met in France during World War I. They later settled in Tahiti, and produced the famous trilogy, *Mutiny on the Bounty, Men Against the Sea,* and *Pitcairn's Island.* They also wrote *The Hur-*

ricane and *Doctor Dogbody's Leg*, a delightful collection of short
stories about life in the Royal Navy.

Another Englishman who must be included here is C. S. Forester,
who lived in the United States for about the last 35 years of his
life. In *The Captain From Connecticut* he wrote the story of an
American merchant raider in the War of 1812. Forester wrote many
stories with the Royal Navy as a background, including *Beat to
Quarters, Ship of the Line, Flying Colours, To The Indies*, and
The Ship, most of which were laid in the eighteenth century.

The days of frigates and broadside gun battles are always good
for rousing sea stories. Two books produced in recent years with
the Revolutionary War as a background are *Three Harbours* and
Rivers of Glory, both by F. van Wyck Mason. Two outstanding
stories with a historical background in the War of 1812 are *The
Lively Lady* and *Captain Caution*, by Kenneth Roberts.

Once the clippers and whale ships had gone, no one could write
about them from direct experience; nevertheless, some excellent
books have been turned out by writers skilled at taking the reader
into times past. One such book is *Pieces of Eight*, by the English
author, Richard Le Gallienne, which has been compared favorably
with *Treasure Island*. Other books filled with the flavor of sailing
days are *Java Head*, a story about whaling by Joseph Hergesheimer,
When Guns Thundered at Tripoli by Charles J. Finger, *Long Pen-
nant* by Oliver La Farge, and *Sea Witch*, a fictionalized account of
the famous clipper, by Alexander Laing.

A writer who did know the last of the big sailing ships was Felix
Riesenberg, who was born in Milwaukee in 1879. During many
years at sea he acquired the background for *Under Sail*, which is
considered nearly the equal of *Two Years Before the Mast*. Riesenberg later joined the Navy and served in the USS *Chase* and USS
Newport.

As the sea gave some men material for books, it furnished others
with material for plays. Eugene O'Neill, one of the greatest play-
wrights of this century, spent several years as a sailor in tramp
steamers. His first play, "Thirst," was set in the South Seas. "The
Hairy Ape" took place in the stokehold of an ocean liner. "Anna
Christie," which won a Pulitzer Prize and is considered one of the
great American sea plays, also had to do with "dat ol' devil sea."

War at sea almost always furnishes material for books, and
sometimes for good books. But not all good books are written as
soon as the war is over. Marcus Goodrich enlisted in the Navy in
World War I, and after the war spent ten or fifteen years working
on his fictionalized account of life aboard a destroyer. The result,
Delilah, was published in 1941, just before World War II began,
and consequently was not well known for many years. It ranks
among the best sea stories ever written, and is one of the finest
accounts of life in the steam Navy. Another sailor, Richard Mc-
Kenna, spent many years on an old riverboat in China. After he

retired he wrote *The Sand Pebbles*, an excellent account of life in the "old Navy" along the Yangtze River before World War II.

World War II, during which literally millions of men went to sea with the Navy, Marine Corps, Coast Guard, and merchant marine, has been the subject of hundreds of books. One of the first good books about that war was a novel based on life aboard an old Navy cargo ship, *Mr. Roberts* by Thomas Heggan. An old destroyer, USS *Southard*, gave Lieutenant Herman Wouk the background experience out of which he wrote an account of great personal conflict aboard a fictional destroyer named *Caine*. His book was *The Caine Mutiny*, which, like *Mr. Roberts*, was produced both as a stage play and a movie.

An officer who wrote professional books on navigation, Captain Arthur Ageton, also wrote a good novel titled *Jungle Sea* based on combat operations in the South Pacific. A fine, sensitive short novel with postwar China as the background is *China Station*, written by Lieutenant Donald Morris. A good historical account of submarine operations in World War II is *Run Silent, Run Deep* by Captain Edward Beach, who recently published a very good novel based on combat submarine operations, *Dust on the Sea*. An excellent suspense novel about cold-war operations aboard a nuclear submarine is *The Brink*, by Admiral Daniel V. Gallery.

Figureheads In sailing-ship days, no ship was complete without a carved figure decorating her bow. This practice originated long before the beginning of the Christian era. The Phoenicians sometimes placed a sea monster at the prow of a ship, while the Greeks and Romans favored gods or goddesses. In the eighteenth century, ships of the Royal Navy sometimes carried at their bows whole groups of figures, elaborately decorated at great cost.

Colonial shipbuilders kept up the custom, and for some 150 years Americans developed a unique form of art. From about 1775 to around 1886, more than seven hundred craftsmen were at work in seaport towns along the Atlantic coast and on the Great Lakes. Much of their work disappeared as ships were wrecked, burned, or left to rot and fall apart in some backwater, but fortunately, some fine examples are still preserved in various maritime museums.

The earliest record of an American figurehead is dated 1720. The figurehead was a "seven and one-half foot lyon" carved for a ship built in Kittery, Maine. Lions were always popular as figureheads— the ancient Romans also liked them—but other subjects were alligators, American eagles, horses' heads, and, of course, people. Favorite people included George Washington, Benjamin Franklin, Daniel Webster, Alexander Hamilton, Thomas Jefferson, Admiral Farragut, Commodore Perry, David Crockett, Jenny Lind, Christopher Columbus, and Julius Caesar. American Indians were frequently depicted as figureheads, as were Hope, Hercules, Columbia, and Peace and Plenty. Some figureheads represented the person whose name was given to the ship, some the wife or daughter of the builder.

As figureheads were life-sized, or larger, it was not always possible to carve one from a single piece of wood: arms, for example, might be carved separately and fastened on. The eagle figurehead of the USS *Lancaster*, which measures 18 feet from tip to tip, is in the Mariners Museum, Newport News, Virginia. Usually blocks of pine were glued together to build up a rough form. Figureheads were painted in lifelike colors and kept in tip-top condition. Before a ship entered port from a long voyage, her figurehead would be touched up.

In estimating the cost of a ship, the figurehead was always included. A figurehead for a ship of the Continental Navy cost as much as $1,620, at a time when unskilled laborers made less than half a dollar a day. Although clipper ships invariably carried them, figureheads gradually died out of use in the U.S. Navy. In 1909 the Navy Department banned them from all naval vessels. There was one exception to that regulation: the *Olympia*, Admiral Dewey's flagship in the Battle of Manila Bay, was allowed to keep her "Winged Victory," which had been sculptured by Augustus Saint-Gaudens and cost $12,000. It is now on display at the U.S. Naval Academy.

Figureheads have been the subject of literary endeavor and have been used for political purposes. One figurehead is best known for its connection with sports.

In his narrative poem, "The Building of the Ship," Longfellow describes the craftsman's final touch:

And at the bows an image stood,
By a cunning artist carved in wood
With robes of white, that far behind,
Seemed to be fluttering in the wind.

The political figurehead belonged to the USS *Constitution* and represented Andrew Jackson, who was then President of the United States. Her original figurehead, which represented Hercules, was shot away at Tripoli, and when she was rebuilt in Boston in 1834, her captain decided a figurehead of President Jackson would be appropriate. But many Bostonians disliked Jackson because of his handling of legislation concerning banking, and they violently objected to seeing him aboard "Old Ironsides." One dark night someone slipped aboard the ship and sawed off Jackson's head. The episode was the subject of considerable celebration before the severed head was finally turned over to the Navy Department.

The figurehead connected with sports is probably better known than any other in the United States. When the USS *Delaware* was completed in 1820, she was given a figurehead depicting the Chief of the Delaware Indians, Tamanend. When the *Delaware* was burned by Confederate forces at Norfolk in 1861, her figurehead was saved and later moved to the U.S. Naval Academy. In 1930 the crumbling wooden bust was replaced by a bronze casting, which has inside of it "the original wooden brains and heart" of Tamanend. No one knows just how Tamanend became known as Tecumseh, or exactly why Tecumseh takes part in football games, but before every Army-Navy football game, midshipmen give Tecumseh a fresh coat of war paint, which is intended to frighten the cadets of West Point.

Although there are no more than a dozen ships left in the United States to recall the great days of sail, several hundred figureheads still stand in museums throughout the country. Silent and dusty now, they once watched dolphins leap beneath the bow of a ship and felt the clean salt wind in all the oceans of the world, as described by Elizabeth Barrett Browning:

Once long ago I sailed the sea,
At the prow of a sailing ship was I,
Bearing the brunt of crested wave,
Fighting the seas when winds were high. . . .

Scrimshaw An art form practiced by a very limited group of people—whalers —was called *scrimshaw*. The term refers to both the decoration of teeth of the sperm whale and to the various objects made of whale teeth or whalebone. It developed in this country around the beginning of the nineteenth century, and virtually disappeared, of course, when the whaling industry ended. The carving of elephant ivory had been an art since the eleventh century. It was perfected by French artists, and when whalers from Nantucket first visited Dunkirk in 1785 they adopted the art.

The word *scrimshaw* probably comes from a Dutch expression for a lazy fellow that came to be applied to a man aboard ship who had nothing much to do. A cruise on a whaler might last for three years and, for days at a time, men had little to do; as there were few books and few men who could read, some form of handicraft helped pass the time. Every man had a knife, and whittling or wood carving helped them to keep busy. The right kind of wood was not always at hand, but once a whale had been caught, there were always plenty of ivory teeth to work on.

In *Moby Dick* Herman Melville mentions men at work on scrimshaw, but sailors had been carving teeth long before that. The oldest known pieces of scrimshaw are dated 1821 and 1827; another dated 1828 was made aboard the *Susan* of Nantucket.

Many items of household use were made from whalebone: rolling pins, napkin rings, knitting needles, clothes pins, crimping wheels for making designs in pie crust, coat racks, spool-holders, work boxes, and cribbage boards. Articles for personal use included collar buttons, cuff links, pins, brooches, and corset stays.

Purely decorative work, usually done on whale teeth, was set off by filling carved lines with colored ink, lamp black, tar, or soot. Designs included beautifully detailed clippers and whaleships, whaling scenes, and floral patterns. Sometimes portraits or scenes in books or magazines were traced and reproduced with infinite detail.

Because many of the men who carved had no artistic talent, much of the work was primitive. But there were also artists among the whalers who, although uneducated, had a real appreciation of line and form and turned out designs of highest quality. Fortunately, some of their work has been preserved and may still be seen in museums throughout the country. There are over 1,200 items of scrimshaw in the museum at Mystic, Connecticut.

Knot-tying is older than the art of sailing. Long before the dawn of recorded history, primitive man learned to make knots that held stone axe heads on wooden handles. When he ventured onto the water, he learned to tie more knots to hold his rude rafts together. By the beginning of the eighteenth century, seamen aboard ship had to know dozens of different knots and hitches. These were used in the lines and rigging and were called working knots. The men also used many other kinds of knots, in their spare time, to produce useful and decorative items for the ship—bell ropes, mats, lanyards, chest handles, and fenders. In long, quiet watches at sea, men also produced "fancy work." They would unravel a piece of canvas and use the threads to tie belts, bags, samplers, and picture frames.

Marlinspike seamanship

Seamen took great pride in their knowledge of knots and how to use them. This sort of work is called *marlinspike seamanship*, because a conical piece of wood, called a marlinspike, is used in working on heavy lines. In the Navy, purely decorative knot work, such as is used in making the canopy trimming for a barge, is called MacNamara's lace. Many books have been written about the history and use of knots; they describe more than 3,500 different knots.

Very recently—since the beginning of the space age—knot-tying has come ashore. Old salts would be dumbfounded to know that their art is now practiced in polite society under the name *macrame*, and that more books have been written telling women how to tie knots than were ever written for sailors.

Music   Over the years, sailors developed a simple form of folk music known as the *shantey*, or *chantey*. A chantey resembled a ballad in that its author was not known and it was not recorded in writing; it was sung and handed down from man to man. A chantey combined a bit of verse—not the best in the world—with a simple tune sung in two parts: melody by one man, chorus by all hands. There are literally thousands of chanties with many variations in words and music. Their words are simple and appealing, and their tunes are catchy and easy to remember. Many of them are of historical interest because of their subject matter. Some referred to famous ships, famous shipping lines, or especially notorious skippers; some were about the California gold rush, sailing-ship races, ports and harbors sailors liked, or women they remembered for one reason or another.

Chanties were work songs, the same sort of songs later used by the gandy dancers who built the railroads across the country, or the circus roustabouts who drove stakes and put up the "big tops." They helped all hands to heave around together on a particular job. Ashore or off watch, sailors sang popular ballads or love songs. In the Navy, chanties were not used at all; a boatswain's call set the pace for work; off-watch sailors, of course, sang the same songs everyone else sang.

A chantey had a definite form. "Hauling" songs consisted of two single solo lines and two alternating refrains. There were several different types of hauling songs, depending on the work to be done, but they were all used for hauling on sheets—working on the lines that handled sails. "Heaving" songs consisted of a four-line solo verse followed by a chorus of four or more lines. They were used for slow, hard work, such as raising the anchor with a capstan or windlass, hoisting heavy gear with a capstan, handling lines to take a ship out of dock, or running the pumps. The last was a job that might go on for days, so a "heaving" chantey had to have lots of verses.

A sailor, called a chanteyman, led off a chantey by singing a solo line, and the crew joined in on the chorus; all hands pulled together on the last word, in this manner:

Chanteyman: When I come ashore and get my pay,
Crew: Walk with me, Miss Edie, *do!*
Chanteyman: On that bright and always sunny day,
Crew: Oh, my Edie, walk with me, *do!**

A good "hauling" chantey was based on the famous Black Ball Line, one of the earliest of American shipping lines:

* This and the following three examples of chanteys are quoted from *American Sea Songs and Chanteys*, by Frank Fay, with special permission of W. W. Norton & Company, Inc.

Chanteyman: 'Twas on a Black Baller I first served my time.
Crew: To my yeo, ho! Blow the man *down!*
Chanteyman: And on that Black Baller I wasted my prime.
Crew: Oh, give me some time to blow the man *down!*

A rousing capstan chantey was "Away, Rio!" It was customary to sing this chantey when a ship took in her anchor before sailing from the United States:

The anchor is weighed and the sails they are set,
    Away, Rio!
The maids we are leaving we'll never forget,
    And we're bound for the Rio Grand. . . .

It was also customary, when a ship picked up her anchor in some foreign port to start the long voyage home, to let ships nearby know this fact by singing the chantey "Shenandoah." This had undoubtedly the loveliest melody of all sailor songs, and perhaps the most variations:

Oh, Shenandoah, I love your daughter,
    Away, my rol-ling ri-ver.
I'll take her 'cross yon rolling water,
    Away, we're bound away,
'Cross the wide Missouri!

No sailing ship bound from anywhere in the world to anywhere else in the world ever went near the wide Missouri, so there is some mystery about why sailors sang about it. However, a bit of confusion in the lyrics has not kept the music from being well known; even now, when a ship gets under way in a movie or on television, the chances are that the background music will be "Shenandoah!"

As sailors had a chantey for everything that involved work aboard ship, they also had one for doing nothing at all. This was generally used to indicate discontent, dissatisfaction, or pure boredom. A man would sing "I've got a sister nine foot high" and the chorus would come in with "Way down in Cuba!" But instead of hauling on a line all hands would make three short jumps on the deck. This was usually the signal for a mate to bellow "Now knock that off!"

The songs sailors sang are not nearly as well known as the chanteys, possibly because the music was not as catchy, and the songs were much longer and more difficult to memorize. Generally, they were narrative accounts of sad love affairs, exciting races, or great battles. One book of songs and ballads lists more than 75 songs written about the War of 1812 alone, and at least ten of them were about Perry and the Battle of Lake Erie. These songs were sung by merchant sailors and Navy men alike.

There was also an interesting variation of the sea ballad, called a "Come-all-ye." No matter what the subject, these ballads all began with the same words—possibly because their authors had difficulty writing a good lead. Once the first line was out of the way, the rest of the song sailed right along—some of them having verses enough to last all night. At times the literary quality of these works was high—some were written by well-educated people—but their opening lines could grow monotonous, as these excerpts from six "Come-all-ye's" show:

Come all ye lads who know no fear. . . .
Come all ye Yankee sailors. . . .
Come all ye Yankee heroes. . . .
Come all ye jolly seamen. . . .
Come all ye hardy sailors. . . .
Come all ye sons of Liberty. . . .

There would have been little enthusiasm for listening to a Hit Parade in 1812.

Band music Wars at sea seldom result in good music ashore. Fighting ships move across vast stages in a majestic cadence that only another Wagner or Bach might hear. The music that moves people—the tunes that inspired the Minutemen, Yankees, doughboys, and dogfaces of several wars to pick 'em up and put 'em down again—is a march, and good marches are not written every day.

The War of 1812 produced no marches worth mentioning, and only one good song. Everyone remembers the first few lines of "The Star-Spangled Banner," but very few people can get all the way through our anthem, which Francis Scott Key composed after watching ships of the Royal Navy bombard Fort McHenry in Baltimore. The well-known Marines' Hymn refers to the war with Mexico (1846–1848) in "From the Halls of Montezuma . . ." and to the war with the Barbary pirates (1805) in ". . . to the shores of Tripoli." The Marines have been marching to that tune for half a century but, oddly enough, no one in the Marine Corps knows where either the words or the music came from.

The Marines have had a band ever since they marched to the shores of Tripoli. In fact, they brought it back with them after that war. Marine Captain John Hall of the USS *Constitution* went ashore in Sicily and virtually shanghaied a roaming band of musicians, including a 12-year-old clarinetist. When he arrived in Washington with them, no one knew what to do with them, but they kept on playing for the Marines. The boy, Venerando Pulizzi, stayed with the band for 47 years.

The Civil War produced a full quota of sentimental ballads,

"fight" songs such as the "Battle Hymn of the Republic," and some good marches—again because the soldiers in that war did a lot of marching. Sailors are not good at marching; they usually ride to battle. Two of the best-known marches of the Civil War were "Tramp, Tramp, Tramp, the Boys are Marching," and "When Johnny Comes Marching Home Again." It is quite possible that the victorious Union Army marched up Pennsylvania Avenue to those tunes, and it is equally possible that one of the small boys tagging along behind the band was John Philip Sousa, who was born in Washington in 1854.

Sousa joined the Marine Band when he was 13 years old, became its leader 13 years later, and remained its leader for the next 37 years. He made the Marine Band famous, and became famous himself by composing great marches filled with heavy brass: "El Capitan," "King Cotton," "Washington Post March," "The Thunderer," and "Stars and Stripes Forever." Those compositions were not "listening music," but "marching music," and they were for all the world; in some countries, "Stars and Stripes Forever" is better liked than is the flag it refers to.

Critics might not class Sousa with the great classical composers, but he comes close behind them. Deems Taylor, the genial critic who wrote *Of Men and Music*, asserted that Sousa's place in the musical hall of fame was assured, not by critics, but by "marching men. The men who had to go long miles on an empty belly, under a hot sun, or through a driving rain. . . . They said he made things easier for them."

John Philip Sousa died in 1932 but still, whenever a Marine band tunes up on a grinder, or a Navy band lines up for a ceremony aboard a fleet flagship, sooner or later it will strike up a Sousa march. No one ever asks "What Sousa march?" So long as Sousa wrote it, who cares?

Ship models

Ship models are nearly as old as ships. Archeologists have found intricate and beautiful models of Nile River boats in the tombs of Egyptian kings buried 4,500 years ago. From such models, a great deal has been learned about the ancient craft of shipbuilding. The Egyptian models were preserved over the centuries by extremely low humidity in the tombs; undoubtedly other models fell apart because of dampness, extreme heat, and careless handling.

English shipbuilders in the early seventeenth century, when drawing plans for a new ship, also made a model of the proposed ship. This was done partly to help people who could not read plans to understand what the ship would look like, but also to help the shipbuilder plan certain details of construction. Such models were called "official models," or Admiralty models. They were not complete, and had part of the side and hull open to show the framework of the ship. The standing and running rigging was usually omitted from these models. Even now, fairly simple models of new ships are made, in order to allow details of the superstructure arrangement, placement of guns, or cargo-handling gear to be worked out.

Shipbuilders sometimes used a half model for the purpose of developing the hull lines of a new ship. A half model shows only the hull, split down the middle from bow to stern. Another type of model, used especially for steamships, shows considerable detail for the entire ship, but only as she would appear floating in the water. These are called waterline models.

Ship models seen in museums are usually either sailors' models or shipbuilders' models. Sailors who created models of their own ships, whether frigates, clippers, or whalers, worked without plans, but paid great attention to detail. They were so familiar with all the lines, rigging, spars, and blocks of their ships that they could build models from memory. Some especially fine sailors' models were produced by British sailors imprisoned by the French during the Napoleonic wars (1793–1815) and by Americans imprisoned by the British during the War of 1812. These delicate and detailed models, called *bone models* because they were made of many small bits of bone the sailors saved from their rations, were built plank by plank, exactly as a real ship would have been built. Sometimes their builders used horsehair from their mattresses, or their own hair, for lines in the rigging. Bone models, like many later models of clippers and whalers, merely represented a type of ship but not any particular ship.

Few of the many beautiful models of clippers and whalers that exist in museums were built by men modeling the ships in which they sailed. Sailors had little room and not much opportunity for model-making at sea—scrimshaw was better suited to their cramped quarters. Most of the fine models were built ashore by retired sea dogs who had plenty of time for fine whittling and intricate work in rigging details, or by craftsmen who prepared them for owners of the ships.

The finest, and most authentic models, are built from the original plans of a ship. These, whether of sailing ships or steamships, merchant or naval vessels, show every detail to exact scale, and are marvels of miniaturization. A craftsman might spend hundreds of hours on one model; some museum models are valued at thousands of dollars.

A unique kind of ship model, more colorful than it is accurate, is the ship-in-a-bottle, usually a waterline model of a full-rigged ship with all sails spread. Most good sailing-ship models do not show the sails spread; it is difficult to make them appear natural, and they hide many details of the rigging. The practice of building ships in bottles began early in the nineteenth century. Although bottle ships are not especially accurate in detail, it requires great skill and patience to build a very small ship, complete with masts, spars, and a bit of rigging, in such a manner that it can be slid through the neck of a bottle and then rigged with masts properly erect. Possibly a few bottle-ship builders had as good a time getting the bottle empty as they did putting the ship inside it. Bottle ships have one good feature; they are preserved from dust, humidity, and damage, and hundreds of very old ones survive in various museums.

Ship models represent a fascinating pageant of maritime history over the past centuries. The hundreds of them on display in museums throughout the country depict every kind of ship built in America, from the earliest fishing sloops to the latest nuclear-powered carriers and automated LASH ships. Ship models are a distinctive art form; many an old one is a wordless expression of some man's deep love for the sea. Careful examination of an old ship model can produce the unique sensation of peering backward in time—somewhat like looking through the wrong end of a telescope—to the day when the ship was fresh from the building yard and ready to go to sea for the first time.

Paintings

Maritime art is as old as the literature of the sea. As in all creative endeavors, some was good and some was not. Some of the paintings are very good and now hang in museums and galleries where they may still be enjoyed. There must have been many paintings that never reached any gallery, and probably there is no need to speculate about what happened to them.

Marine paintings include many subjects: harbor scenes, sea shores, fishing, whaling, sailing, ships, and shipwrecks. The history of shipbuilding and design is preserved in great detail in paintings. Such paintings are the best sources of information on the early colonial schooners, the frigates of the Continental Navy, the first steamboats, the Atlantic packets, the clipper ships, whalers, and the Mississippi River steamboats.

A certain type of marine painting shows great sweeps of empty ocean over which a couple of seagulls might hover or romantic "red sails at sunset." Such paintings are known as *calendar views*. There are also *narrative paintings*, which show ships as the center of interest—ships being smashed up in a storm, wrecked on a lee shore, shot up in battle, going down with all hands and the colors flying, or, with every sail spread, pounding along at a speed never reached anywhere but on an artist's easel.

Another form of marine art is a ship painting that shows every line, every block in the rigging, and every detail of the sails, but with all sails spread fore and aft, like a butterfly pinned on a board. Then there are *ship portraits*, most of which depict clipper ships or whalers. These were not done by amateur sailor-painters, but by trained shoreside artists, and they are technically reliable. All such paintings—especially those made before photography became general—serve as valuable records of the past. If it were not for them, we would have little idea of how ships really looked. The most famous clipper ship, the *Flying Cloud,* was never photographed or drawn from life, although there are paintings depicting her as some artist "reconstructed" her.

Maritime America, as it appeared in the eighteenth and nineteenth centuries, was recorded for all time by such painters as Washington Allston, William James Bennett, George Ropes, and Thomas Birch. These were not primitive painters; some had had intensive art training in Europe before commencing work in America. Two excellent "record views" of the period are "The Crowninshield Wharf, 1806," a Boston view by Ropes, now in the Peabody Museum of Salem, and "Boston from City Point, near Sand Street, 1833," by Bennett, now in the Museum of Fine Arts, Boston. Thomas Birch specialized in marine and naval subjects, and produced many fine paintings based on battles at sea in the War of 1812. A waterfront scene of New York, done in 1828 by Thomas Thompson, shows not only sailing ships and a steam ferry in use then, but the kinds of hats and dresses worn by women at that time.

Other painters of that period were Robert Salmon, whose paintings of ships and waterfront architecture, dating from 1800 to 1843, were finely detailed; John F. Kensett, whose marine paintings had a romantic flavor, now called the "Hudson River School," and Albert Bierstadt, and Fitz Hugh Lane. Bierstadt's "Wreck of the Ancon in Loring Bay, Alaska," is in the Museum of Fine Arts, Boston. Lane was considered the first native American painter of real stature; like the earlier Flemish painters, he knew how to fill his paintings with light. His work became highly prized, although when he died in 1865 it had not yet become widely known. His paintings now hang in the Cape Ann Historical Association Gallery, Gloucester, Massachusetts; the Shelburne Museum in Vermont; the Mariners Museum, Newport News, Virginia; and the Museum of Fine Arts, Boston.

In the clipper-ship era, Americans built the most beautiful sailing ships ever seen. They were romantic and exciting, and artists of all kinds labored to satisfy the public demand for paintings, drawings, and prints of the graceful ships. The results were varied; there are some excellent paintings of clipper ships, but there are also calendar views, romantic treatments, and a particular type called *owners' portraits.*

Owners' portraits were usually based on the builder's plans and were sometimes painted before the ship ever sailed. They always presented a ship broadside, with every detail of her rigging showing and all sails spread. All the ships sat on an even keel; they were never shown beset by storm, ice, or any other danger of the sea. These views were sometimes ready for the public at the time the ship was launched and served to attract the interest of people who wanted a fast trip to California. Some of them were reproduced by Currier & Ives.

One of the best clipper ship artists was James E. Butterworth, who came to the United States in 1845. His works hang in many galleries, and were also reproduced in the famous Currier & Ives prints. Edward Moran came to the United States in 1844 and also became famed as a marine painter, noted for realistic seascapes and historic naval engagements.

Few people could afford an original painting, but the development of lithography in the nineteenth century made it possible for almost everyone to buy cheap prints of paintings. A lithograph was drawn on stone, then printed in black on paper, after which women hand-colored each print. The firm of Currier & Ives began producing prints in New York about 1834, and from then until 1907 sold thousands of prints. Dealers bought them for as little as six cents each. Currier & Ives prints are preserved in museums; many of them are very valuable. Over the years Currier & Ives produced prints of clipper ships, whalers, ocean races, steamboat disasters, and waterfront scenes, all of which serve now as visual records of the history of the time.

Aside from their artistic value, these prints also had news value. When the steamer *Lexington* burned and sank in Long Island Sound on 13 January 1840, over a hundred persons died. Currier & Ives produced a hand-colored lithograph of the burning ship, complete with a list of casualties and a statement by her captain, and had it on sale in New York three days later. Such prints were the late-late news of their day.

Another special form of marine art was devoted to paintings of steamboats. These smoky craft began operations in the very early 1800s, and were still busy on American rivers a hundred years later. Clippers could be seen only in the ports of Boston, Philadelphia, New York, Baltimore, and San Francisco, but steamboats were seen in any little riverfront town in the country that had water deep enough to float one. James Bard was one of the foremost steamboat painters, and Currier & Ives produced steamboat prints. Almost everyone could afford a print of his favorite steamboat loading, racing, burning, or blowing up. As was the case with other types of marine art, some steamboat paintings were authentic and technically correct, while others were glamorous, multi-colored spectacles that never happened.

Even though the great frigates, clippers, whalers, and steamboats finally vanished, artists still paint them. Other artists work at painting one of the most challenging subjects in all marine art, the sea itself. Winslow Homer painted the stormy seas of the New England coast, the sunny Caribbean Seas, and fishermen at work. Albert P. Ryder was noted for romantic, moonlit, marine scenes. Frederick J. Waugh painted bright, colorful seascapes, filled with sparkling sunlight and great smashing breakers. His works were exhibited in Paris and London, and hang in many museums in the United States, including the Metropolitan Museum in New York and the Corcoran Gallery of Art and the National Collection of Fine Arts in Washington, D.C. Edward Hopper's painting "The Lighthouse at Two Lights" hangs in the Metropolitan Museum in New York, and John Sloan's "In the Wake of the Ferry" is in the Phillips Gallery in Washington, D.C. Paintings by Homer, Hopper, and Sloan have also been reproduced in full color on U.S. postage stamps. Gordon Grant faithfully recorded New England waterfront scenes, fishermen and their boats, sailing ships, and beautifully detailed clipper ships. Another artist who brought the old frigates and clippers back to life long after they had gone was Charles R. Patterson. He went to sea at the age of thirteen and spent ten years in sailing ships. His first paintings were on the lids of sea chests. In the early 1930s he was the only living American painter with sailing experience in the old windjammers. Patterson was a "sailors' painter"—he painted to please sailors. His works are preserved in many museums; some particularly striking murals of naval engagements are in Bancroft Hall, at the U.S. Naval Academy.

Not all the good paintings of ships are to be found in art galleries or museums. Many excellent views of ships have been reproduced on postage stamps, and some of them can still be bought for only a few cents each.

The United States issued its first regular postage stamps in 1847. They were a 5-cent stamp portraying Benjamin Franklin and a 10-cent stamp portraying George Washington. From that time until 1922, when an American Indian chief named Hollowhorn Bear appeared on a 14-cent stamp, people at the Post Office stamp counters spent their time licking and sticking a long series of presidential portraits, with an occasional general or admiral for variety. When this unimaginative procession was interrupted, stamps of a very different nature began to appear, and the change eventually resulted in stamps that depicted naval and maritime subjects with great technical accuracy. The first "topical" stamps were issued by the United States in 1869. One of them depicted the steamship *Adriatic* of the Collins Line and three of them depicted the landing of Columbus. Next, for the 1893 Columbian Exposition in Chicago, a series of commemorative stamps was issued; there were sixteen of them and they depicted events in Columbus' life, his voyage to the New World, and his ships *Santa María, Pinta,* and *Niña.*

Since that time, many famous ships and many events in naval and maritime history have been represented on postage stamps. The *Virginia of Sagahadock,* which was built in 1607 and was the first to be built in the colonies, appeared on a stamp in 1957. Other "first" ships on stamps are the *Clermont,* the first successful steamboat in the United States, and the *Savannah,* the first steam-powered ship to cross the Atlantic.

One of the events that led to the Revolutionary War, the Boston Tea Party, was recently depicted on a block of four stamps. The various flags carried by the ships of the Continental Navy have been reproduced on stamps, as have the portraits of men from other lands who fought on the American side in that war: General Comte de Rochambeau, Admiral Comte de Grasse, Marquis de Lafayette, and Count Casimir Pulaski. The naval heroes of the Revolution, John Paul Jones and John Barry, are portrayed on stamps, as is James Fenimore Cooper, who wrote an early history of that war.

Postage stamps have depicted a wide range of ship types, from square-riggers to nuclear-powered ships. Ships on stamps include the old sailing ship *W. F. Babcock* entering the Golden Gate, the whaler *Charles W. Morgan*, steamboats *Grey Eagle* and *St. Paul* on the Mississippi River, the sightseeing steamer *Maid of the Mist* at Niagara Falls, the ore boat *Griffin* on the Great Lakes, the towboat *H. D. Williams*, a World War II Liberty ship, and the steamships *Northwest, City of Alpena, St. Paul*, and *Andrea F. Luckenbach*.

The Spanish ships Columbus brought to the New World are not the only ones from other lands that have appeared on stamps issued by the United States. Stamps have also depicted the *Halve Maen (Half Moon)*, in which, in 1609, Henry Hudson explored the river bearing his name; the *Nieuw Nederland* that brought Dutch settlers to Manhattan in 1624; the *Restaurationen* that brought Norwegian settlers in 1825; the *Kalmar Nyckel* that brought Swedish-Finnish settlers in 1638; the *Ark* and the *Dove* that brought English settlers to Maryland in 1634; the British frigate *Carolina* that brought colonists to Charleston in 1670; and the French frigate *Victoire* that helped Americans in the Revolutionary War.

Ships of the Navy on stamps include the *Bonhomme Richard* and the *Lexington* of the Revolutionary War; the *United States* and the *Constitution* of the War of 1812; the *Susquehanna, Mississippi, Saratoga*, and *Plymouth* that sailed in the Perry Expedition to Japan in 1854; the attack transport *Arthur Middleton* and transport *Dorchester* of World War II; and the nuclear-powered submarine *Nautilus*. The U.S. Coast and Geodetic Survey has had three ships—*Pathfinder, Explorer*, and *Surveyor*—grouped on a stamp.

As the United States has depicted men and ships of other nations on its postage stamps, so have other nations depicted many American ships. One of the most noted in recent years was the USS *Missouri*, which Turkey pictured on three stamps when the battleship visited that country after World War II. The USS *Nautilus* has appeared on stamps issued by France and Monaco. Monaco has also pictured the SS *United States*. Panama has shown the USS *Nereus* on a stamp, Samoa has pictured the USS *Nipsic*, Sharjah & Dependencies has pictured the nuclear merchant ship *Savannah*, and the Netherlands Antilles has pictured on a stamp the *Santa Rosa* of the Grace Line. Even the Confederate States Navy provided a stamp subject; Tristan da Cunha has pictured the raider *Shenandoah* on one of its stamps.

Because interest in ships is worldwide, literally thousands of stamps showing ships have appeared in the past century. The careful representation of ships on stamps often surpasses technical accuracy and attains true artistic quality. These stamps show every type of ship that ever sailed the seas, along with many excellent paintings of the sea and of maritime subjects. The entire history of seagoing exploration and discovery, shipbuilding, fishing and whaling, and oceangoing commerce over the centuries could be told in a colorful mosaic of thousands of bits of paper called *stamps*—a museum and library no bigger than this book.

Combat art   A somewhat specialized form of marine art was developed in World War II, when the Navy sent professional artists to sea to produce what was called "combat art." Much of this work was done quickly, almost before the smoke and dust had settled. While it sometimes lacked the finished perfection of nineteenth-century realism, it was filled with the urgency and clamor of battle. Combat art is authentic, and brings out more of the human side of battle at sea or on the beaches than did the old views of broadside frigate actions, which glamorized ships, not men.

But even the most accomplished artist in the world could never hope to capture, within the limits of a framed canvas, more than one moment of time, a few ships, and a sweep of salt water. World War II naval battles sometimes lasted for days and involved dozens of ships, hundreds of aircraft, and thousands of men spread across limitless reaches of sea. The biggest mural ever conceived could in no way depict the suspense, drama, action, terror, destruction, pain, and jubilation that men experienced in the Battle of Midway, or at the Normandy landings and the subsequent breakout. No two men who took part in any combat action ever saw it in the same light, and no one of them could ever hope to remember, afterwards, exactly what happened.

Fortunately, for those who saw no part of it, World War II was witnessed, on both sides, by the same impartial observer—a camera lens. From the first days in the opening phase of the Battle of the Atlantic, to the final moment of the Japanese surrender on board the *Missouri* in Tokyo Bay, cameras recorded the action. Photographers filmed troops hitting the beaches, surface-ship engagements, combat in the air and beneath the sea, and all the turmoil and tedium that went with those actions. When the war ended, the results of their work filled archives in many nations. Canned film, of course, is of little value until someone sees it, so the Navy, after World War II, spent years in preparing an authoritative visual history of America's vast maritime war, as shot by combat photographers.

The result was the award-winning television documentary titled "Victory at Sea," produced in cooperation with the National Broadcasting Company and first telecast in 1952. The film was accompanied by an impressive musical score composed by Richard Rodgers, who also wrote the music for "South Pacific."

"Victory at Sea" is possibly the longest motion-picture film ever produced. It consists of 26 thirty-minute episodes; a total running time of 13 hours. Its editors reviewed more than 60,000,000 feet of film from 10 different nations in order to compose the final sequence. The titles of some episodes read like the chapter headings of a great adventure story, as indeed they are: "Sea and Sand" (the invasion of North Africa), "Full Fathom Five" (submarine warfare), and "Suicide for Glory" (the battle for Okinawa). The *New York Herald Tribune* acclaimed "Victory at Sea" as "A comprehensive and sweeping documentary that should be repeated again and again." That it has been. Two decades after the series was first telecast it still appears on television programs.

But "Victory at Sea" is more than a documentary. The combination of filmed action, moving narrative, and sometimes haunting music produces a dramatic and, at times, emotional experience that mere words alone could never create. One must *see* the grand sweep of action across a troubled ocean and the sudden blaze of battle, as recorded by many cameras, to comprehend the full meaning of war at sea.

There is a never-ending fascination with the sea. For over two centuries, Americans have produced numberless books and paintings with the sea as a background. Even now, artists and writers are busy trying to depict all the many facets of life at sea. This is a timeless task; it will never end.

CHAPTER 20
SEA POWER
AND NATIONAL
SURVIVAL

"They came by sea. . . ." That was how this book began, and that was how the first American colonies began. Ever since the landings at Jamestown and Plymouth Rock, the history and development of America has been closely tied to the sea. The maritime history of the nation involves many aspects, as do its military and political history. A discussion of any one involves literary treatment appropriate to the subject, and each subject develops its own particular terminology. In any discussion of the place the United States now holds among the world powers, invariably there will come a time when the subject will be sea power.

Sea power is a term used more often than it is understood, yet national economy and national security depend on its proper exercise. In fact, the comfort and well-being of every individual in the country, as well as their peaceful future, depend on some aspect of sea power. For nearly two thousand years, sea power has changed the course of history, although the nations involved were not exactly aware of this at the time; no one had heard of sea power until the U.S. naval historian, Alfred Thayer Mahan, coined the term in his book *The Influence of Sea Power upon History, 1660–1783*, which was published in 1890.

Mahan's study of history led to the observation that great maritime nations had certain basic common characteristics. These were: geographical position, physical conformation, extent of territory, size of population, character of the people, and character of the government. A nation with no sea coast, or one remote from world trade centers, or one with no good harbors, would lack one or more of the elements necessary for a leading maritime nation. But even a nation that has all three elements must also have a population

On previous page: The World War II development of underway replenishment enables ships to operate at sea for long periods. In this 1959 photograph, the oiler *Caloosahatchie* fuels the cruiser *Salem* and the carrier *Lake Champlain*. Two destroyers wait their turn.
Photo: U.S. Navy.

large enough to carry on seagoing commerce and, at the same time, defend itself against any aggression. Success in this area depends, too, on the character of the people and of their government; if they have an aptitude for seagoing commerce and their government favors protecting national interests, they will achieve maritime dominance and become a nation with the ability to exercise sea power and ensure its own security.

Through history, maritime nations—those with sea power—have enjoyed national privacy, in contrast to continental powers, which are subject to enemy attack across common geographical borders. The latter nations have generally maintained standing armies for protection against invasion, whereas maritime nations, most of which front on the sea, have not had invasion fears, and their people have developed a different outlook. "Isolated and thereby well-defended men," wrote Clark Reynolds in *Command of the Sea*, "have tended to be free men, free to think and apply their ideas to machinery and to government." Navies, he maintains, are the bedrock of individualism.

While the territorial limits of continental powers extend not one foot beyond their geographic boundaries, the same has not been true of those of maritime nations. For centuries, maritime nations have applied the "three-mile limit" to give themselves control over the waters within three miles of their shores. That limit was established because three miles was the range of a cannon.

Some nations have held that their territorial seas take in all waters within 12 miles of their shores, but the United States has observed the three-mile limit since 1783—with exceptions. For example, during the time the 18th Amendment, which established prohibition, was in effect, the Coast Guard was permitted to seize rumrunners caught with liquor inside a 12-mile limit.

By custom, all ships have the right to "innocent passage" through waters within the 12-mile limits of any nation. If a nation chose to restrict traffic in such waters, many important sea routes would be barred to international commerce. In recent years some nations, in an effort to preserve fishing rights for their own use, have established claim to all waters within 200 miles of their own shores. Negotiations on 12-mile limits and 200-mile limits, which are international in scope, are handled by the United Nations' Law of the Sea Conferences.

Acceptance of such limits would benefit some "developing" nations, but it would deprive others of resources that have long been the heritage of all people. It might create more problems than it would solve. One problem would be that of maintaining jurisdiction over vast areas of territorial waters, which would be most difficult without sea power.

It must be thoroughly understood that sea power is not just another name for a big navy. Admiral Mahan defined sea power very simply in 1897 when he wrote: "Navy, plus bases, plus merchant marine, equals sea power." But putting together those three basic elements of sea power involves almost numberless subordinate activities. *Navy* means more than just fighting ships; *bases* mean more than just the coaling depots that existed in Mahan's day; and *merchant marine* means more than just freighters.

Elements of sea power   Today the full sea-power inventory includes tankers and cargo ships of all kinds, fishing craft, and ocean-research vessels. Sea power also takes in shipbuilders, shipowners and ship operators, ship repair yards, dry docks, harbors and related facilities, waterways, piers, terminal facilities, and cargo-handling equipment. It takes in the U.S. Coast Guard, the Maritime Administration, the Army Corps of Engineers, longshoremen, merchant sailors and their seafaring unions, the various academies, maritime training schools, and union training schools. Such peaceful operations as fishing, mariculture (farming the sea), extracting minerals from the sea, and offshore oil-drilling, can be undertaken only if the nation has control of the sea in which these operations take place.

Sea power means more than just sending fighting fleets to sea to win a war against an enemy. It means peaceful use of the sea too; our nation must have sea power to send ships anywhere in the world, to carry on commerce and bring back the more than 70 strategic raw materials necessary to modern industry and economy. It also means the nation has the ability to control the seas for its own use by protecting trade routes around the world and keeping open the sea lines of communication to friendly nations. But sea power means more than controlling the seas; it also means being able to deny their use to an enemy. That is where navies come in; the best merchant fleet in the world is useless if it is not free to use the sea; strong talk by diplomats means little to an aggressor nation on the other side of the ocean, if words cannot be backed up by action.

Naval quarantine   Sea power, of course, wins wars, but a nation able to use sea power effectively is in a position to effect national policy without having to go to war. A striking example of this concept was displayed in the quarantine of Cuba laid down by the United States in 1962, when aerial reconnaissance revealed that launching pads for intercontinental ballistic missiles (ICBMs) were being erected on Cuban soil and that some ICBMs were deployed there. As only the United States and Soviet Russia had the technology to build ICBMS, it was plainly apparent where the material was coming from.

To eliminate the missile threat, the United States had two obvious choices of action: either bomb the sites or land an invasion force and capture them. But the United States did not want to go to war with Cuba, and any direct military action against Cuba might well result in hostilities with Soviet Russia. A third, and the best, alternative was to use naval force and blockade Cuba.

The president, accordingly, ordered the Navy to set up a patrol to search for, intercept, and turn back any missile-carrying vessels en route to the Cuban area—in other words, to quarantine Cuba. Within a few days 180 Navy ships and 85,000 men, plus ten Marine battalions, were in the area. Navy forces began searching 3.5 million square miles for merchant ships and submarines. Ships carrying missiles were turned back, others picked up the missiles already landed in Cuba, and in a short while the crisis was over. Not a shot had been fired, but it was plainly evident that the United States had sufficient naval strength afloat in the area to handle any situation that might have developed. In the face of such force, of course, no situation did develop. It was a dramatic example of how to use the "big stick" Roosevelt had mentioned in a similar situation nearly three-quarters of a century earlier.

Functions of the Navy   In Mahan's time the U.S. Navy had one primary duty: to control the sea for the use of the United States and to deny its use to enemies. Since then, the nation's military and political considerations have become vastly complicated and involve functions that could not have been conceived of even fifty years ago. In modern war, there may be considerable overlapping of duties where three military services are involved. Accordingly, the Department of Defense Reorganization Act of 1958 laid down the primary functions of the modern Navy, as follows:

"The Navy and the Marine Corps are to organize, train, and equip Navy and Marine Corps forces for the conduct of prompt and sustained combat operations at sea, including operations of sea-based aircraft and land-based naval air components—specifically, forces to seek out and destroy enemy naval forces and to suppress enemy sea commerce, to gain and maintain general naval supremacy, to control vital sea areas and to establish and maintain local superiority (including air) in an area of naval operations, to seize and defend advanced naval bases, and to conduct such land and air operations as may be essential to the prosecution of a naval campaign."

The U.S. Navy, in carrying out its mission to maintain control and command of the sea as required in the national interests, keeps many of its combatant craft at sea. These ships cruise in parts of the world where political unrest may be best offset by the knowledge that at sea, somewhere nearby, there is a naval force strong enough to discourage any change in the status quo. Ships on the high seas are in "international waters," where they are free to move anywhere they may be needed.

The Navy must also provide forces for joint amphibious operations and it is responsible for training all forces in amphibious doctrine. Other responsibilities include: reconnaissance, antisubmarine warfare, protection of shipping, minelaying, and controlled minefield operations. In conjunction with other services, the Navy must provide forces to defend the United States against air attack.

At present the Navy maintains fleets in the Atlantic and the Pacific oceans. Ships within a certain fleet, when assigned to a specific task, are organized as a *task force*. Smaller groups of ships within a task force are called *task units*. The Navy operates several hundred ships of many different types.

Ship classifications   A modern warship is a highly complicated machine that has its own propulsion plant, weapons for attack and defense, communication and navigation systems, electrical system, repair shops, and all the facilities to house, feed, and care for a crew. Because the basic missions of ships are different, the ships must be different; a destroyer cannot do an aircraft carrier's job, and a guided-missile cruiser cannot replace an assault transport to put troops ashore for a landing. It is not practical to build an all-purpose ship, so each type is built to carry the best possible combination of features to help the ship perform its specific mission. Yet all ships must possess certain essential qualities—armament, protection, seaworthiness, habitability, maneuverability, speed, and endurance.

Ships are classified by major categories (warship); types within categories (aircraft carriers); and classes within types (*Forrestal*-class carriers) as follows:

Warships
  Aircraft carriers
  Surface combatants (cruisers, frigates, destroyers)
  Command ships
  Submarines
  Patrol ships
  Amphibious warfare ships
  Mine warfare ships
  Combatant craft
Auxiliary ships
Service craft

All ships are assigned *designations*—a group of letters which indicate their type and general use—and *hull numbers*, which are usually assigned in sequence to ships of a type as they are built. These identifying designations are used in correspondence, records, plans, communications, and sometimes on ships' boats, because letter and number designations are shorter than the ships' names— *Mission Capistrano* (AG 162)—and help to avoid confusion between such similar names as *Horne* (DLG 30) and *Hornet* (CVS 12) or *Phoebe* (MSC 199) and *Phoebus* (YF 294).

Most ships operate individually only when making a passage from one port to another; even then, if two or more ships sail together they conduct training exercises en route. Fleet operations involve many ships of various types; some operations are explained here.

Amphibious warfare   Amphibious warfare operations are conducted to establish a military force on an enemy shore in order to conduct further combat operations, capture ground for a base, and deny the use of an area or facilities to an enemy. Marines are normally included in landing operations; units from all the armed forces may take part.

A modern amphibious landing is a highly complicated operation that may involve hundreds of ships and small craft and thousands of men. *Planning* for such an operation may take months. After planning is completed, an *operation order* is issued. It covers organization, ships and units assigned, communications, minesweeping, naval gunfire and bombardment, air strikes, actual assault operations, and logistics. There will then be *training* operations, perhaps even "rehearsal" landings before the remaining steps in an amphibious operation take place.

Embarkation takes place when troops are embarked in transport or assault ships, and vehicles and equipment are combat-loaded into ships. "Combat-loading" is a technique whereby materials needed ashore first are loaded last.

Movement to the objective area requires that ships sail from many different ports. Planning enables each ship to arrive at the right place at the right time.

Pre-assault operations include shore bombardment, air strikes on enemy defenses, minesweeping, and underwater demolition of beach obstacles.

Assault of sea approaches takes in the actual landing, which commences on D-day when the force arrives in the objective area.

Ship-to-shore movement begins at H-hour, when troops are loaded into landing craft which move to the beach in waves. Troops land under cover of gun and rocket fire by ships and aircraft.

Establishing the beachhead involves gaining control of enough ground to allow additional troops, weapons, and cargo to be landed to support further operations.

Underwater Demolition Teams (UDT) take part in pre-assault operations. Their primary mission is reconnaissance; secondary missions include demolition, sneak attacks, salvage operations, and emergency rescues.

Antisubmarine warfare   The basic mission of antisubmarine warfare (ASW) is to deny the enemy the effective use of his submarines. Destroyers are the most effective ASW ships, but destroyer escorts, frigates, and guided-missile frigates all have ASW capabilities. ASW operations include both protective and offensive phases.

Protective ASW includes escorting merchant convoys to protect them from enemy submarine attack. Offensive ASW includes strike operations and hunter-killer (HUK) operations.

A typical HUK operation centers on an aircraft carrier (CVS) which employs fixed-wing ASW search aircraft, helicopters, and submarines in a search patrol; the CVS is screened by several destroyers. Carrier-based attack aircraft and fighter aircraft, long- and medium-range patrol aircraft, and land-based search aircraft all have a part in ASW.

The principal ASW weapons are depth charges, hedgehogs, torpedoes, antisubmarine rockets (ASROC), submarine rockets (SUBROC), and the light airborne multi-purpose system (LAMPS).

The principal method of submarine detection is sonar which is used passively—receiving underwater sounds—or actively—transmitting sounds that will be reflected by a target. This is called "pinging," from the noise the transmitter makes. Sonar is used by surface ships and submarines. Helicopters hunt submarines by hovering in one spot and lowering into the water a cable holding a transducer, with which it can listen or echo-range on a target. Fixed-wing aircraft can drop expendable radio-sonobuoys equipped with hydrophones, which pick up and broadcast underwater sounds. Each sonobuoy is on a different frequency, enabling the plane to pinpoint the source of sound. They also use the magnetic airborne detection device (MAD) to sweep a 1,200-foot-wide path, primarily to pinpoint a submarine's location prior to attack.

Carrier task forces   The mission of a carrier task force is to establish control of an ocean area. Such a force, which is built around a carrier, may include cruisers, destroyers and destroyer escorts, picket ships, picket submarines, and AEW (airborne early warning) aircraft to operate between the task force and the location of any possible enemy. The task force will be backed up by logistic support and replenishment vessels.

In the latter part of World War II, a fast carrier task force might consist of 15 carriers, half a dozen battleships, a dozen cruisers, and as many as 75 destroyers. Such a task force is much smaller now, but is faster and has greater offensive power, mainly because it includes missiles.

A striking force is a task force armed for a particular operation. It may consist of a carrier task force, or be composed only of surface ships, in which case it is called a surface strike force.

Logistic support   Logistics is the job of the service forces—the oilers, ammunition ships, supply ships, and their escorts. The ships engaged in amphibious warfare, ASW, carrier operations, HUK operations, shore bombardment, escort and patrol, or blockade duties depend on the service force ships for oil, ammunition, and food, which is usually supplied in an operation called *underway replenishment*.

Underway replenishment (UNREP)   Ships must be able to stay at sea for weeks at a time, yet they must have fuel, provisions, and ammunition. To supply ships at sea, the Navy has developed the technique of underway replenishment, using ships fitted with special cargo-handling equipment to transfer supplies to other ships while they steam alongside each other. Another kind of underway replenishment is *vertical replenishment* (VERTREP), which uses cargo-carrying helicopters to move supplies from one ship to another.

Ships are designed to perform certain missions and duties; accordingly, there are many different types of ships, depending on whether their primary mission is to handle aircraft, perform shore-bombardment, carry troops or cargo, or repair other ships and aircraft. The principal types are described here.

Ship types

Aircraft carriers   Carriers, or "flattops," have replaced battleships as the main strength of the fleet. Other combatant ships are armed with guns or missiles; the carrier's armament consists of aircraft, which in turn are armed with guns, missiles, or bombs. The chief function of a carrier is to serve as a floating airport from which all types of air operations may be conducted around the clock and in all kinds of weather.

Cruisers   Designed to conduct antiair and antisubmarine missions, cruisers are fast ships that act as scouts, protect task forces from surface attack, serve as control ships or flagships, bombard shore targets, and support and cover amphibious operations.

Frigates and Destroyers   About as speedy and powerful as cruisers, frigates and destroyers protect carrier task forces and amphibious forces from air, submarine, and surface attack, engage in submarine hunter-killer operations, attack light enemy surface forces, and provide missile support or gunfire support in amphibious landings.

Submarines   Modern nuclear-powered submarines have an importance in naval warfare far out of proportion to their size. Their ability to launch nuclear weapons with ranges of thousands of miles make them the most powerful ships in the world. Some conventional submarines still operate with the fleet, but the ballistic-missile, nuclear-powered submarines (SSBNs) operate independently. They patrol for two months at a time, submerged.

Amphibious warfare ships   Many basic types of ships have been developed for use in amphibious operations. These include ships with communication facilities, transports equipped to carry and land troops, cargo ships, assault ships, and tank-landing ships, which can actually run ashore in order to unload equipment. Many amphibious ships are equipped to carry and unload smaller amphibious boats in which troops and equipment are carried to the assault beaches.

Mine warfare ships   Mine warfare operations in World War II employed hundreds of minelayers and minesweepers. Mines can now be laid by aircraft or submarines, and effectively swept by helicopters towing electronic and sonic devices. In 1974 Egypt asked the United States to help clear mines and other explosives from the Suez Canal; Navy helicopters did the job.

Auxiliary ships   The Navy uses hundreds of auxiliaries, ranging from 50,000-ton fast combat support ships to 300-ton hydrofoils. The auxiliary fleet includes destroyer tenders, submarine tenders, ammunition ships, store ships, tankers, research ships, survey ships, cargo ships, oilers, transports, hospital ships, and tugs.

Service craft   The "work horses" of the Navy are the service craft. More than 2,500 small tugs, barges, floats, floating dry docks, and various unclassified craft are at work in harbors and at fleet bases. These craft are not seagoing.

Lifelines   In two hundred years the United States has become one of the great industrial nations of the world. Mills, plants, and factories produce a steady flow of manufactured products for use at home and for export to overseas markets. Over 50,000 ships enter and leave U.S. ports every year, carrying more than 2,000,000,000 tons of cargo worth more than $50 billion.

To support this vast industry, the United States consumes millions of tons of raw material every year, much of which is not produced in this country. Every day, ships from the far corners of the world reach our ports, carrying the raw materials needed to keep our national economy healthy.

Without such imports, factories would close down, transportation would come to a near standstill, businesses would fail, and the economic life of the country would be endangered. The long lines of ships bringing imports to this country are so vital to our national well-being that they are sometimes called our "lifelines." Without them, life in the United States might well return to the conditions our colonial ancestors faced—cold and miserable.

Actually, colonial America would not have been nearly as cold and miserable without imports as people would be today. To a large degree, they were self-sufficient; they raised their own food, made their own clothing and furniture, provided their own light, fuel, and housing. They would not have missed the raw materials we are now dependent on, because they had never heard of most of them.

Critical materials   Many of the minerals and chemicals essential to modern industry are not found in this country at all. The United States produces no chromite, cobalt, manganese, rubber, or tin, all of which must be imported. Imports of critical materials, which range from antimony to zinc, amount to millions of tons a year.

It is difficult to relate shiploads of imported ores to the routine of daily living, unless one can visualize the hundreds of items now considered necessities that are produced from such imports. From toothpaste tubes to television tubes, spark plugs to jet engines, bug sprays to bedsprings, and razor blades to radios, nearly everything used in the home, school, and office includes some basic material that came from overseas. Even the type, ink, and paper that went into this book contain metals and chemicals that were imported to this country by ship.

Almost every aspect of our daily routine is dependent, in some part, on ships. By protecting and controlling the sea-lanes, the Navy makes it possible for the merchant marine to carry on that essential ocean trade.

The merchant marine

The history of the American merchant marine goes back more than 300 years, to when the first colonists started sending ships to sea. For a long while, merchant shipping operated pretty much on its own. In the last century, the government began to help merchant shipping by granting subsidies—payments for contracts to carry mail—and by permitting shipbuilding materials to be imported tax-free. Even so, at the beginning of this century, there was only one American transatlantic line in operation, and American ships were carrying less than 10 percent of all U.S. ocean trade.

When World War I broke out in Europe in 1914 there was an acute shortage of shipping, as warring nations withdrew their ships from trade runs to the United States. The situation grew more serious when the United States entered the war, because there were not enough transports and cargo ships to carry the U.S. Expeditionary Force to Europe and maintain it there. The Shipping Act of 1916 set up the U.S. Shipping Board which then organized the Emergency Fleet Corporation, a shipbuilding complex that built more than 2,000 ships between 1918 and 1922. Most of the ships, however, were delivered too late to be of use in the war and many of them were not suited to peacetime operations, so they were soon sold, stored, or scrapped.

After the national and international depression of the 1930s, the U.S. merchant fleet dwindled to the point where, in 1936, the United States ranked sixth in the world in the number of ships 10 years old or less. Congress then enacted the Merchant Marine Act of 1936 which stated: "It is necessary for the national defense and development of its foreign and domestic commerce that the United States shall have a merchant marine . . . capable of serving as a naval and military auxiliary in time of war or national emergency, owned and operated under the United States flag by citizens of the United States insofar as may be practicable, and, composed of the best-equipped, safest and most suitable types of vessels constructed in the United States and manned with a trained and efficient citizen personnel."

Some twenty years later, Admiral Arleigh Burke put it this way: "Sea power is not just men-of-war. It includes cargo ships, passenger liners, tankers, and the many other craft and auxiliaries that make up the Merchant Marine. Our experiences in World Wars I and II demonstrated beyond question our dependence upon our Merchant arm, our 'Fourth Arm of Defense,' and we must strive always to keep our merchant fleet virile and strong."

As the fourth arm of defense, the merchant marine performs these functions for the Navy:

Logistic support: Logistics, a word in general use only since World War II, refers to the process by which the material and human resources of a nation are mobilized and directed toward accomplishing a military objective. In World War II, logistics involved moving hundreds of thousands of men and millions of tons of material into combat zones overseas. Hundreds of merchant ships carried 268,252,000 tons of cargo to all the major combat theaters. During the actions in Korea and Vietnam, similar amounts of cargo were moved overseas.

Ocean transportation is necessary to get men and materials where they are needed. Airlift can move a few essential people or very small amounts of highly critical material, but when it comes to moving whole armies and millions of tons of supplies and equipment, a bridge of ships is necessary. Many U.S. merchant ships are specially designed to be capable of serving as naval auxiliaries and can be rapidly fitted with defense features when needed.

Combat augmentation: Although in the modern world of instantaneous communication and near-supersonic travel, a small "brush fire" action or even an all-out combat situation can develop in hours, it still takes months or years to build a large ship. As Admiral William D. Leahy stated in World War II, "When you need the ships it's too late to build them." So, when hostilities require rapid expansion of the fleet, large numbers of merchant ships are called on to perform urgent naval combat tasks. The U.S. Navy used merchant ships in the Civil War, in World War I, in World War II, in the Korean War, and in the Vietnam War. During World War II, over a hundred merchant ships were converted to small "jeep" aircraft carriers.

The principal effect of the Merchant Marine Act of 1936 was to establish the U.S. Maritime Administration (MARAD), which handles a wide range of duties covering the design, building, and operation of U.S. merchant ships; subsidies for U.S. operators in the shipping business; the training of merchant marine officers; the development of port facilities; the enforcement of safety and navigation regulations; and pollution control. A commission set up by the Maritime Administration surveyed the maritime industry and then initiated a long-range building program that called for 500 new ships to be built at the rate of 50 a year. That was considered a big program, but when the United States entered the war, a truly mammoth shipbuilding program began. From 1942 through 1945, the country built more than 5,500 merchant ships. At the end of the war, the United States was a world leader in total tonnage of merchant ships and in total tonnage of naval vessels, but there was no apparent need for a huge merchant marine or a huge navy. Consequently, hundreds of ships were "mothballed," or placed in reserve, until they might be needed again. Unfortunately, for lack of routine maintenance and upkeep, ships in mothballs deteriorate even faster than do those in service, so in the following 25 years hundreds of ships were sold or scrapped.

At the same time, Russia was rapidly expanding her navy and merchant marine, and her ships were beginning to operate far beyond their normal sea areas—in the Mediterranean, the South Atlantic, the Caribbean, and the Indian Ocean. That was a calculated plan for increasing Soviet influence around the world, at a time when the U.S. merchant marine was rapidly dwindling in size.

During the War of 1812 the United States learned, and during the Civil War the Confederate States learned, that a country dependent on ocean transport for her commerce must provide the ships; if her commerce is to be carried by ships of another nation, it can readily be cut off, should that nation choose not to carry it.

In 1951, when the war in Korea greatly increased the U.S. need for merchant shipping, ships were pulled out of the mothball fleet and sent to sea again. At the same time the Maritime Administration ordered 35 new, Mariner-type, 20-knot ships, designed for rapid conversion to military use. Most of these ships were sold to private ship operators.

By 1958, older ships were becoming obsolete and a new shipbuilding program had been developed. The program called for nearly 300 ships to be built over a period of twenty years. This represented about $5 billion worth of work for American shipyards. However, before many of these ships were in the water, strong foreign competition for U.S. trade made it imperative that the merchant fleet again be strengthened. A determined move in this direction was made when the president signed the Merchant Marine Act of 1970, which put into effect another program for building 300 ships in the next ten years. The total carrying capacity of the new ships, which will be much larger than any built before World

War II, will be equal to that of at least 500 of the older ships. Even so, as of 1974, the entire U.S. merchant fleet of 568 ships, whose total tonnage approximates 12.5 million tons, can carry no more than 5 percent of all U.S. ocean commerce.

Besides the ships mentioned above, there are many that are owned by U.S. citizens but are registered in and fly the flags of foreign countries. Such ships are known as "flag-of-convenience" ships, and some 450 of them are registered as follows: Liberia, 238; the United Kingdom, 109; and Panama, 95. The remainder are registered in 16 other countries, from Australia to Venezuela.

Flag-of-convenience ships include more than 350 tankers owned by major U.S. oil companies. Most of these ships were built in overseas yards, where construction costs are lower, and all are manned by foreign crews because they work for less than do U.S. crews, whose salaries are determined by various maritime unions. The U.S. owners of flag-of-convenience ships must assure the United States that in time of war their ships will be turned over to the United States for service, and in return they receive government insurance on their investment. The catch in this arrangement is that, under international law, a ship belongs to the nation whose flag she flies; therefore, the owner might not be able to fulfill his obligation. Cargo carried by such ships—oil, rubber, or other critical material—might be ordered by and paid for by a U.S. firm, but it does not actually belong to that firm until it has been landed in a U.S. port. An unfriendly nation that might divert the cargo of a foreign-flag ship would not take such action against cargo carried in a ship flying the American flag, because to do so would be to interfere directly with U.S. rights under international law.

The building and maintenance of a big U.S.-owned merchant fleet is of vital importance to national economy and security. Nations that depended on the ships of other nations to move their exports and imports have always been vulnerable to starvation, in the event unfriendly nations decided to stop such traffic. This was a leading cause of the Confederate defeat in the Civil War. Because countries with standards of living lower than that of the United States can build ships more cheaply and operate them at less expense, U.S. shipbuilders and ship operators would be forced out of business if the gap in building and operating costs could not be narrowed.

This differential is offset by subsidies—in other words, the government supports U.S. shipbuilders and shipping lines through payments based on certain conditions governing construction, safety, and routes to be sailed. Firms subsidized by the government must agree to replace obsolete ships with new ships suitable for emergency use as naval auxiliaries. The law allows up to 43 percent of the cost of such ships to be paid by the government. In 1973, about twenty ship operators with some 200 ships in service received subsidy payments of about $230 million.

The Coast Guard, having come into being in 1790 as the Revenue Marine, is one of the oldest services organized under the federal government. Since 1967 it has operated under the Department of Transportation. In time of war or of national emergency it operates as a part of the U.S. Navy.

U.S. Coast Guard

The Coast Guard enforces laws on the high seas and on the navigable waters of the United States. It places and maintains some 44,000 aids to navigation along the coasts and on inland waters. The aids over which it has jurisdiction include lighthouses, lightships, radio beacons, fog signals, buoys, range lights, and loran stations.

Rules of the Road—the seagoing traffic laws—are enforced by the Coast Guard. There are different sets of rules for international waters, inland waters, and certain rivers and canals. The rules set safe speeds for ships and boats, specify what lights and other safety features vessels must carry, and establish the right-of-way for various types of ships, so as to avoid danger of collision. A Coast Guard patrol may stop a small outboard-motor boat and give it a safety inspection.

Safety is a big concern of the Coast Guard. Safety regulations for dangerous cargoes carried by the largest ships afloat and for all types of commercial ships, whether on the Great Lakes or in overseas trade, are set by the Coast Guard. All accidents at sea are investigated by the Coast Guard. Distress messages, whether from a small sloop or from the largest passenger ship, are answered immediately. In any one year, the Coast Guard answers some 60,000 requests for assistance and saves some 3,000 lives in water-connected accidents.

All the waterways of the nation—navigable rivers, harbors, and canals—are maintained by the Army Corps of Engineers. The Engineers have had this responsibility since 1824, when Congress gave the president the authority to make plans and estimates for roads and canals of national importance from a commercial or military viewpoint.

The Army Corps of Engineers

The Engineers build dams to control the flow of rivers and to keep the water at proper levels for towboat operations; they construct and maintain the locks that allow boats going upstream or downstream to move from one level to another; they dredge river and harbor channels to keep them as deep and wide as they are supposed to be; they maintain in good condition all navigable channels; and they remove such obstructions to navigation as sandbars, wrecks, and submerged rocks. The Engineers build breakwaters and jetties, and inspect plans for private and commercial piers and jetties to ensure that such structures will not interfere with waterborne traffic.

Port facilities   There are about 130 seaports in the United States which can handle oceangoing ships that draw 25 feet or more. The basic function of these ports is to provide the facilities and services required for transferring cargo and passengers from ship to shore and from shore to ship. Without such facilities, those would be time-consuming processes and much heavy cargo could not be moved at all.

A port, whose primary requirement is a sheltered harbor, contains man-made breakwaters and, among other things:

Offshore harbor facilities, such as navigational aids, anchorages, and main channels providing access for vessels entering or leaving port. The Army Corps of Engineers and the U.S. Coast Guard construct, maintain, and operate these services.

Shoreside terminal facilities, which consist of piers, wharves, mechanical handling equipment, storage sheds, warehouses, roadways for trucks, and tracks for rail carriers.

Marine terminal facilities are either publicly or privately owned. Most of the private facilities are used primarily to handle single bulk commodities, such as coal, oil, grain, iron ore, etc. Publicly-owned terminal facilities handle general cargo on a "common-carrier" basis; they serve the many shippers and consignees whose volume of cargo is not great enough to justify their building and operating their own terminal. There are about 2,400 marine terminal facilities in use in all U.S. ports.

The port industry, like other elements of the American merchant marine operation, is big business. The 130 main U.S. ports handle more than 1.6 billion tons of cargo annually, generate more than $30 billion in income, and contribute more than $3 billion to the U.S. Treasury in customs collections. Port facilities employ more than 1.2 million people and provide an indirect livelihood to another 2.9 million people, who are engaged in rail, highway, and other types of transportation.

U.S. seaports   The ports of Boston, New York, Philadelphia, Baltimore, Norfolk, Charleston, and New Orleans are older than the United States. Baltimore, a salt-water port for deep-draft ocean ships, is more than a hundred miles from the ocean, at the upper end of Chesapeake Bay. New Orleans, which handles a vast river barge traffic and oceangoing ships, is a fresh-water port; it is on the Mississippi River and more than a hundred miles from the Gulf of Mexico. On the Pacific coast, the principal ports are San Diego, Los Angeles (the harbor is actually in San Pedro), San Francisco, and Seattle. Seattle, like Baltimore, is an ocean port far inland—ships sail for more than 150 miles through Puget Sound before they reach Seattle.

San Diego is the oldest port, in terms of usage, in the United States. It was first used in 1542 when the Portuguese explorer Juan Rodríguez de Cabrillo anchored a ship there, and it was given its present name in 1602, by Sebastian Vizcaino. Seattle, in contrast, was not founded until 1852, and began to grow only after gold was discovered in the Klondike region of Alaska in 1900. West coast shipping favors Seattle because it is 1,100 miles nearer Japan than is San Francisco.

The newest "port" in the United States, and the one that handles more steamship passengers than any other, is Port Everglades, Florida. After transatlantic jet air service killed the passenger-liner trade, "cruise boats" began taking tourists to sea from Florida. Ultramodern ships flying the flags of half a dozen nations depart frequently from Port Everglades, carrying vacationing Americans on round trips to the islands of the Caribbean and to ports in Central and South America.

When Admiral Mahan defined sea power as "Navy, plus bases, plus merchant marine . . ." he simplified matters just a bit. A strong navy, big bases, and a modern merchant marine are useless without people who know what to do with them. Sea power has also been defined as "ships, sailors, and salt water," and it is various combinations of those three essential elements that have, over the past three centuries, produced America's maritime heritage.

The men who contributed most to our maritime heritage were people who could see beyond the nearest horizon. There were such men in Maine in 1607. Faced with plenty of salt water between where they were and where they wanted to go, they had the imagination and determination to do something about it.

As they cut the timbers for the little 30-ton *Virginia of Sagadahock*, they began an era in history unlike any the world had known before. From that day on, as American ships crossed the seas to carry trade and commerce around the world, the country began to grow and expand. The vast pageant of history that has brought the United States to the two-century mark might fill ten thousand books, yet no single subject, whether it be whalers, clippers, or port operations, has ever been fully covered. While historians and scholars seek to learn what has happened, people with imagination and determination are making more things happen.

The sea brought the first colonists to America, and ever since it has been the source of a rich heritage of commerce, history, tradition, and culture. Yet the sea offers more than that: out where the frigates, whalers, and clippers once sailed is the last unknown frontier on earth. Beyond our shores, there is still mystery, adventure, and wealth for those who look into the future. Beyond the shore, the sea is always there.

MARITIME MUSEUMS, EXHIBITS, AND LIBRARIES

There is no single national maritime or naval museum. Bits and pieces of our maritime heritage are scattered about the United States in dozens of cities. The most conspicuous links with our maritime past are battleships, square-rigged ships, riverboats, and replicas of historic ships. There are many priceless collections of great interest, but some of them fill only a small room and can easily be passed by. The following pages list the best-known museums, maritime displays, galleries, collections, exhibits, libraries, and memorials, but the list cannot be considered complete or up to date, because exhibits and displays vary from time to time.

This listing is based on *Treasures of America* published by The Reader's Digest Association of Pleasantville, New York; *Marine Museums in the United States*, published by the U.S. Department of Commerce, Maritime Administration; *Historic Ship Exhibits in the United States*, published by the Naval History Division, Navy Department; and the United States Naval Institute *Proceedings* (various issues) published by the U.S. Naval Institute, Annapolis, Maryland. The foregoing publications list street addresses, admission fees, hours of operation, and, in some cases, telephone numbers to call for detailed information.

Alabama
Dauphin Island—Fort Gaines Museum, anchor of USS *Hartford* (Civil War steam frigate).
Mobile—USS *Alabama* (WWII battleship), USS *Drum* (WWII submarine), USS *Tecumseh* (Civil War monitor, sunken wreck).

Alaska
Juneau—Relics of USS *Juneau* (WWII cruiser).

California
China Lake—Michelson Museum and Laboratory at Naval Ordnance Test Station.
Long Beach—SS *Queen Mary*.
Los Angeles—California Museum of Science and Industry.
National City—Museum of American Treasures.

Oakland—Oakland Public Museum.

Port Hueneme—Seabee Museum.

San Diego—*Star of India* (1863) square-rigger; Maritime Museum of San Diego; Naval Training Center Historical Museum.

San Francisco—USS *San Francisco* memorial (bridge of WWII cruiser); San Francisco Maritime Museum (ship models, artifacts, library); *Balclutha* (1886) square-rigger; *C. A. Thayer,* schooner; *Eureka,* side-wheel ferryboat; *Wapama,* steam schooner; *Alma,* hay scow; Spreckles Museum, Treasure Island.

San Marino—Henry E. Huntington Library and Art Gallery.

San Pedro—Cabrillo Beach Marine Museum.

Vallejo—Mare Island Naval Shipyard Museum.

Connecticut

Groton—Submarine Library and Museum, Submarine Base, New London.

Hartford—Figurehead of USS *Connecticut,* anchor and bell of USS *Hartford,* relics of USS *Tarawa* (WWII cruiser); Marine Room, Wadsworth Atheneum.

Mystic—Mystic Seaport, a restored nineteenth-century seaport; *Charles W. Morgan,* whaleship; *Australia,* schooner; *Dorothy A. Parsons,* schooner; *Joseph Conrad,* ex-Danish sail training ship; *Gundel,* ketch; *Regina M.,* schooner; *L. A. Dunton,* schooner; *Brilliant,* schooner.

New London—U.S. Coast Guard Cutter *Eagle,* ex-German sail training ship *Horst Wessel* (1936); U.S. Coast Guard Museum; New London Historical Society; USS *Flasher* (WWII submarine); deck guns of USS *Narwhal* (WWII submarine); Japanese midget submarine.

District of Columbia

Arlington Cemetery—Mainmast of USS *Maine;* Maritime Administration, Department of Commerce, ship model collection; Pentagon, skylight of USS *Hartford,* ship models; Truxtun-Decatur Museum, documents, ship models, uniforms; Smithsonian Institution, over 200 models of American merchant ships; U.S. Naval Museum, guns, ship models, artifacts; USS *Gyatt* (WWII destroyer); USS *Torsk* (WWII submarine); *Intelligent Whale* (Civil War submarine).

Florida

Fort Lauderdale—*Golden Doubloon,* replica of Spanish galleon of 1680; SS *Queen Elizabeth.*

Key West—Turret-sight hood of USS *Maine;* Japanese midget submarine.

Miami—University of Florida Marine Laboratory Marine Museum.

Pensacola—Naval Aviation Museum, U.S. Naval Air Station.

St. Petersburg—HMS *Bounty,* restoration of original ship.

Georgia

Columbus—Confederate Naval Museum; CSS *Muscogee* (Civil War ironclad); CSS *Chattahoochee* (Civil War gunboat wreck).

Richmond Hill—CSS *Nashville,* relics at Fort McAllister.

Savannah—Model of SS *Savannah* at City Hall; Ships of the Sea Museum.

Hawaii

Honolulu—Bernice P. Bishop Museum, *Falls of Clyde* (full-rigger).

Pearl Harbor—USS *Bowfin* (WWII submarine); USS *Utah* (1909) sunk WWII; USS *Arizona* (1915) Memorial, with model of ship; Japanese midget submarine.

Illinois

Chicago—Museum of Science and Industry, German submarine *U-505* captured by U.S. Navy in World War II; George F. Harding Museum; Chicago Historical Society; Lincoln Park, replica of Viking ship *Raven*.

East St. Louis—USS *Cero* (WWII submarine).

Hines—Armor plate from USS *Indiana* at VA Hospital.

Lockport—Illinois and Michigan Canal Museum.

Indiana

Bloomington—Mainmast and guns of USS *Indiana*.

Fort Wayne—Anchor of USS *Indiana*.

Jeffersonville—Howard National Steamboat Museum, early Ohio River steamboats.

Iowa

Clinton—*Showboat*, stern-wheel steamboat, with theater and museum.

Keokuk—Keokuk River Museum on board *George M. Verity*, old stern-wheel towboat.

Kentucky

Louisville—*Belle of Louisville*, stern-wheel steamboat.

Louisiana

Baton Rouge—CSS *Arkansas*, ironclad sunk during Civil War.

New Orleans—Louisiana State Museum; CSS *Pioneer* (Civil War submarine).

Maine

Bath—Bath Marine Museum (depicts history of Maine shipbuilding); Percy & Small Shipyard (restoration of nineteenth-century yard).

Boothbay Harbor—Grand Banks Schooner Museum; *Sherman Zwicker*, schooner; *Sequin* (1884), oldest steam tug in United States.

Camden—USS *Bowdoin*, schooner.

Castine—Maine Maritime Museum.

Gardiner—Gardiner Library Hall Museum (model steamboats).

Isleboro—Sailors Memorial Museum.

Kittery—Conning tower of USS *Squalus* (submarine).

Portland—Maine Historical Society; Cape Elizabeth Lighthouse (1828); Portland Head Light (1791); mast, bridge, and bell of USS *Portland* (WWII cruiser).

Searsport—Penobscot Marine Museum.

Maryland

Annapolis—Historic Annapolis, Inc., records pertaining to shipping in colonial port of Annapolis; State House grounds, bell of USS *Maryland* (1916); U.S. Naval Academy Chapel, crypt of John Paul Jones, anchors of USS *New York*; U.S. Naval Academy Museum, ship models, flags, paintings, relics; U.S. Naval Academy grounds, guns, figureheads, aircraft, memorials to naval heroes, foremast of USS *Maine*.

Baltimore—USS *Constellation* (1797); Maryland Historical Society, Maritime Collection, pertaining to Chesapeake Bay watercraft; University of Baltimore, The Steamship Historical Society of America Library, models, photographs, and sketches of steamboats.

Landover Hills—Nautical Research Guild.

Piney Point—*Dauntless*, steam yacht.

St. Michaels—Chesapeake Bay Maritime Museum; *Barnegat* lightship; *J. T. Leonard*, topmast sloop.

Massachusetts

Andover—Addison Gallery of American Art, Phillips Academy.

Barnstable—The Donald G. Trayser Memorial Museum.

Beverly—Beverly Historical Society.

Boston—Boston Marine Society; Museum of Fine Arts, Marine Room; Bostonian Society, Old State House; Museum of Science, Science Park; Marine Collection of the State Street Trust Company; Stebbins Marine Collection, Harrison Grey Otis House; USS *Constitution* ("Old Ironsides") at Boston Naval Shipyard.

Cambridge—Francis Russel Hart Nautical Museum; Massachusetts Institute of Technology.

Chatham—Whaling Museum.

Cohasset—Maritime Museum.

Edgartown—Thomas Cooke House (1765), ship models, scrimshaw, whaling relics; Dukes County Historical Society, Martha's Vineyard.

Fall River—Fall River Historical Society Museum; USS *Massachusetts* (WWII battleship) at State Pier; USS *Lionfish* (WWII submarine).

Falmouth—USS *Trout* (WWII submarine) Memorial.

Gloucester—Gloucester Art Institute.

Mattapoisett—Mattapoisett Historical Society.

Milton—Museum of American China Trade, 1833 home of a China trader, with paintings of ships, harbors, men in China trade.

Nantucket—Nantucket Whaling Museum; Peter Foulger Museum.

New Bedford—Whaling Museum and Old Dartmouth Historical Society; half-size replica of whaler *Ladoga*.

Newburyport—Newburyport Historical Society.

Plymouth—*Mayflower II*, replica of original *Mayflower*.

Salem—Peabody Museum, over 500 ship models; Salem Maritime National Historic Sites, Custom House and Derby House; Essex Institute; Derby Wharf, reconstruction of 1760 docking facilities.

Sharon—Kendall Whaling Museum.

Michigan

Dearborn—Edison Institute; Greenfield Village, *Suwanee* (1880), paddle-wheel steamer.

Detroit—Detroit Historical Society, Dossin Museum of Great Lakes History, Belle Isle.

Menominee—Mystery Ship Seaport.

Saginaw—Gig of USS *Saginaw*, wrecked in Pacific in 1871.

Sault Ste. Marie—Museum Ship *Valley Camp*, Great Lakes freighter.

Minnesota

Brainerd—Lumbertown, USA; *Blue Berry Belle*, river steamboat.

St. Paul—USS *Swordfish* (WWII submarine) memorial.

Winona—Transportation Museum; *Julius C. Wilkie*, steamboat.

Mississippi

Biloxi—USS *Biloxi* (WWII cruiser) memorial.

Vicksburg—Mississippi River Museum and Hall of Fame on board riverboat *Sprague* ("Big Mama"); USS *Cairo* (Civil War ironclad) under restoration.

Missouri

Hannibal—*Mark Twain*, reconstruction of Mississippi River steamer.

Hermann—Historic Hermann Museum, including Riverboat Room.

St. Louis—Missouri Historical Society, River Room; *Golden Rod* (1909) showboat, restored; USS *Inaugural* (WWII minesweeper).

Nebraska
Wahoo—Memorial to USS *Wahoo* (WWII submarine).

New Hampshire
Portsmouth—Portsmouth Athenaeum, library, paintings, ship models.

New Jersey
Beach Haven—*Lucy Evelyn*, schooner; Marine Museum.
Paterson—City of Paterson Museum; *Fenian Ram*, early submarine.

New York
Amagansett—Town Marine Museum, model ships.
Brooklyn—The Brooklyn Museum; USS *Maine* plaque at Naval Station.
Buffalo—Buffalo & Erie County Historical Society.
Clayton—Thousand Islands Shipyard Museum.
Cold Spring Harbor, Long Island—Whaling Museum.
East Hampton, Long Island—East Hampton Town Marine Museum;
    Clinton Academy, whaling gear.
Glen Cove, Long Island—Webb Institute of Naval Architecture.
Huntington, Long Island—Vanderbilt Marine Museum.
Hyde Park—Franklin D. Roosevelt Library and Museum.
Lake Champlain—Fort Ticonderoga Museum.
New York City—India House, Hanover Square; Metropolitan Museum
    of Art; Museum of Science and Industry, Marine Transportation Sec-
    tion, Rockefeller Center; Museum of the City of New York, Mari-
    time Museum; New York Historical Society; Seamen's Bank for Sav-
    ings; Seamen's Church Institute; New York Public Library; New York
    Public Library, St. George Branch, Staten Island; New York Yacht
    Club (over 1,000 yacht models).
Oswego—Oswego County Historical Society Museum.
Sag Harbor—Suffolk County Whaling Museum.
Staten Island—Staten Island Museum.
Stoneybrook, Long Island—USS *Ohio* figurehead.
Syracuse—The Canal Museum.
Ticonderoga—Fort Ticonderoga, colonial water craft.
West Brighton, Staten Island—Sailor's Snug Harbor.
Whitehall—Skenesborough Museum; USS *Ticonderoga* (1812), schooner.

North Carolina
Beaufort—Alphonse Whaling Museum.
Carolina Beach—Blockade Runner Museum.
Elizabeth City—Museum of the Albemarle, models of U.S. Coast Guard
    vessels since 1790.
Kinston—CSS *Neuse* (sunk during Civil War, hull restored).
Wilmington—USS *North Carolina* (WWII battleship); Patriot's Point
    Museum, under development.

Ohio
Canal Fulton—Old Canal Days Museum; *St. Helena II*, canal-boat
    replica.
Cleveland—Great Lakes Historical Society Museum; Western Reserve
    Historical Society.
Fairport—Fairport Marine Museum.
Marietta—Rivermen's Museum; *W. P. Snyder*, stern-wheel steamboat.
Vermilion—Great Lakes Historical Society Museum.
Youngstown—Butler Art Institute.

Oklahoma
Catoosa—USS *Sea Dog* (WWII submarine).

Oregon
Astoria—Columbia River Maritime Museum; Lightship *Columbia*.
Hood River—USS *Banning* (WWII patrol craft).
Newport—Old Yaquina Bay Lighthouse (1871), marine artifacts.

Pennsylvania
Doylestown—Marine Room, Bucks County Historical Society.
Erie—USS *Niagara* (1812) brig, reconstructed.
Philadelphia—USS *Olympia* (Spanish-American War cruiser); *Welcome*, replica of William Penn's ship; Franklin Institute; Atwater Kent Museum; Historical Society of Pennsylvania; Insurance Company of North America Museum.

Rhode Island
Bristol—Herreshoff Model Room.
East Greenwich—Varnum Military and Naval Museum.
Newport—New England Naval and Maritime Museum; Newport Historical Society; USS *Constellation* anchor; HMS *Rose,* reconstructed Revolutionary War frigate.
Providence—Rhode Island Historical Society.

South Carolina
Charleston—USS *Maine* capstan.
Georgetown—USS *Harvest Moon*, wrecked 1865, being restored.

South Dakota
Sioux Falls—USS *South Dakota* memorial, museum, model of ship, WWII mementoes.

Tennessee
Johnsonville—USS *Key West*, USS *Tawah*, USS *Elfin*, sunk during Civil War, restoration planned.

Texas
Fredericksburg—Fleet Admiral Chester W. Nimitz Naval Museum.
Houston, San Jacinto Battleground—USS *Cabrilla* (WWII submarine); USS *Seawolf* memorial; USS *Texas* (1912) battleship.

Utah
Clearfield—USS *Utah* bell.
Salt Lake City—USS *Indiana* armor plate at Medical Center.

Vermont
Shelburne—Marine Museum; *Ticonderoga*, restored steamboat.

Virginia
Jamestown—Jamestown Festival Park, restoration of *Susan Constant, Discovery, Godspeed*.
Newport News—The Mariners Museum; propeller of USS *South Dakota*.
Norfolk—USS *Franklin* (WWII aircraft carrier), bridge of ship; SS *United States*.
Portsmouth—Norfolk Naval Shipyard Museum; *Portsmouth* (lightship); Portsmouth Coast Guard Museum, Inc.
Richmond—USS *Cumberland* relics; CSS *Virginia* relics.
Virginia Beach—Cape Henry Lighthouse, first lighted 1792.
Yorktown—Colonial National Park Museum.

Washington
Bremerton—Puget Sound Naval Shipyard Museum; USS *Missouri* (WWII battleship).
Olympia—USS *Washington* bell and wheel.
Seattle—The Museum of History and Industry, Joshua Green-Dwight Merril Maritime Wing; Northwest Museum, *Wawaona*, three-masted schooner.

West Virginia
Clarksburg—USS *West Virginia*, flagstaff.
Morgantown—USS *West Virginia*, mast.

Wisconsin
Manitowoc—Manitowoc County Historical Society; USS *Redfin* (WWII submarine).

BIBLIOGRAPHY

Adamson, Hans Christian. *Keepers of the Light.* New York: Knopf, 1962.

Albion, Robert G. *Forests and Sea Power; the Timber Problems of the Royal Navy, 1652–1862.* Cambridge: Harvard University Press, 1926.

———. *Square Riggers on Schedule.* Princeton: Princeton University Press, 1938.

———, and Pope, Jennie B. *Sea Lanes in Wartime.* New York: W. W. Norton, 1942.

———, with Baker, William A.; Labaree, Benjamin W.; and Brewington, Marion V. *New England and the Sea.* Middletown: Wesleyan University Press, 1972.

Allen, Everett S. *Children of the Light.* Boston: Little, Brown and Company, 1973.

American Heritage. *Clipper Ships and Captains.* New York: American Heritage Pub. Co., 1962. (American Heritage Junior Library.)

———. *Commodore Perry in Japan.* New York: American Heritage Pub. Co., 1963. (American Heritage Junior Library.)

———. *Naval Battles and Heroes.* New York: American Heritage Pub. Co., 1960. (American Heritage Junior Library.)

———. *Pirates of the Spanish Main.* New York: American Heritage Pub. Co., 1961. (American Heritage Junior Library.)

American Waterways Operators, Inc. *Big Load Afloat.* Washington: 1972.

Anderson, Bern. *By Sea and By River; the Naval History of the Civil War.* New York: Knopf, 1962.

Bailey, Thomas A. *The American Pageant.* Boston: D. C. Heath & Co., 1966.

Baldwin, Leland D. *The Keelboat Age on the Western Rivers.* Pittsburgh: University of Pittsburgh Press, 1941.

Barbey, Daniel E. *MacArthur's Amphibious Navy: Seventh Amphibious Force Operations, 1943–1945.* Annapolis: U.S. Naval Institute, 1969.

Bauer, K. Jack. *Surfboats and Horse Marines: U.S. Naval Operations in the Mexican War, 1846–1848.* Annapolis: U.S. Naval Institute, 1969.

Beach, Edward L. *Submarine!* New York: Holt, 1952.

Beck, Horace. *Folklore and the Sea.* Middletown: Wesleyan University Press, 1973.

Behrman, Daniel. *The New World of the Oceans.* Boston: Little, Brown and Company, 1969.

Beirne, Francis F. *The War of 1812.* New York: Dutton, 1949.

Bell, Frederick. *Room to Swing a Cat.* New York: Longmans Green & Co., 1938.

Berry, Erick. *You Have To Go Out!* (Story of the U.S. Coast Guard.) New York: McKay, 1964.

Bloomster, Edgar L. *Sailing and Small Craft Down the Ages*. Annapolis: U.S. Naval Institute, 1940.

Brinnin, John Malcolm. *The Sway of the Grand Saloon*, A Social History of the North Atlantic. New York: Delacorte Press, 1971.

Bryant, Samuel W. *The Sea and the States*. New York: Crowell, 1947.

Buchanan, Albert R., ed. *The Navy's Air War*. New York: Harper, 1946.

Buehr, W. *Ships of the Great Lakes*. New York: G. P. Putnam's Sons, 1956.

Bulkley, Robert J. *At Close Quarters: PT Boats in the United States Navy*. Washington: GPO, 1962.

Bunker, John Gorley. *Liberty Ships*. Annapolis: U.S. Naval Institute, 1972.

Cagle, Malcolm W. and Manson, Frank A. *The Sea War in Korea*. Annapolis: U.S. Naval Institute, 1957.

Carrison, Daniel J. *The United States Navy*. New York: Praeger, 1968.

Carse, Robert. *Ports of Call*. New York: Scribners, 1967.

Carson, Rachel L. *The Sea Around Us*. New York: Oxford University Press, 1951.

Carter, Worrall R. *Beans, Bullets and Black Oil; The Story of Fleet Logistics Afloat in the Pacific During World War II*. Washington: GPO, 1953.

————. *Ships, Salvage, and Sinews of War; The Story of Fleet Logistics Afloat in Atlantic and Mediterranean Waters During World War II*. Washington: GPO, 1954.

Chappelle, Howard I. *The History of American Sailing Ships*. New York: Norton, 1935.

————. *History of the American Sailing Navy*. New York: Norton, 1949.

Clark, William Bell, ed. *Naval Documents of the American Revolution*. Washington: GPO, 1966.

Clarke, William H. *Ships and Sailors, the Story of the Merchant Marine*. Boston: C. L. Page Co., Inc., 1938.

Colcord, Joanna C. *Roll and Go, Songs of American Sailormen*. Indianapolis: Bobbs-Merrill, 1924.

Colman, John S. *The Sea and Its Mysteries*. London: Bell, 1952.

Cooper, James Fenimore. *The History of the Navy of the United States of America*. Philadelphia: Lea & Blanchard, 1839. (Reprinted 1970 by Gregg.)

Cowen, R. C. *Frontiers of the Sea: The Story of Oceanographic Exploration*. Garden City: Doubleday, 1960.

Cutler, Carl. *Greyhounds of the Sea*. Annapolis: U.S. Naval Institute, 1961.

————. *Queens of the Western Ocean*. Annapolis: U.S. Naval Institute, 1961.

Daly, Robert W. *How the Merrimac Won: The Strategic Story of the CSS Virginia*. New York: Crowell, 1957.

Dana, Richard Henry. *Two Years Before the Mast*. New York: Harper & Brothers, 1840.

Downey, Joseph T. *The Cruise of the Portsmouth, 1845–1847: A Sailor's View of the Naval Conquest of California*. Ed. by Howard Lamar. New Haven: Yale University Press, 1958.

DuBois, William E. B. *The Suppression of the African Slave Trade to the United States, 1638–1870*. New York: Social Service Press, 1954.

Dulles, Foster R. *Lowered Boats, a Chronicle of American Whaling*. London: Haddap, 1934.

Duncan, Fred B. *Deepwater Family*. New York: Pantheon Books, 1969.

Durant, John and Alice. *Pictorial History of American Ships: On the High Seas and Inland Waters*. New York: A. S. Barnes, 1913.

Engle, Eloise. *Medic.* New York: John Day Company, 1967.

Ewart, W. D. and Fullard, H., eds. *World Atlas of Shipping.* New York: St. Martin's Press, 1972.

Farris, Martin T. and McElniney, Paul T. *Modern Transportation, Selected Readings.* Boston: Houghton Mifflin Co., 1973.

Fassett, Frederick G. *The Shipbuilding Business of the United States of America.* New York: The Society of Naval Architects and Marine Engineers, 1948.

Frere-Cook, Gervis, ed. *Decorative Arts of the Mariner.* Boston: Cassell and Company, Ltd., 1966.

Furnas, Joseph C. *The Americans, A Social History of the American People.* New York: Putnams, 1969.

Goldsmith-Carter, George. *Sailing Ships and Sailing Craft.* New York: Grosset & Dunlap, 1970.

Goodrich, Carter, ed. *Canals and American Development.* New York: Columbia University Press, 1961.

Gordon, Bernard L., ed. *Man and the Sea.* Garden City: Natural History Press, 1970.

Graebner, Norman R., Fite, Gilbert C., and White, Philip. *A History of the United States.* New York: McGraw-Hill Book Co., 1970.

Greenbrie, Sydney and Marjorie. *Gold of Ophir: The Lure That Made America Famous.* Garden City: Doubleday, Page & Co., 1925.

Guillet, Edwin C. *The Great Migration: The Atlantic Crossing by Sailing Ship Since 1770.* Toronto: University of Toronto Press, 1963.

Hancock, Harry E. *Wireless at Sea: The First Fifty Years.* London: Marconi International Marine Communication Co., 1950.

Hansen, Hans Jurgen, ed. *Art and the Seafarer.* New York: Viking Press, 1968.

Harmor, George M., ed. *Transportation: The Nation's Lifelines.* Washington: Industrial College of the Armed Forces, 1968.

Havighurst, Walter. *The Long Ships Passing: The Story of the Great Lakes.* New York: Macmillan, 1961.

Heinl, Robert Debs. *Soldiers of the Sea, the United States Marine Corps, 1775–1962.* Annapolis: U.S. Naval Institute, 1962.

Hohman, E. P. *The American Whaleman.* New York: Longmans, Green & Co., 1928.

Horseman, Reginald. *War of 1812.* New York: Knopf, 1969.

Howeth, L. S. *History of Communications-Electronics in the United States Navy.* Washington: GPO, 1963.

Hugill, Stan. *Shanties from the Seven Seas.* New York: E. P. Dutton & Co., Inc., 1961.

Hunter, Louis C. *Steamboats on the Western Rivers.* Cambridge: Harvard University Press, 1949.

Hurd, Edith Thacher. *Sailors, Whalers, and Steamers.* Menlo Park: Lane Publishing Co., 1964.

Jennings, John E. *Tattered Ensign.* New York: Crowell, 1966.

Johnson, Robert E. *Rear Admiral John Rodgers, 1812–1882.* Annapolis: U.S. Naval Institute, 1967.

————. *Thence Round Cape Horn: The Story of United States Naval Forces on Pacific Station, 1818–1923.* Annapolis: U.S. Naval Institute, 1963.

Jones, Virgil C. *The Civil War at Sea.* 3 vols. New York: Holt, 1960–1962.

Karig, Walter, and others. *Battle Report.* 6 vols. New York: Farrar & Rinehart, 1944–1952.

Keeler, William F., ed. by Daly, Robert W. *Aboard the USS Monitor: 1862.* Annapolis: U.S. Naval Institute, 1964.

Kemble, John H. *The Panama Route, 1848–1869.* Berkeley: University of California Press, 1943.

Kennedy, John F. *A Nation of Immigrants.* New York: Harper & Row, 1964.

King, Ernest J. *The United States Navy at War, 1941–45, Official Reports to the Secretary of the Navy.* Washington: GPO, 1946.

Knox, Dudley W. *A History of the United States Navy.* New York: Putnams, 1948.

Laing, Alexander. *American Ships.* New York: American Heritage Press, 1971.

———. *Clipper Ship Men.* New York: Duell, Sloan and Pearce, 1940.

———. *Seafaring America.* New York: American Heritage Publishing Company, Inc., 1974.

Leckie, Robert. *Wars of America.* New York: Harper & Row, 1968.

Lewis, Charles Lee. *Matthew Fontaine Maury: Pathfinder of the Seas.* Annapolis: U.S. Naval Institute, 1927.

———. *Books of the Sea.* Annapolis: U.S. Naval Institute, 1943.

Lloyd, Christopher. *The Navy and the Slave Trade: The Suppression of the African Slave Trade in the Nineteenth Century.* London: Cass, 1968.

Lockwood, Charles A. *Sink 'em All: Submarine Warfare in the Pacific.* New York: Dutton, 1951.

Long, Edward J. *Ocean Sciences.* Annapolis: U.S. Naval Institute, 1964.

Lord, Walter A. *The Dawn's Early Light.* New York: W. W. Norton Co., 1972.

———. *Day of Infamy.* New York: Holt, 1957.

———. *Incredible Victory.* New York: Harper & Row, 1967.

Lott, Arnold S. *Most Dangerous Sea: A History of Mine Warfare and an Account of U.S. Naval Mine Warfare Operations in World War II and Korea.* Annapolis: U.S. Naval Institute, 1959.

———, ed. *The Bluejackets' Manual,* 19th ed. Annapolis: U.S. Naval Institute, 1974.

Lovette, Leland P. *Naval Customs, Traditions, and Usage.* Annapolis: U.S. Naval Institute, 1959.

Maclay, Edgar S. *A History of American Privateers.* New York: Appleton, 1899. (Reprinted 1967 by Books for Libraries.)

Mannix, Daniel P. and Cowley, Malcolm. *Black Cargoes: A History of the Atlantic Slave Trade, 1518–1865.* New York: Viking Press, 1962.

McFee, William. *Watch Below.* New York: Random House, 1940.

McNairn, Jac, and MacMullen, Jerry. *Ships of the Redwood Coast.* Palo Alto: Stanford University Press, 1945.

Melville, Herman. *Moby Dick.* New York: Harpers, 1851.

———. *Omoo.* New York: Dodd, Mead, 1924.

———. *Redburn.* New York: Harpers, 1849.

———. *Typee.* New York: Dutton, 1907.

———. *White Jacket.* New York: Harpers, 1850.

Miller, Nathan. *Sea of Glory.* New York: David McKay Co., 1974.

Miller, William. *A New History of the United States.* New York: George Braziller, Inc., 1958.

Milligan, John D. *Gunboats Down the Mississippi.* Annapolis: U.S. Naval Institute, 1965.

Mitchell, Donald W. *History of the Modern American Navy.* New York: Knopf, 1946.

Mitchell, Helen, and Wilson, W. W. *Ships That Made U.S. History.* New York: McGraw-Hill, 1950.

Morison, Elting E. *Admiral Sims and the Modern American Navy.* Boston: Houghton Mifflin, 1942.

Morison, Samuel E., and Commager, Henry S. *The Growth of the American Republic,* 2 vols. New York: Oxford University Press, 1942.

Morison, Samuel E. *The Two-Ocean War: A Short History of the United States Navy in the Second World War*. Boston: Little, Brown and Company, 1963.

————. *Maritime History of Massachusetts*. Boston: Houghton Mifflin, 1921.

————. *The Oxford History of the American People*. New York: Oxford University Press, 1965.

Morris, Richard B. *Encyclopedia of American History*. New York: Harper and Brothers, 1961.

Navy Times, eds. of. *Great American Naval Heroes*. New York: Dodd Mead & Co., 1965.

Neeser, Robert W. *American Songs and Ballads*. New Haven: Yale University Press, 1938.

Nordhoff, Charles. *Life on the Ocean*. Cincinnati: 1874. Reprinted New York: Library Edition, 1970.

————. *In Yankee Windjammers*. New York: Dodd, Mead & Co., 1941.

Parker, W. J. L. *The Great Coal Schooners of New England*. Mystic: Marine Historical Association, Inc., 1948.

Paullin, Charles O. *American Voyages to the Orient, 1690–1865*. Annapolis: U.S. Naval Institute, 1971.

Peters, Harry T. *Currier & Ives, Printmakers to the American People*. Garden City: Doubleday, Doran & Co., Inc., 1942.

Pinckney, Pauline A. *American Figureheads and their Carvers*. New York: W. W. Norton & Co., 1940.

Pohjanpalo, Jorma. *The Sea and Man*. New York: Stein and Day, 1970.

Ponko, Vincent. *Ships, Seas, and Scientists*. Annapolis: U.S. Naval Institute, 1974.

Potter, Elmer B. and Nimitz, Chester W., eds. *The Great Sea War: The Story of Naval Action in World War II*. Englewood Cliffs: Prentice-Hall, 1960.

————. *Sea Power: A Naval History*. Englewood Cliffs: Prentice-Hall, 1961.

Potter, Elmer B. *The Naval Academy Illustrated History of the United States Navy*. New York: Crowell, 1971.

Pratt, Fletcher, and Howe, Hartley E. *Compact History of the United States Navy*. New York: Hawthorne Books, 1967.

Ransom, M. A., and Engle, Eloise Katherine. *Sea of the Bear*. Annapolis: U.S. Naval Institute, 1964.

Roddis, Paul. *A Short History of Nautical Medicine*. New York: Harper & Bros., 1941.

Roscoe, Theodore. *This is Your Navy*. Annapolis: U.S. Naval Institute, 1950.

————. *United States Destroyer Operations in World War II*. Annapolis: U.S. Naval Institute, 1953.

————. *United States Submarine Operations in World War II*. Annapolis: U.S. Naval Institute, 1949.

Scott, Frances and Walter. *Exploring Ocean Frontiers*. New York: Parents' Magazine Press, 1970.

Shay, Frank. *American Sea Songs and Shanteys*. New York: W. W. Norton & Co., Inc., 1948.

Smith, Richard K. *First Across! The U.S. Navy's Transatlantic Flight of 1919*. Annapolis: U.S. Naval Institute, 1973.

Soule, Gardner. *Undersea Frontiers*. Chicago: Rand McNally & Company, 1968.

Stackpole, Edouard A. *The Sea Hunters*. Philadelphia: Lippincott, 1943.

————. *Figureheads and Ship Carvings*. Mystic: Marine Historical Association, Inc., 1964.

Starbuck, A. *A History of the American Whaling Industry . . . to 1876*. Waltham: Author, 1876.

Strauss, Wallace Patrick, ed. *Stars and Spars, The American Navy in the Age of Sail*. Waltham: Blaisdell Publishing Co., 1969.

Toland, John. *But Not in Shame: The Six Months After Pearl Harbor*. New York: Random House, 1961.

Tolley, Kemp. *Yangtze Patrol; The U.S. Navy in China*. Annapolis: U.S. Naval Institute, 1971.

Tucker, Glenn. *Dawn Like Thunder; The Barbary Wars and the Birth of the U.S. Navy*. Indianapolis: Bobbs-Merrill, 1963.

Tuleja, Thaddeus V. *Climax at Midway*. New York: Norton, 1960.

U.S. Department of Commerce. *Historical Statistics of the United States, 1789–1945*. Washington: GPO, 1949.

U.S. Naval History Division. *United States Naval Chronology, World War II*. Washington: GPO, 1955.

Villiers, Alan. *The Way of a Ship*. New York: Scribners, 1970.

Waters, John M. *Bloody Winter, An account of the Battle of the Atlantic during the Winter of 1942–43*. New York: Van Nostrand, 1967.

West, Richard S. *Mr. Lincoln's Navy*. New York: Longmans, Green, 1957.

Westcott, Allan F., ed. *American Sea Power Since 1775*. Philadelphia: Lippincott, 1952.

Wheeler, Richard. *In Pirate Waters*. New York: Longmans, Green, 1957.

Whipple, Addison B. C. *Yankee Whalers in the South Seas*. Garden City: Doubleday, 1954.

Wilmerding, John. *A History of American Marine Paintings*. Salem: Peabody Museum of Salem, Massachusetts, 1969.

Wolfe, Reese. *Yankee Ships*. Indianapolis: Bobbs-Merrill, 1953.

INDEX

The text of this book is set in ten-point Palatino, with two points of leading. The part titles and chapter titles are set in thirty-six-point Palatino Semibold.

The book is printed offset on Consolidated's Paloma Matte paper. The cover cloth is Holliston Roxite B 53540, linen finish.

Design by Beverly Baum.

The book was composed by Monotype Composition Company, Baltimore, Maryland.

The book was printed and bound by George Banta Company, Incorporated, Menasha, Wisconsin.